Allegories of Desire

Esoteric Literary Commentaries of Medieval Japan

Harvard-Yenching Institute Monograph Series, 55

Allegories of Desire
Esoteric Literary Commentaries of Medieval Japan

Susan Blakeley Klein

Published by the Harvard University Asia Center
for the Harvard-Yenching Institute
Distributed by Harvard University Press
Cambridge (Massachusetts) and London 2002

Printed in the United States of America

The Harvard-Yenching Institute, founded in 1928 and headquartered at Harvard University, is a foundation dedicated to the advancement of higher education in the humanities and social sciences in East and Southeast Asia. The Institute supports advanced research at Harvard by faculty members of certain Asian universities and doctoral studies at Harvard and other universities by junior faculty at the same universities. It also supports East Asian studies at Harvard through contributions to the Harvard-Yenching Library and publication of the *Harvard Journal of Asiatic Studies* and books on premodern East Asian history and literature.

Library of Congress Cataloging-in-Publication Data

Klein, Susan Blakeley.

Allegories of desire : esoteric literary commentaries of medieval Japan / Susan Blakeley Klein.

p. cm. -- (Harvard-Yenching Institute monograph series ; 55)

Includes bibliographical references and index.

ISBN 0-674-00956-8 (cloth : alk. paper)

1. Waka--History and criticism. 2. Japanese poetry--1185–1600--History and criticism. 3. Fujiwara, Sadaie, 1162–1241. 4. Buddhism and literature. I. Title. II. Series.

PL728.A2 K54 2002

895.6'12209--dc21 2002027643

Index by the author

Printed on acid-free paper

Last number below indicates year of this printing

12 11 10 09 08 07 06 05 04 03 02

The publisher thanks FontFreak.com for permission to use the design elements

In loving memory of my mother

Abigail Banghart Klein

She is greatly missed

Acknowledgments

I started the research that has come to fruition in this book more than ten years ago; as with any project as long-lasting as this one, the number of people to whom I owe a debt of gratitude is beyond count. Usually friends and family are thanked last in acknowledgments, but I begin with all those whose love and support have made these many years of work possible. A by no means exhaustive list includes my mother and father, Abigail and Gus Klein; my brothers, August and Frank, and their families; my friends Mark Anderson, Sherry Bayouth, Marjorie Beale, Tom Benigson, Julie Burstein, Deidre Stiff Collier, Jim Fujii and Ellen Radovic, Stuart Harten, Hu Ying and Michael Phelan, Richard Kroll and Allison Gary, Tom Looser, Mark Oshima, Anne Sneath Islan, Melly Ivy, Carol Kostik, Anne Salladin, and Wes Sasaki-Uemura; and my fellow co-counselors Maria Brown, Joanne Coleman, Suvan and Steve Geer, Keith Glassman, Mary Gonzalez Veleta, Allan Hansen, Mary Hodgson, Vicki Kain, Kelly Steele, and Sarah Tozer. I also thank Ohno Kazuo and his family, as well as Nakajima Natsu, Meiji Setsuko, and Masuda Hiroshi; in differing ways each opened their lives and took me in during my various stays in Japan, for which I am truly grateful. Most especially I thank my husband, Joe McKenna, whose love and whimsical humor have supported me through the highs and lows of this project.

Next on the list is my dissertation advisor, Karen Brazell. As a teacher, mentor, and thoughtful reader, she was a wonderful role model for me throughout my graduate student years; as a friend, she has continued to always be ready with both intellectual engagement and warm support. I also thank my other dissertation committee members, Brett DeBary, Victor Koschmann, and Jane Marie Law, for their insightful comments and suggestions on the dissertation, as well as their friendly encouragement.

My first foray into the world of medieval commentaries was through a reading group with Mitani Kuniaki, Richard Okada and Lewis Cook at Yokohama Shiritsu Daigaku; their lively discussion and helpful guidance to appropriate texts laid the groundwork for all my subsequent work. In addition, Lewis Cook's extensive knowledge of medieval Japanese commentaries has made him a remarkable resource over the years, and this book has benefited greatly from his critical reading. I made initial contact with Professor Mitani through the Stanford Inter-University Center for the Study of Japanese; the teachers there moved me far forward along the never-ending road to fluency.

I am incredibly lucky to have wonderful colleagues at UC Irvine generally, but especially so in the East Asian Languages and Literatures Department. During my first year at UC Irvine, Michael Fuller went beyond the call of duty and stayed up all night helping me print out my dissertation to meet a deadline; that was just the first of numerous times he has come to my aid as scholar and friend. Michael also participated in an interdisciplinary faculty reading group that gave critical suggestions on my theoretical chapter on allegory. This group included Chris Beach, Charlie Chub, Alice Fahs, Carrie Noland, and Kathy Ragsdale; their friendship has also been a continuing source of support. Steve Carter carefully read various drafts of the manuscript and translations and made excellent suggestions for improvement, but, more important, he was always available to discuss ideas. I could not ask for a better or more generous colleague in premodern Japanese literature. In addition, as chair of the department, he bent over backward to make sure that I had the time and financial support I needed. My friend and colleague in the History Department, Anne Walthall, painstakingly read the entire manuscript and made many thoughtful editorial comments. Mindy Han and everyone in the department office gets a special vote of thanks. And on a personal note, Dean Karen Lawrence (and the entire EALL department) stood behind me when my mother was dying, making sure I had the resources to take a nine-month family leave to help my father take care of her. I will always be grateful to everyone at UC Irvine for their kindness in that difficult time, both to me and my family.

In terms of research support, Yoshiko Lang, Akiba Satoshi, and Amy Blumenthal in the interlibrary loan office at Cornell's Olin Library and Pam LaZarr and Dianna Sahaar at UC Irvine deserve kudos for their tremendous efforts to find out-of-print texts and articles in obscure journals. Toshiko Yokota and Akemi Morioka helped with translations. Junko Matsuura was a wonderful research assistant; I could not have done it without her.

Kate Wildman Nakai edited much of the material in Chapter 11 in its earlier appearance as an article on *Ise monogatari zuinō* in *Monumenta Nipponica*. William LaFleur, Mack Horton, William Bodiford, and Royall Tyler have answered queries, discussed ideas, and pointed me in the direction of Japanese sources. My three anonymous referees provided very constructive feedback on the structure of the book as a whole, as well as on difficult points in the translations. John Ziemer has been everything one could ask for in an editor: knowledgeable, flexible, eagle-eyed, and, above all, patient. His editing improved the book considerably.

This particular project has enticed me into fields beyond my original graduate training in literary analysis, notably into the field of esoteric (even heterodox) Buddhism. I have had a few truly helpful guides as I made my way into those uncharted territories. Richard Bowring and John McCrae read early versions of my translation of *Ise monogatari zuinō* and made many helpful suggestions on that fearfully difficult text. Richard Bowring's work, in particular, helped inspire my interest in the commentaries originally, and his input at an early point in the research was crucial for the direction of my project. James Sanford and Bernard Faure read translations and generously shared unpublished manuscripts on Tachikawa Shingon. Their knowledge has been invaluable in teasing out the esoteric meanings of the more difficult commentaries; Sanford's work on spiritual embryology was especially useful.

In terms of financial support, I also have much to be grateful for. First, I thank the Department of Asian Studies and the Graduate School at Cornell for all the fellowships and assistantships that initially allowed me to pursue my interest in Japanese literature. In this respect, Eleanor Jorden played a crucial role in finding me my first fellowship to study Japanese intensively in Cornell's FALCON program. My dissertation research in Japan (1987–89) was undertaken as a Fulbright Graduate Research Scholar; I also received a Kasumi Kaikan Foundation for Community Services Scholarship during the summer of 1989. My dissertation was underwritten by the Woodrow

Wilson National Fellowship Foundation (Charlotte W. Newcombe Doctoral Dissertation Fellowship) and by a grant from the Joint Committee on Japan Studies of the Social Science Research Council and the American Council on Learned Societies with funds provided by the Andrew W. Mellon Foundation. I returned to Japan on a Northeast Asia Council Travel Grant for two months of research in 1994. In 1995–96 I spent a sabbatical year on a National Endowment for the Humanities Fellowship writing the first draft of this manuscript. While at UC Irvine, I have received a number of fellowships and grants, including a UC Irvine Faculty Research Fellowship, a Faculty Career Development Award, and a Humanities Center Research Grant. Each of these grants and fellowships were vital to the development and completion of this book.

Finally, I thank the late Terashima Shōichi of Kōnan Daigaku. During his year as a Fulbright scholar at Cornell University, we met weekly to discuss esoteric commentaries and Noh theater, and those converstaions remain the high point of my intellectual experience as a budding scholar of medieval Japanese literature. Terashima read through a number of early drafts of my dissertation and strongly encouraged me to take on what at the time seemed to me to be an almost impossible project. Without his friendship and guidance, I could hardly have taken the first step along the path to completing this book.

S.B.K.

Contents

Reference Matter

Names and Dates

Japanese and Chinese names are given in the traditional order, with the family names first, unless the author is publishing in English. Japanese texts often indicate a person by his or her office and rank; to simplify identifications for readers in English I have, for the most part, simply given the name of the person. Official titles, when given, follow the standard translations given in William H. McCullough and Helen Craig McCullough, *A Tale of Flowering Fortunes*, vol. 2.

In giving dates, years are given in both the Gregorian and Japanese calendars, but months and days are given according to the Japanese lunar calendar. In other words, in the date "the twenty-eighth day of the first month of Ten'an 1 (857)," "first month" does not mean "January."

I treat the Kamakura period as "medieval" despite arguments recently advanced by historians such as Jeffrey Mass that the medieval period begins in Japan with the fall of Emperor Go-Daigo in 1336. In some ways my argument supports Mass's contentions; the esoteric commentaries fall out of favor after the 1330s for reasons that are related to the changes in politics, economics, and religion that begin to occur with the establishment of the Ashikaga shogunate. However, it is also clear that these commentaries could have developed only in the post-Heian period. Because their methodology has important corollaries with western medieval allegory, it makes sense to call them "medieval"; I could have settled for "proto-medieval," but that seemed too pedantic. Conventional period names are used in the text, often without dates. For easy reference, here is a list of dates:

Early Nara period	646–710
Late Nara period	710–94
Heian period	794–1185
Kamakura period	1185–1333
Nanbokuchō period	1336–92
Muromachi period	1392–1568
Momoyama period	1568–1600
Edo period	1600–1868
Meiji period	1868–1912

Allegories of Desire

Esoteric Literary Commentaries of Medieval Japan

Introduction

One of the more intriguing developments within medieval Japanese poetic culture occurred in the Kamakura period (1185–1333), when the esoteric Buddhist ordination and transmission system of initiation (Shingon *kanjō* 灌頂) began to be incorporated into the pedagogy of waka poetry. At these initiation ceremonies, a "waka mandala" was displayed along with portraits of Sumiyoshi Daimyōjin (the patron deity of waka poetry) and the poets Kakinomoto no Hitomaro (?–ca. 708–15)[1] and Ariwara no Narihira (825–80),[2] who were considered the founders of the Path of Poetry. Incense was burned, elaborate gifts of money and clothing were presented, and after appropriate poetic mantras were recited, commentaries containing esoteric poetic "secrets" were transmitted to the initiate along with genealogical documents purportedly authenticating an unbroken line of transmission.

A relatively obscure poet, Fujiwara no Tameaki (ca. 1230s–after 1295), son of Fujiwara no Tameie (1198–1275) and grandson of the influential poet

1. Little is known about Hitomaro's life, except that he was a court poet and served under three consecutive emperors and that the earliest official anthology of Japanese poetry, the *Man'yō shū*, contains a number of his poems.

2. Narihira was the fifth son of Prince Abo and a grandson of Emperor Heizei (r. 806–9). He was made a commoner with the surname "Ariwara" in the year following his birth. Ki no Tsurayuki (ca. 872–945) included Narihira in his list of six important ninth-century poets in his kana preface to the *Kokin waka shū*.

Fujiwara no Teika (1162–1241), can be identified as the central figure behind the development of both the pedagogical system of poetry initiations and the production of numerous secret commentaries. Tameaki took orders as a Shingon priest and appears to have been an adept in the infamous Tachikawa sect, which advocated tantric sex as a means to enlightenment. His commentaries transform late Heian period (794–1185) canonical texts such as *Ise monogatari* (The tales of Ise) and the first imperial poetry anthology *Kokin waka shū* (Collection of ancient and modern Japanese poems) into complex tantric allegories.

In order to transform these relatively secular texts into esoteric Buddhist allegories, Tameaki developed a new form of literary interpretation that was widely influential. For example, in the medieval period, *Ise monogatari* was popularly understood to be the autobiography of the poet Ariwara no Narihira, and the phrase "mukashi otoko arikeri" (in the past, there was a man) that appears as the first line of the majority of its episodes was thought to refer to Narihira. In order to reveal the true, esoteric meaning of the phrase, the Reizei school commentary *Ise monogatari shō* (Selected comments on *Ise monogatari*), analyzed the graph for *mukashi* 昔: "When [the primordial deities] Izanagi and Izanami had sex [thereby creating the country of Japan], one female and three males were born in twenty-one days. Since this was the origin of Yin and Yang, when Narihira wrote of eroticism (*irogonomi* 色好) he used the word *mukashi* 昔 because that graph is written with the elements for 'twenty-one days' 廿一日."[3] This example of etymological allegoresis involves paronomasia: the resolution of a *kanji* into its component parts and the rearrangement of those parts to reveal a hidden meaning. Here, the repetitive phrase "mukashi otoko" in *Ise monogatari* is understood to be a clue left deliberately by Narihira. When properly analyzed, this clue reveals that *Ise monogatari*, although superficially a tale about Narihira's frivolous love affairs, is grounded in something much more profound: the origin of Japan through the sexual act of Izanagi and Izanami, an act that serves as a model for enlightened tantric sex.

Various texts associated with Tameaki provide evidence that by the early 1270s he was already performing fairly elaborate poetry initiation ceremonies. The idea caught on quickly. Soon every major poetic house had its own esoteric initiation ceremony, and many of their documents contained material

3. [Kunaichō Shoryōbu shōzō Reizeike-ryū] *Ise monogatari shō* (hereafter cited as Reizeike-ryū *Ise monogatari shō*), p. 193.

that Tameaki had originated. Even after the tantric content was eliminated, the allegorical interpretive methodology continued to be used well into the Edo period (1600–1868) in commentaries transmitted by the various poetic houses.

Tameaki's esoteric commentaries gradually filtered into the popular culture of the fifteenth and sixteenth centuries, forming the basis for numerous Noh plays and prose narratives. For example, *Kokin waka shū jo kikigaki: san ryū shō* (Lecture notes on the preface to the *Kokin waka shū*: selected comments from the three schools) provided anecdotal contexts for phrases from the *Kokin shū* preface.[4] The stories associated with these phrases underlie Noh plays as varied as *Takasago* ("growing old together with the twin pines of Takasago and Suminoe"), *Ominameshi* ("recalling the olden days of Man Mountain and mourning the brief blossoming of the maiden flower"), *Matsumushi* ("yearning for a friend at the sound of the pining cricket"), and *Fujisan* ("comparing one's smoldering passion to Mount Fuji's rising smoke").[5] Important allusions to the commentaries also appear in such Noh plays as *Hakurakuten, Kinsatsu, Naniwa, Ukai, Asagao,* and *Sotoba Komachi.* Commentaries on *Ise monogatari* provided the plot and poetic content for *Izutsu, Kakitsubata, Oshio, Ukon,* and *Unrin'in.* Tameaki's commentaries also provided material for Zeami's (ca. 1364–ca. 1443) and Zenchiku's (1405–?) treatises on Noh (particularly Zeami's *Rikugi* [The six modes] and Zenchiku's *Meishuku shō* [Selected notes on the radiant deity]).[6] And allusions to their material appeared in popular tales such as *Soga monogatari* (Tale of the Soga brothers) and *Arokassen monogatari* (The battle of the crows and her-

4. Unless otherwise noted, the term "*Kokin shū* preface" refers to Ki no Tsurayuki's *kana* preface.

5. *Kokin waka shū jo kikigaki: san ryū shō* (hereafter cited as *Kokin waka shū jo kikigaki*), pp. 259–68.

6. The influence of esoteric commentaries on the writing of Noh plays resurfaced as a focus of interest within Japanese scholarship from the 1970s onward, particularly in the work of Itō Masayoshi and his students. Among others, see the following works by Itō Masayoshi: "*Ise monogatari* to yōkyoku"; "Kokin chū no sekai: sono han'ei toshite no chūsei bungaku to yōkyoku"; "Yōkyoku to chūsei bungaku"; and "Yōkyoku to *Ise monogatari* no hiden: *Izutsu* no baai o chūshin toshite." See also Kumazawa Reiko, "*Kokin shū* to yōkyoku—chūsei Kokin chū to no kanren ni oite."

I say "resurfaced" because early Edo period commentaries on Noh such as *Yōkyoku shūyō shō* and *Utai shō* identify a number of allusions to the esoteric commentaries. See Inui Teijo, *Yōkyoku shūyō shō*; and *Utai shō*.

ons).[7] This is a rich field for exploration: in my next book, a companion volume to this one, I intend to look at the various ways these commentaries influenced popular culture in the Nanbokuchō and Muromachi periods, especially the writing of Noh plays.

Although Tameaki's commentaries were extremely influential at the time and had important consequences for popular culture in later centuries, there has been almost no research in English on them, and research in Japanese has focused primarily on textual problems. It is high time that the development of Tameaki's allegorical commentaries was examined within a comparative framework, as well as within the Kamakura historical context. An analysis of their interpretive methods and content is also long overdue.

In order to think productively in comparative terms about the problem of allegory and allegoresis in Japanese literature, I begin with a general structural account of symbol, allegory, and allegoresis and then present concrete illustrations of allegory and allegoresis from the Japanese Classical (Late Heian) and Early Medieval (Kamakura) periods. There are, of course, thorny political problems attending any attempt to impose contemporary Western critical terms such as allegory on texts from a different culture and time. We need to balance the universalizing tendency necessary if we are to talk meaningfully across cultures against the necessity for historicizing and reading texts "against the grain" of theory.

The core of the book addresses three main areas necessary for an understanding of the medieval Japanese development of allegorical commentaries as part of a system of secret pedagogical initiation. First, I examine the commentarial tradition and the texts themselves to see what in the *Ise monogatari* and *Kokin shū* in particular incited allegoresis in ways that other canonical texts, such as *Genji monogatari* (Tale of Genji), did not. Second, I look at the broader context, the political and economic conditions of the late thirteenth century and relevant developments in the practice of religion. Third, I explore the localized historical contingencies: Who was Fujiwara no Tameaki? Why was he involved in creating the waka initiation ceremony and the commentaries? Who else might have been involved? And how did Tameaki justify his allegorical method and legitimate the initiation system that he developed?

7. See Ishikawa Tōru, "Muromachi jidai monogatari ni okeru *Ise monogatari* no kyōju." See also Bowring, "The *Ise monogatari*: A Short Cultural History."

The rest of the book contains a detailed discussion of six exemplary commentaries. Chapters 9 and 10 focus on four commentaries believed to be by Tameaki, and Chapter 11 examines two later commentaries strongly influenced by material originated by Tameaki but thought to be fourteenth-century texts associated with the Reizei and Nijō schools of poetry. For each commentary, I summarize its contents, present examples of its interpretive method, and discuss its subsequent influence on other texts as well as popular literature of the Muromachi period.

Tameaki's commentaries provide an unusual look at how two important texts were written and rewritten (both literally and through interpretation) by their readers. Through them, we can examine how Heian period texts, embedded in the political and cultural discourses of their own time, were appropriated by scholars and artists of a later period when the discursive context had changed considerably. I am interested not so much in trying to recover the original meaning of texts such as *Ise monogatari* as in examining the ways different readers went about attempting to "retrieve" that meaning. I focus in particular on the allegorizing strategies (allegoresis) that medieval Japanese scholars and poets mobilized to confront and appropriate texts for their own ideological purposes.

Until fairly recently, however, there has been a general consensus among many Japanese and nearly all Western scholars that allegory, and particularly allegorical interpretation, does not exist in Japanese literature in any interesting or significant way. I first discovered the existence of the Kamakura allegorical commentaries on *Ise monogatari* while working on a translation of the Noh play *Kakitsubata* (The iris), which draws on a famous episode from that text. For this project I happened to use a new collection of Noh plays edited by Itō Masayoshi, the first scholar to take the commentaries into account in his annotations.[8] However, when I looked for more information on the commentaries in the English-language histories of Japanese literature, there was no mention of them; the standard Japanese histories were just as silent. Nevertheless, the more work I did on the Noh plays related to *Ise monogatari*, the clearer it became that an understanding of the medieval allegoresis on *Ise monogatari* was central to a historical understanding of what the plays meant to medieval playwrights and their audience. Why the scholarly silence?

---

8. See Itō Masayoshi, ed., *Yōkyoku shū*.

This question was given further impetus as I did more research into the waka initiation ceremony and commentaries themselves and realized their influence on the subsequent development of waka pedagogy. The esoteric commentaries themselves were popular for about fifty years (until the 1330s). Even after they began to be replaced by other kinds of secret commentaries in the second half of the fourteenth century, their interpretive method continued to be used, and a variation of the waka initiation ceremony continued to be performed. Again, if the esoteric commentaries and the waka initiation ceremony were so successful, why the nearly complete scholarly silence?

One reason might be that the standard narrative history of Japanese literature articulated by Japanese scholars of the Muromachi and Edo periods, as well as by contemporary Japanese and Western scholars, has tended to emphasize those texts that are easiest to assimilate into the discourses (political, religious, rhetorical) contemporaneous to the critic. Not surprisingly, the commentaries generally used to construct the tradition of Japanese literary criticism by present-day critics are "rational" (approximating modern secular humanism) and address such issues as philology, the pragmatics of composition, and proper aesthetic appreciation. Since Kamakura commentaries follow none of these guidelines for "proper" interpretation, they are, in that sense, "irrational" or "gnostic" (that is, they depend on religious practices no longer considered appropriate or even plausible). Their philological analyses on obscure words and phrases depend on etymological paronomasia and numerological homologizing no longer accepted as interpretive modes. They show almost no interest in pragmatic issues (except to describe certain secret rituals that must be performed for court ceremonials involving poetry) or aesthetics. In other words, they instantiate religious and literary modes of interpretation completely different from our own and are therefore difficult to assimilate into contemporary critical practices.

Although the standard histories ignore the esoteric commentaries, in the past twenty years there have been a number of excellent articles and books in Japanese on the medieval reception of *Ise monogatari* and the *Kokin shū*. Japanese scholars motivated by "reader reception" theories of the 1960s and 1970s have looked at the medieval commentaries in a new light, as examples of the wide variety of ways that medieval authors represented their world. However, the more general scholarly disinterest in (and the occasional strongly worded distaste for) the esoteric commentaries has thrown up a number of roadblocks to understanding them.

The first roadblock is the unavailability of the commentaries in modern printed editions. In the Muromachi period, some of the esoteric commentaries were incorporated into the system of secret transmission known as the *Kokin denju* (古今伝授 Received transmission on the *Kokin shū*).[9] In the late Edo period, a few of the *Kokin denju*–affiliated commentaries were printed in the anthology *Gunsho ruijū* and became available to anyone who could afford the woodblock editions. However, from the Muromachi period on, the majority of the texts discussed in this study lay forgotten in family and temple archives. Only when postwar changes in the tax laws forced families to donate their libraries to public institutions did these commentaries come to light.[10]

Under the circumstances, Japanese scholars with an interest in the commentaries have had to focus on the enormous task of getting the texts into print. Although most of the commentaries discussed here have been published in typescript, a number still exist only in photographic reproductions of the original manuscript. And there are no annotated editions, although most of the collections published since 1970 have helpful scholarly introductions.

Because the commentaries have only just begun to emerge as a serious object of inquiry in Japanese scholarship, in doing the research for this book, I felt the thrill of a detective uncovering long-buried clues. The obscurity of the texts alone has confounded my efforts to piece together what they meant to the people who wrote and received them. The influence of the heterodox Tachikawa sect of Shingon on the commentaries has been one important source of that obscurity. Tachikawa flourished in court circles in the late thirteenth and early fourteenth centuries. By the late fourteenth century, however, it had been declared heretical by orthodox Shingon authorities,

---

9. The term *Kokin denju* in its widest application could be (and often has been) understood to include all the secret commentaries, transmission lineages, waka initiations, and poetic protocols produced from the twelfth through eighteenth centuries. However, I see a clear difference between the esoteric commentaries and initiations developed in the late Kamakura period and the later corpus of secret poetic transmissions produced by the renga poets Sōgi (1421–1502) and Jōen (or Tō no Tsuneyori, d. 1484?). Hence I use the term *Kokin denju* to refer specifically to the lineage of texts associated with Sōgi and Jōen, which dominated literary pedagogy from the sixteenth to eighteenth centuries. See Lewis Cook's description of the creation of the *Kokin denju* in his lengthy introductory chapter in "The Discipline of Poetry: Authority and Invention in the *Kokindenju*," pp. 1–54. Cook's dissertation is the first English-language treatment of the *Kokin denju* and as such is indispensable reading for anyone working on medieval *Kokin shū* commentaries.

10. See Brower, "The Reizei Family Documents."

and over the next hundred years most of its liturgical texts and documents were destroyed. Tameaki's commentaries undoubtedly survived the purge because they were literary texts as well as religious ones; the copies in scholars' libraries were safely beyond the reach of priests intent on destroying all evidence of the sect. The texts analyzed in this study are some of the earliest datable Tachikawa documents and therefore are of great interest to both religious and literary scholars interested in the development and influence of Tachikawa in medieval Japan. That they have only recently begun to be taken seriously is undoubtedly a result of too narrowly defined disciplinary boundaries, both in Japan and in the west. Another reason is that so few other Tachikawa documents survive to help illuminate their meaning. Much more research remains to be done on this fascinating aspect of Japanese religion; as it becomes better understood, the meaning of the commentaries is certain to become clearer.

A second roadblock has been our ignorance of the origins of the allegorical methodology itself. Japanese literary scholars seldom address this issue directly. When it is mentioned at all, we are simply told that it was a method of interpretation in widespread use in the medieval period. It is, in fact, ubiquitous in medieval religious discourse. It may have been influenced by Taoist divination practices, but it was apparently first developed systematically in Japan within the syncretic sects of esoteric Buddhism (Sannō Shinto and Ryōbu Shinto) in the twelfth and thirteenth centuries. From there it spread into popular religious discourse. As a literary interpretive method, however, the earliest known examples date to the late thirteenth century. This makes it seem likely that Tameaki was one of the first to use it for that purpose. Again, much more research needs to be done to understand the origins of this interpretive method. Again, perhaps one reason why so little work has been done on this important topic is that the allegorical method presupposes a form of reasoning that treats resemblance as an indication of deep-seated causal relations. This form of analogical reasoning is completely foreign to present-day secular scholars' more linear, "scientific" forms of reasoning. The fact that we no longer reason this way, however, is not a good reason for ignoring such a widespread phenomenon.

A third roadblock has been the lack of information about the more localized historical contingencies behind the commentaries' production: their dates, authorship, and transmission. The difficulties in determining even these limited facts is intimately related to the circumstances surrounding the production of the commentaries. For political and economic reasons that hinge directly on modes of authority within the Kamakura pedagogical institution of waka poetry, the true authorship of the commentaries was hidden and spurious genealogies were manufactured that traced their transmission through Fujiwara no Teika back to the Heian period. This has meant that the texts' authorship and dating have presented a real challenge, but it is one that Japanese scholars have made great strides in meeting during the past thirty years.

The first scholar to address this challenge was Otsu Yūichi, whose pioneering scholarship in dating the commentaries and identifying the differences between commentaries written in different periods was presented in his *Ise monogatari kochūshaku no kenkyū* (Research into old-style commentaries on *Ise monogatari*). The greatest amount of research on the texts themselves, both in publishing them and providing the first analysis of their contents, has been done by Katagiri Yōichi in his two-volume *Ise monogatari no kenkyū* (Research into *Tales of Ise*) and his six-volume *Chūsei Kokin shū chūshakusho kaidai* (An annotated introduction to medieval commentaries on the *Kokin shū*). Miwa Masatane has done much of the tedious but essential spadework of comparing the transmission lineages of the various commentaries and looking for clues to their authorship. Using these lineages, Miwa and other scholars such as Inoue Muneo have been able to think productively about the localized contingencies behind the development of the commentaries. Their research has shown that Fujiwara no Tameaki is the most likely candidate for authorship, but that other poets from relatively minor poetic factions associated with Fujiwara no Ietaka (1158–1237) and Rokujō Yukiie (1223–75) probably also played an important role.

Western (and most Japanese) scholarship has focused almost exclusively on the aesthetic dimensions of medieval Japanese literature. Allegory and allegoresis, which force the critic to attend to the politics of culture, has naturally been seen as problematic. At the same time, the medieval Japanese religious experience has been transformed into a reflection of contemporary secular humanism. The interests of scholars condition what they see (in psychological terms this is what is referred to as "transference"). It is no accident that the predominant characteristics of the textual object shift with changes in interpretive strategies. Twenty-five years ago, Japanese poetry, subjected to New Criticism, looked remarkably like modern symbolist poetry; more recent forms of poststructuralist interpretation have tended to present Japanese literature as a form of postmodern *écriture avant la lettre.*

Two of the most provocative and exciting critics in recent years, Richard Okada and Mark Morris, have argued consistently and persuasively that Heian literature cannot be encompassed by (and on occasion resists) expressive-realist and New Critical assumptions. Their politically informed arguments are a much-needed corrective. At times, however, both run the risk that their own characterizations of Heian textuality conform all too neatly to Roland Barthes's characterization of the writerly text, or *écriture.* Whereas before, for example, waka poetry was too often seen as the spontaneous lyric expression of the alienated individual, now we suddenly find unstable subject positions (or the disappearance of the author completely), intertextuality, an emphasis on the opaqueness of the material signifier and the endless displacement of metonymy, and an inherent undecidability in and through which the text thwarts interpretation even as it invites it. Okada and Morris invite the criticism that they have simply shifted the scholarly emphasis: whereas before metaphor was the privileged trope, transparency the privileged quality, and realism the privileged narrative structure, now metonymy, opaque undecidability, and *écriture* suddenly emerge from the text.[11]

Nor can I as a critic escape the charge of shaping the text to fit my own interpretive strategies. My fascination with allegory's punning enigmas and the hidden, noetic meanings that lie within its polysemic play predates my interest in Japanese literature. I was attracted to the esoteric dualisms of medieval European Gnosticism and the inventive exegetical etymologies of Biblical allegoresis. Not surprisingly, when I began studying Japanese poetry and drama, I found myself drawn to texts that were structured by a particularly dense rhetoric and that overtly demanded an intimate knowledge of their specific historical context for interpretation. My love of esoteric texts whose difficulties lie precisely in the density of their semantic play and their profound alterity fulfills Augustine's principle that "when something is searched for with difficulty it is, as a result, more delightfully discovered."[12]

---

11. See Okada, *Figures of Resistance*; Okada's linguistic insights into *Ise monogatari* have been particularly useful in constructing the argument of this book. For an especially cogent attack on "lyric expressivity," see Mark Morris's review of *Hitomaro and the Birth of Japanese Lyricism*; and idem, "Waka as Form; Waka as History."

12. As cited in Fletcher, "Allegory in Literary History," p. 42.

What is elided in both New Critical and poststructuralist accounts of Japanese literature are those literary artifacts that resist being transformed into either symbolist poetry or poststructuralist *écriture* because they are grounded in a belief system quite different from our own critical practices. The following study, which foregrounds a group of commentaries that feature very little in the way of what we would today consider "proper" literary criticism, and which were influenced by a very "improper" religious movement, is a historicizing intervention in the field as a whole. I believe we need to take the alterity of the medieval literary and religious experience much more seriously, and this study is intended as a first step toward that goal.

I

Allegory, Symbol, and Allegoresis

An ideal definition of allegory should be broad enough to encompass historical and cultural differences but not be so broad as to be meaningless. Any definition should enable us to distinguish what is unchanging in the allegorical mode from what is historically contingent. It would, for instance, affirm that Dante's *Commedia*, Thomas Pynchon's *The Crying of Lot 49*, and the commentary *Ise monogatari zuinō* (The essentials of *Ise monogatari*) are "allegorical" in some universal sense, even though they operated in particular historical contexts. "Unchanging" is of course a problematic word—there is nothing natural about the development of a literary mode, and any definition is in the end simply a generalization from specific historical cases.[1] In a sense, all definitions of literary terms are tautological; we abstract certain qualities from examples to create ideal literary categories and then use those qualities to determine whether other cases fit the category. Elsewhere I have given an extended structuralist account of the historical relationship of the terms "allegory" and "symbol."[2] Here I restrict my analysis to the most important defining characteristics of symbol, allegory, and allegoresis and discuss what gives rise to them, before turning to an examination of allegory and allegoresis in medieval Japan.

1. For a discussion of this point, see de Man, "The Epistemology of Metaphor," pp. 16–17.

2. Klein, "Allegories of Desire: Kamakura Commentaries and the Noh," pp. 16–78.

Brief Definitions of Allegory and Symbol

Classical rhetoricians such as Cicero and Quintilian considered allegory to be a series of correlated metaphors that could be understood as one larger extended figure that created a secondary surplus beyond the literal or referential meaning of the text. Quintilian noted that "continued metaphor develops into allegory," and Cicero claimed that "when there is a sequence of metaphors, the sense of the words is totally altered; thus, in this case when the Greeks speak of *allegoria* etymologically, this is correct, but logically it would be better to follow Aristotle and range all these figures under the headings of metaphors."[3] This extremely broad definition of allegory as any continuous figurative language was widely accepted prior to the nineteenth century. In the late eighteenth century, however, the Romantic poets developed a concept of "symbol" that came to replace allegory as figure; allegory was in turn relegated to the status of a specific (and denigrated) case of figural language.[4] In the late twentieth century, poststructuralists have reversed the terms again; allegory has once more become the trope of tropes, and symbol is now devalued as a specialized use of figurative language.[5]

The historical slipperiness of these two terms and the easy substitution of one for the other within theory should lead us to see that on the most basic

---

3. Quintilian, *The Institutes of Oratory*, and Cicero, *The Orator*, as cited in Fletcher, *Allegory: The Theory of a Symbolic Mode*, p. 74.

4. According to Rene Wellek ("Symbol and Symbolism in Literature"), the first application of the term "symbol" to literature, with a meaning clearly defined in contrast to allegory, occurred in Germany in the late eighteenth century. Prior to that, symbol, emblem, and allegory were used almost interchangeably. In 1790 Kant first used the term in a sense that we would recognize today ("Beauty is a symbol of morality"), but it was Coleridge in England and Goethe in Germany who, in the early nineteenth century, developed and refined the notion of symbol.

5. Paul de Man's essay "Rhetoric of Temporality" initiated the rehabilitation of allegory within poststructuralism. According to de Man's critique of the Romantics, allegory's reference to another, temporally anterior signified (it can "consist only in the *repetition* . . . of a previous sign with which it can never coincide"; ibid., p. 190) had a demystified clarity that was distasteful to literary critics who wished to replace faith in a transcendent God as a guarantee of the possibility of closing the subject/object split with faith in the symbol's offer of a potentially sublime aesthetic experience. It is this same demystified clarity, with its display of the arbitrariness of the signifying relation, that has made allegory the critical darling of poststructuralist criticism. For a more detailed critique of the poststructuralist understanding of allegory, see Klein, "Allegories of Desire," pp. 57–71.

structural level there is no difference between allegory and symbol. On this level, both are simply a series of tropes that simultaneously have both a "literal" meaning (determined mostly by linguistic codes) and a secondary meaning that can be interpreted only by its relation to the discursive (textual) context. In the post-nineteenth-century Romantic binary of symbol and allegory, the major differences emerge only in the kinds of discourse a reader uses to create secondary meaning and the level of complexity of rhetorical ornament employed.

For contemporary scholars, the basic difference between symbol and allegory remains that which Coleridge laid out in the nineteenth century: "Of utmost importance to our present subject is this point, that the latter (allegory) cannot be other than spoken consciously; whereas in the former (the symbol) it is very possible that the general truth may be unconsciously in the writer's mind during the construction of the symbol."[6] In other words, the interpretation of a symbolic text appears to require only naturalized discursive conventions that we accept unconsciously, but an allegorical text demands the use of political and/or religious discourse, and this dependence on "extrinsic" discourse forces the process of interpretation into consciousness.

Thus post-Romantic scholars have generally understood symbols as creating an illusion of naturalized identity; that is, the "doubleness" inherent in symbols as tropes is masked by naturalized conventions of verisimilitude that join the writer and the reader in one ontologically unified, synchronous world. This naturalization is achieved in both writing and interpretation by using only rhetorical and literary codes that can be considered intrinsic to the text, and by employing only cultural codes that seem universal (especially the "scientific" logic of cause and effect, and the "psychological" logic of human behavior). For example, conventionalized associations are treated as natural and universally understood: a journey = life, autumn = old age, dew = tears, sleep = death. The structural arbitrariness of symbol is further masked by a deemphasis on rhetorical ornament or any polysemic complexity that directs the reader's attention away from an illusion of transparent referentiality.

Allegory, on the other hand, appears to emphasize the semantic doubling inherent in all tropes by relying on discourses that lie outside the text and are difficult to naturalize: political, philosophical, religious. The reader is incited to use these extrinsic discourses in interpreting a text by a lack of the plausible causal relations and "realistic" natural settings found in symbolic texts.

---

6. Coleridge, *Coleridge's Miscellaneous Criticism*, p. 99.

Gordon Teskey has noted that "allegorical narratives are often, in Aristotelian terms, badly constructed: paratactic, digressive, episodic, and replete with iconographic details that have nothing to do with the story."[7] It is precisely this operational disorder, however, that encourages readers to construct their own meaning through an intricate network of correspondences, based on resemblance, that unifies the allegorical text's superficially unconnected images.

This sustained and conscious interpretive interaction between reader and allegorical text has many of the features of a game: the reader proceeds on the assumption that the author has intentionally left clues to a hidden, noetic meaning, an enigma to be discovered beneath the obvious literal or referential meaning. As Thomas Pynchon's *The Crying of Lot 49* shows, the anxiety that fuels paranoia and conspiracy theories—that superficially unconnected things are in truth bound by a hidden web of correspondences—is the same hermeneutic anxiety that fuels allegorical interpretation. And because these correspondences are based on analogy, it is not possible to reach a hermeneutical terminus: like Pynchon's character Oedipa Mass, we find that the ultimate unifying explanation is endlessly deferred.

In contrast to symbolic figures, allegorical figures emphasize the polysemous side of language through their use of tropes that involve complex wordplay, especially puns on proper names and place-names that give them a semantic force. This kind of wordplay threatens the transparent referentiality of language by focusing on the textual surface and by making language a noumenal reality in its own right. In medieval European texts, the polysemy of punning proper names, personification, and emblem contributed to the construction of allegory. In the Japanese case, polysemic play such as *kakekotoba* (pivot words), *monotsukushi* (poetic catalogues), hidden names, and *engo* (associated words), all of which call attention to language itself and seem to have little referential function, were put to good use in the allegorical mode.

The Medieval Understanding of Language

Allegory's presumed dependence on extrinsic discourses of religion or politics appears to promise that it might be possible to separate the allegorical meaning from the literal; indeed, allegory's supposedly simplistic one-to-one determination of image and referent was one of the post-Romantics' strongest criticisms. This criticism depends, however, on a post-Kantian view of

7. Teskey, "Allegory," p. 18.

language as both arbitrary and ideally transparent that medieval readers did not share. Medieval allegory only superficially appears to be separable into two parallel senses; close analysis of the texts shows that the doubled literal and allegorical levels are inextricably bound together in the figural language of the text.[8] What binds the two levels together, particularly in religious allegory, is the assumption that words have "magical" force. Analogical and/or metonymic correspondences between language and reality are not accidents but "signatures" left intentionally by a transcendent creator. They are marks indicating where interpretation should take place.[9] For a medieval allegorist, language is revelatory: "Words contain wisdom, and the form in which we inherit words from the past is itself not without reason, if we can only discover the inner web of motives that led to the slow formation of that legacy."[10] As Michel Foucault explains in *The Order of Things*, "The truth of all these marks—whether they are woven into nature itself or whether they exist in lines on parchments and in libraries—is everywhere the same; coeval with the institution of God . . . and this is why nature and the word can intertwine with one another to infinity, forming, for those who can read it, one vast single text."[11] For the allegorist, the path to the discovery of the "inner web of motives" that entwines nature and the word is the principle that almost any metaphoric or metonymic link must be meaningful, that "all things mortal are but metaphor."[12] Using this principle as a method, the allegorist "treats the universe as if it were a book."[13]

Even modern secularists may continue to treat the world like a book. Conspiracy theories surrounding the supposed cover-up of an alien crash

---

8. Maureen Quilligan (*The Language of Allegory: Defining the Genre*, p. 68) argues that "the key to the story's meaning lies in the text's language—its most *literal* aspect—not in the translation of the story's events to a different (metaphorical) set of terms" (see also ibid., pp. 25–29). For another discussion of this point, see Van Dyke, *The Fiction of Truth: Structures of Meaning in Narrative and Dramatic Allegory*, pp. 35–37.

9. In *The Order of Things*, Michel Foucault discusses this point in ample detail, arguing that the principle that all knowledge is based on deciphering the meaning of these signatures was a primary category of thought up to the late sixteenth century. According to Foucault, this principle applied equally to the phenomenal world and to language. See esp. chap. 2, "The Prose of the World," in *The Order of Things*, pp. 17–45.

10. Fletcher, "Allegory in Literary History," p. 45.

11. Foucault, *The Order of Things*, p. 34.

12. "Alles Vergängliche / Ist nur ein Gleichnis"; from Goethe, *Faust*, pt. II, last stanza.

13. Fletcher, "Allegory as Literary History," p. 46.

landing at Roswell, New Mexico, or television shows that play on paranoia, such as *The X Files*, depend on a belief in a world interconnected by hidden supernatural correspondences. Most critical observers recognize that the web of correspondences used to fabricate the Roswell conspiracy is produced by the interpreter rather than inherent in historical fact. Perhaps because contemporary scholars tend to see the analogical reasoning behind conspiracy theory as symptomatic of paranoid schizophrenia, they are reluctant to impute such "irrational" reasoning to the subjects of their research.

In fact, medieval European religious philosophy posited an immanent logos that binds phenomenal reality and language (a belief we might now consider irrational); but there was also a strong presumption that language can never fully express that ultimate unifying truth, a belief that accords quite well with our present-day critical understanding of language. According to Gordon Teskey, medieval allegory seems to direct us "through the process of interpretation, toward a point where all mystery is dispelled in the presence of truth. . . . What we encounter instead is a point where all further progress is blocked by the inadequacy of language to express something that is always beyond it."[14]

This ambivalence might be said to take the form of two categories of thought, often mobilized as interpretive strategies, that I will characterize, following Bernard Faure, as "gnosticism" and "rationalism."[15] Like Faure, I argue that these two categories of thought should be understood not as distinct but as two poles along the heterogeneous continuum of medieval thought, neither of which has ultimate priority.

In medieval Japan, rationalism included a strong skepticism about language's ability to express the truth of Absolute Reality; despite this skepticism, however, it was taken for granted that language was the only tool available. (The paradoxical *kōans* of Rinzai Zen were developed with precisely this problem in mind.) However, even "enlightened" thinkers such as Sōtō Zen patriarch Dōgen (1200–1253) were not particularly worried about the question of whether language could express *phenomenal* reality, because phenomenal reality was not "real" anyway. So for these thinkers, language's ability to refer to the real world was, in a fundamental way, a non-problem.

Religious discourses are never homogeneous, however. A second category of thought in medieval Japanese religious discourse (both elite and folk), dia-

---

14. Teskey, "Allegory," p. 16.

15. Faure, *The Rhetoric of Immediacy: A Cultural Critique of Chan/Zen Buddhism*, pp. 3–7.

lectically intertwined with the first and not unlike that of medieval Europeans, assumed the essential underlying unity of language and reality.[16] It was this faith that provided the grounds for Shinto *kotodama* (spirit words), Shingon esoteric dharani based in Sanskrit "seed" syllables, or the Pure Land recitation "Namu Amida Butsu" (All Hail, Amida Buddha). For these sacred words to have the performative power to affect the phenomenal world (for example, to have the power to heal, curse, save), there had to be a conviction that what might appear superficially to be mere analogical correspondences (by resemblance or contiguity) between language and reality were actually signs of a deep unity that could be used by those with proper knowledge.

Thus, for the medieval Japanese, as for medieval Europeans, the correspondences between linguistic signs (words) and phenomena were often *not* arbitrary but natural. They were "signatures," although not signatures put there by one transcendent, all-encompassing God.[17] It should be emphasized, however, that any neat line between "enlightened" and "mystified" views of language in the medieval Japanese context is an artificial one. Despite the apparent antithesis of these views, medieval Japanese often managed to hold both simultaneously. As Thomas Hare has pointed out, even so elevated a religious thinker as Kūkai (774–835), the founder of Shingon Buddhism, believed in the power of a rite that promised that if you recited the "True Words" one million times, you would be able to memorize the meaning of all the sutras. It was also Kūkai who said, in a memorial to the throne in 806, "Dharma has no language, but it is not apparent except through language."[18]

Allegorical Interpretation

Allegoresis is allegory's structural counterpart. As we have seen, allegory is a mode of structuring narrative in such a way that the reader is encouraged to discover a unifying meaning for an apparently disparate series of tropes by means of correspondences with an external religious or political discourse. In

16. By "elite" and "folk," I do not mean to imply that allegorical thought was relegated exclusively to non-elite discourse; in fact, quite the opposite. For a succinct analysis of the difficulties in using the terms "elite" and "folk" with regard to religion, see Faure's chapter "Chan/Zen and Popular Religion" in *Rhetoric of Immediacy*, esp. pp. 79–87.

17. For the western medieval view of "signatures," see Foucault's discussion of Paracelsus in *The Order of Things*, esp. pp. 19–20, 25–30.

18. As cited in Thomas Hare, "Reading Writing Cooking: Kūkai's Interpretive Strategies," p. 256.

allegoresis, a reader attempts to discover a unifying meaning in a text by the same basic method; the significant difference is that the text which is the focus of interpretation is not originally an allegory. The running commentary of allegoresis attempts to get at meanings "hidden" beneath the textual surface by finding puns and other forms of polysemy (including numerological homologies) that the author never intended.

Angus Fletcher sees the two modes of allegory and allegoresis as opposite poles of one basic communicative process: "Secondary meanings may be imposed upon a text, or an author may clearly build them into a text, but no clear distinction separates the interpretive and creative aspects of allegory."[19] Maureen Quilligan, on the other hand, sets up an opposition between allegoresis (or "imposed allegory") and allegory "proper" (which she also refers to as "creative" or "narrative" allegory).[20] Although I agree with Quilligan that allegoresis and allegory "proper" may well emerge for differing historical and cultural reasons, I side with Fletcher when he says that the two cannot be separated. The authority and legitimacy of an allegorical commentary or interpretation depend implicitly on the belief that the text was written as allegory. Before allegoresis can occur, there must already exist a few texts written as narrative allegories that the interpreter can cite as justification for this method.

To contemporary scholars, allegoresis so obviously appears to falsify the meaning of the text (to whatever extent we can understand that meaning in terms of its original historical context) that it is impossible to take it seriously. However, whereas present-day scholars of medieval Europe treat Augustine's or Aquinas's allegorical interpretations of the Hebrew Bible as sincere attempts to make it consistent with Christian scripture and theology, until very recently Japanese literary scholars have denigrated esoteric allegoresis of *Ise monogatari* and *Kokin shū* as interpretations in bad faith. True, the motivation for these texts is somewhat suspect since the initiation ceremonies were quite lucrative. But the difference in views may also have to do with the fact that Christianity continues to be a dominant religious system,

19. Fletcher, "Allegory in Literary History," p. 41.

20. On the relationship between these two terms, see Quilligan, *The Language of Allegory*, pp. 30–33. Quilligan believes that the two forms should be treated separately, although both originate in the allegorist's obsession with polysemy. Throughout the present discussion, I will use "allegoresis" to refer to allegorical interpretation and "allegory" to refer primarily to allegorical figures.

whereas tantric Buddhism in the form of the Tachikawa Shingon sect was declared heretical in the late fourteenth century, and there are no toes left to step on. Perhaps, however, as more religious texts of Tachikawa Shingon and Ryōbu Shinto are uncovered and published and their influence on the writing of the commentaries becomes better understood, it will be possible to see Fujiwara no Tameaki and others involved in the production of these commentaries as sincere participants in a religious movement. At any rate, notwithstanding the suspect motivation of the medieval allegorists, these commentaries are replete with cultural assumptions whose interrogation should provide a fuller understanding of the late Kamakura period.

The simple fact that allegoresis was deemed necessary tells us one important thing about the period: canonical texts were being rendered obscure and outdated by epistemic change. As Fredric Jameson notes, the great allegorical interpretive systems "sprang from cultural need and from the desperate attempt of the society in question to assimilate monuments of other times and other places, whose original impulses were quite foreign to them, and which required a kind of rewriting—through elaborate commentary, and by means of the theory of figures—to take their place in the new scheme of things."[21] Allegorization brings old texts in line with the new, but in some sense it also allows the old to continue unchanged: allegoresis is syncretic rather than synthetic.[22] It allows colloidal mixtures of beliefs to exist in layers without homogenizing them into a single dominant doctrine.[23] As a "diplomatic medium of thought," allegoresis "gathers in rather than expels, but at the same time it preserves the sense of diverse origins and intellectual styles."[24] Allegoresis in particular appears to be fueled by a desire for conciliation and accommodation; it often appears when rival worldviews clash at their borders.

Take, for example, the early Christian fathers' theory of "types": key persons, actions, and events in the Jewish Bible were not only historically real but also prefigured later persons, actions, and events in the New Testa-

---

21. Jameson, "Metacommentary," p. 10.

22. Syncretism differs from synthesis in that "the former preserves the individual traits of the combining beliefs, whereas the latter would achieve a radical transformation of disparate cultural forces, until a single set among them came to dominate and control the assimilation of other sets as minor premises in the logic of the culture as a whole" (Fletcher, "Allegory in Literary History," p. 43).

23. Ibid., pp. 43–44.

24. Ibid., p. 44.

ment.[25] This allegorical reading of the Old Testament was necessitated by the conflict between the new, Christian worldview and the old, Judaic one that obliged early Christians to develop typology as a way to accommodate the Old Testament into their new world order. They justified this radical rereading of the Old Testament in terms of the New by claiming that the events narrated in the Old Testament had been part of the Christian God's plan from the beginning. As we shall see, the Japanese allegorical commentaries that arose in the Kamakura period followed this pattern in recuperating Heian texts for a new and different age.

It is easy to believe, given the serious political and religious changes faced by downwardly mobile aristocrats in the thirteenth century, that allegoresis was fueled by a desire to stem the rapid loss of court culture, even if it meant transforming canonical works into religious texts more in keeping with the esoteric Buddhist proclivities of the time. Before we examine that possibility, however, the question of what creates the demand for new interpretive strategies needs to be theorized.

Triggers for Interpretation

Allegory tends toward the fragmentary as a way to incite interpretation; allegorical interpreters are attracted to the gaps, ellipses, and fragmentary structure of a text in the belief that they themselves are able to supplement its textual aporias and fractures. In *Symbolism and Interpretation*, Tzvetan Todorov divides such difficulties, which he calls "triggers" for interpretation, into two categories: syntagmatic and paradigmatic. Syntagmatic triggers are those within the text itself, such as textual contradictions, lacunae or discontinuities, tautologies, and superfluities. Paradigmatic triggers arise from a confrontation between the text and what Todorov terms "the collective memory" of a society, the cultural discourse (in the broadest sense of the term) synchronic to the interpreter.[26] Here interpretation is called into play by (1) whatever is unintelligible or ungrammatical according to contemporary

25. Augustine expressed this principle with typical epigrammatic wit: "In the Old Testament the New Testament is concealed; in the New Testament the Old Testament is revealed" (cited in M. H. Abrams' discussion of typological interpretation in *A Glossary of Literary Terms*, p. 89). See also Mark Taylor's discussion of typological interpretation in *Erring: A Postmodern A/theology*, pp. 52–61; and Tzvetan Todorov's discussion in *Symbolism and Interpretation*, pp. 116–19.

26. Todorov, *Symbolism and Interpretation*, pp. 28–32.

linguistic and rhetorical codes; (2) whatever seems implausible given the contemporary cultural codes that make up the interpreter's commonsense understanding of the world; (3) whatever seems inappropriate given the contemporary codes (cultural, political, religious) that determine norms and values.

For exegetes, the most serious contradiction tends to be intratextual. As John Henderson points out in *Scripture, Canon, and Commentary,* it is vital that any internal contradictions in a canonical text be only apparent, since "truth, even if it is not really one and indivisible, must, by most estimations, at least be non-self contradictory, internally consistent."[27] Intertextual contradiction with other canonical works can be a serious problem as well. The discomfort triggered by discontinuity (and/or lack of sufficient detail to make narrative sense) and superfluity (and/or redundancy) in texts can incite a wide variety of interpretive explanations. These include everything from the transcendent (oracular revelations are *meant* to be obscure) to the historical (I have secret knowledge of what *really* happened). A sense that the text is implausible and inappropriate is most likely to be triggered in a reader whose cultural and religious discursive codes differ significantly from those of the context in which the text was originally written. A passage may strike a reader as implausible or inappropriate when it conflicts with her "commonsense" notions of how the world is structured or when the characters act in ways that go against her religious and moral codes. Words that are obscure and difficult for the interpreter to understand may simply incite etymological explication, but when the interpreter's attempt to make sense of an archaic word is inspired by the belief that obscurity is a sign left intentionally to signal a hidden meaning, etymological allegoresis is likely to follow.

As we shall see, *Ise monogatari* manifests every one of these triggers—a lapidary, elliptical style; obscure words and phrases; a paratactic structure filled with narrative gaps; the enigmatic use of generic nominals ("a woman" and "a man") instead of proper names; no clear author (who might be invoked to explain some of these problems). Even its title is a mystery. The *Kokin shū* also provided plenty of opportunity for interpretive play: the *kana* preface by Ki no Tsurayuki (ca. 872–945) in particular posed numerous

---

27. Henderson, *Scripture, Canon, and Commentary,* p. 115. Henderson provides an excellent discussion of what he calls "commentarial assumptions and strategies," which in many ways support the points I make in the following chapters.

problems for later exegetes. According to Fletcher, the allegorist proposes to smooth over any apparent discrepancies by contextualizing them within a broader framework, thereby supplanting "the literal inconsistency by a spiritual equivalent possessed of inner truth, precisely in short, what had been veiled by the inconsistent literal surface."[28] This is exactly the approach taken by Kamakura commentators: they strove to provide an overarching framework that supplemented and thus explained the textual aporias in *Ise monogatari* and the *Kokin shū*. And although at times it may seem, in the chapters that follow, that the medieval exegetes went to extremes in their attempts to "rationalize" these texts, we should always keep in mind Frank Kermode's point that "it probably requires more strenuous effort to believe that a text lacks coherence than to believe that it [is coherent]."[29] Even today, a number of scholars continue the tradition of trying to find coherence and rational purpose in *Ise monogatari*'s fragmented, gap-ridden structure.

---

28. Fletcher, "Allegory in Literary History," p. 45.
29. Kermode, *The Genesis of Secrecy: On the Interpretation of Narrative*, p. 53.

2

Allegory and Allegoresis in Premodern Japanese Literature

In order to understand how allegoresis developed in Kamakura Japan, we need to look first at examples of allegory proper, because they helped legitimate allegorizing interpretation. By the Heian period, a shared body of allegorical images were beginning to be constructed: particular puns and other kinds of wordplay were regularly assumed to allude to "external" political and religious discourse. At the same time shared conventions of allegorical writing and reading were developing: authors themselves, particularly poets, placed hints (triggers) in their texts to encourage readers into the interpretive play of allegorical correspondences.

Once interpretive conventions for allegory were in place, gaps in contextual information tended to trigger commentary. One common response was to supplement the text with narrative details that reduced the text's ambiguity. To the extent that the creative production of details points to religious and political discourse, this move can be seen as a spontaneous form of interpretive allegorization on the part of readers. The thirteenth-century commentaries, however, are distinguished by the use of more complex forms of etymological and numerological allegoresis that have no counterparts in the Heian period composition of allegorical poetry and prose.

Political Allegory and Allegoresis

When rhetorical ornament is understood in relation to religious and political discourse, the text becomes a mirror of ideology: as "figurative cosmologies" allegories tend to sum up worldviews. To the extent that medieval religious and political cosmologies were hierarchical, we will find reflected images of hierarchy within an allegorical text's ornamental surface. Its verbal ornaments (emblems) are often a cosmos in miniature, signifying the relation of the microcosmos to the macrocosmos. Such hierarchic cosmologies create emblematic chains of command that indicate the place of a person (or class of persons) within the political and religious order.

Although political allegory is most often embedded in a religious cosmology, it can also appear as allegory's secularized form, and as such, political allegory has continued to appear into the twentieth century. Secularized political allegory can still be recognized as allegory by its use of puns and wordplay to hide a secondary meaning whose proper interpretation depends on the reader's knowledge of contemporary political discourse. In the Heian period, this kind of secularized political allegory seems to have been used primarily in the context of eulogistic congratulations to those stationed above the author or in public poetry expressing the author's discontent. Take, for example, two poems from the *Kokin shū*. The first (*Kokin shū* 1095) is an anonymous "Hitachi song":

> *tsukubane no / kono mo kano mo ni / kage wa aredo*
> *kimi ga mikage ni / masu kage wa nashi*
>
> On Tsukuba Peak, there is shade (*kage*) from the sun here,
> there, and everywhere,
> but nowhere is there protection (*kage*) surpassing the shelter
> of our sovereign's benevolence (*mikage*).

This eulogistic poem, whose meaning centers on a wordplay on *kage*, teaches us how to read the political meanings that lie hidden in the word's seemingly antithetical meanings of "shade" 陰 and "reflected light" 景. In its meaning of "light," *kage* becomes a figure for reflected glory of political power; as "shadow," it acts as a figure for the shelter provided by a powerful person. This figural reading is made literal in Japanese with the word *mikage* 御影, the sovereign's benevolent protection of his subjects. The political hierarchy is held securely in place by homophonic correspondences that naturalize the relationship between ruler and ruled.

A second poem from the *Kokin shū* (966, by Miyaji no Kiyoki), may have been written with the other poem in mind:

> *Tsukubane no / ko no moto goto ni / tachi zo yoru*
> *haru no miyama no / kage o koitsuru*
>
> Searching beneath each and every tree on Tsukuba Peak,
> I long for shelter within the springtime mountains.

This poem, which the prose foretext (*kotobagaki* 詞書) informs us was "composed [by Kiyoki] when told he had been derelict in his duties and was to be dismissed from the crown prince's guards," does not spell out the wordplay on *kage* for us; we are left to interpret the doubled meaning for ourselves. To do so, the reader calls on her knowledge of the political meanings for *kage*, as well as a hint given in the foretext: Kiyoki was one of the crown prince's guards. The crown prince was metonymically identified with spring because he lived in the Spring Palace. Thus the mention of the lovely mountains of spring (*haru no miyama*) is a veiled reference to the crown prince, and the poem suggests allegorically Kiyoki's desire to once more be blessed with his favor. *Kokin shū* 966 assumes that the reader already understands the multiple meanings of *kage* and that there is no need to spell out its secondary meaning explicitly. In its use of implicit metaphor and metonymy, along with the extrinsic reference provided by the prose foretext, it therefore functions as a more complex allegory.

It was because such poems existed, written as allegories by means of polysemic play, that medieval commentators could justify using an allegorical reading strategy on what we might now consider non-allegorical poems from *Ise monogatari* or the *Kokin shū*. As an example of such political allegoresis, let us look at the Reizei school's analysis in *Ise monogatari shō* (Selected comments on *Ise monogatari*) of episodes (*dan* 段, literally "steps") 7 through 9. According to the opening line of episode 7, the Man of Old (identified in the medieval period as Ariwara no Narihira), feeling weary of the capital, takes one or two friends on a journey to the Eastern Provinces. Quite early on in the history of the reception of *Ise monogatari*, this journey was understood to have been undertaken because Narihira was in disgrace with the powerful Fujiwara family. Readers generally assumed that Narihira felt it expedient to remove himself from the capital after his affair with Fujiwara no Takako (also read Takaiko or Kōshi, 842–910), the niece and adopted daughter of the Regent Fujiwara no Yoshifusa (804–72), came to light. Takako later became the Empress of the Second Ward (Nijō no Kisaki).[1] Since Yoshifusa was intending to present Takako as a consort to Emperor Seiwa (r. 858–76), Narihira was interfering with his plans and therefore became *persona non grata* to Yoshifusa and his clan. Although the common assumption among readers, even today, is that Narihira and the Fujiwara were at odds politically, the Reizei school *Ise monogatari shō* reads the relationship between Narihira and Yoshifusa very differently, and it does so by means of a similar analysis of puns and tropes to that seen in the interpretations of the poems discussed above.

Ise monogatari shō argues that Narihira never went to the Eastern Provinces but was instead kept under house arrest near the capital:

> With regard to the opening line, "Long ago there is a man who having grown weary of life in the Capital, travels to the East," in truth, [Narihira] did not, feeling weary, travel to Azuma (東, the Eastern Provinces). When his abduction of the Empress of the Second Ward became public knowledge, it is said that he was placed under house arrest in Regent Yoshifusa's villa in Higashiyama (東山, the Eastern Hills). The character for "east" in Azuma was taken [from Higashiyama].[2]

Here *Ise monogatari shō* argues that the phrase "Eastern Provinces" is simply a cover for the "Eastern Hills" of the capital. During the time Narihira was supposedly traveling in lonely exile in the Eastern Provinces, he was actually staying as the guest of his "enemy," Fujiwara no Yoshifusa, who felt sorry for the couple and wanted to let them continue to meet. Yoshifusa helped Narihira produce the episodes describing his travels in order to fool the emperor, who had ordered Narihira's exile. And throughout the time Narihira was under house arrest at Yoshifusa's villa, Yoshifusa continued to argue his case before the emperor. According to *Ise monogatari shō*, Yoshifusa's impassioned pleas on Narihira's behalf shortened his term of "exile" to only three years.

---

1. The fact that this was the understanding of almost any reader from the late Heian period onward can be seen by a reference to *Ise monogatari* in the historical chronicle *Ōkagami* (ca. 1085–1125), in which the narrator describes Narihira's relationship with Takako as though it were historical fact and then defends his gossip: "It is presumptuous for a nobody like me to talk about such things, but they are all matters of common knowledge. Is there anybody nowadays who hasn't read the *Collection of Early and Modern Times* [*Kokin shū*] and *Tales of Ise*?" (Helen McCullough, trans., *Ōkagami: The Great Mirror*, p. 73). Note that most contemporary scholars read 高子 as "Takaiko." I have used "Takako" because that is how both the medieval commentaries and Noh plays read her name. See, e.g., Reizeike-ryū *Ise monogatari shō*, p. 360; and *Kakitsubata*, in Itō, *Yōkyoku shū*, vol. 59, p. 262.

2. Reizeike-ryū *Ise monogatari shō*, p. 305.

By making this claim, *Ise monogatari shō* transforms episodes 7 through 9 into pure allegory; every phrase, every piece of natural scenery, is simply an allegorical refraction of Narihira's political and amatory situation. This enables a highly politicized form of allegoresis, such as the following analysis of the prose text of episode 9. In this episode Narihira and his friends reach Yatsuhashi, where they see a splendid mass of iris blooming at the edge of a marsh. They get down off their horses to admire the irises while eating lunch under the shade of a tree:

> The marsh (*taku* 沢) [at Yatsuhashi] represents Yoshifusa's family. A person's rising fortunes are signified by a marsh. We call the benevolence (*on* 恩) of a sovereign "*ontaku*" 恩沢, signifying that his favor is as deep and wide as a marsh. . . . A marsh is a place that is "enriched with moisture." So this marsh signifies the flowering fortune of Yoshifusa's family. The phrase "in the shade of a tree" (*ki no kage* 木の陰) signifies the flowering fortune of Yoshifusa as a tree. As the fortunes of Yoshifusa flower, his house becomes like a large tree that many people gather under for shelter (*kage* 陰) from the sun. The phrase "get down [off their horses] and sit" means Narihira came down from above the clouds [i.e., the palace] and was kept under house arrest in the Eastern Hills.[3]

Here the Reizei analysis identifies puns on "marsh" (*taku* 沢) and "shade" (*kage* 陰) to transform *Ise monogatari* into a celebration of Fujiwara power and benevolence.

One might well ask why the Reizei school took such a counterintuitive position with regard to Narihira's political situation. One possibility is that since the Reizei were themselves Fujiwara, they had every reason to downplay antagonism between Narihira and their own family. If there were animosity, it would be less likely that they would have access to Narihira's supposed secret commentaries on *Ise monogatari*. Another reason might be that for the allegorical readings to be true secrets and hence valuable to the initiate who paid for them, they had to be counterintuitive; that is, the allegorized reading had to go against the grain of what an ordinary reader could guess simply from reading the text. By applying the methods of poets who produced political allegory proper, the Reizei were, ironically, able to retroactively neutralize a politically volatile reading and replace it with a new reading that politicized *Ise monogatari* in a way more useful to their house.

---

3. Ibid., p. 308.

Religious Allegory and Allegoresis

My first example of religious allegory is an anonymous poem and its foretext from the imperial anthology *Goshūi waka shū* (Later gleanings of Japanese poems; 1086). It is a witty allegory whose correct interpretation depends on the reader's knowledge of the *Lotus Sutra* (*Myōhō renge kyō*), the most important religious text of medieval Japan.[4]

Three ladies-in-waiting were on the way to a lecture in separate carriages, but having got caught in the rain, all climbed into one carriage and reached the hall successfully.

> *morotomo ni / mitsu no kuruma ni / norishikado*
> *ware wa ichimi no / ame ni nureniki*
>
> Our party rode out in three vehicles,
> but all of us got dampened by the impartial rain.[5]

The initial clue that this poem was intended as more than a literal narrative of three women on an outing is conveyed by the story's apparent lack of inherent interest: Why write a poem about getting caught in a rainstorm? In addition, the topic of the poem fails to conform to any of the secular conventions of the time (love, the seasons). Given this hint that the blandness of the anecdote may hide some other, allegorical, meaning, the reader looks more closely at the figural language of the foretext and the poem. Here one finds two more clues: the first is the phrase *kuruma* (車 vehicle), which, as in English, can be taken in both a literal sense, as a cart or carriage, and a metaphorical sense, as the conveyance of an idea. The foretext's image of trading three vehicles for one, for any reader acquainted with the *Lotus Sutra*, immediately evokes the "Parable of the Burning House." In this story, the Buddha tempts his three children, who are playing in a burning house (this sinful world), with promises of three carts (the three "vehicles" of Buddhism). When they emerge from the house, however, instead of the promised separate carts, he gives them one larger cart (the one Great Vehicle of Mahayana Buddhism). The *Lotus Sutra* thus conveys its *raison d'être*: to harmonize a fractured religious community by asserting a single vehicle of enlightenment that assimilates three competing visions of Buddhism. The second key phrase, "ichimi no ame" (一味の雨 literally, "one-flavor rain," or

4. For a discussion of this poem, see LaFleur, "Buddhism and Japanese Literature," p. 180.

5. *Goshūi waka shū*, 1187. Translation from LaFleur, "Buddhism and Japanese Literature," p. 180.

as William LaFleur translates it, "impartial rain"), evokes the "Parable of the Medicinal Herbs." The central figure of this story, that a rain cloud's showers benefit equally a wide variety of plants and trees, is used to explicate the principle of expedient means (*hōben* 方便): the Buddha adjusts his single teaching to a wide variety of recipients. When the figures of "vehicle" and "rain" are understood properly, the women's successful arrival at the hall becomes the achievement of enlightenment, which will occur if one chooses the Great Vehicle of Mahayana.

The Heian poet Izumi Shikibu's (976?–?) most famous poem, number 1342 in *Shūi waka shū* (Gleanings of Japanese poems; ca. 1005–11), provides a more ambiguous example. Here the poem was written as allegory but since not enough context is given to make it determinate, the reader is pushed to create a narrative that explains the poem's allegorical reading:

Sent to the High Priest Shōkū:

> *kuraki yori / kuraki michi ni zo / irinubeki*
> *haruka ni terase yama no ha no tsuki*
>
> The path I must follow goes from darkness unto darkness;
> Oh moon on the mountain rim, illuminate my way.

Even without the foretext, the reader would have difficulty supposing that this poem describes the poet wandering at night, asking the moon for light to see the way ahead. The idea of a well-bred Heian woman wandering in the mountains alone at night would stretch most readers' credulity and cause the trigger of implausibility to engage immediately. This implausibility combined with the information in the foretext that the poem was sent to a Buddhist priest (her spiritual advisor) predisposes the reader to look for religious meaning in the poem. In that frame of mind, the reader would examine the natural images to see if they can be correlated to create a coherent alternative interpretation appropriate to the apparent context.

The basic imagery is a path of darkness that the poet must enter and a brightly shining moon that she hopes will illuminate her way. Within Heian and medieval Japan, the word *michi* (道 path, way) had a number of metaphorical meanings, including the path of life, death, and rebirth/reincarnation, a religious or spiritual path (the Buddhist Path, the Way of the Warrior), and eventually, artistic vocation (the Way of Poetry), often understood as a religious path in itself. The reader's sense that this poem must have a religious meaning would be further strengthened by the recognition that the line "from darkness unto darkness" (*kuraki yori kuraki*) alludes to a passage in the "Parable of the Phantom City" from the *Lotus Sutra*: "Through the long night increasingly they follow evil paths, reducing the multitude of heavenly beings; from darkness they enter into darkness, to the end never hearing the Buddha's name."[6] In other words, those who have not experienced the Buddhist teaching grope blindly in the darkness of evil. In contrast, the moon is a trope for Buddhist enlightenment, and perhaps a metonym for High Priest Shōkū himself, whose teaching illuminates Shikibu's path through life.

For much of the premodern and modern periods, it has been widely believed that this poem was written on Izumi Shikibu's deathbed. The phrase "irinubeki" (I must enter) was understood as indicating that she was describing her imminent death, and the general interpretation of the poem was as follows: "I must now go from one dark path (life) into a still darker path (death); I am asking you, priest Shōkū (an earthly representative of the moon of enlightenment), to light my way through the darkness that lies ahead." Their attempt to unify the imagery has even led some readers to argue that the moon on the mountain rim was setting (mountains can be a trope for death) and to see this as another hint that the poem was written at the end of her life.[7] Recently, however, scholars have questioned this interpretation because of the identification of the author in *Shūi shū* as "Shikibu, the daughter of Masamune."[8] They take this as evidence that when she wrote the poem she had not yet married Michisada, the governor of Izumi, and so was about sixteen or seventeen years old. In this case, the poem must be rather differently translated: "I (like all human beings who have not heard the Buddha's words) follow a path that goes from darkness unto darkness; I count on you, priest Shōkū, to help me find my way to enlightenment in this life." Here the moon on the mountain rim might be interpreted as rising and analogous to a young girl who is just at the beginning of her life.

Present-day scholars may feel that their interpretation is more objective (although the assumption that the *Shūi shū* attribution should be taken as

---

6. Watson, *The Lotus Sutra*, p. 121.

7. For example, Jane Hirshfield and Mariko Aratani (*The Ink Dark Moon*, p. 208) interpret the poem as follows: "As she moves from the darkness and confusion of human life and suffering towards the darkness of the unknowable future, Shikibu asks for the clarifying moon of enlightenment to remain with her for a few moments longer before disappearing."

8. Keene, *Seeds in the Heart*, p. 331*n*40.

definitive proof is questionable), but the point is that both medieval and contemporary readers have used inter- and intratextual evidence in an attempt to create a hypothetical context for Shikibu's composition of the poem. For example, Donald Keene rejects the deathbed story and suggests instead that "perhaps, as has been conjectured on the basis of what we know of her later life, she had already suffered the torment of an unhappy love affair and was seeking guidance . . . from the priest to whom the poem was offered."[9] The drive to narrativize the scene of composition as a way to imbue the poem with a more richly complex, yet still coherent allegorical meaning is clearly at work even today. Thus, Izumi Shikibu's poem testifies to the intricate interaction of the author's original use of allegorical imagery that subtly alludes to religious and cultural discourses and the reader's desire to produce narratives that further that allegorical meaning.

In the medieval esoteric commentaries, poems that originally had little or no allegorical meaning were transformed into complex religious allegories by reading puns as religious allusions. *Kokin shū* 409, listed as anonymous but tentatively attributed to the eighth-century poet Kakinomoto no Hitomaro in the *Kokin shū* preface, was often singled out for allegorical interpretation:

> *honobono to/Akashi no ura no/asagiri ni*
> *shimagakure yuku/fune o shi zo omou*
>
> In the faint glimmering of the dawn at Akashi Bay,[10]
> my thoughts go with the boat that disappears among the
> islands into the morning mist.

The poem is listed as having no known topic (題知らず *dai shirazu*), and to most present-day readers it would seem to be a simple yet graceful description of a view out to sea in the early morning. There is only a single obvious pun to mar a smoothly symbolic reading: *akashi* read as "glimmering" (明し) and as a place name, Akashi Bay 明石の浦. The fact that the poem has no explanatory foretext, however, leaves the reader with just a touch of enigma—Why does the implied viewer yearn for the boat? Is his or her lover

---

9. Ibid., pp. 288–89.

10. An anonymous reader of this manuscript argued that "Akashi Bay" is not an accurate translation for "Akashi no ura"; that "ura" actually means "the marine equivalent to *sato* (village)." This is an unwieldy translation, however, and I have settled, as so many other translators before me, for "bay."

on board?—and invites the reader to imagine narrative details for this dawn parting. The commentary *Kokin waka shū kanjō kuden* (Oral transmission of the initiation on the *Kokin waka shū*) takes up the challenge and answers any and all questions that we might have about the poem. It is not, as we might have thought, a poignant scene of lovers parting. Instead, *Kanjō kuden* explains, it is a Buddhist eulogy for a dead emperor or prince.[11] The commentary proves that explication with an allegorical reading of an interrelated series of metaphors, metonyms, and puns. The boat signifies the emperor/prince, hidden from our view by death. The islands (*shima* 島) are no ordinary islands; they are the four evils (*shi ma* 四魔) of birth, old age, illness, and death. The phrase "honobono to akashi" describes the mind that becomes serene and bright as it watches the scene (on the literal level we are witnessing a funeral). This serenity is gained when the viewer is enlightened and comes to understand the four evils, which afflict even emperors who manifest the ten virtues. As an extra bonus, the poem is shown to be a primer of the Six Poetic Modes (*rikugi*) by which poetry expresses meaning, enumerated in the *Kokin shū* preface.[12]

The "Honobono to Akashi" poem was a favorite object of allegorical interpretation in the Kamakura commentaries. One reason may simply have been its fame: besides being singled out by Ki no Tsurayuki in the *Kokin shū* preface, it was also named by Fujiwara no Kintō (966–1041) in *Waka kuhon* (Nine styles of waka) as one of three examples of the highest grade of poetry, and by Minamoto no Toshiyori (1055–1129; AKA Shunrai) in *Toshiyori zuinō* (Toshiyori's poetic essentials) as one of ten superlative poems. The fact that it was traditionally attributed to Hitomaro, who in the medieval period was worshipped as a patron deity of poetry, would also have contributed to its popularity.

---

11. *Kokin waka shū kanjō kuden,* p. 510. The commentary indicates that the poem could be an elegy for either Emperor Monmu (r. 696–707) or Prince Takechi (654–96), eldest son of Emperor Tenmu (r. 673–86) and a hero of the Jinshin War (672). The latter identification is more common in the Kamakura commentaries on this poem. Such an identification would have been reinforced by Hitomaro's long elegy for Takechi in the *Man'yō shū* (199–202). Reading the poem as an elegy made sense, given the number of poems by Hitomaro in the *Man'yō shū* that are elegies for important members of the imperial family. *Kokin waka shū kanjō kuden,* p. 510.

12. Ibid., pp. 510–11.

Three Forms of Allegoresis in Kamakura Commentaries

These examples of religious and political allegory in Heian poetry contain hidden meanings whose correct interpretation depends on the reader's knowledge of religious and political discourse. The examples of allegoresis are interpretive counterparts to the examples of constructed allegory; the interpretive methods employed in these allegorical interpretations are simply an extension of the methods used to create narrative allegory. For example, in the analyses of the "Honobono to Akashi" poem, the commentator began by looking for puns and other possible double meanings that allowed him to argue that the poem's hidden meaning (its *kokoro*) was a demonstration of esoteric Buddhism. In other commentaries associated with Fujiwara no Tameaki, however, the methodology of allegoresis is developed much further. Tameaki employed techniques such as etymological paranomasia, in which graphs are analyzed into their component parts and shown to have hidden "esoteric" meaning, and numerological allegoresis, in which homologies based on certain numbers are used to show hidden correspondences between Buddhist concepts and waka's rhetorical structure. These more elaborate forms of allegoresis have no precedent in either secular or religious poetry written as allegory; they appear to have emerged in the context of attempts to syncretize native deities and rituals into esoteric Buddhism. Chapters 8 and 9 explore the historical and religio-philosophical bases for this form of interpretation in Tendai and Shingon efforts to syncretize Shinto and Buddhist deities. Here I want simply to introduce the main forms of allegoresis.[13]

In the commentaries we can discern two types of etymological and one type of numerological allegoresis. This form of interpretation focuses on

---

13. See Stone, *Original Enlightenment and the Transformation of Medieval Japanese Buddhism*, pp. 156–67, for some of the basic forms of what she calls "*kanjin*-style interpretation" found in medieval Tendai oral transmissions (*kuden*). She describes three general hermeneutic categories: wordplay, correspondence and association, and reversal. Maeda Eun was probably the first modern scholar to attempt an explanation of this form of interpretation. He argued (*Maeda Eun zenshū*, vol. 1, see esp. examples on pp. 389–93) that it developed because in Japan priests commonly chanted Chinese texts in a *bō-yomi* style (棒読み, reading in a straight line, "like a stick") without reference to Chinese grammar. Maeda believed treating texts with this kind of freedom encouraged priests to develop some innovative new methods of interpreting texts, including etymological allegoresis.

proper names of both humans and deities, on the titles of the works themselves, on numbers (two, three, and five receive special attention), and on words or phrases repeated throughout the text (in *Ise monogatari*, for example, *mukashi otoko*, "the Man of Old"). Tameaki's choice of the segments of the text to subject to allegoresis follows the principle outlined by Tzvetan Todorov in *Symbolism and Interpretation*: "The *poorer* the *linguistic meaning*, and thus the more limited its comprehension, the more easily *symbolic evocation* is grafted onto it, and thus the *richer* the interpretation."[14] Todorov lists proper names, numbers, and technical nouns as word classes particularly poor in linguistic meaning and so particularly prone to allegorical interpretation.

In one form of etymological analysis, groups of graphs are pulled apart into their constituents and then rearranged to create meaningful sentences that substantiate the author's argument.[15] For example, in "The Meaning of the Two Graphs" (*Niji no gi*) from *Ise monogatari engi* (Commentary on *Ise monogatari*), the idea that Narihira was actually Kakinomoto no Hitomaro reborn is substantiated by an etymological analysis of the graphs for I 伊 and Se 勢:[16]

(1) hito 人　　(4) masa ni 平
(3) umarete 生　　(2) maro 丸
(5) tsutome ari 力

In other words, when you write 伊勢, it is read: "Hitomaro umarete masa ni tsutome ari" (Hitomaro was born and naturally made efforts). The phrase "to make efforts" (*tsutome*) means "to propagate the Way of Poetry."[17] These two characters have various readings, but this is their true meaning: "Hitomaro was born as Narihira and propagated the Way of Poetry, leading living beings to the profound secret of Yin and Yang."[18]

14. Todorov, *Symbolism and Interpretation*, pp. 101–4.

15. This process is similar to the *notarikon* form of interpretation in biblical commentaries whereby each letter of a word is interpreted as the initial letter of another word, and these words are then combined to form meaningful phrases. See ibid., p. 104.

16. According to this analysis, the kanji 伊 is made up of 人 and 平; the kanji 勢 is made up of 生 and 丸 over 力.

17. *Tsutome* may also have the supplementary meaning here of performing a Buddhist service.

18. *Ise monogatari engi*, p. 580.

This is a particularly clear instance of the commentaries' argument that wordplays were deliberately planted in the text (here by Narihira) as a signal to the initiated reader. They therefore act as tautological textual evidence that corroborates the commentary's explication. And for this interpretation to have force, one must believe that graphs have a hidden esoteric meaning that, if properly understood, reveals transcendent truths.

In a second form of etymological allegoresis, pillow words (*makura kotoba* 枕詞) and other phrases whose meaning had by the late thirteenth century become obscured with time are assigned homophonic graphs (*ateji* 当て字). These assigned graphs clarify the phrases' true meaning. For example, in *Ise monogatari zuinō* (The essence of *Ise monogatari*), one section is devoted to the pillow word *chihayaburu*, which usually prefaces (pillows) the word "kami." In the medieval period, *chihayaburu* was widely written with the graphs 風速振る, "wind-swift-brandishing," and taken as signifying the mighty power of the gods. However, *Ise monogatari zuinō* assigns it the graphs 千葉破る, "thousand-leaves-tearing":

> The phrase "chihayaburu" means "emerging from the womb." It refers to the process by which the soul, having been conceived in a human form, is born. The form of the Five Viscera and the Six Entrails of the mother closely resembles petals of the lotus flower. Conceived in the lotus, when born in the tenth month, the child emerges by tearing (*yaburu* 破る) those thousand-petaled (*chi ha* 千葉) membranes. . . . Thus the phrase "chihayaburu kami" refers to the soul.[19]

This unusual reading is used to substantiate *Ise monogatari zuinō*'s argument, based in Tachikawa "spiritual embryology," that the native kami do not exist other than as our own souls (*tamashii* 魂).[20]

Numerological allegoresis can take various forms. Waka are easily divided in two, creating an "upper" part (*kami no ku* 上の句) of 5–7–5 syllables and a "lower" part (*shimo no ku* 下の句) of 7–7 syllables. This division allows for innumerable binary homologies, including that of heaven and earth, Yang and Yin, male and female, and most important, the Diamond and Womb-Storehouse Realm mandalas, which were considered central to

19. [Kariya Chōritsu Toshokan zō] *Ise monogatari zuinō* (hereafter Kariya *Ise monogatari zuinō*), p. 431.

20. For Tachikawa "spiritual embryology," see Chapters 10 and 11. See also Klein, "Allegories of Desire: Poetry and Eroticism in *Ise monogatari zuinō*"; and James Sanford, "Wind, Waters, Stupas, Mandalas: Fetal Buddhahood in Shingon."

Shingon Buddhism. Significant words made up of two graphs, such as "Ise" 伊勢 in *Ise monogatari* or "Kokin" 古今 in *Kokin waka shū*, are also easily homologized this way. For example, in *Gyokuden jinpi no maki* (Jeweled transmission of deep secrets), in a section entitled "The Deep Secret of the Two Graphs *Ko* and *kin*" (*Kokin niji no himitsu*), each graph is assigned six meanings that reveal the true Buddhist significance of waka poetry. The sixth meaning of "kin" is said to reveal that:

The Path of Poetry may appear superficially to be merely frivolous play, but within it are marvelous Dharma sermons on the True Reality, Disciplined Practice, and the Dharma Body. A person who composes a single poem will close the gate on the three evil paths [of reincarnation], and if one hears a poem, even for an instant, one is assured of successively better rebirths. By chanting the thirty-one syllables of a waka, one obtains the merit of praising the thirty-one deities. Thus, beginning with the Lord Hitomaro [as] Sumiyoshi Daimyōjin, the Thirty-six [Sages of Poetry] are all embodiments (*kegen*) of the kami and of Dainichi Nyorai. This precious path is an expedient means to salvation, pacifying the hearts of the multitudes, [and clearing their] bad karma. Without it, the wonderful path of Buddhism is difficult to enter indeed.[21]

And in "Explanation of the Inner Path" (*Naidō ron*), we find an analysis of the graphs for "Ise" from an esoteric Buddhist perspective:

The two graphs, *i* and *se*, are Yin and Yang. Yin and Yang are the origin of the manifold Dharma. Thus, what is there that has escaped the benefits of these two graphs? In other words, all the manifold phenomena are the two characters of *i-se*.

Query: Of course, all the manifold phenomena, even the grasses and trees, dust and sand, are the Buddha Body. So how is it that *Ise monogatari* was written as the profound meaning of Shingon? . . .

Reply: Manifesting as Yin and Yang, essentially one with the Dharma Realm, the myriad things appear as the Dharma Body. The Absolute Reality and phenomenal reality are equally Dharma and dust, dust and Dharma. To know the Buddha is no different from becoming the Buddha. Thus whether one calls it the Buddhist Dharma or *Ise monogatari*, it is the same essence, with a different name. Narihira transformed himself and having been born in this world, he filled a frivolous tale (*monogatari*) with the profound meaning of Shingon in order to enlighten and benefit all living beings. This tale is none other than a profoundly esoteric practice of Shingon.[22]

---

21. *Gyokuden jinpi no maki*, pp. 549–50.
22. Ibid., pp. 536–37.

Here the characters *i* and *se* are identified with Yin and Yang, the primordial dualism that originated phenomenal reality but is ultimately essentially one with Absolute Reality. According to *Gyokuden jinpi no maki,* since there is no ultimate distinction between Absolute Reality and phenomenal reality, a frivolous tale like *Ise monogatari* can be the means to enlighten all living beings if its true allegorical nature is understood correctly.

Waka poetry's five phrases (*ku* 句) also become the focus of much attention. The preface of the Kunaichō Shoryōbu *Waka chiken shū* (Collection of revealed knowledge of waka) argues that writing a poem in five phrases is equivalent to creating a five-storied pagoda (itself equivalent to the Buddha Body):

> When you create a well-formed poem, you create a Buddha of the Five Roots of Goodness and the Five Powers; the Five Wisdoms, the Five Instructions, the Five Aspects, and the Five Periods of the Dharma all arise from this source. But if you compose a bad poem, then you are faced with a body of this mortal world, and it becomes the Five Aggregates, the Five Passions, the Five Misunderstandings, and the Five Senses.[23]

Waka chiken shū ups the stakes considerably for writing good poems; a lot more is on the line than simply the author's reputation.

Numerological homologies often seem to be produced for no reason other than a sheer delight in multiples of five. In the opening section of *Gyokuden jinpi no maki,* each of the five phrases of a waka poem is identified with a season, a direction, an element, a color, a Confucian virtue, a kami, one of the Five Wisdom Buddhas associated with the Diamond Realm mandala, and a stage of enlightenment. For example, the second line is identified with summer, south, fire, red, Courtesy, the Leech Child (Hiruko no Mikoto), the Hōshō Buddha, and Disciplined Practice.[24] Finally, the thirty-one syllables of a waka poem (5–7–5–7–7) also come in for attention. As we saw above, in *Gyokuden jinpi no maki* the thirty-one syllables are treated as equivalent to thirty-one kami. The *Waka chiken shū* manages to homologize the 31 syllables with the 32 identifying marks of a Buddha:

> The fixing of syllables at thirty-one must be by analogy with the thirty-two aspects of the Tathāgata. Among these thirty-two aspects is that known as the Unseen Peak;

23. [Kunaichō Shoryōbu den Tameuji hitsu] *Waka chiken shū* (hereafter Kunaichō *Waka chiken shū*), p. 98. Translation (modified) from Bowring, "The *Ise monogatari,*" p. 440.

24. *Gyokuden jinpi no maki,* pp. 522–24.

in other words it cannot be seen by the eye, so only thirty-one aspects are actually visible. A poem always contains a meaning (*kokoro*) that does not appear in the syllables but lies hidden. Hence we should think of both poem and Tathāgata as having thirty-two aspects.[25]

This deft interpretive footwork does double duty. First, it manages to make the numbers thirty-one and thirty-two equivalent and thereby provides a solid Buddhist source for the number of syllables in a waka poem. Second, it argues that there is always a hidden meaning to a poem, probably Buddhist; the implication is that one needs the help of a commentary such as *Waka chiken shū* to ferret it out. In the chapters that follow, I discuss in much greater detail the Buddhist underpinnings of the development of this kind of etymological allegoresis, as well as the economic benefits that such arguments conferred on those, like Fujiwara no Tameaki, who produced the commentaries. First, however, let us examine the commentary tradition itself.

---

25. Kunaichō *Waka chiken shū*, pp. 97–98. Translation from Bowring, "The *Ise monogatari*," p. 440.

3
The Commentary Tradition

As an inveterate reader of comic books (or graphic novels) published by the Vertigo Press of DC Comics, I have watched a commentarial tradition develop around Neil Gaiman's *The Sandman* on the internet usenet group devoted to Vertigo (rec.arts.comics.dc.vertigo). *The Sandman* was originally published monthly from January 1989 to March 1995. The entire run was also republished in a series of ten volumes, of four to thirteen issues each. It has a relatively large adult readership (at this point, numbering in the hundreds of thousands), a substantial proportion of whom are college-educated and have access to the internet. Over the course of 75 issues, the plot involved dozens of characters (both fictional and historical) and allusions to a wide variety of cultural artifacts and historical events. Because the issues were spaced out at monthly intervals, the story tended to be episodic and yet characterized by extremely dense layerings of plot lines and characters. Readers responded by annotating each issue as it came out. These annotations were generally intended (1) to show how the new plot developments tied in with older ones, as well as with story threads from other comic books; (2) to identify the characters by noting their previous appearances in the story, whether they were historically "real" or whether they were characters from another comic book "universe"; and (3) to explain allusions to texts (literary and otherwise), cultural artifacts, and historical events.

Generally one person was responsible for annotating each book as it came out and publishing it on the usenet group. Other people would add their knowledge and expertise to fill any gaps; this often generated considerable discussion. Once most of the problematic points had been resolved, the annotations were archived on a website devoted to Neil Gaiman.[1] However, as revelations about characters and plot developments appeared in new issues, they were used to explicate character and plot points in earlier issues. The annotations were continuously revised until the entire run of the series was completed.[2] The end result has been a page-by-page, and sometimes frame-by-frame, analysis of both the graphics and the text.

The second most common form of reader response to Gaiman's work has been aesthetic commentary; that is, arguments on the critical value of particular issues, whether the artist's work supported or detracted from Gaiman's text, and so forth. Discussions on these issues could become heated. It was difficult for readers to reach a consensus about what factors should be used as a measuring stick for critical evaluations, and the discussions often were diverted from the ostensible point of aesthetic value and became mired in personal issues.

As noted in Chapter 1, the earliest interpretive responses to a text tend to be triggered by problematic aspects of the text itself. These syntagmatic triggers include textual contradictions, lacunae or discontinuities, tautologies, and superfluities. Texts that readers treasure almost inevitably generate commentary, and the first step in the development of commentary is usually an annotation of the text. Most of the annotations and commentary on Gaiman's text were clearly a response to syntagmatic triggers; there has not been enough time for the paradigmatic triggers to kick in. As we shall see, the earliest commentaries on the *Kokin shū* and *Ise monogatari* developed in a similar way, among a community of readers responding to perceived difficulties in those texts. And personal issues were never far below the surface of even the most "objective" commentaries.

---

1. David Goldfarb and Greg Morrow were the originating editors. The annotations are archived on a website maintained by David Wald at <http://theory.lcs.mit.edu/~wald/sandman-index.html>. The site can also be reached via the FAQ (frequently asked questions) for DC Vertigo at <http://www.idyllmtn.com/rac/dc/vertigo>. See also *The Wake* website maintained by Dylan Verheul at http://www.dyve.net/sandman. For another example of how a community of annotation can develop around a difficult (some would even say esoteric) yet treasured text, see the website on Grant Morrison's *The Invisibles* series at <http://www.barbelith.com/bomb>.

2. As of summer 2001, the annotations are only complete up to issue 57; those for issues 58–71 are still in the first draft stage, and those for 72–75 have not been done yet.

The Development of a Commentary Tradition

The first commentaries to the *Kokin shū* and *Ise monogatari* were literally "on" those texts: annotations written in the margins or between the lines. These marginalia were then transcribed along with the original text when it was copied by later readers and often inadvertently became part of the text. Thus the situation of textual production in the Heian period was quite different from what it is today, when copyright considerations tend to keep text and commentary firmly separated.[3] For example, early in the dissemination of the *Kokin shū* someone (Fujiwara no Kintō is the most likely candidate) wrote interlinear notes in the preface identifying allusions or clarifying points that he found obscure. These were subsequently transmitted as part of the text. Although in contemporary editions these interpolations are marked as such, medieval scholars were divided over the authorship of these comments. Some thought the emendations were by the original author, Ki no Tsurayuki; others attributed them to a later reader such as Kintō.

The case of *Ise monogatari* is even more complex. The text appears to have been produced over the course of two hundred years (ca. 900–1100) by multiple readers-editors-transcribers. Each apparently felt little or no compunction about revising, interpolating, or abridging material. These reader-editors were, once again, responding mainly to syntagmatic triggers, for the most part textual difficulties. Contemporary scholars have identified traces of at least three waves of revision in the form of interpolated commentary. Not until the late twelfth century, when the great poet and scholar Fujiwara no Teika took it upon himself to collate his own recension, did the text become stabilized to the point that commentary about (i.e., extraneous to) the text began to develop. By then enough time had passed for the cultural and political context to have changed significantly, and we start seeing commentaries incited by paradigmatic triggers as well.

By the late Heian and Kamakura periods, four main kinds of commentaries on classical texts such as the *Kokin shū* and *Ise monogatari* were being

3. One analogue, however, might be the creative response of readers to the fictional worlds of Gaiman's *Sandman* or the television show *Star Trek*. Readers write their own stories to fill in perceived gaps in narrative or character development and publish them on the internet or in fanzines.

transmitted among families who specialized in poetry (*uta no ie* 歌の家): "pragmatic" commentaries that were basically indexes to useful information for aspiring poets, including aesthetic evaluations; "philological" commentaries that explained obscure vocabulary and figures of speech; "anecdotal" or "historical" commentaries that attempted to provide information on the origin and history of poems; and "religious" commentaries that interpreted the poems from a religious viewpoint, often esoteric Shingon or Tendai Buddhism.[4] Although a commentary often included elements of all four types, as a whole it can usually be classed as one of these categories.

The first kind of commentary, pragmatic, cannot be called interpretation as such, since such commentaries were interested not in explicating the meaning of the poems but in providing guidelines for composing poetry. These commentaries generally provided examples of "good" and "bad" poems as models for the beginning poet and so might be seen as forebears of later forms of aesthetic criticism. However, pragmatic commentaries within the aristocratic families that participated in the medieval institution of secret transmission often included information on how a particular family performed certain rites and activities associated with poetry, such as meetings (*kai* 会), lectures (*kōshiki* 講式), poetry contests (*uta awase* 歌合), and memorial ceremonies (*eigu* 影供). These esoteric family traditions continued to be considered important throughout the Muromachi period and into the Edo, because knowledge of the secrets of proper etiquette could be parlayed into patronage by emperors and high-ranking samurai in the Kamakura and Muromachi shogunates. The following excerpts from *Guhi shō* (Selected humble secrets) are good examples of secret traditions commonly found in commentaries from the Kamakura period onward:

When imperial anthologies are being presented, images of the deities Sumiyoshi and Tamatsushima must be present in the meeting room. Their images are to be placed to the left and right of the emperor.[5]

It is crucial that Hitomaro's image be hung correctly in the poetry meeting room. Unless you have received proper instruction, you are likely to commit a grave error of etiquette. . . . Hitomaro's image should be hung on the left, and Akahito's image on the right. . . . Images of the deities Sumiyoshi and Tamatsushima are to be hung

4. Katagiri (*Chūsei Kokin shū chūshakusho kadai*, vol. 2, p. 37) categorizes the commentaries into the first three classes; I have added the fourth.

5. *Guhi shō* (*tei-bon*), p. 308.

in the same way. This protocol must be transmitted correctly; it is a treasured secret of our school.[6]

Pragmatic commentaries often included elements of philological analysis, as a composition guide to important sources of poetic imagery. This second category of commentary was triggered by words, phrases, and certain kinds of cultural references that had become obscure over time and so interfered with their proper use in poetic composition. An anecdote from Kamo no Chōmei's (1155–1216) *Mumyō shō* (The nameless treatise; ca. 1209) illustrates this problem. During a gathering of poets, the discussion turns to the meaning of the term "masuho no susuki" (*susuki* is a kind of pampas grass). When an old man mentions that he has heard there is a monk at a place called Watanobe who knows about it, the Monk Tōren immediately gets up and prepares to leave, although it is pouring rain outside. When the others ask him what he is doing, he replies: "I am off to Watanobe. I have heard there exists a man who knows something that has been on my mind for years. How can I refrain from visiting him?"[7] Tōren goes to see the man and treats the answer as "a very precious treasure." Chōmei indicates that he himself received the transmission from a disciple of Tōren and identifies the plant (it has "a long ear about one foot high"). This is just one of many anecdotes in *Mumyō shō* that identify the meaning of obscure terms or the location of obscure places. Clearly by the thirteenth century, knowledge of such arcane terminology was highly valued.

Haruo Shirane notes how this same problem led to commentaries on *Genji monogatari*: "The early commentaries first emerged out of a need to explicate words and court customs in the *Genji* that had become obscure with the passage of time and the disappearance of Heian Court society, but Kamakura commentators, who were influenced by the views of Shunzei and Teika, had a particular interest in the rituals, incidents, and characters found in the *Genji*."[8] It is not surprising that two to three hundred years after *Ise monogatari*, *Genji monogatari*, and the *Kokin shū* were written, the meaning of certain words and phrases had become obscure. Given the extremely small number of people involved in the writing and reading of texts, virtually all of

---

6. Ibid., p. 310. Also cited in Miwa Masatane, "*Chikuen shō* karon no seisei to hatten: kashin toshite no Sumiyoshi myōjin o megutte," p. 53.

7. Hilda Katō, "The *Mumyōshō* of Kamo no Chōmei and Its Significance in Japanese Literature," p. 366.

8. Shirane, *The Bridge of Dreams*, p. xvii.

whom belonged to the same elite homogeneous group, writers could use what amounted to "in-group" slang. And given the means of reproduction, confusion could also easily develop because of simple transcription error. When philological interpretation was incorporated into religious or historical commentaries, however, its goal was not primarily pragmatic; it was generally used to reinforce those commentaries' allegorical readings.

The last two kinds of commentaries—the "anecdotal" and "religious"—are the major focus of this book, for it was these commentaries that allegorized *Ise monogatari* and the *Kokin shū* via medieval political and religious discourse. The authors behind the anecdotal and religious commentaries took the rhetorical techniques used in allegorical poetry as methodological justification for their own allegoresis. The commentator's attention was generally focused, however, not on poems intentionally produced as allegories (after all, any properly trained reader could interpret those correctly) but on poems, such as *Kokin shū* 409 ("Honobono to Akashi"), that in their original context may have had little or no allegorical meaning.

These anecdotal and religious commentaries are known in Japanese scholarship as Kamakura *kochūshaku* (古注釈 old-style commentaries), a phrase often shortened for simplicity to *kochū*.[9] Although I will argue that the genesis of these commentaries is symptomatic of changes in the religious, political, and cultural context, I by no means see a one-to-one correspondence between changes in literature and a periodization drawn from political history; in fact, these kinds of commentaries continued to be produced in the Muromachi period (and, to a much more limited extent, the Edo).[10]

---

9. I use the term *kochū* to mean any of the Kamakura commentaries that employ etymological and numerological allegoresis. Note, however, that Katagiri Yōichi (*Ise monogatari no kenkyū [kenkyūhen]*, pp. 514–20) argues that when discussing *Ise monogatari* Muromachi scholars such as Ichijō Kaneyoshi and Sōgi used the term *kochū* to designate interpretations from the Reizei school *Ise monogatari shō*; they used *Chiken shū* to designate interpretations from *Waka chiken shū*. Katagiri does not analyze the use of *kochū* with regard to *Kokin shū* commentaries, nor does he consider texts such as *Gyokuden jinpi no maki* that predate *Ise monogatari shō*. See also Otsu Yūichi, "Kochū to iu wa nani ka," in idem, *Ise monogatari kochūshaku no kenkyū*, pp. 141–48.

10. The transmission lineages of commentaries included in the *Kokin denju*, which first appeared in the Muromachi period and was popular throughout the Edo period, show that the *Kokin denju* was a direct outgrowth of the earlier Kamakura *Kokin shū* commentaries. Nevertheless, there are major differences: Kamakura commentaries employ a religious allegoresis that draws on Shingon and Tendai Buddhism as well as esoteric Shinto and Onmyōdō (Taoist Yin-Yang divination). Although traces of these remain in the *Kokin denju*, on the whole

Nevertheless, the *kochū* commentaries were for the most part created in the late Kamakura period and are marked by a common interpretive approach that I believe is symptomatic of a specific historical context.

The most obvious characteristic of the Kamakura commentaries is their interest in finding esoteric Buddhist meaning in waka poetry and poetics. In this, they were symptomatic of a general trend, which I discuss in more detail in Chapter 7. Idiosyncratic to the Kamakura commentaries are their deployment of the form of interpretation that I have called "etymological allegoresis" and their use within a well-developed esoteric initiation system borrowed from Shingon Buddhism.

A Brief Outline of Tameaki's Commentaries

The texts associated with Tameaki or his disciples can broadly be divided into three levels of initiation. These levels move from fairly exoteric secrets on how to write poetry and the etiquette for poetry meetings to increasingly esoteric knowledge involving complex etymological allegoresis meant to reveal the true religious content of waka poetry. The only text that does not fit these categorizations is *Waka chiken shū*, which does not employ etymological allegoresis. This lack makes it likely that the text did not originate with Tameaki. Instead he probably copied it early in his career from a text produced by the poetic faction of Fujiwara no Ietaka centered in the Kantō area and revised and expanded the introduction to fit his new purposes.

The first level of initiation includes two of the earliest Tameaki commentaries, *Tameie kuden* (Tameie's oral transmission) and *Chikuen shō* (Edited selections from a bamboo grove), both of which were probably produced and transmitted between 1265 and 1270.[11] In these texts Tameaki claimed to be passing on poetic knowledge inherited from his father, Tameie. *Tameie kuden* contains a variation on Tameie's theory, later elaborated in *Eiga no ittei* (The foremost style of poetic composition; 1275), that certain poetic phrases have "owners" (*nushi aru kotoba* 主ある詞) and should not be used by contempo-

---

it tends toward a historical allegoresis under the sway of Neo-Confucianism and proto-nationalism.

11. *Chikuen shō* is published in both the *Zoku Gunsho ruijū* and the *Nihon kagaku taikei*. *Tameie kuden*, also known as *Kuden shō Tameie* and *Waka kuden shō* (not the same text as the Ietaka school *Waka kuden shō* discussed below), has not been published. For discussions, see Miwa, *Kagaku hiden no kenkyū*, pp. 244–45; and Inoue, *Chūsei kadanshi no kenkyū*, p. 885.

rary poets.[12] The colophon to one manuscript of *Chikuen shō* asserts that since Tameie transmitted the contents to Tameaki in a bamboo grove when Tameaki was quite young, the text is appropriate for a beginning poet.[13] *Chikuen shō* has sections on such standard topics as the six poetic illnesses, the theory of "close and distant linking" of upper and lower verses (*kami* and *shimo no ku*), an explanation of the *Kokin shū* preface's theory of the Six Poetic Modes by which poetry expresses meaning, the proper use of allusive variations (*honkadori* 本歌取り), and the composition of a reply poem. Both texts also include some "secret" material on the proper etiquette for poetry meetings, which was considered an essential part of poetic knowledge at the time: *Chikuen shō* describes a waka lecture ceremony (*kōshiki*), which was probably a preliminary to Tameaki's later more highly developed waka initiations. In addition, the allusions in both texts to "important matters" (*daiji* 大事) and "separate oral transmissions" (*bechi kuden* 別口伝) correlate well with material presented in Tameaki's more esoteric commentaries.[14]

Another text transmitted about this time, *Waka kanjō den* (Transmission of a waka initiation), may be based on an Ietaka school commentary, *Waka kuden shō* (Selected oral transmissions on waka).[15] Tameaki appears to have

---

12. Brower, "The Foremost Style of Poetic Composition: Fujiwara Tameie's *Eiga no ittei*," pp. 421, 425; and Nijō Tameie, *Eiga no ittei*, pp. 398–99. *Eiga no ittei* is usually dated to around 1275 because the text with the earliest colophon has this date. The fact that Tameaki appears to have produced *Tameie kuden* and *Chikuen shō* in the 1260s may indicate that as a child he was, in fact, instructed by Tameie himself.

13. See Miwa, *Kagaku hiden no kenkyū*, pp. 73–74.

14. Miwa Masatani (ibid., pp. 73–88) points out three connections between *Chikuen shō* and higher-level texts affiliated with Tameaki. First, *Chikuen shō*, in its discussion of close and distant linking, refers to a secret transmission called "Kushō" (Nine fascicles) that might be the "Kushō mitsuden" (Secret transmision in nine fascicles) in *Gyokuden jinpi no maki*. Second, *Chikuen shō*'s discussion of the Six Poetic Modes refers to the extremely secret "tei" (体 appearance) and "kei" (形 form) versions of these modes. A spinoff of the *Gyokuden jinpi no maki*, *Gyokuden shū waka saichō* (Collection of the highest-level jeweled transmission on waka), explains these secret *tei* and *kei* versions of the Six Poetic Modes in detail. Third, when *Chikuen shō* discusses how to use the special folded poem paper known as *fukurogami*, it says to see *Teikin shū* (An imperial collection of teachings) for more details. This matches a discussion in *Shinsen teisetsu shū* (An imperial collection of explanations, newly edited).

15. On the relationship of the two texts, see Miwa Masatani, "Ietaka katakusho no kentō: *Waka chiken shū*, *Waka kuden shō* o megutte" (which has a text of *Waka kanjō den*); and idem, *Kagaku hiden no kenkyū*, pp. 221–36. For a text of *Waka kuden shō*, see *Nihon kagaku taikei*, vol. 4, pp. 386–94. In the article, Miwa suggests that the Ietaka school *Waka kuden shō* was based on Tameaki's *Waka kanjō den*; in *Kagaku hiden no kenkyū*, Miwa appears to reverse his position.

taken *Waka kuden shō* and expanded it by interpolating more detailed material and more examples of poems. According to the colophon of *Waka kuden shō*, the commentary was written by Ietaka when he was about thirty-five, but the contents make that seem highly unlikely; it is possible that it was written by his son Takasuke (1180s–after 1251), but more likely it was written by someone else connected to the Ietaka school. The basic contents of the two commentaries are similar; both discuss close and distant linking of upper and lower verses and the theory of how to develop the topic of a waka over the course of the five lines (*hen-jo-dai-kyoku-ryū ron* 篇序題曲流論).[16] Both theories later became part of the *Kokin denju*. *Waka kanjō den* also has what may have been the first description of a waka initiation ceremony. The obvious paradox of the secret commentaries was that to a certain extent their existence had to be made public in order to entice students. By describing waka lecture and initiation ceremonies and giving only the titles of some of the secrets transmitted during those ceremonies, these introductory texts whet the appetite of initiates, encouraging them to continue studying with the teacher and possibly bring in other students as well.

Perhaps because the primary emphasis of these texts was the pragmatics of writing good poetry and they contained little of the kind of esoteric material that tends to stretch the limits of our credulity today, they have continued to be treated with relative respect by later scholars. The theory of close and distant linking is probably the most important idea advanced in these commentaries since it played a significant role in Muromachi renga poetics.[17] It is possible that Tameaki got his influential theory of close and distant linking from the Ietaka school *Waka kuden shō*, and put it forward as his own in both *Chikuen shō* and *Waka kanjō den*.

All the texts in the next level—the "esoteric" level of initiation—have lineage documents that claim a divine origin in oracular revelations from Sumiyoshi Daimyōjin and employ etymological allegoresis as their primary

16. A complex theory of how to structure the five phrases of a waka in order to make the most effective use of the topic. It is briefly mentioned in both lineages of *Waka chiken shū*, and more lengthy explications of it appear in the Ietaka school's *Waka kanjō shidai himitsu shō* (Selected secrets on the protocol for waka initiations), as well as in the Fujiwara no Tamezane–affiliated *Waka mitsu shō* (Selected secrets on waka) and *Sango ki* (Record of thrice five nights). In the Muromachi period Shinkei (1406–75) applied it to the problem of linking in renga in *Sasamegoto* (Murmured conversations; 1463).

17. See Kami Hiroyuki, "Shinku, soku setsu no keisei to hatten."

interpretive strategy. These commentaries can be divided further into intermediate and advanced initiations.

Kokin waka shū jo kikigaki (Lecture notes on the *Kokin shū* preface) and *Shinsen teisetsu shū* (An imperial collection of explanations, newly edited) belong to the intermediate level.[18] *Kokin waka shū jo kikigaki* focuses on the many allusions to poems in the *Kokin shū* preface, going through the text line by line and identifying the secret names, dates, and stories behind each phrase, thereby establishing a historical and religious basis for the poetic imagery used. The preface to *Shinsen teisetsu shū* states that it contains material transmitted to Narihira by Sumiyoshi Daimyōjin, material that was then re-edited and expanded by Fujiwara no Shunzei (1114–1204) in 1157 at the request of Emperor Go-Shirakawa (r. 1155–58). It contains a good deal of pragmatic material from *Chikuen shō* with some slightly more religious interpretations of poetic techniques added. For example, there are twelve sections explaining how to write poems on *tanzaku* (narrow strips of stiff paper). Given that this style of paper for poetry writing had only just been developed, these explanations must have been considered very useful at the time. Lower-level texts such as *Chikuen shō* refer the reader to separate oral transmissions in *Kokin waka shū jo kikigaki* and *Shinsen teisetsu shū*, but these texts themselves often include the phrase "bechi kuden ari" (there is a separate transmission on this point) indicating that there are other even more advanced texts for the properly initiated student. For example, in both *Shinsen teisetsu shū* and *Kokin waka shū jo kikigaki*, we find versions of a commentary on episode 117 of *Ise monogatari* in which Narihira receives secret transmissions from Sumiyoshi Daimyōjin. These secret transmissions are named ("Gyokuden," "Akone no ura kuden," "Kushō") but are not explicated in either *Kokin waka shū jo kikigaki* or *Shinsen teisetsu shū* themselves. Instead these oral transmissions are found in *Gyokuden jinpi no maki* and its related texts.

Gyokuden jinpi no maki (Jeweled transmission of deep secrets) appears to have been considered suitable for only the highest-level initiates. It is basically a collection of separate oral transmissions which, like those in *Kokin waka shū jo kikigaki* and *Shinsen teisetsu shū*, were supposed to have been transmitted to Narihira by Sumiyoshi Daimyōjin. Because of its miscellaneous character, there are numerous versions of *Gyokuden jinpi no maki*, with

---

18. *Shinsen teisetsu shū* has not been published; for a discussion, see Miwa, *Kagaku hiden no kenkyū*, pp. 81–88.

varying amounts of material in different orders. This was probably because Tameaki (and those who followed him) selected oral transmissions according to the needs and interests of the chosen disciple. There are also a number of shorter spinoffs that appear to have been compiled out of selected oral transmissions from *Gyokuden jinpi no maki.*[19] The general interpretive approach of these oral transmissions continues to be etymological allegoresis, and their content is influenced by syncretic forms of esoteric Buddhism and Shinto.

Waka Kokin kanjō no maki (Initiation on waka of the *Kokin shū*) is a somewhat more coherent text than *Gyokuden jinpi no maki*. It organizes and consolidates material found in earlier texts and brings the reading of poems as allegories of Tachikawa secrets to its furthest development. Every poetic technique discussed, every poem interpreted, is shown to have profound esoteric meaning. An extremely dense and difficult text, *Waka Kokin kanjō maki* probably represents the culmination of Tameaki's lifework and would have been the ultimate text for initiates.

The Muromachi Response

Commentaries such as these were first designated "old-style commentaries" (*kochū* 古注) by Muromachi poet-scholars such as Ichijō Kaneyoshi (1402–81) and Sōgi, who were attempting to distinguish their own form of criticism from the older style. *Kochū* was a term of critical disparagement, implying that these commentaries were outmoded and irrelevant to contemporary concerns. However, to the extent that the term recognizes a common interpretive approach taken by a number of different commentaries, it can also be taken as a sign that there is a historical basis for grouping these commentaries.

The first real break with the *kochū* style of commentary comes with Kaneyoshi's *Ise monogatari guken shō* (Selection of humble views on *Ise monogatari*; 1474). And it solidifies around Sōgi's lectures on *Ise monogatari* found in *Ise monogatari Shōmon shō* (Selected notes from Shōhaku on *Ise monogatari*), transcribed by Shōhaku (1443–1527), and *Ise monogatari Sōchō kikigaki* (Sōchō's lecture notes on *Ise monogatari*), transcribed by Sōchō (1448–1532). Commentaries from this period are generally designated by modern scholars as *kyūchū* (旧注 literally, "former commentaries," but probably better trans-

19. See the section on *Gyokuden jinpi no maki* in Chapter 10, pp. 236–37, for a more detailed discussion of these spinoff texts.

lated as "transitional"). Finally we have the "new commentaries" (*shinchū* 新注) of the nativist scholars (*kokugakusha* 国学者) in the Edo period, beginning around the seventeenth century.[20] The *kyū* and the *shin* styles of commentary are much closer to what contemporary scholars would call "literary criticism": they address primarily problems of philology (the correct meaning and pronunciation of difficult words substantiated by comparative examples of usage) and other pragmatic issues of interest to aspiring waka and renga poets. It was at this time that something approximating modern aesthetic appreciation developed as well. However, although the *kochū* were disparaged by Kaneyoshi and (to a lesser extent) by Sōgi, Sōgi and his disciples recognized the *kochū* commentaries' pedagogical and perhaps historical import in their use of *kochū* material as a basis for the *Kokin denju*. Although much of the esoteric content was removed, the commentaries transmitted in the *Kokin denju* continued to stress secret knowledge of ritual practice and obscure terminology, which could be used as a lucrative form of cultural capital.

As used by these later Muromachi scholars, the term *kochū* did not mean any commentary written in the Kamakura period. And although today we think of the *kochū* as forgeries, in the sense that they were clearly not written by the poets to whom they were attributed (Fujiwara no Teika, Fujiwara no Ietaka, Minamoto no Tsunenobu [1016–97]), not all of the commentaries that we now consider forgeries were referred to as *kochū* by Muromachi scholars. Texts such as the so-called *Usagi* (Cormorant and heron) commentaries attributed to Teika, or Fujiwara no Tameaki's *Chikuen shō* (which Tameaki claimed was based on his father's writings), continued to play an important role in the development of Muromachi aesthetics, especially renga criticism, long after the *kochū* had been discredited. One reason may be that these texts are primarily pragmatic commentaries. Although they were cloaked in secrecy like the *kochū*, most of their content was relatively orthodox, dealing with standard topics such as the theory of Ineffable Beauty (*yūgen* 幽玄), the theory of the Six Poetic Modes, the Ten Poetic Illnesses, and so on. Although by no means completely free of historical and religious allegoresis, this was not their main interpretive strategy, and Muromachi scholars could ignore those sections in which allegoresis did come into play

---

20. This division of *Ise monogatari* commentaries into *kochū*, *kyōchū*, and *shinchū* was first developed by Otsu Yūichi; see his *Ise monogatari kochūshaku no kenkyū*, p. 25; see also Katagiri Yōichi, *Ise monogatari no kenkyū (kenkyūhen)*, pp. 514–15.

with relative ease. For example, Shōtetsu (1381–1459), who showed little patience for either the pedanticism or the allegoresis of the *kochū*, was happy to quote one of the *Usagi* forgeries, *Guhi shō*, in support of his version of the theory of *yūgen*.[21]

Twentieth-century scholars have paid these more pragmatic forgeries of the Kamakura period a fair amount of critical attention, both because the core parts of these texts are thought to be based on Teika's teachings and because they had an important influence on Muromachi poets and scholars. However, because the *Usagi* forgeries have long been thought to derive from the battle for poetic authority between Teika's poetic descendants, the Nijō and the Reizei, any content that does not fit contemporary critical standards has tended to be written off as a cynical exercise in poetic politics. Robert Brower and Earl Miner, for example, argue that the Reizei filled their forged manuscripts "with commonplaces, trivial 'secret traditions' such as the 'proper' way to pronounce a certain name, the number of grand ministers represented in the *Kokin shū* but not so identified, and other meaningless statements calculated to appeal to the pedantic interests of the Nijō poets."[22] They imply that other, more legitimate poetic commentaries do not provide this kind of "pedantic" and "trivial" information, and the inclusion of such "secret traditions" is one clue that the treatises are forgeries.

It was just such "trivial" information, however, that made these treatises so valuable to their readers. From the mid-thirteenth century on, knowledge of the correct etiquette for poetry meetings was increasingly seen as the most important component of a poetry school's authority (and thus its economic power). The differences of detail between the Nijō and Reizei may strike us as trifles, but it was precisely these small but crucial differences in the ritual forms of poetic practice that distinguished the two schools (perhaps even more than any aesthetic poetic differences that could have been discerned at the time). By Shōtetsu's time some of these differences already seemed pedantic. For example, in *Shōtetsu monogatari* (Conversations with Shōtetsu), Shōtetsu comments on the fact that the Reizei and Nijō differed in how

21. Muromachi poet-scholars affiliated with the Reizei school such as Imagawa Ryōshun (1326–1417?), Shōtetsu, and Shinkei believed that the *Usagi* texts were written by Teika and incorporated them into their theories on poetic form and *yūgen*. See Brower, *Conversations with Shōtetsu*, pp. 161–22; Steven Carter discusses Shōtetsu's use of *Guhi shō* in his introduction to ibid., pp. 52–54.

22. Brower and Miner, *Japanese Court Poetry*, p. 349.

they wrote the character for poetry (謌 and 歌, respectively), and it is clear that he thinks the distinction unimportant.[23] Nevertheless, Shōtetsu's name appears in the transmission lineages of a number of *kochū*, including one of the highest-level secret commentaries, *Gyokuden jinpi no maki*. Even as he criticized the content, he continued to participate in its transmission. And since much of *Shōtetsu monogatari* is devoted to discussing the proper etiquette for poetry gatherings and the like, the pragmatic knowledge of proper court etiquette was obviously still considered essential for a poet.

If we want to get a true sense of what it was like to practice poetry in the Kamakura and Muromachi periods, we should look at those aspects of the commentaries that seem strangest to us today. And the strangest of the commentaries from this period are, without a doubt, the *kochū* that employ historical and religious allegoresis to explain *Ise monogatari* and the *Kokin shū*. It is these commentaries, which have so little in common with what we call poetic criticism today, that are most likely to give us clues to the world of the Kamakura poets.

The question remains: Why should these commentaries have suddenly appeared in the late thirteenth century in the possession of a few courtier families, securely guarded from the view of outsiders and carefully legitimated through direct oral and written transmission within the lineage? A related question is: Why did these supposedly secret commentaries just as abruptly lose their privileged esoteric status in the mid-Muromachi period and become the object of openly disparaging criticism by the leading scholars of the day, not to mention widely available for use as thematic sources by relatively low-ranking Noh playwrights and authors of popular prose tales (*otogizōshi*)? To address these questions, the next three chapters focus on two main areas. The first is syntagmatic: What was it about *Ise monogatari* and the *Kokin shū* that triggered allegoresis in a way that other texts, such as *Genji monogatari*, did not? The second focus is paradigmatic: How was the development of the literary institution of secret transmission within certain court families symptomatic of more general political and cultural changes in the Kamakura period, as well as the particular historical circumstances from which most of the commentaries emerged?

---

23. Brower, *Conversations with Shōtetsu*, p. 111.

4
Textual Triggers

The *Kokin waka shū* and Its Preface

The *Kokin waka shū* or *Kokin shū* was the first of twenty-one imperially commissioned anthologies of waka poetry. Although scholars disagree strongly about its date, we can at the least say that it appears to have been commissioned by Emperor Daigo (r. 897–930) sometime in the first few years of the tenth century. The four compilers were Ki no Tsurayuki, Ki no Tomonori (d. before 905?), Ōshikōchi no Mitsune (d. ca. 925?), and Mibu no Tadamine (b. ca. 850?). The anthology is organized into twenty thematic chapters that deal with the progression of the seasons; the progress of love, from first glimpse to last lingering regret; celebrations of the living and laments for the dead; the pleasures of travel and the grief of parting from loved ones; and miscellaneous categories such as poems constructed around word games, poems written in one of the less common poetic forms, and folk songs as poems.

There are two prefaces, one in Japanese by Ki no Tsurayuki and one in Chinese attributed to Ki no Yoshimochi (d. 919). The Japanese preface was of particular interest to commentators. It was accepted as the first and most influential statement of Heian period waka poetics in Japanese, and as such it was absolutely central to any aspiring poet's classical education. At the same time, its allusive, heavily rhetorical style presented a number of interpretive difficulties that called for comment and explication.

For example, almost immediately there were questions about Tsurayuki's discussion of the Six Modes by which poems express meaning. Some contemporary scholars suppose that Ki no Tsurayuki simply borrowed them from Chinese literary theory (specifically, the "Major Preface" to the *Book of Songs*) without much thought, in order to make his own poetic theory sound good.[1] If the explanations of the Six Poetic Modes are vague and the poems given as examples do not seem to fit the explanations, we can simply write them off. Within Heian period poetry circles, however, disregarding them was not a possible solution. This may explain the series of interpolated comments, perhaps by Fujiwara no Kintō, that were meant to help clear up the obscurity of the terms, but that often further obfuscated them. The preface also alludes to poems without identifying them, which almost immediately incited attempts to specify which poems were meant. Today a suitable candidate for each allusion has been found, and for the most part these identifications follow interlineal and marginal comments made by the earliest *Kokin shū* readers.

The *Kokin shū* contains a number of anonymous poems (*yomibito shirazu* 読み人知らず) whose topic is no longer known (*dai shirazu* 題知らず). A waka's thirty-one syllables arrayed in five phrases can be frustratingly abstract and cryptic; when a poem is severed from the circumstances of its composition, its enigmatic brevity demands an explanatory context. In addition, in the medieval period the poems of the *Kokin shū* were models for aspiring young poets, and they were frequently used as the basis for allusive variations. Almost any noun (concrete or proper) in them was fair game for use as a topic (*dai* 題), but that necessarily entailed the poet's understanding of its *hon'i* (本意 original or essential meaning). Obscure words, especially names of places, flora, and fauna that had fallen into disuse and so could not be properly identified, were therefore troublesome and needed to be elucidated. These syntagmatic triggers resulted in commentaries such as *Kokin waka shū jo kikigaki* and its descendents, the Bishamondō *Kokin shū chū* (Bishamon Hall commentary on the *Kokin shū*) and *Kokin waka shū kanjō kuden*, which went to great (and largely unsubstantiated) lengths to identify the authors of anonymous poems and to offer anecdotal explanations of the circumstances under which poems with no known topic had been written.

1. See Wixted, "Chinese Influences on the *Kokin shū* Prefaces," pp. 393–94. Although the term "rikugi" appears only in the Chinese preface (Tsuraki uses "sama"), it was nevertheless the term regularly used in commentaries.

But even simpler textual inconsistencies could trigger interpretation, such as the *Kokin shū*'s inconsistent treatment of poems for which both author and topic are unknown: some prose foretexts indicate that both author and topic are unknown, others say only "author unknown," and still others only "topic unknown." (These poems could have lost their original identifications in a myriad of ways. On the one hand, the author may not have wanted the true circumstances of the poem to be known; this would have especially been the case for poems originally exchanged in private. On the other hand, the processes of oral transmission and transcription meant that names and dates were easily lost, especially for lower-class authors.) Apparently even minor inconsistencies in how the *Kokin shū* indicated *dai shirazu* and *yomibito shirazu* poems was enough to trigger interpretations such as the following example from *Kokin waka shū kanjō kuden*: "If the prose foretext indicates that both the topic and the author are unknown, the poem is by a high-ranking court lady or empress. If it says only that the author is unknown, it is by someone under imperial censure. If it says only that the topic is unknown, it is by a low-ranking person."[2] Here the categorizing of anonymous authors as high-ranking court women, low-ranking people in general, or the politically tainted rationalizes the vagaries of the editing and transmission process. The slightest inconsistencies in the *Kokin shū* are read as clues to a secret coherence that only properly initiated readers can understand.

Since a number of poems in *Ise monogatari* appear in the *Kokin shū* as well, the *Ise monogatari* and *Kokin shū* commentaries overlapped and influenced each other. Because the *Kokin shū* was an imperial poetry anthology, it was generally accepted that its identifications and prose foretexts were factual. Any contradictions between it and *Ise monogatari* had to be resolved in a way that showed the *Kokin shū* version to be correct. This was probably one of the motivating triggers behind the reading of *Ise monogatari* as a fictionalization whose purpose was to obfuscate historical truths that were otherwise politically sensitive or unpalatable.

The *Ise monogatari* Text

Ise monogatari is a collection of 125 short episodes, each of which provides a narrative context for one or more poems (the standard total is 209). Although the core of the text may have existed earlier, a text that resembled

2. *Kokin waka shū kanjō kuden*, p. 501.

what we think of today as *Ise monogatari* was probably first compiled in the early tenth century, at about the same time as the *Kokin shū*. It continued to be developed throughout the tenth and eleventh centuries by an unknown number of anonymous hands. It was not until Fujiwara no Teika collated a recension in the thirteenth century that the text became stable. Teika's role as editor and compiler was thus crucial to the development of the commentary tradition. First, by selecting, collating, and editing versions of certain Heian texts, most particularly *Ise monogatari* and *Genji monogatari*, he created an authoritative text that was sufficiently stable that commentaries could be written about it (rather than be absorbed into it). Second, as the foremost poet of his day, his position on the proper education for a poet was extremely influential: "Regularly focus your thoughts on and imbue your mind with the general effect of old poems. You should pay particular attention to the best poems in the *Kokin shū*, *Ise monogatari*, *Gosen shū*, *Shūi shū*, and in the collections of the Thirty-six Poets (Hitomaro, Tsurayuki, Tadamine, Ise, Komachi and so on)."[3] This decree, which Teika put forward in *Eiga no taigai* (An outline for poetic composition; ca. 1222), effectively canonized *Ise monogatari* and the three tenth-century imperial anthologies, and was taken as normative for waka poets who followed him.

Although Teika's recension almost immediately became the standard text, because of the transmission process there remained a large number of variants. Medieval commentators found these variant texts problematic and worthy of extensive exegesis; they continue to vex modern critics.[4] Indeed, the choice of which *Ise monogatari* text to analyze in itself constitutes an interpretive act.

In Japanese scholarship, *Ise monogatari* is classified as *uta monogatari* (poem tale), a collection of brief prose narratives providing contexts for song-poems. Because poem tales strike a precarious balance between an emphasis on waka and an emphasis on fictional prose, as a genre they are usually desig-

---

3. Fujiwara no Teika, *Eiga no taigai* in *Karon shū*, *NKBZ* vol. 50, p. 495. In English, see Hiroaki Sato and Burton Watson, *From the Country of Eight Islands: An Anthology of Japanese Poetry*, pp. 202–4.

4. See my discussion of the *Waka chiken shū* and Reizei school *Ise monogatari shō* explanations for these variant texts in Chapters 9 and 11. Because the earliest extant text dates from the late Heian period and information on the text of *Ise monogatari* in the Heian period is practically nonexistent, scholars have been prone to wild speculation about its textual development. In fact, one might say that the critical obsession with origins, that is, with coming up with the original form of *Ise monogatari*, has made *Ise* studies a stifling dead end until very recently.

nated as a transitional form between poem collections and narrative literature (*tsukuri monogatari* or "fabricated/fictional narrative"). Although it is easy to understand why scholars see poem tales as a transitional form, chronologically the text of *Ise monogatari* was still very much in flux when the most famous fictional narrative, *Genji monogatari,* was being written at the beginning of the eleventh century. In fact, although it is generally accepted that *Ise monogatari* had a strong influence on the thematic structure and plot of *Genji,* retroactively *Genji* also had a strong effect on the reading of *Ise monogatari* and thus on the rewriting and reordering of *Ise* that continued to take place throughout the eleventh century.[5]

Poem tales probably developed out of a combination of two poetic practices. The first is the prose foretext in poetic anthologies. As pointed out above, the enigmatic brevity of waka poetry practically demands that an explanatory context be supplied. The poem tale's prose narrative provides that context. As we shall see, however, the waka often continues to resist the interpretive closure of its surrounding prose, and in some cases the prose context itself poses more interpretive problems than it solves.[6]

A second poetic practice that apparently contributed to the development of poem tales was the composition of poems for screen paintings (*byōbu uta* 屏風歌). This often took place as a group activity, a kind of social game in which poets made up stories about the people depicted on the screens and took turns reciting poetry from the characters' point of view. In episode 147 of *Yamato monogatari* (Tales of Yamato), a late tenth-century poem tale, for example, after a passage in which a young girl drowns herself in the Ikuta River because she cannot decide between two suitors, the story comes to an abrupt stop:

These tragic events of long ago were depicted in a painting. When it was presented to the late empress, everyone imagined themselves in the place of one of the figures in the painting and composed poems. Lady Ise, expressing the feelings of one of the men (*otoko*), composed:

> *kage to nomi / mizu no shita ni / aimiredo*
> *tama naki kara wa / kai nakarikeri*

---

5. For a discussion of the influence of *Ise monogatari* on *Genji monogatari,* see Field, *The Splendor of Longing in the Tale of Genji,* pp. 34–40.

6. See, e.g., Richard Okada's (*Figures of Resistance,* pp. 144–46) discussion of this point with regard to episode 4, and Richard Bowring's ("The *Ise monogatari,*" pp. 3–5) discussion of episode 6.

Our shadows are seen meeting beneath the waters;
but a body without a soul is worth nothing.

The First Princess replied in the role of the woman (*onna*):

kagiri naku / fukaku shizumeru / waga tama wa
ukitaru hito ni / mienu mono ka wa

How can my soul, sunk to the fathomless depths,
ever be seen by someone frivolously adrift?[7]

Mitani Kuniaki has argued persuasively that assuming the identity of a character in a screen was an important step in the development of fictional narratives.[8] A second step occurred when the identification of particular waka as screen poems was elided. For example, the foretext of *Kokin shū* 293 and 294 reads: "Composed at a time when Nijō no Kisaki (the Empress of the Second Ward) was still known as the Mother of the Crown Prince, on the topic of a screen painting of autumn leaves floating down the Tatsuta River." The author of *Kokin shū* 294 is identified as Ariwara no Narihira, but when the same poem appears in *Ise monogatari* episode 106, the foretext reads: "Sometime in the past a man, on an excursion with a few imperial princes, composed a poem on the bank of the Tatsuta River." A screen poem has been narrativized by the removal of any reference to the original circumstances of production and by the addition of a fictional prose foretext (developed from a description of the screen) that explains the poem. This may well have been the process behind a number of the *Ise monogatari* episodes.

There are other excellent reasons besides the hint provided in episode 106 for supposing that the core text of *Ise monogatari* was made up, at least partially, of poems written for screen paintings.[9] Screen poems use the generic

---

7. *Yamato monogatari*, pp. 313–14; in English, see Tahara, *Tales of Yamato*, p. 95.

8. See Mitani Kuniaki, "*Ise monogatari* no hyōgen kōzō: dōka no bungaku aruiwa jijitsu to kyokō," in idem, *Monogatari bungaku no hoho*, pp. 265–81.

9. For more extended discussions in English on the question of whether *Ise monogatari* was developed from screen poems, see Okada, *Figures of Resistance*, pp. 114–16; and Bowring, "The *Ise monogatari*," pp. 9–14. Both Okada and Bowring suggest that the poet Ise (874?–939?), whose personal poetry collection included a number of screen poems whose foretexts used the generic "a woman" and "a man" to refer to the figures in the paintings, may have had a hand in shaping the ur-text of *Ise monogatari*. The Kamakura commentaries usually identified Lady Ise as the editor of at least one version of *Ise monogatari*, and some such explanation continued to be maintained throughout the Muromachi period. However, from the early Edo period, beginning with Keichū (1640–1701), the majority of scholars rejected Lady Ise's authorship, usually on the grounds that the style of *Ise monogatari* (as well as its supposed political content)

"woman" (*onna* 女) and "man" (*otoko* 男) to designate figures in the paintings; this rhetorical device facilitated the reciting of poetry from the point of view of the characters in the screen. This theory also fits well with a recent theory about the use in *Ise monogatari* of the grammatical aspect marker *keri*, as a kind of storytelling, or historical, present tense.[10] Someone standing in front of a screen talking about the events depicted on it would quite naturally have used a historical present tense. Imagine, for example, someone standing before a screen depicting the events of episode 7: "The man [we see before us] is feeling tired of life in the capital and so, taking a few good friends along, he travels to Azuma (the Eastern Provinces)." The historical present tense allowed past events to come alive in the narrative present. In addition, the screen poem theory explains the occasional appearance of deictic markers such as *koko* (here), which indicate that the "narrator" is in the Heian capital even as he or she describes scenes in the Eastern Provinces.[11] Finally, the screen poem theory explains why *Ise monogatari* contains a number of episodes that seem to be simple variations on a theme: the same screen may have inspired poems on more than one occasion.[12] Incidentally, a similar explanation appears in a Muromachi commentary. According to *Ise monogatari nangi chū* (Commentary on difficult points in *Ise monogatari*), a group of courtiers (including Archbishop Henjō [816–90] and Ki no Aritsune [815–77]) gathered in a room of the Eastern Palace that contained a screen painting of all the famous places in

---

was not "feminine." For a discussion of this point, see Vos, *A Study of the Ise monogatari*, vol. 1, pp. 56–58.

10. For a summary of recent Japanese scholarship on this issue, see Okada, *Figures of Resistance*, pp. 15–20, 35–42.

11. In episode 9, for example, right after a poem about Mount Fuji, we find, "sono yama wa koko ni tatoeba Hie no yama hatachi bakari kasaneagetaran hodo shite" (If we compare that mountain to one here [in the capital], it is about as high as twenty Mount Hiei's piled one on top of another). Richard Okada (*Figures of Resistance*, pp. 151–52) also makes this point.

12. Katagiri Yōichi (*Ise monogatari no shinkenkyū*, pp. 61–64) argues, however, that the redundancy in *Ise monogatari* is a function of its two-tiered structure of a superficial "phenomenal appearance" and an underlying "Absolute Reality." Katagiri is careful to maintain that this underlying Absolute Reality does not reflect historical reality (i.e., the "real" Narihira's life); rather, he sees it instead as a formal structure composed of a limited number of conventional themes into which the Narihira persona is inserted (e.g., young love, unrequited love, love between persons of unequal status, and so on). He sees *Ise monogatari* as having been built from variations on these themes, variations that expanded and stabilized the underlying "Absolute Reality" so that it came to take on a life of its own. One problem with this argument is that Katagiri assumes a certain amount of chronology (earlier episodes form the basis for later variations) that is difficult to sustain.

Japan, including the Eastern Provinces (Azuma). The group devised the poems and stories of episodes 7–15 while looking at this screen; the result was that the main character (the "Man of Old") appeared to travel to Azuma, whereas he was really being held under house arrest not far from the capital.[13]

Narihira as the Man of Old

Nearly every episode of *Ise monogatari* opens with the phrase "mukashi otoko arikeri." The word "mukashi" in this phrase has traditionally been read in at least two ways. It is sometimes taken simply a temporal marker: "sometime in the past." It is also read as an adjective modifying "otoko," to give the commonly quoted epithet, "the Man of Old." This "Man of Old" was already, while the text was still in flux in the mid- to late Heian period, identified with the ninth-century poet Ariwara no Narihira. The "Agemaki" chapter of *Genji monogatari*, for example, refers to *Ise monogatari* as *Zaigo ga monogatari* (Tale of the fifth-ranked [captain]).[14] The identification is not, in fact, without foundation. The collection contains a disproportionate number of poems attributed elsewhere to Narihira or to people with whom Narihira is known to have associated. Thirty-four of the poems composed by the main character, the Man of Old, are attributed to Narihira in the imperial poetry anthologies *Kokin shū* and *Gosen waka shū* (Later selected collection of Japanese poetry; ca. 950s), and a number of the stories in *Ise monogatari* closely parallel *Kokin shū* prose foretexts to his poems. In addition, the court offices held by the Man of Old correspond to those held by Narihira (that is, director of the Stables of the Right and middle captain of the Imperial Guards of the Right). Although it is possible that *Ise monogatari* borrowed directly from the *Kokin shū*, most contemporary scholars believe that both the *Kokin shū* and *Ise monogatari* drew on a pre-existing collection of Narihira's poems (now lost) and combined the poems in this collection with others, including screen poems, from collections also no longer extant.

The man known as Ariwara no Narihira was born in 825, the son of Princess Ito and Prince Abo, and the grandson of Emperors Kanmu (r. 781–806) and Heizei (r. 806–9). Narihira was made a commoner with the surname "Ariwara" in the year following his birth. He never ascended far in the

---

13. *Ise monogatari nangi chū*, pp. 482–83.

14. In *Sagoromo monogatari* (The tale of Sagoromo; mid-eleventh century), it is referred to as *Zaigo chūjō no nikki* (The diary of the fifth-ranked middle captain).

court bureaucracy; at his death in 880 he had achieved only the rank of Junior Fourth Upper. However, in the year before his death, he had been named to the prestigious position of head chamberlain. The holders of this position usually advanced into the ranks of the senior bureaucrats. Had he lived longer, he probably would have done much better for himself.

Narihira's obituary in *Sandai jitsuroku* (The true history of three reigns) describes his life in four short Chinese phrases. He was "elegant and handsome in appearance" (*taibō kanrei*), and he was "self-indulgent and unrestrained" (*hōjū kakawarazu*), a phrase that Helen McCullough translates as "disregarded established conventions" and takes to mean that he was promiscuous. The *Sandai jitsuroku* then adds, "He had almost no [Chinese] scholarship" (*hotondo saigaku nashi*) and "he composed very good Japanese poems" (*yoku Yamato uta o tsukuru*).[15] These descriptive phrases are quite unusual in a historical work that focuses mainly on political achievements, and their use indicates that Narihira's reputation as a brilliant poet and gallant lover, irresistibly attractive to women, was already beginning to be established by the start of the tenth century.

Narihira's reputation was given a boost when Ki no Tsurayuki singled him and five other poets out for special attention in the preface to the *Kokin shū*. Although it was not until much later that this group of six poets came to be called the "Six Sages of Poetry" (*rokkasen* 六歌仙), the inclusion of thirty of Narihira's poems in the *Kokin shū* indicates the compilers' high regard of him as a poet. Tsurayuki may have faulted Narihira's poems for containing "too much sentiment and too little diction" (*sono kokoro amarite kotoba tarazu*), but his best poems combine an excellent command of poetic diction (*kotoba* 言葉) with an extraordinary poetic sensitivity and imagination (*kokoro* 心). Narihira's reputation as lady's man, hinted at in the *Sandai jitsuroku*, is based on much more speculative grounds. Heian and medieval Japanese took as fact the love poems attributed to Narihira in the *Kokin shū* and reinforced them with the adventures ascribed to Narihira as the Man of Old in *Ise monogatari* to create a "Narihira" persona caught up in a complex web of romantic attachments.

The narrative "biography" of Narihira pieced together by readers of *Ise monogatari* (using interpretive methods discussed in more detail below) sketches the life of a Heian courtier spent mainly in amorous pursuit of a variety of women (who are, for the most part, referred to simply as "a woman"

15. Translations (adapted) from Helen McCullough, *Tales of Ise*, pp. 42–44.

but are occasionally identified with historical women through later interpolations in the text). In the opening episode, he comes of age and dons the "first cap" (*uikōburi* 初冠) of young manhood. Then he goes hunting on his estate near Nara, where he experiences his first poetic dalliance with two beautiful sisters. Next he falls in love with the young Fujiwara no Takako (episode 3).[16] Takako is a problematic love object, since her family is determined to make her the consort of Emperor Seiwa. While Takako is living with her aunt (the Empress of the Fifth Ward, Fujiwara no Junshi), the man takes to visiting her through a gap in the palace's earthen wall, but the aunt finds out and posts a guard to prevent their meeting (episode 5). Her family discovers the affair and separates the couple (episode 4; a variation on this theme is given in episode 65); he tries to abduct her but is foiled in the attempt by her two brothers (episode 6; a variation is given in episode 12). Deciding that he is tired of living in the capital, he takes a few good friends and travels to the Eastern Provinces (episodes 7–9). His sadness at leaving Takako behind does not keep him from exchanging poems and pledges with women in Musashi and Michinoku (episodes 10–15). Later, when he returns to the capital, he continues his habit of amorous exchanges with any woman who crosses his path, going with friends on pleasure junkets to famous scenic spots, and composing poetry for friends and patrons on a wide variety of social occasions. At some point he is sent as the imperial huntsman to the Ise Shrine, where he has a secret tryst with the Ise Priestess (episodes 69–72). In his later years, Narihira accompanies Takako (now the dowager empress known as Nijō no Kisaki) on an imperial visit to her ancestral shrine, and he takes the opportunity to recite a poem recalling their youthful love affair (episode 76). Around this episode the man begins to be described as an old man (*okina* 翁), and the number of poems lamenting both the swift passage of time and his own lack of political advancement begin to increase. He

---

16. Fujiwara no Takako is better known as Nijō no Kisaki (Empress of the Second Ward). She was the niece and adopted daughter of the first Fujiwara regent, Yoshifusa, and at age 24 became the junior consort of Emperor Seiwa. In *Ise monogatari*, episodes 3, 5, 6, 29, and 76 have direct references to Nijō no Kisaki (although these references are now mostly believed to be late Heian interpolations), and episodes 4, 26, and 65 are generally also taken to be about Nijō no Kisaki, although they do not name her specifically. *Kokin shū* poems 747 (episode 4), 632 (episode 5), and 871 (episode 76), which have foretexts similar to the *Ise monogatari* episodes and are attributed to Narihira, were seen as providing a historical basis for the affair. *Kokin shū* poems 410 and 411, which appear in episode 9, are treated as the historical basis for Narihira's travels to the Eastern Provinces.

is surprised and upset when his patron, Prince Koretaka, takes orders after losing the succession to Emperor Seiwa (episode 83). The tale ends when the man takes ill and, realizing the end is near, composes his deathbed poem (episode 125).

This traditional reading of *Ise monogatari* as a biography, or even autobiography, of Narihira is a clear example of what Mark Morris has called the "subject effect" in Japanese literature, whereby a body of legends gradually builds up around a historical figure, often a Heian court poet.[17] This process includes not only dubious retroactive attributions of poems but also the fabrication of historical contexts for those poems. Each subsequent generation of readers makes its own modifications and additions to the cult of personality that attends these quasi-historical figures, additions that depend on the dominant ideal of that age. The development of Narihira's image up to the Muromachi period involved a number of factors, both textual and cultural. Some of those factors remained constant, whereas others changed drastically. One must therefore be careful about making generalizations about the inherent "nature" of the text, which might then be used as an explanation for the development of the Narihira persona. Nevertheless, it seems clear that certain aspects of the *Ise monogatari* text triggered interpretive strategies that ultimately encouraged just such a development.

Triggers for Interpretation in *Ise monogatari*

One of the most important structural problems in dealing with the history of the reception of *Ise monogatari* is that in the Heian period, especially, it is practically impossible to separate the act of reading from that of writing. Partly because of the prevalence of oral transmission, texts were not yet viewed as inviolable "organic" wholes. In the early textual history of *Ise monogatari*, the anonymous readers were also writers who felt free to add more episodes and reorganize (or disorganize) their order according to their own chronological and thematic concerns.

There seem to have been at least two waves of rewriting.[18] The first came around the time of the *Kokin shū*, when the basic text was put together from

17. See Mark Morris, "Waka as Form; Waka as History."

18. For a succinct summary of the three-stage theory of the development of *Ise monogatari* (i.e., stage 1 = Narihira collection; stage 2 = ca. 905 and the *Kokin shū*; and stage 3 = ca. 950s and the *Gosen shū*), see Katagiri Yōichi, ed., *Ise monogatari, Yamato monogatari*, pp. 11–19. In English, see Marra, *The Aesthetics of Discontent*, pp. 36–37.

a variety of sources (see above). At this stage, each episode of *Ise monogatari* would have included one or more poems embedded in a prose context. Some episodes commented on the characters' feelings and actions, from the position of a narrator who brings us into the storytelling present tense. The narrator occasionally identifies the poetic reference of the character's use of certain metaphors. For example, in episode 1 the narrator explains the term *shinobu* (a randomly patterned design imprinted with moss-fern) and comments that "people were remarkably elegant in those days"; in episode 41 he or she identifies the poetic allusion behind the use of *murasaki* (deep purple). In episode 9 the narrator breaks away from the story of Narihira's travels in the East to compare the height of Mount Fuji to Mount Hiei (see note 11 to this chapter), thereby reminding us that the story is being told in the capital. In episode 19 the narrator explains the meaning of a poem for us ("He meant that there was another man in her life"). In episodes 33 and 44 the narrator hazards poetic criticism ("Not bad for someone living in the provinces"; and "Given the circumstances, this is a most interesting poem. [For the recipient] just to savor the lingering aftertaste in silence would be enough; no reply was necessary"). This level of narrative intervention was probably created at the same time that the episodes were first produced, and it signals the text's origin in some form of oral recitation.

The second wave of revision followed the compilation of *Gosen shū*. It was during this second wave of revision that readers familiar with the *Kokin shū* poems attributed to Narihira who wished to create a more satisfying sense of biographical closure began to interpolate comments identifying the "real" names of the anonymous women with whom the Man of Old had affairs. An examination of episode 6 will make this process clear.

Sometime in the past there was a man. For years he had been courting a most inaccessible lady. One pitch-black night, he finally spirited her out of her apartments and ran off with her. As they passed along the Akuta River, she caught a glimpse of a dewdrop on a blade of grass and asked him what it was. The journey ahead was long, the hour had grown late, and a torrential rain was pouring down, punctuated by frightful peals of thunder. The man put the lady inside a ruined storehouse and stationed himself in the doorway with his bow and quiver on his back, never dreaming that the place was haunted by demons. But while he was standing there longing for daybreak, a demon ate the woman up in one gulp. A thunderclap muffled her scream of terror. When the sky finally began to lighten a bit, the man peered inside and saw that the lady was gone. Frantic with helpless grief, he recited:

> *shiratama ka / nani zo to hito no / toishi toki*
> *tsuyu to kotaete / kienamashi mono o*
>
> When my love asked, "What is it? A jewel?"
> I wish I'd replied "dew" and vanished.

This occurred when the Empress of the Second Ward was still in attendance upon her cousin, the imperial consort. Because she was so beautiful, someone stole her away and carried her off on his back. Her brothers, the Horikawa Minister Mototsune and Major Counselor Kunitsune, still minor officials at the time, happened to be on their way to the imperial palace. They heard someone wailing, halted the abductor, and took her back. They were the so-called demons. This all happened when the lady was still very young and had not yet ceased to be a commoner, or so they say.[19]

As Richard Bowring has pointed out, the poem probably came first; its strange vision of a woman asking about jewels practically demands supplementary information for the reader to make sense of it.[20] The prose foretext attempts to provide that information, but in the process it raises more questions than it resolves. The prose text following the poem (*atogaki* 後書) adds a second layer of supplementary interpretation. The first story is rationalized with a "historical" interpretation, including the names of the demons. This kind of second-level narrative interpolation is called *danmatsu fukachū* (段末付加注, literally, "comments attached at the end of the episode"). We see here, in these interpolated identifications, the initial seed of the allegorical commentaries to come: the assumptions are that generic nominals had been intentionally substituted for personal names and that historical events had been fictionalized to cover up a scandalous affair. Allegoresis thus lies at the very heart of the text's production.

In the case of *Ise monogatari*, then, we have a text that manifests traces of its own reception. However, these identifications were rather random and desultory at best. No concerted effort was made to reorder the episodes into a truly coherent "biography"; the biographical impulse seems to have been

19. Although I am persuaded by Richard Okada's argument for translating *keri* as a historical present tense, I have also been persuaded by my various readers (anonymous and otherwise) that its use in English is so cumbersome that it presents more problems than it solves. Although I have decided to keep the traditional past tense, the reader should keep the historical present tense in mind. Translation (modified) from Helen McCullough, *Tales of Ise*, pp. 72–73.

20. Bowring, "The *Ise monogatari*," pp. 3–5.

just one among a number of thematic concerns that subtend the paratactic sequencing.[21] Although some segments, for example, episodes 7–15 (the so-called *Azuma kudari*, in which the Man of Old travels through the Eastern Provinces) and episodes 69–72 (in which the Man of Old has an affair with the Ise Priestess), do seem to be linked by biographical codes, each episode could just as easily be read as a self-contained whole; there is no necessary relationship of narrative cause and effect between consecutive episodes.

Moreover, the perennially enticing interpretation of *Ise monogatari* as a pseudo-biography of Narihira is constantly undercut by a number of internal contradictions, as well as historical and geographical discrepancies. These discrepancies became particularly noticeable after Fujiwara no Teika had standardized (and thus canonized) the text so that readers no longer felt free to tamper with it (in other words, to correct any perceived problem themselves). The development of the Kamakura commentaries can partially be explained as an attempt to resolve these newly apparent contradictions, which became "triggers" for allegorical interpretation.

First and foremost among these is that *Ise monogatari* has poems and stories that both predate and postdate Narihira's life. The foretext for the second episode indicates that the events occur "sometime after the move from Nara, at a time when people were still not settled in the new capital"; the transfer of the capital from Nara to Kyoto happened some thirty years before Narihira was born. On the other hand, episode 114, which describes Emperor Kōkō's (r. 884–87) hunting expedition to the Serikawa River, is known to have taken place in 886, six years after Narihira's death. This is one of the first problems raised in the *Waka chiken shū*: "It is written that Narihira died in 880, during the reign of Emperor Yōzei [r. 876–84], and yet this tale includes descriptions of incidents such as the Imperial Progress to Serikawa, which is known to have occurred in 886. . . . What kind of person was Narihira that he could write about something that happened seven years after his own death?"[22]

---

21. Other thematic concerns besides biography include stories grouped by season, by place (the Eastern Provinces [including Michinoku and Musashi], places along the way to Ise, etc.), around the same person (Ki no Aritsune, Prince Koretaka, the Ise Priestess), or about the same topic (thwarted young love, marital strife and separation, life in the countryside, the inaccessible woman).

22. Shimabara Kominkan Matsuhira Bunko shozō *Waka chiken shū* (hereafter "Shimabara *Waka chiken shū*"), p. 105.

Second, a number of episodes depict a Man of Old who does not fit the standard image of Narihira. For example, episodes 23, 40, and 86 are variations on the theme of young love thwarted. A young boy, the son of ordinary parents (in episode 23 he is the child of an itinerant peddler), is desperately in love with a young girl who lives nearby, but his parents have a higher-class bride in mind and try to separate them. Another thematic variation that does not fit well with Narihira's "life" is presented in episodes 24, 60, and 62, all of which depict a wife of a minor official, who leaves him for another man because of his neglect and then is embarrassed to see her former husband again. Even when the story does fit the idealized character of Narihira, the reader still runs into contradictions between episodes that seem to be subtended by the same story. For example, there are problematic contradictions between episodes 3–9 and episode 65, which were already by the late Heian period understood as describing the affair between Narihira and Fujiwara no Takako.[23]

Third, there are certain geographical discrepancies. An especially bothersome one for the commentators occurs in the episodes in which the Man of Old travels through the Eastern Provinces. Kamakura poets and readers were able to travel with greater ease than Heian period courtiers and, perhaps for that reason, were much more aware of geography. They were vexed by the fact that in episode 8 Narihira sees Mount Asama from the Eastern Sea Road (Tōkaidō), when it is, in fact, not visible from there.[24]

Finally, there were discrepancies between the *Kokin shū* and *Ise monogatari* that problematized the straightforward use of the *Kokin shū* to provide evidence for identifications in *Ise monogatari*. For example, episode 65's

---

23. See note 1 to Chapter 2.

24. As suggested above, the *Azuma kudari* episode may well have been composed in response to a series of pictures of the Eastern Provinces painted on a screen. Since it is unlikely that either the poet(s) or the patron would have ever traveled to Azuma, geographical accuracy would not have been a particularly important concern to them. By the late Heian period, however, we already begin to see instances of disappointment on the part of travelers when they see in "real life" the places they have previously known only through poems. In *Sarashina nikki* (Sarashina diary; mid-eleventh century), for example, the author complains that Musashi, famous in poetry for its *murasaki* plants, is "a province without a single charming place to recommend it. On the beach the sand was not white but a sort of muddy color; in the fields, there were none of the *murasaki* plants I had heard about, but just a mass of reeds growing so high that the tips of our horseman's bows were invisible" (translation from Ivan Morris, *As I Crossed a Bridge of Dreams*, p. 43).

summary of the Fujiwara no Takako and Narihira affair outlined in episodes 3–6 includes a poem attributed in the *Kokin shū* to Fujiwara no Naoiko.[25] A second example is from episode 12, a variation on the abduction theme of episode 6, and so again assumed to be about Narihira and Takako:

Sometime in the past there was a man who abducted someone's daughter. He was on his way to Musashi Plain with her when some provincial officials arrested him for theft. He had left the girl in a clump of bushes and run off, but the pursuers felt certain that he was on the plain and prepared to set fire to it. In great agitation the girl recited this poem:

> *Musashino wa / kyō wa na yaki so / wakakusa no*
> *tsuma mo komoreri / ware mo komoreri*
>
> Do not set fire to Musashi Plain today, for among the young grasses
> my beloved and I lie hidden.

They heard the poem, seized the girl, and marched the two of them off.[26]

This story poses two interpretive difficulties. First, all the medieval commentaries assumed that the story was about Narihira and Takako. Since Musashi Plain is in the Kantō region, the idea that Narihira managed to spirit Takako that far away must have seemed unrealistic. Luckily, however, a similar poem and story appear in the *Kokin shū* (17, anonymous); there the setting of the story is the Kasuga Plain, a much more plausible location if the episode is understood to be about Narihira and Takako. The problem confronting the commentators was to resolve the apparent geographical and intertextual discrepancies. The Reizeike-ryū *Ise monogatari shō* solves the problem with an elaborate story about a man from Musashi who died in the capital. His last request to his son was that he be buried on Musashi Plain. Since that proved impossible, his son had soil transported from Musashi Plain to build a tomb on Kasuga Plain; this burial site came to be called the "Musashi Tomb." Since this is where Narihira and Takako were hiding when they were discovered, in the episode the area was referred to as "Musashi Plain."[27]

---

25. *Kokin shū* 807: the Reizei commentators resolved the problem by claiming that Naoiko (直子) was Takako's childhood name (Reizeike-ryū *Ise monogatari shō*, p. 360).

26. Translation (modified) from Helen McCullough, *Tales of Ise*, p. 78.

27. Reizeike-ryū *Ise monogatari shō*, pp. 317–18. There are references to this story in both the old and new versions of the Noh play *Unrin'in* (Unrin temple), as well as in the nonstandard (*bangai*) Noh play *Musashino tsuka* (The tomb of Musashi).

As can be seen from these two examples, the Kamakura commentaries generally attempted to resolve a discrepancy between *Ise monogatari* and *Kokin shū* so that neither work would appear simply mistaken. Nevertheless, the *Kokin shū* was always given authoritative precedence because the *Kokin shū*'s "historical" status had to be maintained for it to continue to be used as a key to read through the fictive appearance of *Ise monogatari*.

Heian period author-reader-editors of *Ise monogatari* were not, however, all that concerned about such inconsistencies (after all, they were at least partially responsible for them). In fact, another reason for using the generic "a man" and "a woman" rather than proper names may have been that it allowed the initial author-editors the freedom to play, to mix historical events with fictionalized ones, rather than to cover up a scandal. Although some poems and prose contexts may have been lifted directly from the *Kokin shū*, with just the proper names replaced, other episodes join two unrelated preexisting poems within a completely new, fictional context. For example, episode 25 was formed by taking *Kokin shū* poems 622 (anonymous) and 623 (Ono no Komachi), which are unrelated except for juxtaposition, and creating a prose foretext that binds them together narratively. If the writers had used specific names in the historically based episodes, the other fictional ones would have stood out. This would particularly be the case in segments such as episode 65, which combined poetry composed by people who were not even contemporaries.

One result of mixing quasi-historical accounts with completely fictional episodes is that the issue of whether *Ise monogatari* is fact or fiction becomes basically undecidable.[28] Nevertheless, because the medieval commentaries based their entire interpretive method on the assumption that *Ise monogatari* was written as a fictional refraction of historical fact, they had to assume that *Ise monogatari* belonged in the same factual category as the *Kokin shū* and in a different category from the fictional *Genji monogatari*. The anecdotal commentators were therefore concerned chiefly with discovering interpretive keys that allowed them to directly translate the narrative of *Ise monogatari* into historical data.

28. This question still comes up even in twentieth-century discussions. For example, Masao Miyoshi ("Against the Native Grain," pp. 541–42) points to this quality of undecidability as being the antecedent of the twentieth-century genre of the *shishōsetsu*, or "I-novel," a genre that also transgresses the boundaries between autobiographical fact and fiction.

Textual aporias (syntagmatic triggers) in *Kokin shū* and *Ise monogatari* tended to lead to philological commentaries that deal with obscure words and phrases or to anecdotal and historical commentaries that attempted to fill in the missing circumstances under which the poems were created. In the case of *Ise monogatari*, one can discern in the text itself traces of a set of interpretive principles that Heian readers employed to read *Ise monogatari* so as to reveal its supposed historical subtext. With the commentaries affiliated with Fujiwara no Tameaki, however, we begin to see much more elaborate and systematic efforts to render *Ise monogatari* historical.

Heian and Kamakura Readers' Interpretive Principles

Both Heian and Kamakura readers shared a few important assumptions as to how episodes in *Ise monogatari* might be linked to reveal their supposed historical subtext:[29] (1) the *Kokin shū*, as an imperially sanctioned collection, must be historically accurate; (2) the fact that *Ise monogatari* and *Kokin shū* had a number of the same poems, with similar prose foretexts, in common was evidence for treating at least some of the *Ise monogatari* episodes as a fictionalized smokescreen for historical events; and (3) repetition of any kind was meaningful. This third interpretive principle was deployed by Kamakura readers in two forms: (a) thematic variations between episodes indicated that the episodes referred to the same historical events; and (b) a repeated epithet indicated the same person. These three interrelated assumptions meant that the reader was justified in assuming that if the anonymous "woman" of episode A could be identified with a historical figure by comparison with the *Kokin shū*, then the woman in episode B, which seemed to be a variation on the same theme, was the same woman. Simple repetition served to link episodes in which causal chains were missing. An example of this train of reasoning is the Reizei school's identifications of Ono no Komachi.[30] Episode 25 contains a poem attributed to Ono no Komachi in the *Kokin shū* (623). This episode refers to the woman as "a woman of passionate temperament" (*irogonomi naru onna* 色ごのみなる女).[31] The

29. I have extrapolated these general principles of interpretation from Katagiri's (*Ise monogatari no shinkenkyū*, pp. 41–52) more concrete discussion of how the Kamakura commentary identifications may have been generated.

30. See ibid., pp. 41–42.

31. *Irogonomi* 色好 means "love of sex." In the rest of the book, depending on the context, I also translate it as "eroticism."

Reizei commentaries then identify any other woman designated as "passionate" (*irogonomi*) as, *ipso facto,* Ono no Komachi (episodes 28, 37, and 42). Since episode 28 tells of a passionate woman who suddenly leaves her lover or husband, women in other episodes in the same kind of situation are also identified as Ono no Komachi (episodes 21, 60, 62, and 113). And since episodes 37 and 42 characterize the woman as shallow and untrustworthy, women so characterized in other episodes are also Ono no Komachi (episodes 18 and 50).

It is important to note that although it is the interpolated identifications in each episode (or the external identifications made in the *Kokin shū*) that enable the reader to link these episodes, there is no overt linkage *between* episodes in the text itself. Although the basic impulse to identify the reality beneath the tale's fictional appearance was present in the Heian period and continued full force into the Kamakura period, there were also changes in the ways that readers responded to *Ise monogatari.* For one thing, Heian readers who were interpolating identifications would have known that their comments were being added to a previously existing text. However, from the twelfth century onward, particularly after Teika had stabilized the text in the form we know today, readers treated the Heian interpolations as a part of the text, which was, to a greater or lesser extent, read as Narihira's biography (or autobiography). From Teika's time into the Muromachi, readers did not see the Heian interpolations as a secondary layer of commentary. Instead they generally thought that these comments had been placed there intentionally by either Narihira or his supposed wife (and editor) the poet Ise (874?–939?), as tantalizing hints of the historical reality hidden beneath the tale's fictional surface.

Thus *Ise monogatari*'s paratactic structure (which refused narrative relations of cause and effect), its use of the enigmatic "a woman" and "a man" (even when the characters were identified as historical persons elsewhere), its thematic repetition with variation (which led to many internal contradictions), and its intimate relationship to the *Kokin shū* (which readers assumed was historically accurate) both encouraged and frustrated readers' attempts to discern the unified outlines of a life spent in amorous pursuits and thus acted as triggers for allegorical interpretation. Further, both the ritualistic repetition of "mukashi otoko arikeri" at the beginning of each episode and the paratactic structure of the work as a whole give *Ise monogatari* an allegorical quality. According to Angus Fletcher, parataxis and ritualistic repetition are fundamental elements of the earliest forms of allegory, especially in places where oral tradition is still influential. They are considered allegorical because rhythmic repetition in and of itself seems to establish an enigma that the reader has to figure out. This certainly has been the response of readers of *Ise monogatari* through the ages.[32]

32. See Fletcher, *Allegory*, pp. 162–80.

5

Extratextual Triggers

As we have seen, certain substantive and stylistic features of *Ise monogatari* and the *Kokin shū*, which disrupted and resisted the efforts of readers to read the text as a coherent whole, invited the reading strategies employed by Heian and Kamakura readers. In the Heian period, these features led to interpolated comments within the texts themselves, which were often treated by later readers as part of the original text. After the texts had been stabilized, however, the features incited philological and anecdotal commentaries that clearly stood apart from the text.

A number of features of the Kamakura commentaries, however, cannot satisfactorily be explained by textual triggers alone. For example, the commentaries went to wild lengths in their search for the hidden "history" of *Ise monogatari*. The commentaries' accumulation of superfluous "historical" detail included meticulous identifications of dates of events and the names of people and places, on the basis of no known historical evidence and indeed often enough in conflict with whatever evidence was available. For example, the Reizeike-ryū *Ise monogatari shō* commentary on the first episode begins with Narihira's coming-of-age ceremony: the date, the reigning emperor, the location, even what Narihira was wearing, are all carefully recounted.[1] *Ise monogatari nangi chū* fabricates stories to fill in such obvious gaps as how Narihira and Takako met in the first place (she watched him perform the

1. Reizeike-ryū *Ise monogatari shō*, pp. 293–94.

Gosechi dances at the palace; when he dropped his dancing comb, she had an opportunity to address him).[2] And once the *Kokin shū*'s usefulness as a source of corroborating evidence had been exhausted, the commentators simply invented other historical documents, such as Heian diaries and commentaries, to back up their stories. Or they claimed that the commentary itself originated in a Heian oracular revelation. The historical data the commentators were purporting to uncover obviously was not very historical. If one assumes that the original impulse toward identification was a sincere belief in the facticity of *Ise monogatari* and the *Kokin shū*, then there would seem to be a contradiction between the commentators' seeming intolerance for "pure" fiction and their willingness to invent these dates, places, and events out of whole cloth. The aporias of the text are simply not enough to explain this contradiction.

Another development that first appears in the commentaries of the late thirteenth century is the religious interpretations and allegorizations of both the *Kokin shū* (especially the Japanese preface) and *Ise monogatari*. There is nothing in either text that prepares us for the interpretive approach of commentaries such as *Gyokuden jinpi no maki* or *Waka Kokin kanjō no maki*, which interpret these texts as revelations of the profoundly esoteric secrets of Shingon Buddhism. And beginning with the religious commentaries of the 1270s and 1280s and spreading quickly to the historical commentaries of the early

---

2. The Gosechi 五節 dances were performed at the "Flushed Faces Banquet" (*toyo no akari no sechie*) as part of the Great Thanksgiving Service (*daijōsai* 大嘗祭) for the enthronement of a new emperor. Although usually performed by carefully selected young girls, the Muromachi commentary *Ise monogatari nangi chū* (p. 466) claims that Narihira was one of the dancers: "The matter of the Gosechi Middle Captain. In the past, at the time of the Gosechi dance at the Flushed Faces Banquet, Narihira performed as one of the dancers, wearing a robe imprinted with moss fern [the robe the Man of Old wore in the first episode of *Ise monogatari*]. In the midst of the dance . . . he dropped his Gosechi comb. Nijō no Kisaki saw this and had someone replace it [in his hair]." The "Gosechi comb" was a special comb worn by the dancers during a private dress rehearsal performed before the emperor; at the end of the dance he would choose one of the combs as a mark of special favor. The commentary appears to reverse the usual gender/power roles, with Takako showing her partiality for Narihira by returning his comb. The commentary goes on to analyze the character for comb (節) into its component parts to show that "Gosechi Middle Captain" (五節中将) actually refers to Narihira being the fifth son (gorō 五郎) of Prince Abo. Note that the Noh play *Kakitsubata* also includes a reference to Narihira as a Gosechi dancer: "As for this court cap, it is the cap Narihira wore for the Gosechi dance at the Flushed Faces Banquet" (Itō Masayoshi, *Yōkyoku shū*, vol. 57, p. 262). For more information on the Gosechi dances, see W. H. McCullough and H. C. McCullough, *A Tale of Flowering Fortunes*, vol. 1, pp. 375–78, supplementary note 18.

fourteenth century, we find etymological allegoresis: the analysis of graphs, words, and whole phrases as complex puns and wordplays intentionally woven into the text to hint at a hidden layer of meaning. Etymological allegoresis appears to have been employed first by the religious commentaries. This is difficult to explain by textual triggers alone, since there is little in the *Kokin shū* or *Ise monogatari* that calls for religious allegoresis. Once etymological allegoresis was established as a methodology, however, it became an effective tool for harmonizing intra- and extratextual contradictions.

Textual aporias also do not explain the new emphasis on secrecy. By the thirteenth century, even commentaries that were mainly pragmatic and philological ended with strict prohibitions against indiscriminate access to family secrets. And, of course, aporias do not explain the introduction of the Shingon Buddhist initiation ceremony (*kanjō*) as a way to transmit secret traditions.

Features such as these appear to have been encouraged by what I have been calling paradigmatic or extratextual triggers; that is, triggers for allegoresis that have less to do with the text itself than with the changed context in which that text was read. As with inter- and intratextual triggers, their existence would not necessarily result in allegorical interpretation, but they certainly facilitated it.

In order to understand why Kamakura commentators were so intent on translating the events of *Ise monogatari* and the poems of *Kokin shū* into a hidden historical or transcendent religious "fact" that they were willing, in effect, to invent those facts, one has to examine the early Kamakura political and cultural context. In the manner of Todorov, we are looking for the reasons that the Kamakura reader of *Ise monogatari* and the *Kokin shū* no longer felt comfortable with those texts: triggers of implausibility (the text conflicts with one's commonsense view of the world) and inappropriateness (it conflicts with one's moral and religious values) are the most pertinent here. In this respect, the change that seems decisive is the widespread popularization of Buddhism that was occurring throughout the Kamakura period. I examine this changed religious context in Chapter 7. Here and in the next chapter, I examine changes in the political and economic context that had a profound impact on the poetic families: the localized historical contingencies of the late thirteenth-century disenfranchisement of the aristocracy, particularly the political and literary struggles of the poetry factions (歌壇 *kadan*) in Kyoto and Kamakura.

Although at the end of the Gempei War (1180–85), many governmental functions had been moved to Kamakura, the Kyoto court still remained the center of aesthetic culture. Court aristocrats who had progressively less political power retained at least a modicum of social status through their role as the jealous guardians of the Heian literary tradition. These poetry families (*uta no ie* 歌の家; that is, families that specialized in Japanese poetry) had a pressing need to claim possession of the "secret truths" of Heian court literature—they could use them as economic and political bargaining chips to preserve their status. The contemporaneous appearance in other artistic traditions, such as gardening and music, of secret treatises reinforces the supposition that the development of secret traditions within families was symptomatic of broader social changes. The increasing demand for secret commentaries would have provided a powerful economic motivation for the development of an allegorical reading strategy that searched for hidden meanings in wordplays on names and places and within poetic imagery. In other words, their need to find hidden meanings guaranteed that members of poetry families would find them.

The commentaries might also be seen as a response to a feeling of great distance—not merely temporal, but religious and social as well—from the stable world of Heian court culture and the idealized hero, Narihira, who exemplified that culture. Samurai patrons who aspired to the elegance of court society would have been curious about anecdotal details of life in the Heian court; they wanted the "inside scoop," so to speak. And the Kamakura commentators seem to have been more than willing to fabricate interesting details to satiate that curiosity.

The intended audience of the commentaries is thus, I suspect, an important consideration in our understanding of their development. I will return to this point when I discuss Fujiwara no Tameaki, the figure most closely connected to these commentaries, who was located in Kamakura rather than Kyoto and who seems likely to have been economically dependent on the patronage of samurai poet/scholars. First, however, let us examine an example of how political and economic pressures may have played a role in developing a poetry family that had family secrets, a "founder" of the house whose image was passed down as an emblem of authority, and a ritual that becomes the forerunner of the esoteric waka initiation ceremony later developed by Fujiwara no Tameaki.

The Development of the Rokujō as a Poetry Family

The earliest examples of literary families were those attached to the imperial university (*daigakuryō* 大学寮). Originally professorships at the university were obtained through merit, as measured by a series of examinations, based on the Chinese model of government bureaucracy. However, as kinship and personal ties to the Fujiwara family began to take precedence over merit at court, a similar process occurred at the university; from the tenth century on, professors of Chinese literature were chosen from only three families, the Sugawara, Kiyowara, and Ōe. By the late Heian period, a Sugawara professor of literature passed his position to his son as if it were a private possession rather than a public office.[3] Each of the families that supplied university professors developed its own esoteric methods for reading Chinese texts.[4] Having been squeezed out of political power by the Fujiwara, they were able to stabilize and justify their economic position by claiming to be purveyors of a specialized corpus of knowledge (*saigaku* 才覚) to the court. Possession of a secret tradition helped protect the family's status in competition with other families since, as Konishi Jin'ichi has pointed out, it could be instrumental in obtaining one of the limited number of prestigious and lucrative government posts.[5] As we shall see in the Kamakura period as well, a secret family tradition could overcome a lack of aptitude in the heir.

By the late tenth century, there were already what we might call scholars of secular Japanese literature, for example, Fujiwara no Kintō and Minamoto no Shitagō (911–83). However, the Rokujō house, founded by Fujiwara no Akisue (1055–1123) and named after his mansion in the Sixth Ward, is probably the first example of what we would today think of as a poetry family. Akisue, who was a highly regarded waka poet in his time, came from a family famous for its knowledge of Chinese and Confucian studies, and it may be that his familiarity with the secrets taught by the families associated

---

3. See Borgen, *Sugawara no Michizane and the Early Heian Court*, p. 87. Borgen notes: "Such secretive practices helped protect a family's status but were detrimental to the intellectual vitality of the university."

4. According to Konishi Jin'ichi (*A History of Japanese Literature*, p. 150), this code of specially placed marks (dots or short lines) was first developed by Buddhist monks to help them read Chinese.

5. Ibid., pp. 152–53. See also Cook, "The Discipline of Poetry," pp. 58–67.

with the university encouraged him to develop a tradition of secret poetic knowledge for his own family. It appears that, at least for a time, Akisue was successful in giving his family a competitive edge; subsequent generations of the Rokujō house were well known for their learned knowledge of waka and waka history. In the early thirteenth century, Kamo no Chōmei quoted a comment by Lay Priest Shōmei (1112?–?) about Rokujō Kiyosuke (1104–77) that "no one could compare to him when it came to breadth of knowledge about poetry."[6]

In order to establish the Rokujō as a poetry family, Akisue created the "Hitomaro eigu" (人麻呂影供), a memorial ceremony venerating the early Nara poet Kakinomoto no Hitomaro. The original ritual was based on a ceremony known as *sekiten* (or *shakuten* 釈奠) in which Confucius and his disciples were venerated. In time it took on a more syncretic Shinto-Buddhist coloration and formed the basis for waka lecture ceremonies (*kōshiki* 講式) that venerated poets such as Hitomaro and Narihira as incarnations of the guardian *kami* of waka poetry, Sumiyoshi Daimyōjin.[7] Sumiyoshi was in turn considered a manifestation of various Buddhist deities, including the bodhisattva Kōkitokuō[8] and Dainichi Nyorai.

The first Hitomaro memorial ceremony was performed at Akisue's Higashi no Tōin mansion in the Sixth Ward on the sixteenth day of the sixth month in 1118. A fairly detailed description of the events appears in the section on waka in *Kokon chomon jū* (Anecdotes heard from writers ancient and modern; 1254) by Tachibana no Narisue (fl. 13th century). There is also an account written by Fujiwara no Atsumitsu (1063–1144) entitled *Kakinomoto*

---

6. Kamo no Chōmei (*Mumyō shō*, p. 89) continues, "If you approach him with a question about something you deliberately searched for and thought out, in the belief that he could not possibly have encountered it before, it always turns out to be something that he has already investigated long ago" (translation [modified] from Hilda Katō, "The *Mumyōsho* of Kamo no Chōmei," p. 394).

7. See, e.g., *Kakinomoto kōshiki*, pp. 55–58. Note that the head administrator of the Sumiyoshi Shrine, Tsumori Kunimoto (1023–1102), who was a good poet and close friend of Akisue, Minamoto no Toshiyori, and Fujiwara no Mototoshi (1060–1142), was at just this time encouraging the worship of Sumiyoshi Daimyōjin and Tamatsushima Myōjin as the guardian deities of waka poetry. I discuss the development of the waka deities Sumiyoshi and Tamatsushima in more detail in Chapter 8; see also Aso Mizue, "Hitomaro shinkō: sono keisei to hatten," p. 23.

8. "Noble Virtue Bodhisattva": one of the bodhisattvas to whom the Buddha expounded the *Nirvana Sutra* (*Nehan-gyō*).

eigu ki (Record of the Kakinomoto memorial ceremony).[9] The two accounts do not always correspond perfectly, but the basic outline of what occurred is clear.

Akisue had an image of Hitomaro created specifically for the occasion. It was painted on a scroll about one yard (three *shaku*) high. Hitomaro was shown wearing an *eboshi* 烏帽子 court cap and a courtier's robe, in his left hand he held paper, in his right hand a writing brush, and he appeared to be about sixty years old. Akisue also composed an inscription for the scroll. It included a brief introductory biography of Hitomaro, an explanation for the image, and a eulogistic poem in Chinese:

His family name was Kakinomoto; his given name was Hitomaro. He served Empress Jitō and Emperor Monmu and associated with Princes Nitta[10] and Takechi. When the empress was visiting the Yoshino Mountains as the spring breezes blew, Hitomaro offered a poem of blessing;[11] in the autumn mist at Akashi Bay he expressed his feelings in a poem through the image of a small boat.[12] Is it not truly said that this poem is a masterpiece of the *Kokin shū*'s Six Modes by which poetry expresses meaning, a praiseworthy anecdote of the *Man'yō shū* period? Lately people have valued the ineffable beauty (*yūgen*) of the classic style of painting; I have had the painting done in the newer style. Because I have been so moved, I have composed the following poem praising the virtues of Hitomaro:

> The nature of this Sage of Poetry
> was received from heaven.
> His talent for poetry was great;
> his arrangement of verses was ceremonious.
> In thirty-one syllables

---

9. Tachibana no Narisue, *Kokon chomon jū*, pt. I, section 178, pp. 231–34; and Fujiwara no Atsumitsu, *Kakinomoto eigu ki*, pp. 53–54. The following discussion is indebted to Yamada Shōzen's article "Kakinomoto no Hitomaro eigu no seiritsu to tenkai." See also Aso Mizue, "Hitomaro shinkō." In English, H. E. Plutschow discusses the *Hitomaro eigu* in relation to ancestor worship and the Shinto-Buddhist synthesis in the arts in *Chaos and Cosmos: Ritual in Early and Medieval Japanese Literature*, pp. 187–88.

10. "Nitta" probably refers to Prince Niitabe, the seventh son of Emperor Tenmu and half-brother of Takechi.

11. *Man'yō shū* 36–39: "Poems written by Kakinomoto no Hitomaro at the time of the imperial procession to the palace at Yoshino"; see Levy, *Man'yōshu: A Translation of Japan's Premier Anthology of Classical Poetry*, pp. 56–58.

12. This alludes to the "Honobono to Akashi" poem (*Kokin shū* 409), popularly attributed to Hitomaro, which is recited at the close of the ceremony.

his diction flowered brilliantly.
For more than four hundred years
[his poetry] has been transmitted.
The laureate of this Path [of Poetry],
Hitomaro is a founding sage of our court.
It is not possible to criticize
or find fault [with his poetry].
It is as rare as the phoenix's feathers;
as unique as the unicorn's horn.
As has been said before, he walks alone
[among poets past and present];
no one has yet attained his level of achievement.[13]

It is not clear whether Akisue composed the inscription in Chinese himself, or had Fujiwara no Atsumitsu, the head of the Bureau of [Chinese] Education (*daigakubu* 大学部), translate his ideas into Chinese; the latter seems more likely. Akisue then had the noted calligrapher Fujiwara no Akinaka (1059–1129) inscribe it above the painting.

On the day of the ceremony, a low table was placed before the image, with offerings of sweet cakes and various artificial fish and fowl carved from water buffalo horn. After the banquet trays were brought out, there was a ceremony in which three offerings of sake were presented to the portrait of Hitomaro. The attendants served small "parrot" cups[14] and bottles of sake, then retired to wait on the veranda. Akisue suggested that the first offering should be made by the leading poet among those present, and Minamoto no Toshiyori agreed to drink the first cup. Akisue's son Akisuke set out the cups before the image, Akisue's nephew Michitsune poured sake, and then the first ritual offering was made. After the sake was passed around the room three times, sweets and soup were served. Then Akisue asked whether the inscription praising Hitomaro should be read before or after the poetry meeting, and there was some disagreement among the participants. Eventually Akisue decided that the inscription should be read first, and he had a

13. Tachibana Narisue, *Kokon chomon jū*, pt. I, pp. 231–32.

14. 鸚鵡の盃: Thomas Rimer and Jonathan Chaves (*Japanese and Chinese Poems to Sing: The Wakan rōei shū*, p. 147) note that this term refers to cups made from the chambered nautilus, which was called a "parrot shell" (鸚鵡貝) because of its resemblance to the head and beak of a parrot. The wine cups used here were apparently made from nautilus shells and were probably chosen (or manufactured especially) to go with a poem on sake wine from the *Wakan rōei shū* recited later in the ceremony.

round cushion placed at the lectern for the reader, a scholar of Chinese named Fujiwara no Yukimori. Saneyuki (Akisue's son-in-law) placed the inscription on the lectern, and Yukimori read it aloud. Then they moved on to the poetry meeting. Everyone composed poems on the theme of "a breeze on the water as evening approaches." Atsumitsu wrote a preface for the poems, Fujiwara no Munekane (the brother-in-law of Akisue's son Ieyasu) took the role of lector (*kōshi* 講師), and Saneyuki performed the role of marshal (*dokushi* 読師).[15]

After the poetry meeting, some people went directly home, but others lingered to talk. Atsumitsu recited a Chinese poem:

> The colors of the Hsin-feng wine
> glow fresh and pure in the parrot-nautilus cup!
> The sounds of Eternal Joy Palace music
> murmur softly in the phoenix-flutes.[16]

Akisue repeated the poem, and then both he and Atsumitsu recited a pair of waka that at the time were popularly attributed to Hitomaro: "Honobono to Akashi"[17] and "Tanometsutsu."[18] The poems functioned as a ritual closure to the ceremony; afterward everyone agreed that they had enjoyed themselves thoroughly and promised to meet again.

One of this event's more striking points is that it appears to have been mainly a family affair. Of the thirteen people who attended, ten were related by either blood or marriage to Akisue.[19] Only three non-family members

---

15. The marshal collected the poems and checked them for errors and then passed them to the lector to read aloud.

16. *Wakan rōei shū* 479, by Kung-Ch'eng I, in Kawaguchi Hisao, *Wakan rōei shū zenshakuchū*, p. 360; translation from Rimer and Chaves, *Japanese and Chinese Poems to Sing*, p. 147.

17. The attention given here to "Honobono to," which is also alluded to in Atsumitsu's preface, may have influenced later commentaries that made this poem a focus of nearly obsessive attention.

18. *Shūi shū* book 13 (love poems), Hitomaro; *Wakan rōei shū* (love).

> *tanometsutsu / konu yo amata ni / narinureba*
> *mataji to omou zo / matsu ni masareru*

> These many nights you've promised to visit, but still you don't;
> deciding not to wait is better than waiting.

19. Yamada Shōzen ("Kakinomoto no Hitomaro eigu," p. 94) gives a family tree that shows the various kinship relations. Some of them are quite attenuated. For example, Fujiwara no Tametada was Akisue's sister's great-grandchild; Akinaka was Akisue's sister's husband's brother's child.

were present: Minamoto no Toshiyori, Fujiwara no Atsumitsu, and Fujiwara no Yukimori. It is also clear that although the ceremony was planned beforehand, the order of events and the roles to be played by various participants were still somewhat uncertain on the day of the ceremony. This is not surprising given that this was the first time such a ceremony had been performed. However, it also seems evident that Akisue was accepted as the leader of his family; when he declares that the eulogistic inscription and poem should be read at one point, his will prevails. Thus the ceremony itself is marked by Akisue's assertion of his right to leadership and the family's acceptance of that leadership.

However, Akisue's assertion of leadership within his family is not a sufficient explanation for why he created the Hitomaro memorial service. Immediate economic gain also seems unlikely. Unlike the esoteric initiations developed later, which were aimed mainly at those outside the family and were quite lucrative, the memorial ceremony was performed primarily for Akisue's own family and involved no significant economic exchange. In addition, despite his moderate court ranking (senior third rank), Akisue was not in need of money. His mother had been wet nurse to Emperor Shirakawa (r. 1072–86), and he was on intimate terms with the retired emperor, a relationship that gave him access to political power and wealth not obvious from his court rank alone. For an explanation of his creation of the Hitomaro memorial service, we should look instead to the political and cultural competition at court.

According to Yamada Shōzen, lying in the background was the development of two competing poetic factions at court. One centered on Akisue and the people surrounding Retired Emperor Shirakawa. The other centered on Fujiwara no Tadamichi (1097–1164), who was palace minister at the time but who eventually served as regent (both *kanpaku* and *sesshō*). Tadamichi's group seems to have consisted mainly of younger poets of high rank affiliated with his own branch of the Fujiwara. Tadamichi and Akisue created two exclusive salons and refused to invite members of the rival group to their poetry meetings. However, Minamoto no Toshiyori and Fujiwara no Mototoshi (1060–1142), well-respected poets who belonged to neither family, were welcome in both groups. Later, in the Kamakura period, this kind of exclusivity and competitiveness became the norm, but at this point it was a new development. Since Akisue's power rested mainly on his personal relationship with Shirakawa, it may be that Akisue's competition with Tadamichi, both politically and socially, served as an incitement for him to commission the Hitomaro image and to develop the Hitomaro memorial service. Realizing that he had several promising poets in his family, Akisue may have seen the Hitomaro portrait and memorial service as a way to unify his family and provide it with the kind of cultural capital that would survive his personal relationship with the retired emperor.

In this sense, the ceremony was undoubtedly meant as a signal to the court that the Rokujō were now a poetry family. This explains why so many members of the extended family were invited. For the ceremony to have the kind of legitimacy that Akisue wanted, however, there had to be a few witnesses from outside the family who could testify to others about them. Toshiyori, as a leading poet of the day and approximately the same age as Akisue (mid-sixties), was an obvious choice as a guest-participant who could provide the appropriate legitimizing testimony. Atsumitsu also served as a witness with his written account of the event, *Kakinomoto eigu ki*.

Atsumitsu was a noted Chinese scholar, a useful talent since the format of the Hitomaro ceremony was directly modeled on a Confucian memorial service popular at the time among Japanese who wrote Chinese poetry. In this ceremony, usually performed at a hall in the Bureau of Chinese Education, images of Confucius, his favorite disciple Yen Hui, and nine other Confucian philosophers were displayed with offerings of sweets and artificial fish and fowl arranged before them. Three ritual offerings of sake were made; this was followed by a question-and-answer period on the Confucian classics, and then Chinese poems were composed on a set topic from *The Analects*, the Five Classics, *The Classic of Filial Piety*, or another text from the Chinese canon.[20] Akisue and Atsumitsu, who seem to have planned the ceremony, made appropriate modifications to this basic format: the reading of the Hitomaro biography substituted for the discussion, and Japanese rather than Chinese poems were composed on a line from Chinese poetry.[21] In

20. I am following the description of medieval Japanese *sekiten* given in ibid., pp. 88–90. See, however, the description of eighth- and ninth-century versions of the ceremony in McMullen, "The Worship of Confucius in Ancient Japan." By the medieval period the ceremony had apparently become primarily a social occasion.

21. This practice, *kudai* (句題) waka, was very popular at the time. According to Brower and Miner (*Japanese Court Poetry*, p. 197), "The object of this mode was to re-create the atmosphere of the original poem, by means of either 'translation' or variation, and to fill out the emotional context of the passage by exploring hints in the text." The quotations were often

China, the *sekiten* was initially used to establish a school and was thereafter performed in spring and fall to commemorate that establishment. It purported to be a Zhou dynasty ritual and probably was imported to Japan late in the Northern and Southern Dynasties period or in the Tang (its first recorded performance was in 701). Since the Hitomaro memorial ceremony was modeled on the Confucian ceremony, it appears that Akisue was attempting to establish his family as a poetry school, as well as create the various ritualistic implements and images associated with a school that could be passed down only within the family. The veneration of Hitomaro in this ancestral memorial service thus transformed Hitomaro into a tutelary deity of the Rokujō house.

Although the order of events was not completely worked out in advance, the physical arrangements of the meeting room were planned down to the last detail: it may even be that the parrot-nautilus sake cups were used because of the Chinese poem that Atsumitsu recited from the *Wakan rōei shū*. Of course, the most time-consuming item was Akisue's commission of a portrait of Hitomaro for the occasion. In *Kokon chomon jū*, Tachibana no Narisue described how Akisue obtained this portrait:

> The governor of Sanuki, Fujiwara no Kanefusa, deeply loved the Path of Poetry, and was saddened that he did not know what Hitomaro looked like.[22] Hitomaro came to him in a dream and said, "Because you love me, I am revealing myself to you." Since Kanefusa was not adept at making pictures, the next morning he went to a painting master and instructed him to paint the portrait according to his dream. Overjoyed with it, he treasured the painting for years. Retired Emperor Shirakawa loved the Path of Poetry, and so requested the portrait [from Kanefusa] and had it stored in the treasure house of Shōkōmyō-in.[23] Rokujō Akisue, who was among the emperor's intimates, requested that he be allowed to copy it, but he initially was refused. He persisted until at last he got permission. His eldest two sons, Nagazane and Ieyasu, were not particularly talented at poetry, so he gave it to his third son, Akisuke.
>
> As for Kanefusa's original, the Ono Grand Empress asked to borrow it. Most unfortunately, while she had it in her possession, it was burned in the same fire that destroyed a copy of the *Kokin shū* in Ki no Tsurayuki's own hand. So Akisuke's copy is all that remains of the original. It is rumored that there is a pledge to the gods at-

---

taken from poems by the Tang poet Po Chū-i found in the *Wakan rōei shū* and other collections of Chinese poetry.

22. Fujiwara no Kanefusa (1001–69) was Regent Michikane's grandson.

23. A temple within the Toba Detached Palace.

tached that you not transmit it or allow it to be copied by anyone who is not a talented poet, even if he or she is your own child. This pledge [which along with the portrait conferred the authority to perform the ceremony] was transmitted to Yasusue [Akisue's great-grandson], and subsequently to Narizane. Narizane was called into service with Retired Emperor Go-Saga [r. 1242–46], and since the Kenchō era [1249–56] Go-Saga has held memorial services. The ritual implements were transmitted from Iehira[24] to his son Iekiyo. After Iekiyo died they went to his son [Moriie], who also was called into service with Retired Emperor Go-Saga. There was a lectern (*bundai* 文台) used in poetry meetings, which was made from the posts of the Nagara bridge [mentioned in the *Kokin shū* preface] and which had been transmitted from the Priest Minamoto no Shun'e. In Retired Emperor Go-Toba's time it was used for poetry meetings. Retired Emperor Go-Saga placed it in front of the Hitomaro portrait and lectured from it at his poetry meetings. This story has many points of interest.[25]

This story does indeed have a number of points of interest. First, there is the question of why the Hitomaro portrait came into being. By the late twelfth century, the study of Hitomaro was a central part of any poet's education. There is here as well a kernel of the thinking that lay behind the worship of Sumiyoshi as a guardian deity of waka: the idea that by praying to Hitomaro's image Kanefusa would be able to create better poetry.

During the medieval period, the claim that a poet or deity had appeared in a dream revelation was a standard way to lend authority to an image used as an object of veneration or worship. However, since Hitomaro apparently died relatively young, art historians today have some reason to be skeptical about the authenticity of this dream revelation of Hitomaro as an old man and have looked for a more concrete model.[26] Ōgushi Sumio has argued persuasively that the typical Hitomaro portrait of a white-haired old man with paper and brush in hand is based on a landscape screen depicting the Tang poet Po Chü-i (772–846).[27] Since at the time Po Chü-i's popularity was at its peak, his image was an appealing prototype. And given that the ritual

24. Iehira (1179–1245) was Tsuneie's eldest son (Kiyosuke's nephew). The ritual implements probably included the parrot-nautilus cups used in the original ceremony.

25. Tachibana no Narisue, *Kokon chomon jū*, pt. I, section 204, pp. 262–63.

26. In an article on the development of the medieval image of Hitomaro, Ōgushi Sumio ("Hitomaro zō no seiritsu to Tō-ji Sansui byobu," p. 98) refers to a number of different scholars who believe Hitomaro died in his forties.

27. Ibid., pp. 85–110. Ōgushi's argument is also summarized in Yamada, "Kakinomoto Hitomaro eigu," pp. 90–93.

functioned as a memorial service, the use of a "godly old man" (*okina* 翁) image would have reinforced Akisue's implicit goal of transforming Hitomaro into the Rokujō family's symbolic poetic ancestor. Ōguchi argues that the image of Sumiyoshi as the guardian deity of waka poetry also derived from the landscape screen depicting Po Chü-i.[28] If the Hitomaro and Sumiyoshi images were based on the same model, the strong resemblance would have furthered the connections between the two.

A second point emphasized in the description of the origin of the Hitomaro portrait is the transmission pledge (*kishomon* 起請文), which warns that the portrait should be transmitted only to a poet of talent, regardless of familial ties. If Akisue indeed wrote such a pledge to go with the portrait, it is one of the earliest examples of its type. Later it became common for secret commentaries to end with a pledge of this kind, which had the tautological effect of turning the recipient, *ipso facto*, into a talented poet. Here, too, it has that effect; transmission of a portrait signifies the transmission of authority within a poetry family. Despite the admonition that the portrait be bequeathed to the best poet in each generation, this transmission of poetic authority managed to bypass two of the best poets in the Rokujō family: Akisuke's adopted son Kenshō (ca. 1130–1210?) and Akisuke's grandson Ariie (1155–1216). On the other hand, Kenshō wrote the first critical biography of Hitomaro in 1184: the *Kakinomoto no Ason Hitomaro kanmon*. And Ariie, whom Retired Emperor Go-Toba (1180–1239) chose as one of the compilers of the imperial anthology *Shin Kokin waka shū* (New collection of ancient and modern Japanese poetry; 1205), was probably closely involved in promoting Go-Toba's veneration of Hitomaro at the highest levels of the court. Go-Toba displayed the portrait in the Waka-dokoro, the official Bureau of Japanese Poetry of the imperial government, where he held numerous poetry meetings and contests in the years just prior to the completion of the *Shin Kokin shū*. H. E. Plutschow suggests that the Bureau of Japanese Poetry may have adopted the worship of Hitomaro as a tutelary deity to pray for the success of the forthcoming imperial anthology.[29] By encouraging Hitomaro poetry contests, Rokujō Ariie was encouraging the retired emperor to venerate a poet who had by that time become, for all intents and purposes, his family's poetic ancestor. This could only have enhanced the Rokujō's status as a poetry family.

---

28. Ōgushi, "Hitomaro zō no seiritsu," pp. 102–3.
29. Plutschow, *Chaos and Cosmos*, p. 188.

At any rate, the creation of the Hitomaro memorial service played an important role in the subsequent development of secret poetic commentaries. The ceremony, although originally Confucian, gradually took on more syncretic coloration, forming the basis for the deification of Hitomaro as a guardian deity of waka along with Sumiyoshi Daimyōjin. And certain elements of the ritual format continued to play a role in the later waka initiation and lecture ceremonies. Fujiwara no Tameaki acknowledges that debt when he wrote in *Waka kanjō den*, "The format for the initiation ceremony was transmitted from Kiyosuke's family."[30] The strong influence of the Rokujō family's Hitomaru ceremony is corroborated by a description of Tameaki's waka initiation ceremony in *Waka Kokin kanjō maki*, which quotes in its entirety the eulogy to Hitomaro used in the original Hitomaro ceremony held by Akisue in 1118.[31]

The Mikohidari Attitude Toward the Master-Disciple System

It is an obvious fact (to us at least) that poetic talent cannot be transmitted; although training plays a role, without innate talent it is impossible to become a great poet. As a natural corollary to this assumption, most contemporary scholars see the development of secret family traditions and the emphasis on exclusive master-disciple relationships as a primary factor in the degeneration of waka poetry in the thirteenth and fourteenth centuries. Thus, the Rokujō family's development of the Hitomaro memorial ceremony and its promotion of secret family transmissions are taken as signs that they did not have the innate talent to be great poets. Kamo no Chōmei's statement in *Mumyō shō* that no one could match Rokujō Kiyosuke's knowledge of poetry is understood to be a backhanded compliment; the implication is that he was a great scholar but only a so-so poet. The Rokujō substituted scholarly knowledge, something that it was possible to transmit, for poetic talent.

Such scholarly antagonism toward the development of the pedagogical system of secret transmission is undoubtedly justified. It is quite clear that the emphasis on secrecy and exclusivity promoted within the poetry families, begun by the Rokujō but actively promoted by the various descendents of

30. As quoted in Miwa Masatane, *Kagaku hiden no kenkyū*, p. 34.

31. Ibid., pp. 460–61.

the Mikohidari house founded by Fujiwara no Shunzei, did indeed have deleterious effects on the practice of composing waka poetry. By the Muromachi period, exemplary poets such as Shōtetsu who were forced to participate in this system of family privilege were justifiably incensed by it: "It may be true that I am the heir of Tamehide and Imagawa Ryōshun [two poets of the Reizei school], but in my poetry I seek only for the deep secrets of Teika and Jichin. For those degenerate houses of our own day—the Nijō and the Reizei—I have no allegiance."[32] Shōtetsu is generally applauded for, as Steven Carter puts it, "disavowing his own genealogy in favor of affiliation with more distant ancestors."[33] His originality and talent, in an age of mostly mediocre waka poets, are understood as functions of his intellectual liberation from the oppressive conservatism of the master-disciple system as it was practiced in his time.

Instead of looking to his contemporaries, Shōtetsu sought authority in the originators of the Mikohidari house, Fujiwara no Shunzei and Teika, in the belief that they would not have approved of the factional strife and conservatism of his own age. It is certainly true that Teika would have been appalled at the degeneration of the Mikohidari house, but I believe that both Teika and Shunzei were more ambivalent about the development of family traditions than either Shōtetsu or contemporary scholars give them credit for.

In the preface to *Kindai shūka* (Superior poems of our time; ca. 1209), Teika quoted Shunzei as saying, "Poetry is not an art which can be learned by looking afield and hearing far; it is something that proceeds from the heart and is understood by the self."[34] In *Eiga no taigai* (An outline for poetic composition; ca. 1222) Teika pointed out: "In Japanese poetry there are no teachers. Simply take revered old poems as your teachers. If you immerse your sensibility (*kokoro*) in the old styles and learn diction (*kotoba*) from great poets who have led the way, how can you not compose successfully?"[35] This statement is usually applauded by scholars as an unequivocal rejection of the master-disciple system; Shōtetsu certainly understood it that way when he

---

32. Translation from Steven D. Carter, "'Seeking What the Masters Sought': Masters, Disciples, and Poetic Enlightenment in Medieval Japan," p. 51; *Oi no kurigoto*, in *NST*, vol. 23, p. 417.

33. Carter, "'Seeking What the Masters Sought,'" p. 51.

34. Fujiwara no Teika, *Kindai shūka*, p. 101. Translation from Brower and Miner, *Fujiwara Teika's Superior Poems of Our Time: A Thirteenth-Century Poetic Treatise and Sequence*, p. 43.

35. Fujiwara no Teika, *Eiga no taigai*, p. 495.

quoted it in *Shōtetsu monogatari.*[36] Teika is understood to be saying that you cannot learn the intuitive feel of a poem from someone else—it can come only through intensive study of poems themselves. However, Teika also raised the problem of diction: "Learn diction from great poets who have led the way." As noted above, medieval poets often found it difficult to read Heian poems because certain words, particularly the proper names of places or flora and fauna, had become obscure with time. In *Kenchū mikkan* (Secret annotations of Kenshō's commentary on the *Kokin shū*), Teika related his attempt to read the *Kokin shū* without instruction: "When I was young, I looked through the *Kokin shū* and found many passages I could not decipher (*yomitokanu tokoro*). I asked [my father] and was told, 'The *Kokin shū* is to be received! How could one read it by force?' "[37] In other words, the *Kokin shū* is not understandable without a direct transmission of instruction (*denju* 伝授) in how to read it. Both in this anecdote and in his emphasis on the importance of studying the diction of old poems, Teika was implicitly opening the backdoor to those commentaries that explicate obscure phrases and difficult rhetorical figures (*nangi* 難儀) and whose authority relied on the continuity of a family transmission dating back to the Heian period.

And in fact, although both Shunzei and Teika argued that poetic talent could not be taught, they nevertheless fully participated in the master-disciple system both as teachers and students. An anecdote in *Mumyō shō* recounts how Shunzei became Fujiwara no Mototoshi's disciple:

The lay priest Gojō Sammi [Shunzei] told the following story: "When I reached the age of 25, I wanted to become a disciple of Mototoshi, and with the former governor of Izumi, the lay priest Michitsune, as mediator, I took a carriage together with him and set out toward the residence of Mototoshi, who was at that time 85. That night was, moreover, the fifteenth night of the eighth month and therefore the host was in the right mood and made the first part of a poem:

> *naki no aki / tōka itsuka no / tsuki o mite*
>
> When in the eighth month on the fifteenth day we look at the moon

He was reciting this in a serious vein, so I continued

> *kimi ga yado nite/kimi to akasan*
>
> Yours is the house at which you and I will spend the night.

---

36. Brower, *Conversations with Shōtetsu*, p. 104.

37. Fujiwara no Teika, *Kenchū mikkan shō*, p. 138; translation (slightly modified) from Cook, "The Discipline of Poetry," p. 123.

> . . . Thus we established our teacher-disciple relationship, but as far as poetic composition was concerned he could not compete with Toshiyori. Toshiyori was a man of extraordinary ability."[38]

Although he thought Minamoto no Toshiyori the better poet, Shunzei seems to have felt it necessary to establish a master-disciple relationship with Mototoshi in order to advance his scholarly knowledge. Since Shunzei was Rokujō Kiyosuke's main rival, he may have felt compelled to find a teacher who could rival Kiyosuke for knowledge of difficult points and obscure words. We know the knowledge he gained through this relationship was passed on to Teika, since in texts such as *Eiga no taigai* and *Hekian shō* (Selected biased opinions), Teika cites Mototoshi as the authority for his readings of obscure and difficult words.[39] So although on one level both Shunzei and Teika objected to the idea that poetic talent could be transmitted within a master-disciple relationship, they saw the usefulness of acquiring arcane poetic knowledge. They participated fully in a system that awarded them substantial income and prestige and furthered that system by transmitting a large library of poetic treatises and manuscripts within the family.

On the other hand, Retired Emperor Juntoku (r. 1210–21), a contemporary of Teika, was unambivalent in his antagonism toward the idea of master-disciple relationships. In *Yakumo mishō* (Imperial notes on the art of the eightfold clouds), he wrote: "The composition of poetry begins in the heart. This is something that cannot be taught. Because a father has talent, this does not mean his child will inherit it. And although a teacher may have the bones of style, he cannot transfer it to his student."[40] Here Juntoku was denying two kinds of teacher-disciple relationships. First, he rejected the idea that a child inevitably inherits the poetic talent of a parent and thereby undercut the rationale for poetic houses. Second, and more radically, he rejected the idea that poetry can be taught even by teachers to disciples unrelated by family. Scholars generally applaud Juntoku as a lone voice attacking the degenerative effects of secret family traditions on poetry, but one should consider what he had to gain from taking this tack. For one thing, since he

---

38. Hilda Katō, "The *Mumyōshō*," pp. 371–72.

39. Interestingly, Teika also cites Kiyosuke. Evidence from *Kenchū mikkan shō* indicates that Teika got access to the erudition of his family's rival through a commentary by Kenshō (Kiyosuke's brother by adoption) that Mototoshi transmitted to Shunzei.

40. *Yakumo mishō*, in *NKT*, supplementary vol. 3, p. 427.

did not belong to a family of poets, he did not have easy access to the secret traditions that he rejected. Second, as a retired emperor and an acknowledged poet, he did not need the status and economic benefits that family traditions brought. In this sense, his opposition to the idea of a poetic tradition that can be passed down from teacher to disciple within the family corroborates my hypothesis that the development of secret traditions had much to do with the political and economic situation of the court families involved.[41]

With the development in the late thirteenth century of spurious commentaries that based their authority on oracular revelations from the gods, however, the master-disciple system moved into a new phase. It is doubtful that Fujiwara no Shunzei and Teika, or even Rokujō Kiyosuke, would have approved. The authority for commentaries that elucidated obscure terms and difficult points of etiquette was at least apparently rational. Poets in the Heian period presumably understood the meaning of the words they used, and that knowledge could be transmitted to their descendants (in fact, of course, much of this "knowledge" was manufactured). With the creation of oracular commentaries, the source of poetic knowledge became irrational, in the sense that the insights presented were irreproducible by pragmatic logic or aesthetic principles. When deities become the primary authority on poetry, the waka teacher's position degenerates; he or she becomes someone who merely disseminates that secret oracular tradition. Teachers no longer teach by virtue of their talent, but because of their family's access to the *kami*'s revelation. It is this system that Shōtetsu so vehemently protested, and rightfully so.

The Teika Forgeries

Until recently, scholars have assumed that the context for the sudden appearance in the late thirteenth century of the spurious commentaries based on oracular revelation was the breakup of Fujiwara no Teika's Mikohidari house into the competing Nijō, Reizei, and Kyōgoku factions. The assumption has been that both the *kochū* and the *Usagi* forgeries spuriously attributed to Teika were originally fabricated by the factions to shore up their po-

41. Ironically enough, *Yakumo mishō* was transmitted to Teika's son Tameie and then to Tameie's eldest son, Nijō Tameuji, becoming a valued text within the Nijō family transmission.

etic authority and substantiate their poetic positions. I believe, however, that the assumption that the *kochū* forgeries arose out of the Reizei-Nijō-Kyōgoku split has obscured their emergence from smaller poetic factions active at the time. Perhaps because the Nijō, Reizei, and Kyōgoku so dominated later poetic history (particularly by monopolizing the all-important function of editing the imperial anthologies), the existence of these smaller poetry factions has often been ignored in the standard histories of Japanese literature. However, as we shall see, the complex interactions of poetry factions affiliated with Fujiwara no Tameaki, Rokujō Yukiie, and Fujiwara no Ietaka's granddaughter were the most significant influence on the development of the *kochū* commentaries. In order to clarify this point, I will briefly summarize both the circumstances of the Nijō-Reizei-Kyōgoku split and the traditional explanation given for the commentaries.[42]

Tameie, the son of Fujiwara no Teika and grandson of Fujiwara no Shunzei, inherited at least two generations of rare manuscripts and critical commentaries. Over the course of his long life, Tameie continued to augment that collection with his own acquisitions and critical writings. In the late thirteenth century, this was precisely the kind of library that, by adding the weight of tradition to one's teaching, was becoming increasingly crucial to a scholar's authority. Although excellence as a poet certainly helped in gaining prestigious teaching positions, important political figures, whose patronage was vital to court success, apparently demanded that one have access to secret texts as well. For example, Kyōgoku Tamekane (1254–1332) used secret commentaries supposedly given him by either Tameie himself or his uncle Reizei Tamesuke to instruct such notables as Emperors Fushimi (r. 1288–98), Go-Fushimi (r. 1298–1301), and Hanazono (r. 1308–18).[43] Under these circumstances, the Mikohidari family library was an extremely important legacy for Tameie's heirs. In addition Tameie also had proprietary

42. For the usual explanation of the connection between the Nijō-Reizei conflict and the creation of these forgeries, see Brower and Miner, *Japanese Court Poetry*, pp. 343–52; and Brower, "The Reizei Family Documents," pp. 445–61.

43. In his diary, *Hanazono tennō shinki*, Retired Emperor Hanazono described how Tamekane entrusted him with secret teachings and eventually certified him as a poetry master. And according to Robert Huey (*Kyōgoku Tamekane*, pp. 23, 159), Tamekane's diary indicates that he and his sister Tameko used special texts of the *Kokin shū* with marginal notes to teach Fushimi, Go-Fushimi, and Eifukumon-in.

(領家 *ryōke*) and stewardship (地頭 *jitō*) rights to the Hosokawa estate, from which the Mikohidari family derived most of its income.[44]

In 1256, stricken with a life-threatening illness, Tameie took the tonsure and began deeding his poetic and economic legacy to his children, primarily to his eldest son, Tameuji (1222–86). Tameie recovered, however, and shortly afterward married a young woman now commonly referred to by the name she took after Tameie's death, Abutsu Ni (Abutsu the Nun, 1222?–83).[45] Abutsu soon bore Tameie two sons, Tamesuke (1263–1328) and Tamemori (1265–1328). She managed to persuade Tameie to change his will and to award the valuable Hosokawa estate to Tamesuke. Not surprisingly, when Tameie died in 1275, a bitter battle over this estate immediately arose between Tameuji on one side and Abutsu and Tamesuke on the other. It was these two factions that became the Nijō and Reizei, respectively. Kyōgoku Tamenori (1227–1279), who was born after Tameuji by the same mother but who never got along with his older brother, formed the third, Kyōgoku, faction.

There were, at that time, two legal systems in the country. Imperial court law permitted a parent to bequeath property as he or she wished, but once it had been willed to one person, the property could not be transferred to anyone else. The law of the military government at Kamakura, on the other hand, allowed for revisions in wills. In addition, the law of the imperial court dealt with proprietary rights, whereas military law dealt with stewardship rights.

For obvious reasons, Tameuji chose to take his case to Kyoto; Abutsu and Tamesuke went to Kamakura. Tameuji was initially more successful; in 1286 the court of Retired Emperor Kameyama (r. 1259–74) awarded the proprietary rights to the disputed Hosokawa estate to him.[46] At this time the court also ordered Tamesuke to turn over to the Nijō line the corpus of manuscripts he had acquired from Tameie through his mother. It is not

---

44. As Robert Huey (ibid., p. 21*n*) points out, "*Jitō* [stewardship] rights were usually reserved for Kamakura vassals. But the Bakufu [shogunate] had awarded them to Teika for, among other things, his service as poetry teacher to the Shogun Sanetomo (1192–1219). Having both proprietary and *jitō* rights to an estate amounted to virtually absolute control over its income." This made the estate extremely valuable to Tameie's heirs.

45. Abutsu Ni was also known as Ankamon-in Echizen, Ankamon-in Uemon no Suke, and Ankamon-in no Shijō. Abutsu Ni began service with Ankamon-in, the second daughter of Retired Emperor Go-Takakura, when she was about fourteen or fifteen. For a biography of Abutsu Ni in English, see Wallace, "Abutsu-ni."

46. In 1313, however, Tamesuke was granted stewardship rights by the military government; the proprietary rights were given to his descendants about a century later.

surprising that in addition to the estate, Nijō Tameuji would have explicitly asked for the return of these documents. As Brower and Miner point out,

> As long as they rested in Kyōgoku-Reizei hands, the manuscripts could only embarrass the Nijō poets. They were priding themselves on conserving Teika's tradition without possessing all of the tangible literary evidence for it. . . . As long as the Kyōgoku-Reizei faction had some of the most precious of Teika's writings in their possession, they could challenge Nijō doctrine on the basis of documents they refused to show their opposition.[47]

The Reizei, for their part, knew that if they lost possession of Teika's treatises and canonical manuscripts, their poetic authority would be greatly lessened.

Faced with this unacceptable decision, the Reizei supposedly devised a scheme to outwit their adversaries. According to the account of the poet and scholar Kitabatake Chikafusa (1293–1354) in *Kokin shū jo chū* (Commentary on the Japanese preface to the *Kokin shū*), Tameie had two sets of documents written by Teika in his possession. One was kept in a box with a figure of a cormorant inlaid on the cover, the other in a box inlaid with a heron. These texts were taken by Abutsu to Kamakura after her husband's death. In 1286, when the imperial court ordered Reizei Tamesuke to turn over to the Nijō line the Teika manuscripts, the Reizei "surrendered all the writings that had been catalogued long ago and were well known to various people, but apparently because not even Lord Tameuji had any clear idea of the contents of the Cormorant and Heron boxes, they retained the secret writings, filled the boxes with forgeries, and handed those over instead."[48] Of course, for this ruse to work to the Reizei family's advantage, not only did they have to retain the true manuscripts, but also they had to "secretly" show them to selected patrons and trusted disciples, with assurances that these were the authentic treatises. That this is precisely what the Reizei did is substantiated to some extent by Genshō (1224–1303), a son of Tameie who criticized everyone in the dispute. In his poetic treatise, *Genshō waka kuden* (Genshō's oral transmission on waka), Genshō fumed, "The Nun Abutsu and the Great Counselor [Tameuji] quarreled over the poetic documents. . . . Abutsu hid the catalog of poetic writings written in the former Middle Counselor's [Tameie's] own hand and held back a number of important documents that

47. Brower and Miner, *Japanese Court Poetry*, p. 349.

48. Translation from ibid., p. 351.

she began to display to all and sundry. She was twice warned in a dream, and then she and her two sisters died in rapid succession."[49]

The usual interpretation of these passages is that the four spurious Teika treatises known today as the "Cormorant and Heron" (*Usagi* 鵜鷺) texts were created in the context of this battle between the Nijō and the Reizei.[50] These texts include *Guken shō* (Selected humble views), *Guhi shō*, *Sango ki*, and *Kirihioke* (The paulownia brazier). They are generally considered to be the Cormorant and Heron treatises mentioned by Chikafusa because *Guhi shō*'s alternative title is *U no honmatsu* (鵜の本末 The roots and branches of the cormorant) and *Sango ki*'s alternate title is *Sagi no honmatsu* (鷺の本末 The roots and branches of the heron). Evidence from lineage documents and analysis of their contents bears out Chikafusa's explanation that these commentaries may have arisen in the general context of the Nijō and Reizei conflict, but their relationship to it would seem to be somewhat more complex than Chikafusa allows. According to Fukuda Hideuchi, *Guken shō* tends toward a Reizei view of poetry and was probably produced by someone affiliated with Abutsu and Tamesuke. The earliest extant manuscript has a date of 1259, but since this predates the Reizei-Nijō conflict by more than twenty years (Tamesuke was not even born until 1263), it would throw the whole explanation for these texts into doubt. Therefore scholars who accept Chikafusa's account argue that the most likely date for its creation would be the late 1280s, sometime after the 1286 court decision, and that the date of 1259 is an example of deliberate predating.[51] *Guhi shō* and *Sango ki* (the two texts linked by name to the supposed *Usagi* forgeries) are said to favor the Nijō side. They are now generally thought to have been written by Nijō Tameuji's younger son, Tamezane (1266–33) between 1312 and 1317. Given this much later date, they cannot be explained by the court order of 1286, although one could argue that these texts were simply a delayed reaction to the Reizei forgery. In line with this train of thought, Fukuda sees *Guhi shō* as a direct rebuttal of *Guken shō*. For evidence he points out that there exist

49. Ibid.

50. Chikafusa was not yet born when the 1286 judgment came down, and only twenty at the time of the 1313 judgment. Although Konishi Jin'ichi (*A History of Japanese Literature*, pp. 259–60) admits that it is not known how Chikafusa acquired his information, he nevertheless accepts Chikafusa's account as an explanation for the emergence of spurious commentaries on both the Nijō and Reizei side. We need to keep in mind, however, Chikafusa's possible polemical motives in accusing the Reizei of forgery.

51. See Fukuda Hideuchi, "Guken shō," p. 57.

Guhi shō texts in which passages from *Guken shō* have been inserted in order to be rebutted. Fukuda's explanation for the origins of these texts complicates Chikafusa's account but does not undermine the basic assumption that the texts were forged as part of a polemical battle for poetic authority. In other words, when the Reizei wrote *Guken shō*, they took the opportunity to slant "Teika's" arguments to support their poetic position; when the Nijō forged *Guhi shō*, they provided arguments that rebutted the Reizei.

I believe, however, that these texts may not have been created by the Reizei to fool their adversaries. In fact, if that had been the sole motivation for their creation, then it would be hard to understand why Nijō-affiliated scholars in the Muromachi (such as Chikafusa and Tonna [1289–1372]) had doubts about these texts whereas Reizei-affiliated scholars (such as Shōtetsu and Shinkei) accepted them. If the Reizei were attempting to fool their adversaries, it would appear that they ended up fooling only their own descendants and disciples.

Another question is whether Tamezane, now credited with being the author of the forgeries, was even affiliated with the Nijō. Fukuda assumes he was, but Miwa Masatane prefers to think of Tamezane as having his own school, which would in many ways have operated independently of the more powerful Nijō, Reizei, and Kyōgoku factions. Miwa argues that all four of the *Usagi* forgeries were the work of Tamezane because his name appears in the transmission lineages of all of them.[52] If this is the case, then the texts arose not because of the Nijō-Reizei conflict but because of Tamezane's attempt to establish poetic authority for himself. In the same way, one of the chief reasons Japanese scholars have moved away from assuming that the Nijō-Reizei conflict was the sole origin of the *kochū* is because a number of the names that appear on the transmission lineages for the commentaries (Fujiwara no Tameaki, Ietaka's granddaughter, Rokujō Yukiie) do not easily fit into a simple two-way split (Nijō-Reizei) or even a three-way split (Nijō-Reizei-Kyōgoku).

Although the factional struggles among the descendants of Teika were clearly important to the emergence of spurious commentaries, laying the blame simply on the Nijō and Reizei conflict makes the struggles look much simpler than they actually were. It also obscures the numerous factions in existence at the time in addition to the Nijō, Reizei, and Kyōgoku lineages.

52. Miwa Masatane, "Ietaka gisho no sakusha, kyōjusha wa ikanaru hitobito ka."

There are as well a number of other difficulties with the hypothesis that the *kochū* forgeries arose simply because of the Nijō-Reizei split.

First of all, the earliest *kochū* commentary, *Waka chiken shū*, is thought to predate Tameie's death by more than ten years; since Reizei Tamesuke was still in his infancy, its creation can have had little to do with the Nijō-Reizei conflict. Second, a good number of the *kochū* are not attributed to Teika, but to Fujiwara no Ietaka, Minamoto no Tsunenobu, or most commonly, to Sumiyoshi Daimyōjin. This is one clue that at least some of these texts were created by poets outside the main lineages of the Mikohidari house. In addition, references to Teika in texts attributed to Ietaka generally give him much less authority than Ietaka; that would be a highly unlikely position for anyone related to the Mikohidari house to take. Third, although not completely unconcerned with the issues of protocol and aesthetics that the Nijō, Reizei, and Kyōgoku fought over, the main focus of the *kochū* commentaries is elsewhere, and it seems clear that their interpretive judgments were not forged as part of the Nijō-Reizei battle.

Although the use of allegoresis as a literary interpretive method had become firmly entrenched in both the Reizei and Nijō schools by the early fourteenth century, it does not seem to have been incited by the split itself. Instead, it appears to have developed in the Kantō region within a small group of poetry factions centering on poets who were shut out of the benefits accruing to the prestigious Mikohidari school. The poets who led these factions seem to have played the central role in the development of the *kochū* commentaries, and it was another of Tameie's many sons, the minor poet Fujiwara no Tameaki, who appears to have been the key figure.

6

Fujiwara no Tameaki and the Kamakura Commentaries

Fujiwara no Tameaki, the man most responsible for the Kamakura commentaries, was the son of Fujiwara no Tameie and an unknown mother who is thought to have been a lady-in-waiting at court.[1] He was born in the 1230s sometime after Nijō Tameuji (1222), Genshō (1224), and Kyōgoku Tamenori (1227) but long before Reizei Tamesuke (1263) and Tamemori (1265). The following list shows Tameie's sons by each of his consorts.

Utsunomiya Yoritsuna no Musume (d. 1250s?)	Nijō Tameuji (1222–86) Genshō (1224–1303) Kyōgoku Tamenori (1227–79)
Unknown lady-in-waiting[2]	Tameaki (1230s–after 1295)

1. Much of the following basic material on Tameaki's life comes from descriptions in Hisamatsu Sen'ichi, "*Chikuen shō* kō," pp. 194–97; and Inoue Muneo, *Chūsei kadanshi no kenkyū*, pp. 82–86, 266–76. Parts of this chapter appeared in my "Fujiwara no Tameaki."

2. The identification of Tameaki's mother as a palace lady-in-waiting comes from *Genshō waka kuden*, by Tameaki's older brother. In one variant of the text she is identified as "Naishi no Onna" (内持女), which would make her a lady-in-waiting at the palace; but in another variant she is identified as "onaji jijo" (同侍女), which might indicate she was an attendant in Tameie's own household (Inoue Muneo, *Kamakura jidai kajin den no kenkyū*, p. 288).

Abutsu Ni (1222?–83) —— Reizei Tamesuke (1263–1328)
└ Tamemori (1265–1328)

In a sense, Tameaki was caught squarely in the middle of the struggle between his older brothers Nijō Tameuji and Kyōgoku Tamenori and his younger brother Reizei Tamesuke, losing the battle for his father's attention. At any rate, from the little information we have on his life, it appears that he did not join any of the factions but kept his poetic options open.

Although Tameaki's name first appears in the historical record in conjunction with poetry contests at the Sumiyoshi and Tamatsushima shrines in the third month of 1263, probably under the auspices of his father, his connection to his father was probably not particularly close in the 1260s. In 1265 Tameie served as one of the compilers of the imperial anthology *Shoku Kokin waka shū* (Collection of ancient and modern Japanese poems continued; 1265), but he chose not to include any of Tameaki's poems. Since Tameaki's contemporaries considered his waka at least comparable to those of his brothers Tameuji and Tamenori, it seems likely that at the time Tameaki was estranged from his father. This suspicion is substantiated in *Genshō Waka kuden* by Tameaki's older brother.[3] According to Genshō, Tameaki's mother lost favor with Tameie after he took up with Abutsu. After Abutsu gave birth to Tamesuke, her first acknowledged son by Tameie, supposedly she did her best to alienate Tameie from Tameaki as well, and Tameie acquiesced. The anecdote appears in the context of Genshō's attack on Abutsu (as another example of the kind of wicked behavior that led to the karmic retribution of her death), but it is probably a fairly accurate description of the relationship between Tameaki and his father. Another reason to suspect that Tameie took little interest in Tameaki is that unlike his more favored brothers Tameuji and Tamesuke, who achieved important court positions (Dainagon [major counselor] and Chūnagon [middle counselor], respectively) and court ranks (both ended at Senior Second Rank through their father's support), Tameaki never advanced further in the court bureaucracy than Junior Fifth Rank Upper.

Tameaki seems to have reconciled at least nominally with his father in later years, since in 1271 he accompanied the poet-priest Jakue (fl. 1271–1241) on a visit to Tameie in Saga.[4] However, in a poem from a hundred-poem sequence

3. Hisamatsu quotes the pertinent passage in "*Chikuen shō* kō," pp. 196–97.

4. Kubota Jun, "Junkyōbō Jakue ni tsuite," p. 48.

that he compiled in 1278 (*Kōan hyakushu*),[5] Tameaki made clear his continuing sense of estrangement from the Mikohidari branch of the Fujiwara:

> *mukashi waga / na o sae kakenu / Mikasayama*
> *ikanaru fuji no / shita ha naruramu*
>
> In the past, I wasn't even allowed to hang my name on Mount Mikasa,
> so what sort of lowly leaf of wisteria might I become?[6]

This poem is typical of the overall tone of the hundred-verse sequence: many of the poems lament his bad fortune and lack of advancement in the court bureaucracy. Here Tameaki uses an allusion to Mount Mikasa (the home of the Fujiwara clan deity) and a pun on *fuji* (wisteria) to indicate his dissatisfaction with his position as an outsider within his own family and may be implying that for a time Tameie refused to acknowledge him.

Tameaki must have become a Shingon priest before 1278, because he referred to himself by his Buddhist name Myōkaku in the *Kōan hyakushu*. One poem provides evidence that he took orders at a relatively young age:

After taking the tonsure:

> *ika ni waga / musubi okikeru / motoyui no*
> *shimo yori saki ni / kawari hatsuramu*
>
> Why did my bound hair have to change so soon,
> before it even started to be threaded with white frost?[7]

Tameaki's complaint that he had to take the tonsure at so young an age may indicate a lack of economic resources.

A transmission lineage from the *Kingyoku sōgi* variant of *Gyokuden jinpi no maki*, "*Ise monogatari* shishi sōjō kechimyakufu" (Transmission lineage from masters to disciples on *Ise monogatari*), claims that Tameaki took the tonsure on the thirteenth day of the third month of 1273.[8] Although we have no in-

---

5. A request from Retired Emperor Kameyama that Tameaki submit a hundred-verse sequence for consideration during the compilation of the imperial anthology *Shoku Shūi waka shū* is one indication that Tameaki was well-regarded as a poet at least by his peers, if not treated well by his family.

6. *Shin Shoku Kokin shū* 3207.

7. *Shoku Shūi waka shū* 1240.

8. Ishigami Hideaki, "Kunaichō Shoryōbu-zō *Kingyoku sōgi*," pt. II, p. 46; see also the *Kokin shū* transmission lineage in ibid., pt. I, p. 48. But note that a lineage document attached to *Kakinomoto no Hitomaro no koto* indicates that Tameaki took the tonsure in 1270 (Miwa Masatane, *Kagaku hiden no kenkyū*, p. 499).

dependent verification for this date, it seems fairly credible since some of the poems in the hundred-verse sequence indicate that by 1278 he had already been living in the Kantō region for an extended period. For example:

> *Azumaji no / okute no yamata / kari ni nomi*
> *omoishi io mo / suminarenikeri*
>
> I only intended to stay briefly in the hinterlands of Azuma, just
> until the late rice was harvested in the mountain paddies,
> but somehow I've grown used to living here in this hut.[9]

This poem confirms a line from *Shami Ren'yu shū* (Novice Ren'yu's collection) that says Tameaki lived in a small hermitage in Kamakura where he often held poetry meetings.[10] It is also typical of Tameaki's style, which employs numerous puns and pivot words (*kakekotoba* 掛詞). Here the two important pivots are on *oku/te* (奥 the interior of Azuma; 奥手 late rice) and on *kari ni* (刈り to harvest; 仮に briefly, temporarily). Since Tameaki's most distinctive interpretive strategy was to identify puns and show through etymological allegoresis that they had hidden religious meanings, it makes sense that in his own poetry he would use complex puns to create overlapping layers of meaning.

Tameaki's move to Kamakura is not particularly surprising. The Nijō and Asukai families dominated Kyoto during the 1270s, and without support from his father there probably was not much room for a younger son like Tameaki. The Kamakura area was still fairly sparsely populated, and the level of culture there was generally lower than in Kyoto. Nevertheless, samurai poets were strongly interested in waka and renga. Fujiwara no Teika had had excellent relations with the Kamakura shogunate; given the scarcity of good poets in Kamakura, Teika's grandson Tameaki would have been welcomed.

Although Tameaki had only reached the rank of Junior Fifth Upper, he apparently was accepted into the highest levels of samurai society in Kamakura. Sometime in the 1280s, Tameaki married his daughter Senshi[11] to Nijō

9. *Shin Senzai waka shū* 2065.

10. Ren'yu (1225–98) came from a powerful family connected to the shogunate. The poems in his collection were mostly written between 1288 and 1299 and include exchanges with Tameyo, Tamezane, Tamesuke, and Asukai Masaari. Ren'yu apparently circulated in court poetry circles in both Kyoto and Kamakura; as a samurai poet, he would have been a likely person to participate in poetry meetings at Tameaki's hermitage.

11. Senshi (or Nobuko, ?–1321) was an excellent poet in her own right and was affiliated with the Kyōgoku school. Thirty-three of her poems were selected for inclusion in the impe-

Kanemoto, the son of Nijō Morotada, minister of the left from 1275 to 1288, and regent from 1287 to 1289.[12] Kanemoto held a series of high offices and became regent (*sesshō*) in 1298.[13] Kanemoto's son Michihira, Tameaki's grandson, was born in 1287. Like his father, Michihira held a series of high offices; he became regent (*kanpaku*) in 1316 under Emperor Hanazono.[14]

More than 150 years later, Tameaki's great-great-great-grandson, Regent Ichijō Kaneyoshi wrote that *Waka chiken shū* was filled with utter nonsense; written by "someone obsessed with the erotic" (*irogonomi*), it could only lead the reader toward evil and was therefore not to be trusted. Had he known that his great-great-great-grandfather had been involved in its authorship, Kaneyoshi might not have been quite so harsh.[15]

Tameaki's Poetic Affiliations

Tameaki's poetic affiliations are the subject of some dispute. When he wrote his hundred-poem sequence in 1278, the Nijō, Reizei, and Kyōgoku "styles" had not yet been established and the relatively few poems available show no clear pattern of influence.[16]

Seven of Tameaki's poems appear in the imperial anthologies compiled by the Nijō, beginning with the "Azumaji no" poem in *Shoku Shūi waka shū* (Collection of gleanings of Japanese poems continued; 1279). Tameaki also had ties to his nephew Tamezane, a younger son of Nijō Tameuji. Tamezane, who is thought to be the main figure behind the *Usagi* forgeries, lived in the Kamakura area at about the same time as Tameaki. Manuscripts of Tameaki's *Chikuen shō* and *Waka chiken shū* have colophons with Tamezane's name on them, and the second half of one of the *Usagi* forgeries, *Sango ki*, was clearly influenced by Tameaki's version of *Waka chiken shū*. Tamezane appears to have felt, however, that Tameaki was unqualified genealogically to

rial anthologies, and she was one of the poets asked by Emperor Go-Uda (r. 1274–87) to submit a hundred poem sequence (*Bunpō hyakushu*, 1320) for the *Shoku Senzai waka shū*.

12. Nijō Morotada (1254–1341) was the son of Regent Nijō Yoshizane (1216–70). He took Buddhist vows in 1294.

13. Nijō Kanemoto (1268–1334) held the offices of minister of the right (1291–96), minister of the left (1296–99), chancellor (1299–1300), and regent (*sesshō* 1298–1300 and *kanpaku* 1300–1305).

14. Nijō Michihira (1287–1335) held the offices of minister of the right (1309–13), minister of the left (1313–16 and 1333–35), and regent (1316–18).

15. Ichijō Kaneyoshi, *Ise Monogatari guken shō*, p. 505.

16. Inoue Muneo (*Chūsei kadanshi no kenkyū*, p. 85) is typical when he temporizes that Tameaki's style is basically Nijō, yet occasionally shows the influence of Kyōgoku Tamekane.

inherit such secrets. Although he was happy to accept Tameaki's commentaries, he generally revised them considerably when he incorporated them into his own work.[17]

There is another textual connection to the Nijō: in the *Kingyoku sōgi* variant of *Gyokuden jinpi no maki*, the names "Tameuji" and "Tameyo" are interpolated into two of the transmission lineages, an indication that the text was transmitted within the Nijō house.[18] Material that originated with Tameaki, particularly selected sections from *Gyokuden jinpi no maki* and poetic criticism from *Chikuen shō*, continued to appear in Nijō commentaries throughout the rest of the medieval period and was eventually incorporated into the Nijō *Kokin denju*.

In later years Tameaki appears to have become close to the Reizei side of the family. He is known to have traveled to Kamakura sometime before 1293 with his youngest brother Tamemori, from the following poem by Tamemori in the *Shūi fūtei waka shō* (Selected gleanings of the styles of Japanese poems; compiled by Reizei Tamesuke, ca. 1303):

When I accompanied Fujiwara no Tameaki to the Eastern Provinces and returned alone:

> *kono tabi wa / miyako ni okuru / tomo mo nashi*
> *namida to naru na / ariake no tsuki*
>
> Dawn moon, although we have no friend
> to send us off on our journey back to the capital,
> let's not shed tears.[19]

Like Tameaki, Tamemori eventually settled in the Kantō region and took orders at the relatively young age of forty.

---

17. Actually, such revision was the norm; one of the side effects of secret transmission was the considerable freedom afforded transmitters to make changes as they wished. See, e.g., the discussion of Tamezane's version of *Chikuen shō* in Miwa Masatane, *Kagaku hiden no kenkyū*, pp. 74–75.

18. For example, the *Kingyoku sōgi* variant of *Gyokuden jinpi no maki* contains two transmission lineages (sections 27 and 60) that indicate Tameie transmitted secret material both to Tameaki and to Tameuji, who in turn transmitted the material to his son Tameyo (Ishigami Hidemi, "*Gyokuden jinpi no maki* kaidai kō," pp. 227, 229). And section 23 has: "The exalted Daimyōjin transmitted the material to Narihira, and since then it has become an important treasure of the Nijō house. It should not be shown to [members of] any other house" (*Kingyoku sōgi*, pt. I, p. 46).

19. *Shūi fūtei waka shō* 235.

In 1293 Tameaki wrote a hundred-poem sequence with Reizei Tamesuke, and in 1294 and 1295 he participated in Reizei poetry meetings held by Tamesuke (the 1295 meeting is Tameaki's last recorded public appearance). Tameaki's poems were included in both of the imperial anthologies compiled by the Reizei-Kyōgoku faction. He has five poems in the imperial anthology compiled by Kyōgoku Tamekane, *Gyokuyō waka shū* (Collection of jeweled leaves of Japanese poetry; 1312) and two in *Fūga waka shū* (Collection of elegant Japanese poetry; 1349) compiled by Emperor Kōgon (r. 1332–33) with the help of Emperor Hanazono. In addition, his poems were included in Tamesuke's personal collection, *Shūi fūtei waka shō*, and more than forty of his poems appeared in *Fuboku waka shō* (Selected poems of Japan; ca. 1308–10), compiled by a disciple of Tamesuke, Fujiwara no Nagakiyo (fl. 1293–1310).

These multiple connections to both the Reizei and Nijō factions may explain why material associated with Tameaki can be found in both the Nijō and the Reizei family commentary transmissions. After Tameie died in 1275, Tameaki (or for that matter anyone in the Mikohidari family) could claim to have a secret manuscript transmitted by Tameie and no one would be able to contradict him. And with Kyōgoku Tamenori's death in 1279 and Nijō Tameuji's in 1286, the way would have been cleared for Tameaki, who was considerably older than his brother Reizei Tamesuke or his nephews Tamezane and Nijō Tameyo, to figure as a mentor to these young poets and to establish his authority by means of these secret treatises. For example, since numerous sections from *Gyokuden jinpi no maki* appear in Tamesuke's library catalogue of 1317 and fragments are woven into the Reizei school *Ise monogatari shō*, we can guess that Tameaki transmitted some form of *Gyokuden jinpi no maki* to Tamesuke between 1293 and 1295.[20] Tameaki could have argued that he alone received these esoteric treatises because he was the only one of Tameie's sons to become a Shingon priest.

Tameaki and the Rokujō and Ietaka Factions

The large number of spurious commentaries produced by the poetic houses of the late thirteenth and early fourteenth centuries is usually attributed to the Reizei-Nijō conflict. In the 1260s and 1270s, however, when Tameaki was most active in producing his commentaries, that conflict was still only

20. For Tamesuke's library catalogue (*Reizeike soshimokuroku*), see Katagiri Yōichi, *Ise monogatari no kenkyū (kenkyūhen)*, pp. 576–77.

on the horizon. The distinctive character of the commentaries associated with Tameaki is therefore more likely to have been determined by the circumstances surrounding their production. Here I examine the influence of other poetic factions active at the time, particularly the Rokujō and Ietaka schools. Their importance as competition for Tameaki is clear in the opening lines of *Kokin waka shū jo kikigaki*: "There are three schools of *Kokin shū* commentary. The first is Teika's, the second is Ietaka's, and the third is [Rokujō] Yukiie's."[21] As might be expected, Tameaki argued that the true understanding of the *Kokin shū* is found only in the "Teika" school. However, the development of both Tameaki's distinctive style of commentary and his esoteric waka initiation ceremony seems to owe much more to the Rokujō and Ietaka schools than to Teika's legitimate heirs.

Rokujō Yukiie was selected as a co-compiler along with Tameie of the *Shoku Kokin waka shū* and was the judge of numerous poetry contests. He officially became head of the Rokujō family in 1264, when he received the family's Hitomaro portrait, ritual implements, and secret manuscripts as part of a Hitomaro memorial ceremony poetry contest; he continued holding both Hitomaro memorial ceremonies and poetry contests until his death eleven years later. As noted in the preceding chapter, the Hitomaro memorial ceremony was the basis for Tameaki's waka initiation ceremony. In addition, the Rokujō house's approach to literary criticism was one prototype for Tameaki's "anecdotal" commentaries. Anecdotal commentaries such as *Kokin waka shū jo kikigaki* reveal an especially strong stylistic debt to works such as Kiyosuke's *Fukurozōshi* (Commonplace book; ca. 1157–60), which consists mainly of anecdotes related to poetry. Tameaki also appears to have borrowed the general notion that secret family transmissions are to be shown only to those who have been specially initiated, as well as some specific material used to create the esoteric waka initiation ceremony that marked the disciple's reception of secret material.

One unanswered question is how Tameaki gained access to this Rokujō material. Miwa Masatane has argued that the chapter on waka in Tachibana no Narisue's prose miscellany *Kokon chomon jū* reveals Narisue's partiality toward Ietaka, Ietaka's son Takasuke (ca. 1180s–?), and the Rokujō and his antipathy toward Teika and Tameie.[22] Miwa argues that this decided parti-

21. *Kokin waka shū jo kikigaki*, p. 223.

22. See the discussion of the *Kokon chomon jū* in Miwa Masatane, *Kagaku hiden no kenkyū*, pp. 429–47.

ality makes it highly likely that the Ietaka poetry faction continued to exist in some form after Takasuke's death, and that in the 1250s and 1260s that faction made common cause with the Rokujō in their fight against the Mikohidari. As further proof of their possible cooperation, Miwa cites a transmission lineage for the Ietaka school commentary *Waka kanjō shidai himitsu shō* (Selected secrets on the protocol for waka initiations; ca. 1260s–1270s?) that contains the names Rokujō Akisue, Fujiwara no Ietaka, and Rokujō Yukiie.[23] It may therefore have been through his contacts with members of the Ietaka poetry faction that Tameaki gained access to secret Rokujō materials.

The Ietaka poetry faction naturally developed around Ietaka's son Takasuke. Takasuke was quite a bit older than his main rival, Tameie, and at the time was considered as good (or even better) a poet. After Takasuke's death (probably sometime after 1251) the faction is thought to have continued in the Kantō region and centered around Takasuke's daughter. The evidence for this is the transmission lineage for the Ietaka school version of *Waka chiken shū*, which passes from Ietaka to "Ensho no Nyōbō" (遠所女房). Inoue Muneo hypothesizes that this lady-in-waiting might be Takasuke's daughter or granddaughter.[24]

Waka chiken shū is one of a number of Kamakura commentaries that have two variant lineages: one transmitted via Ietaka (most often to Takasuke) and one via Teika (to Tameie and then Tameaki). Of course, the Ietaka school variant of *Waka chiken shū* was not transmitted by Ietaka or even Takasuke; it was probably produced after Takasuke's death by someone associated with his daughter or granddaughter. The Ietaka version of *Waka chiken shū* (dated around 1265) was probably the original, and Tameaki acquired and revised it to make it appear to be a text transmitted from Teika rather than Ietaka. If this is the case, the Ietaka school version of *Waka chiken shū* may well be the first example of a commentary that asserts a divine origin for its poetic insights. The introduction claims that it was transmitted from Sumiyoshi Daimyōjin to the Heian poet Minamoto no Tsunenobu. It also argues for waka poetics as a profound path to Buddhist enlightenment. Tameaki appears to have revised and expanded this introduction by adding material influenced by Shingon Tachikawa, such as "Narihira is identified as

---

23. Ibid., p. 199.

24. Shimabara *Waka chiken shū*, p. 206; Inoue Muneo, *Chūsei kadanshi no kenkyū*, p. 14. For a comparison of *Waka chiken shū* transmission lineages, see Otsu Yūichi, *Ise monogatari kochūshaku no kenkyū*, pp. 72–73.

two Bodhisattvas: the Bodhisattva of Song and Dance in Paradise and the Horse-Headed Kannon. Seeing the plight of humanity . . . he was born as a human into this world . . . and eventually brought consolation to 3,733 suffering women. He recorded his activities in *Ise monogatari* in order to disseminate the [esoteric] meaning of eroticism (*irogonomi*) to later generations."[25]

Here we see one of the first instances of etymological allegoresis at work: Narihira may well have been identified with the Horse-Headed Kannon because he was head of the Right Horse Bureau. This interpretive strategy is not, however, employed in *Waka chiken shū*'s analyses of the *Ise monogatari* episodes themselves. Those analyses tend to be straightforward identifications of the anonymous men and women in the tales, giving precise locations and historical dates. The complete lack of etymological allegoresis, plus the fact that few of the identifications match those made in later Tameaki-affiliated commentaries such as *Gyokuden jinpi no maki*, makes it unlikely that the main body of the text was written by Tameaki.

Instead, it appears that Tameaki acquired the Ietaka poetry faction's *Ise monogatari* commentary and, after making a few simple changes in style and format and adding some sections more in line with his thinking on the connection between poetry and Buddhism to the introduction, claimed it as a "Teika" family text. Tameaki probably got his start manufacturing spurious "oracular" commentaries with this revision of the Ietaka version of *Waka chiken shū*. In addition, he got three of his most important interpretive strategies from this text. First, he borrowed the concept that a profound religious meaning is hidden within waka and waka poetics and that this meaning is essentially Buddhist (an idea that he subsequently took in a more Tachikawa direction). Second, the oracular authority of deities such as Sumiyoshi Daimyōjin, substantiated by the authority of the poetic house, take precedence over the poet's own insights. Third, the identification of Narihira with the Bodhisattva of Song and Dance and the Horse-Headed Kannon was the model for Tameaki's development of religious allegoresis as an interpretive strategy for *Ise monogatari* and the *Kokin shū*, a strategy fully realized in later texts such as *Gyokuden jinpi no maki* and *Waka kokin kanjō no maki*.

To judge from the *Waka chiken shū*, Tameaki's interaction with the Ietaka poetry faction was crucial in the early stages of the development of his commentaries (1265–80). At least two other Ietaka school commentaries resem-

---

25. Kunaichō *Waka chiken shū*, p. 108.

ble Tameaki's, *Waka kuden shō* (Selected oral transmissions on waka) and *Waka kanjō shidai himitsu shō*. The dating is so problematic, however, that it is difficult for scholars to tell who was influencing whom. Miwa Masatane argues that by the 1280s the Ietaka faction was no longer functioning independently and had been absorbed into the Tameaki faction. He bases his argument on the opening of *Kokin waka shū jo kikigaki* of 1287, which implies that Ietaka's faction is simply a subordinate branch of the Mikohidari.[26] Support for Miwa's argument comes from evidence that the Ietaka faction had faded away within a generation. The late Kamakura period *Guhi shō*, for example, comments: "Lord Ietaka always produced verses of splendid effect, and he had an unusually fine poetic manner. Nevertheless, from time to time are found in his verse elements of a style presaging the extinction of his house, which makes one want to keep one's distance."[27]

Thus the question of how Tameaki came to be involved with the Ietaka poetic faction is an important one. One possible answer lies in the friendship between Tameaki and Tsumori no Kunisuke (1242–99), the forty-eighth hereditary head administrator (*kannushi*) of Sumiyoshi Shrine and a well-regarded poet.[28] Kunisuke's aunt was married to Takasuke, and Kunisuke himself married his cousin, Takasuke's daughter:

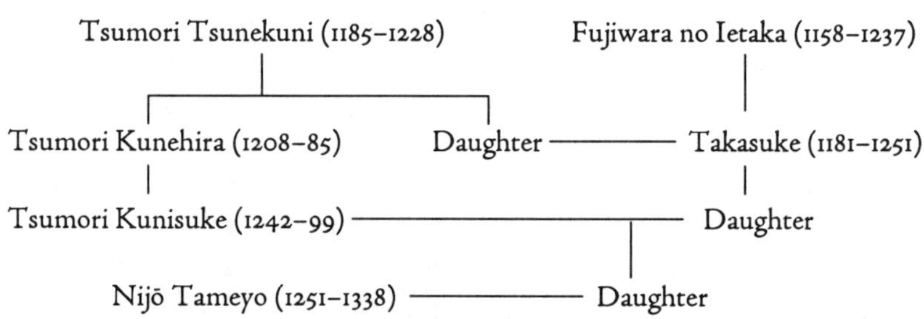

This genealogy makes clear a point that is often neglected in literary studies of medieval Japan: although their names are now unknown, daughters

26. Miwa Masatane, *Kagaku hiden no kenkyū*, pp. 210–11; *Kokin waka shū jo kikigaki*, p. 223.

27. *Guhi shō* (*U no matsu*), in Sasaki Nobutsuna, ed., *Nihon kagaku taikei* (Kazama Shobō, 1973), vol. 4, p. 296; translation (modified) from Brower, *Conversations with Shōtetsu*, p. 63n15. Shōtetsu makes a very similar comment in *Shōtetsu monogatari*: "Teika feared [Ietaka], saying that his style had something about it that presaged the extinction of his house—a poetic manner that indicated his descendants would not long endure" (ibid., p. 63).

28. Kunisuke received this position in 1285. For information on Kunisuke, see Hosaka Miyako, "Tsumori ke no kajin gun (16): Kunisuke no denki."

played a vital role in cementing ties between poetry families and may have played an active role in promoting them.

Although the evidence is slim, it is possible that Kunisuke's wife is the same woman (Ensho no Nyōbō) who appears in the transmission lineage for the Ietaka school *Waka chiken shū*. If so, the fact that *Waka chiken shū* is the earliest Kamakura commentary to claim Sumiyoshi Daimyōjin as its oracular source may be connected to Kunisuke's office. The Tsumori family produced a number of outstanding poets and no doubt encouraged the development of Sumiyoshi Daimyōjin as the guardian deity of waka poetry. If, as claimed in *Waka chiken shū*, Sumiyoshi Daimyōjin was an active transmitter of revelations on the relationship of Shinto, esoteric Buddhism, and waka, the deity's standing in the world of poetry would only have been enhanced, and this would, of course, have benefited the Tsumori family. At any rate, Kunisuke had strong connections to the Ietaka poetry faction, and at the very least he is a likely candidate as conduit of Ietaka school commentaries to Tameaki.

Tameaki probably met Kunisuke at the Sumiyoshi and Tamatsushima poetry contests of 1263; Kunisuke would have been about twenty-one, and Tameaki would have been in his late twenties or early thirties. Twenty-nine years later, both attended the Ikitsushima Shrine poetry meeting of 1292.[29] Evidence of the closeness of their friendship can be found in an exchange of poems (nos. 540 and 541) in the *Shin Gosen waka shū* (New later collection of Japanese poems; 1303):

When I went down to Azuma, I called on Fujiwara no Tameaki, and he promised without fail to accompany me back [to the capital], but something came up, and so I sent him this:

> *onaji yo no / inochi no uchi no / michi danimo*
> *okure saki datsu / hodo zo kanashiki*
>
> Even when you are on the same life path,
> how sad it is when one goes on ahead and the other lags behind.

[Tameaki's] reply:

> *chigiri arite / meguri ainuru / onaji yo no*
> *inochi no uchi no / michi wa hedatsu na*

29. Thirty-three poets participated, including Tameyo, Tamemichi, Tamezane, and Tamemori (ibid., p. 10).

Having made a pledge, we've met in this life;
may our paths never diverge!

Kunisuke's image of one "going on ahead" and the other "lagging behind" on the road back to the capital refers in a playful way to the grief of a person left behind when his friend or lover "goes ahead" to the next life. Tameaki responds that their friendship is undoubtedly founded on a pledge from a previous life and calls for their continued friendship in lives to come.

Like Tameaki, Kunisuke wrote at least one poem that indicates he may have spent a fair amount of time in Kantō (*Shoku Shūi waka shū*):

Written when I'd gone off to Azuma, and all unawares the days piled up until it became autumn:

Shirakawa no / seki made yukanu / Azumaji mo
hi kazu henureba / aki kaze zo fuku

The days have gone by and I haven't even gotten as far as the
Shirakawa checkpoint;
now the autumn winds are blowing here on the Azuma road.[30]

We cannot tell for sure, but this poem may also date to the period Kunisuke spent with Tameaki in Kantō.

Although the opening passage of Tameaki's *Kokin waka shū jo kikigaki* presupposes a rivalry between Ietaka and Teika, the fact that commentaries such as *Waka chiken shū* have both Ietaka and Tameaki school variants could be seen as evidence of cooperation between the two poetic factions, and the most likely point of connection would have been Kunisuke and Tameaki. One possible scenario for the production of *Waka chiken shū* is that Kunisuke and his wife produced it as an Ietaka school commentary and attributed it to oracles from Sumiyoshi Daimyōjin. Tameaki either participated in the production of *Waka chiken shū* or acquired a copy of the text and created

---

30. Here Kunisuke is alluding to *Goshūi shū* 518 by the priest Nōin (988–ca. 1050).

Composed at Shirakawa Barrier:

Miyako oba / kasumi to tomo ni / tachishikado
aki kaze zo fuku / Shirakawa no seki

Though I left Miyako with the [spring] mists,
the autumn wind is already blowing at Shirakawa Barrier.

Kunisuke has not even gotten as far as Shirakawa (the entrance to the Northern provinces), but since he has let so many days go by, the autumn wind is already blowing in Azuma (the Eastern Provinces). My thanks to an anonymous reader for pointing out this allusion.

his own lineage, which he then transmitted to two of his own disciples in the Kamakura area, Ichijō Yoshimoto and Shinsui. As a Shingon priest familiar with the use of etymological allegoresis to substantiate Shinto-Buddhist syncretic identifications and with the esoteric initiation ceremony as a way of legitimating transmission of esoteric secrets, Tameaki introduced those elements into his commentaries, and they in turn influenced later Ietaka school texts that have Tameaki school variants. This is all, however, completely speculative.

One last point that can be gleaned from genealogical charts of the Tsumori family: Kunisuke's daughter married Nijō Tameyo. This connection provides one explanation for how Ietaka and Tameaki school material became incorporated into the Nijō lineage of secret transmissions and why Nijō Tameuji and Tameyo's names are interpolated into the transmission lineages of Tameaki-affiliated texts such as the *Kingyoku sōgi* variant of *Gyokuden jinpi no maki*.

Tameaki's Audience

The distinctive character of the commentaries associated with Tameaki is undoubtedly related to their prospective audience. In Kamakura, where Tameaki appears to have spent much of his adult life, his hermitage was the center of a literary group that included samurai and court officials attached to the shogunate, Buddhist and Onmyōdō priests, and Shinto shrine officials. Unfortunately, other than a few names, we do not have much information on Tameaki's disciples and associates.[31] This audience presumably had a powerful influence on the contents of his commentaries as well as the style of his waka initiation ceremony. The anecdotal quality of commentaries such as *Kokin waka shū jo kikigaki*, with its revelations of the "true" origins and histories of poems, would have played on provincial poets' thirst for knowl-

31. For a listing of names on the various transmission lineages, see Miwa Masatane, *Kagaku hiden no kenkyū*, pp. 323–24. Some names not otherwise discussed here: Yoshinaga ("*Kokin shū* shishi sōjō kechimyakufu") and Ōtomo Tarō Tokichika, who is on the transmission lineage of *Tameie kuden* and in 1266 received a variant of *Kindai shūka* from Tameaki. Inoue Muneo (*Chūsei no kadanshi no kenkyū*, p. 82) suggests that he could either be the son of Hōjō Tokisada, who had poems in the *Shin Kokin shū* and *Fuboku waka shō*, or Fujiwara no Tokichika, who was included in the *Shoku Senzai shū*. In either case, he appears to have been a samurai poet affiliated with the Kamakura shogunate.

edge from the inner circle of court poetics. And in texts such as *Gyokuden jinpi no maki* and *Waka Kokin kanjō no maki*, Tameaki's application of the Shingon *kanjō* system of ordination and esoteric initiation to teaching the secrets of poetry would have catered to the deep desire of his students to find profound religious significance in their poetic tradition.

Besides Tsumori Kunisuke, Jakue is probably the best known of Tameaki's friends and disciples, but even his birth and death dates are unknown.[32] His family name was Abe no Norimoto, and he came to the Kantō region in 1263, where he made his living as a Yin-Yang priest (*onmyōji*) in the employ of the shogunate. He also served as a poetry teacher and personal retainer to Prince Munetaka. Sometime between 1265 and 1273, he took the tonsure. He has nine poems in imperial anthologies from *Shin Gosen shū* on and is known for his two waka treatises, *Jakue hōshi bun* (Writings by the priest Jakue; 1280) and *Jakue hōshi utago* (Poetic words by the priest Jakue; 1314). After visiting Tameie with Tameaki in 1271, Jakue became a disciple of Tameie, and after Tameie's death in 1275, he became a disciple of Nijō Tameuji. Although he had a falling out with Tameuji over the production of the imperial anthology *Shoku Shūi waka shū*, Jakue probably continued to provide a link between Tameaki and the Nijō side of the family. He also appears to have interacted with Reizei Tamesuke; we have a manuscript of *Shūi waka shū* that Jakue copied from Tamesuke circa 1292–93.[33] As a known practitioner of Yin-Yang divination, Jakue may well have had Tachikawa leanings and so influenced the tantric content of Tameaki's commentaries.

Tameaki associated with other religious figures besides Jakue and Tsumori no Kunisuke. For example, he exchanged poems (*Fuga shū* 831 and 832) with the Tendai priest Dōgen (1237–1304):

Once while I was staying in Mudō-ji,[34] I sent the following poem to Tameaki on a snowy morning:

> *Miyako e mo / miyuran mono o / aware to mo*
> *towanu zo tsuraki / mine no shirayuki*

32. The following information comes mainly from Kubota Jun, "Junkyōbō Jakue ni tsuite."

33. See Inoue Muneo, *Chūsei kadanshi no kenkyū*, pp. 80–81.

34. Mudō-ji is a small temple to the south of the Middle Hall in Enryaku-ji, the main Tendai temple on Mount Hiei.

A snow-covered peak: though surely visible from the capital,
no one comes to visit, even for compassion's sake.

His reply:

nagamubeki / sonata no yama mo / kakikurete
Miyako mo yuki no / haruru ma mo nashi

I would gaze in your direction but the mountain is obscured;
even here in the capital snow has been falling without a break.

Dōgen complains of a lack of visitors and hints that Tameaki should pay a visit; Tameaki replies that the snowy weather in the capital has made it impossible even to see Mount Hiei, much less climb it.

During the course of his career, Dōgen was the grand archbishop (大僧正 *daisōjō*) of the Tendai school of esoteric Buddhism and head priest (座主 *zasu*) of the Tendai complex on Mount Hiei. At first glance, it might seem surprising that Tameaki should be on terms of easy acquaintance with such a high-ranking esoteric priest. In fact, Tameaki was related to Dōgen by marriage. Dōgen was the younger brother of the regent Nijō Morotada, who was the father of Nijō Kanemoto, Tameaki's son-in-law. Through the marriage of his daughter Senshi, Tameaki managed to form high-level connections in both the religious and the political spheres of his day.

In Kamakura, the priests who regularly participated in Tameaki's poetry circle were less illustrious. One such priest would have been Yoshimoto (also read Nōki), who appears in the transmission lineages of *Chikuen shō*, *Kokin waka shū jo kikigaki*, the *Kingyoku sōgi* variant of *Gyokuden jinpi no maki*, and *Jinpi kushō* (Nine fascicles of profound secrets), a spinoff of *Gyokuden jinpi no maki*. Given the number of transmission lineages associated with Yoshimoto, he was probably Tameie's most important disciple. Early on, Miwa Masatane tentatively identified him as Ichijō Yoshimoto, a descendent of Fujiwara no Michinaga's (966–1027) great-grandson, the poet Mototoshi. Yoshimoto's family had been connected to the shogunate in Kamakura for generations, and his father Yoriuji (1198–1248), a fairly high-ranking court official living in Kantō, was a good enough poet for eight of his poems to be included in imperial anthologies. As a samurai poet living in Kamakura, Ichijō Yoshimoto would at first appear to be a good match for the Yoshimoto listed in the transmission lineages. There are, however, problems with this identification. Ichijō Yoshimoto died in Kōan 8 (1285). The date given for the transmission of *Kokin waka shū jo kikigaki* to Yoshimoto is Kōan 9 (1286). The *Kingyoku sōgi* variant of *Gyokuden jinpi maki* claims that Yoshimoto transmitted the text to someone named Kaishō in Kōan 10 (1287). One transmission date that postdates Ichijō Yoshimoto's death might be a transcription error, but two call the identification into question.[35]

The transmission lineages in *Kingyoku sōgi* also contain two short biographies that do not square with what we know of the samurai Ichijō Yoshimoto. Section 27, "Transmission Lineage of Masters to Disciples on Waka from the *Kokin shū*" ("*Kokin* waka shishi sōden kechimyakufu"), claims that Yoshimoto was a priest living in Ise and designates him an *ajari* 阿舎利 (Dharma master), a title that indicates he had received the Shingon ordination.[36] This is corroborated by the transmission lineage for *Ise monogatari* in section 60 ("*Ise monogatari* shishi sōjō kechimyakufu"): "[Yoshimoto] received this transmission at Mount Izu on the twenty-eighth day of the twelfth month of 1278. He was a descendant of Regent Fujiwara no Michinaga and Fujiwara no Mototoshi; the grandson of Nōsei; the fifth son of Fujiwara no Asamoto. He was a disciple of Kakugen, a priest from Mitsugon-in on Mount Izu."[37]

If we take this passage seriously, there are at least three points of inquiry: Who was this priest Yoshimoto? Who was his preceptor, Kakugen? What kind of temple was Mitsugon-in?

Interestingly, this second biography places Yoshitomo squarely in the Ichijō lineage: since the samurai poet Ichijō Yoshimoto was Nōsei's brother, the priest Yoshimoto would be his grand-nephew.[38] Since Asamoto does not appear as a son of Nōsei in any of the genealogies, however, the priest Yoshimoto cannot be traced. At any rate, whether he was a samurai poet or a poet-priest, Yoshimoto certainly fits the typical profile of a Tameaki disciple. And if the biography is valid, we can speculate that Shinsui, the recipient of *Gyokuden jinpi no maki*, was also a priest associated with Mitsugon-in, since the date given for its transmission is the same.

As for Kakugen, Kushida Ryōkō presents two Mitsugon-in lineage documents that place him at Mitsugon-in at approximately the right time for Yoshimoto to have been his disciple.[39] The first document does not contain dates, but indicates that Kakugen was the fourth head priest of the

35. For Yoshimoto, see Miwa, *Kagaku hiden no kenkyū*, pp. 143–45; Katagiri, *Chūsei*, vol. 2, pp. 30–31; and Ishigami Hideaki, "Kunaichō Shoryōbu-zō *Kingyoku sōgi*," pt. I, pp. 39–41, 47.

36. Ibid., p. 48.

37. Ibid., pt. II, p. 46.

38. See the genealogies in ibid., pt. I, p. 40.

39. Kushida Ryōkō, *Shingon mikkyō seiritsu katei no kenkyū*, pp. 435–38.

temple, which was founded in the 1180s. A second lineage document gives initiation dates from Kakui (third head priest) to Kakugen (11/27/1256) and then to Kakukai (3/22/1263). The two documents indicate that Kakugen and Kakukai were grandsons of the director of the Right Horse Bureau Katō and sons of the Lay Priest Junior Assistant Minister Ashikaga Yasuuji. In addition, Kushida provides a lineage document that shows Kakugen also received an initiation at Zentei-in in Tō-ji in 1261. Kushida considers this an indication that Kakugen had connections in both the Kantō area and Kyoto and moved freely between them. The fact that Kakugen was an Ashikaga would also tie Mitsugon-in to the Kamakura shogunate and make him an appropriate teacher for Yoshimoto, whose family members were shogunate retainers.

The Mitsugon-in's establishment was deeply embedded in shogunal politics.[40] The founder of the temple, Kakuen (Mon'yō), appears to have met and impressed Minamoto no Yoritomo when Yoritomo was sent into exile in Izu. By this time there already existed a temple-shrine complex on Mount Izu (also known as Sōtō-zan) for priests who for one reason or another (personal or political) found it expedient to leave the capital. According to Martin Collcutt, this temple-shrine complex was devoted to the cult of Izu Gongen, a syncretic Shinto-Buddhist deity revered by the Hōjō family and by Yoritomo and other Izu warriors. When Yoritomo began gathering his forces for an attack on the Taira in 1180, Kakuen helped raise a large contingent of soldiers from among the warrior-priests living in the area of Mount Izu and sheltered Yoritomo's wife, Hōjō Masako, while he was away campaigning. As Yoritomo's spiritual advisor, Kakuen also performed recitations of the *Lotus Sutra* and dedicated an image of Kannon in support of Yoritomo's efforts.[41] When Yoritomo successfully overthrew the Taira and established the Kamakura shogunate, he rewarded Kakuen and Mitsugon-in with extensive estates in Izu and Sagami.

Not much is known about Kakuen's affiliations within Shingon. An anecdote in the historical chronicle *Azuma kagami* (Mirror of the east) indicates that he was at the very least quite adept at numerological homologies. Accord-

40. Most of the following information on Mitsugon-in comes from ibid., pp. 481–86; and Collcutt, "Religion in the Life of Minamoto Yoritomo."

41. See Collcutt, "Religion in the Life of Minamoto Yoritomo," pp. 99–100, for Yoritomo's deep faith in Kannon and the *Lotus Sutra*; he even kept a small silver image of Kannon in his topknot.

ing to the story, Yoritomo had been reciting a thousand passages from the *Lotus Sutra* each day, but the pressures of preparing for his attack on the Taira made it difficult for him to complete the invocations. He therefore summoned Kakuen, who obligingly rationalized a reduction to eight hundred:

> "Although you are not completing one thousand recitations, it shows respect for the Buddha to offer eight hundred." Then, making an offering of incense and flowers before an image of the Buddha, Kakuen explained: "Your Lordship upholds the eight chapters of the Lotus Sutra. Your Lordship, as the recipient of the will of Hachiman Tarō (Minamoto no Yoshiie), is the leader of the brave warriors of the eight provinces of the east. It is within the palm of your hand to subjugate the eight major crimes of the rebel clan of [Kiyomori] the lay priest of the eighth avenue (Hachijō). This your Lordship can do by reciting the eight hundred passages of this sutra."[42]

Pleased with Kakuen's quick thinking, Yoritomo promised him appropriate rewards when the Taira were beaten.

Although Kakuen himself appears to have come from Tō-ji, most of the existing records on the temple in the Kamakura period have been found at Sanbō-in at Daigo-ji in Kyoto; almost from the beginning Mitsugon-in seems to have been under the administrative control of Sanbō-in. This may be significant for two reasons. First, the supposed founder of the Tachikawa "heresy" of Shingon, Ninkan Ajari, was the younger brother and disciple of the founder of Sanbō-in, Assistant Archbishop Shōkaku.[43] In the somewhat murky history of Tachikawa, Ninkan was said to have been exiled to the Izu peninsula in 1113 for his involvement in an aborted *coup d'état* planned by Prince Sukehito against Emperor Toba (r. 1107–23) and Retired Emperor Shirakawa. Supposedly while in exile Ninkan combined Yin-Yang practices with Shingon to create the tantric sect of Tachikawa.[44] Although modern scholars have some doubts whether Ninkan really single-handedly invented Tachikawa, it seems clear that the Izu area was a stronghold of Tachikawa influence.

---

42. Translation from ibid., pp. 94–95.

43. Shōkaku himself was famous for his rainmaking and other magical abilities and regularly shows up on Tachikawa lineages.

44. The primary source for the idea that Ninkan was involved in the origin of Tachikawa is the fourteenth-century Shingon priest Yūkai's *Hōkyō shō* (Compendium of the precious mirror), an attack on the Tachikawa heresy. See Yūkai, *Hōkyō shō*, *T.*, p. 848. I discuss Tachikawa and Ryōbu Shinto in more detail in the next chapter.

Sanbō-in was also the home temple of Hōkyō (Rendō), a major figure in the Shinto-Buddhist fusion movement of Ryōbu Shinto. Hōkyō founded the Miwa sect of Shingon, a form of Ryōbu Shinto permeated with Tachikawa elements.[45] Since Hōkyō was active in the 1270s, Mitsugon-in was under the direct control of a temple that had important Tachikawa and Ryōbu Shinto connections at the time when Tameaki's commentaries were being transmitted to Yoshimoto. Note, too, that the Miwa sect was named after the Miwa region near the Ise shrines, where Hōkyō founded the temple Yakushi-in. Since one of the lineage documents says that Yoshimoto was living in Ise, this may be another source of the Ryōbu Shinto influence found in Tameaki's commentaries.

A more tentative connection to Tachikawa is through the name Mitsugon-in itself. Another Mitsugon-in was founded on Mount Koya around 1130 by Kakuban (Kōgyō Daishi, 1095–1143) as an innovative center for combined Shingon and Pure Land *nenbutsu* practice (it was moved to Mount Negoro in 1288). Kakuban equated Dainichi Nyorai and Amida Buddha and promoted a Shingon version of the Pure Land, the "Pure Land Adorned with Mystery" (*mitsugon jōdo*), from which both temples got their name. Also, it is probably significant that the names of the head priests of the Mitsugon-in on Mount Izu consistently contain the element "kaku." It would be useful if we could find a concrete connection between the two temples, since Kakuban's *Jinshinkan* (Visualizing one's own body) is one of the earliest "spiritual embryology" texts treating the human fetus as a Buddha Embryo. *Jinshinkan* may well have influenced Tameaki's *Waka Kokin kanjō no maki*, which correlates the five stages of gestation with the five lines of *Kokin shū* 409 ("Honobono to"). However, so far I have not been able to establish any connection beyond the name.

Given the strong influence of Tachikawa teachings on Tameaki's commentaries, the role of the Izu-Kamakura area in Tachikawa transmission, and Mitsugon-in's connection to Sanbō-in, it seems likely that Mitsugon-in

45. Hōkyō's commentary *Kakugen shō* (Selections from Kakukai [1142–1223] and Yūgen [fl. 1160]) was severely criticized by Yūkai for its Tachikawa elements: "There are many heretical views in the writings by Hōkyō Shōnin (the monk Rendō) of Miwa in the province of Yamato. The *Itteki shō* [Single drop compendium] and the like are Tachikawa teachings. Such compendiums and collections of oral teachings should be considered as forgeries through and through. In general this school is filled with heretical ideas" (Yūkai, *Hōkyō shō*, *T.*, p. 850; translation [modified] from Pol Vanden Broucke, trans., *Hōkyōshō: "The Compendium of the Precious Mirror" of the Monk Yūkai*, p. 28).

did indeed have Tachikawa and esoteric Shinto leanings. And given its history of connections with the Kamakura shogunate, it was an appropriate place for Tameaki to transmit commentaries to disciples such as Yoshimoto, who also had strong connections with the shogunate.

Evidence from numerous poetic exchanges indicates that Tameaki was well liked and respected by people from a variety of ranks and social positions and on all sides of the Nijō-Reizei-Kyōgoku conflict. His wide range of friends and associates is striking for someone in the Mikohidari family, which certainly had its share of ill-tempered personalities from Teika on. Tameaki's quick wit and affable nature was one likely reason he was so valued as a friend.

Two poems from *Fuboku waka shō* show a certain mischievous sense of humor at work:

> *hakanashi ya / tsutsui no kawazu / ware bakari*
> *hoka o mo shirazu / asaki kokoro wa*
>
> What a waste! His mind is so shallow, he's like a frog in a well,
> unaware of anyone but himself![46]

Here *kokoro* means both "heart" and "mind"; the person (it could be either a man or a woman) is criticized for being shallow and self-centered. The image of the frog refers to the medieval proverb that most human beings are like frogs at the bottom of a deep well: they know nothing of the true reality of things, yet continue to believe their limited knowledge constitutes everything worth knowing.[47] By means of this allusion, a witty criticism takes on a more profound nuance.

The second poem is on the topic of "beasts" (*kedamono*) and was included among a group of poems on foxes:

> *hana o miru / michi no hotori no / furugitsune*
> *kari no iro ni ya / hito mayōran*
>
> Alongside the path for flower-viewing, there's an old fox;
> her shifting color may lead hunters astray.[48]

---

46. *Fuboku waka shō* 1931.

47. *I no naka no kawazu taikai o shirazu* (the frog in the well knows nothing of the great ocean). See the citation in Suzuki Tōzō and Hirota Eitarō, *Koji kotowaza jiten*, p. 84, which includes Tameaki's poem as an example.

48. *Fuboku waka shō* 13028.

Here Tameaki puns on *kari*, meaning both "hunting" (狩り) and "temporary, transient" (仮), and on *iro* (色) in its meanings of "color," "sex," and "phenomenal reality." In addition, Tameaki uses the character 華 for *hana* (flower) rather than the more usual 花. Since "lotus blossom" (understood as the pre-eminent flower of enlightenment by its association with the *Lotus Sutra*) is written 蓮華, the flower-viewing path may be a metaphor for the path of enlightenment. Foxes are known to be bewitching shape-shifters; female foxes are known for their sexual allure (*iro*) as well. One reading of the poem would be that the old fox, whose fur has turned white with age, blends invisibly into the white blossoms alongside the path, thus confusing its hunters. On this level, Tameaki is playing deftly with the timeworn convention of elegant confusion. But on another level, the old fox who bewitches people and leads them astray with her sexuality is a trope for the lure of phenomenal reality (*kari no iro*), which bewitches people and causes them to lose sight of Absolute Truth and so stray from the path of enlightenment. Thus a secondary layer of religious meaning slips surreptitiously into at what at first glance is a frivolous, amusing poem. Another reading, that Tameaki was being cynical about his life's work, would posit Tameaki himself as the crafty old fox leading people astray with the temptations of tantric sex. One can easily imagine the author of these poems as having the combination of playful humor and poetic ability necessary to pull off writing the material in some of the more outrageous spurious commentaries and then managing to convince a number of important Nijō and Reizei poets that they were authentic.

The poems from Tameaki's later years that appear in *Fuboku waka shō* show less of the bitter resentment and disappointment that pervaded the hundred-verse sequence of 1278. The marriage of his daughter might have helped ease his old age; through her marriage to Regent Kanemoto, she achieved the rank of Junior Second. She was also an excellent poet; thirty-three of her poems were included in the imperial anthologies. Tameaki's other children did well too, perhaps because of the influence of his son-in-law. His heir, Tamenaka, surpassed his father and reached the rank of Junior Fourth Lower and the position of lesser captain of the left. He appears to have become the disciple of Tamezane (younger brother of Nijō Tameyo and supposed author of the *Usagi* forgeries). Two of Tameaki's other sons, Kūkei and Tametoshi, followed in their father's footsteps and took the tonsure; both achieved the rank of assistant grand bishop. Tameaki's grandson

Nijō Michihira became regent under Emperor Hanazono and was a member of Emperor Go-Daigo's trusted inner circle of ministers. And Tameaki's descendents include two of the most prominent poets of the Muromachi period: Nijō Yoshimoto and Ichijō Kaneyoshi. Even though—all unknowingly—they tried their best to discredit their forefather's lifework, their poetic talent continues to serve as testimony to him.

7

Basic Religious Concepts Underlying Tameaki's Commentaries

Tameaki's interpretive strategy of allegoresis was not new. There were earlier examples of religious allegory that employed complex puns and other techniques to tease out new meanings. The popularity of acrostics and "hidden word" games—a whole chapter of the *Kokin shū* is devoted to them—set the stage for allegorizing searches for hidden meanings. The analysis of graphs, however, especially the paronomastic technique of breaking them down into their component parts and rearranging those parts to reveal a supposed hidden "inner" meaning, does not appear in Heian period waka. Nor does the obsession with numerical homologies. These more technical forms of etymological paronomasia developed in concert with changes in the religious discourse of the medieval period, as well as in the political and economic environment of religious institutions.

One of the central concerns of medieval poets was the Buddhist argument that the literary arts were nothing but "wild words and ornate phrases" (狂言綺語 *kyōgen kigo*), sins of language that would cause the unwary poet to be reincarnated in one of the lower, more hellish, of the Six Realms. The difficulties for good medieval Buddhists who wanted to write poetry paralleled the difficulties confronting good Buddhists of a slightly earlier period who wanted to worship the native Japanese deities. As we have seen, allegoresis, with its diplomatic syncretism that preserves diverse origins and intellectual styles, often appears when rival worldviews conflict. Allegoresis proved useful in the Japanese context, first, for syncretizing kami and Buddhist deities and, second, for syncretizing the paths of poetry and of Buddhist enlightenment.

Japanese Buddhists deployed a variety of concepts and allegorizing strategies to syncretize native kami with Buddhist deities, a movement known as *honji suijaku* (本地衰弱). The *honji suijaku* theory of hypostasis claimed that kami were "manifest traces" (*suijaku*) of Buddhist deities who formed their "original ground" (*honji*). The Buddhist deities temporarily took the form of kami to prepare the Japanese for the arrival of the more advanced teachings of Buddhism. The most important concepts used to support this theory were nondualism, expedient means, and a belief in the magical efficacy of language. Etymological allegoresis, which developed fairly late within the *honji suijaku* movement, can be seen as a meta-strategy because it builds on these allegorizing concepts. It apparently first developed as part of an attempt by priests at Enryaku-ji, the Tendai complex on Mount Hiei, to assimilate the Hie shrines at the foot of their mountain. These efforts resulted in the development of a syncretic school known as Sannō Shinto, named after the Sannō deity worshipped at these shrines. The esoteric writings of these priests are the first clear examples of etymological allegoresis. The strategy was quickly adopted by the Shingon syncretic school, Ryōbu Shinto, with which Tameaki was undoubtedly familiar.

A second important religious influence on the development of the commentaries was the quintessentially syncretic Tachikawa sect that emerged within Shingon in the eleventh and twelfth centuries. The Tachikawa sect combined Shingon's emphasis on binary oppositions that are interdependent and ultimately nondual with elements of Taoist Yin-Yang divination and Ryōbu Shinto to create a tantric sect that promoted ritual sex as a path to enlightenment. Tachikawa thinking pervades Tameaki's commentaries.

"Wild Words and Ornate Phrases": The Sin of Poetry

The religious allegorization of *Ise monogatari* and the *Kokin shū* was symptomatic of broad cultural changes. The late Heian, early Kamakura period (twelfth to thirteenth centuries) witnessed a broadening and deepening of Buddhist faith. Not only did the esoteric sects of Tendai and Shingon continue to prosper (particularly among the elite), but the newly arisen Pure Land, Nichiren, and Zen sects expanded rapidly among the populace. These religious and political changes manifested themselves in the literature of the period. The canonical Heian court texts (*Genji monogatari, Ise monogatari, Kokin shū*) had revolved around the amorous affairs of the elegant court aristocracy. In the Kamakura period, the literary focus shifted to the suffering and salvation of military heroes or to religious and philosophical reflection deemed more appropriate to the anxieties and concerns of authors living in the "degenerate age" of *mappō* (末法).[1] As William LaFleur has argued in *The Karma of Words*, poets and scholars of this period felt hard-pressed to justify their frivolous pursuit of the literary arts in terms of the religious values of the age.[2]

Although the Nara sects seem not to have objected to secular literature, by the mid-Heian period signs of a felt contradiction between the composition of poetry and fiction and the practice of Buddhism began to appear. A poet was expected to compose poems on such topics as love, from the first pricking of desire to the deep bitterness when all was at an end. Writing poetry or fiction filled with descriptions of passionate attachment was hard to justify in view of the Buddhist emphasis on detaching oneself from this world of delusion. Moreover, the act of writing poetry in and of itself could be viewed as a deflection of purpose from the path of religious vocation. The competition for praise and prestige within court literary circles was considered a sign of delusory attachment to worldly goals. A remonstration by the Zen patriarch Dōgen makes this point quite clearly: "If in the short space of this existence you would cultivate some art or pursue some line of learning, then let it be the Way of the Buddha that you practice, the Law of the Buddha that you study. Literature, poetry, and the like are useless pursuits. I need hardly say they are best abandoned."[3]

---

1. The Buddhist idea that history was divided into three periods, *shōbō* (正法 true Dharma), *zōhō* (像法 imitated Dharma), and *mappō* (末法 declining Dharma), gained a strong grip on the Japanese imagination in the late eleventh and early twelfth centuries, when the political and social anarchy occasioned by the Gempei Wars seemed to bear out the idea that the world had entered *mappō*, the degenerate age, in the year 1052.

2. See particularly LaFleur's discussion of these issues in his first chapter, "'Floating Phrases and Fictive Utterances': The Rise and Fall of Symbols," in *The Karma of Words: Buddhism and the Literary Arts of Medieval Japan*, pp. 1–25. Plutschow also addresses the problem of *kyōgen kigo* in "Is Poetry a Sin? *Honjisuijaku* and Buddhism Versus Poetry."

3. Dōgen, *Shōbō genzō zuimonki*, pp. 341–42; translation from Thomas Harper, "Motoori Norinaga's Criticism of the 'Genji Monogatari': A Study of the Background and Critical Content of His 'Genji Monogatari Tama no Ogushi,'" p. 49.

A third issue was the use of language for nondidactic purposes. According to the central sutra of Pure Land Buddhism, *Muryōju kyō* (The Buddha of Infinite Life sutra), among the ten categories of evil (*jū aku* 十悪) are four that involve words: falsehood (*mōgo* 妄語), equivocation (*ryōzetsu* 両舌), slander (*akku* 悪口), and ornate, frivolous speech (*kigo* 綺語). Since any rhetorical ornament constitutes frivolous speech, almost any form of secular literature could be considered sinful. The writer of fiction was further damned by the sin of falsehood. According to the *Kegon* ("garland") *Sutra*, such sins could lead the writer to an afterlife spent in hell or to rebirth as an animal or hungry ghost (*gaki* 餓鬼). The mid-Kamakura priest and literatus Mujū Ichien (1226–1312) summed up the three Buddhist objections to literature in his preface to the prose miscellany *Shaseki shū* (Sand and pebbles; ca. 1279–83): "Now, we refer to the poetry of 'wild words and ornate phrases' as 'defiled poetry,' because it lures us to attachment, imbues us with vain sensuality, and decks us out with empty words."[4] The phrase "wild words and ornate phrases" (*kyōgen kigo*) alludes to an anecdote about the Chinese poet Po Chü-i. Toward the end of his life, Po Chü-i presented an anthology of his poetry to a Buddhist library. In the preface to this set of poems, he wrote: "My devout prayer is that the karma of writing worldly literature in this life, the error of wild words and ornate phrases, be transformed in lives to come into an instrument of praise for the Vehicle of Buddha, a link that turns the Wheel of Law."[5] Fujiwara no Kintō included this couplet in his collection of Chinese and Japanese verses for chanting, *Wakan rōei shū* (ca. 1013), under the heading "Buddhist matters" (*butsuji* 仏事). Its subsequent popularity can be seen from a description of a "meeting for the encouragement of learning" (*kangakue* 勧学会) in Minamoto no Tamenori's collection of didactic tales, *Sanbōe* (Illustrations of the three jewels; 984).[6] This meeting was held by students from the Northern Hall of the Imperial University in conjunction with monks from the Enryaku-ji temple on Mount Hiei. The Northern Hall was concerned mainly with the study of secular Chinese literature, and from the description in *Sanbōe* it appears that the participants saw the meeting as a means to atone for the "sins" of frivolous speech and falsehood in-

4. Translation (modified) from Morrell, *Sand and Pebbles*, p. 163.

5. Kawaguchi Hisao, *Wakan rōei shū zenshakuchū*, p. 440.

6. See "The Kangakue of Sakamoto on Hie," in Kamens, *The Three Jewels: A Study and Translation of Minamoto Tamenori's Sanbōe*, pp. 295–98.

volved in their pursuit of the study of literature. This atonement was accomplished by chanting verses from the *Lotus Sutra* and by Po Chü-i.

The appropriation of Po Chü-i's poems into this ritual context undoubtedly entailed a reinterpretation of his words. As Thomas Harper has pointed out, Po Chü-i was lamenting a life wasted on worthless literary pursuits and counted himself fortunate if even the smallest affinity with enlightenment could be salvaged from his poetry. Japanese writers, on the other hand, applied the *Lotus Sutra*'s concept of expedient means to the verse to yield the interpretation that Po Chü-i believed even the most vulgar of his writings might serve as an expedient means and form a link to salvation.[7] Po Chü-i might have appreciated the irony in the university students' belief that reciting his "wild words and ornate phrases" couplet had enough ritual efficacy to erase the bad karma that they had acquired through studying Chinese literature and writing poetry.

In literary criticism, the new intensity of religious faith seems to have been one inspiration for Fujiwara no Tameaki's allegorical reinterpretation of the canonical Heian texts in an attempt to find religious meaning where little or none had originally existed. By doing so, he successfully transformed a text like *Ise monogatari*, whose emphasis on love affairs would seem to make it a particularly egregious example of "wild words and ornate phrases," into an "instrument of praise for the Buddha." There is some evidence that he was simply giving his students what they wanted. For example, Emperor Hanazono, in his eulogy for Kyōgoku Tamekane in *Hanazono tennō shinki* (Diary of Emperor Hanazono; 1310–32), made it clear that he was a student of Tamekane rather than of Nijō Tameyo, precisely because he felt that Tameyo had no sense of the important relationship between the Buddhist Dharma and the Way of Poetry:

> Ordinary people do not understand these religious truths. [Nijō] Tameyo, who claims the main descent from Shunzei and Teika, has no idea of such things. They just made no impression on him. He jealously holds to the Six Poetic Modes and cannot see the true meaning of the art. Yet most of the world follows him, and the true Way of Poetry is gradually being abandoned. . . . In recent years I have met with the holy man of Sōko and learned the tenets of religion. I have also met with Shinsō Hōnin and heard the doctrines of Tendai. I have perused the Five Classics and have come to understand the doctrine of Confucianism. With this knowledge I

---

7. See Harper's discussion of these issues in "Motoori Norinaga's Criticism of the 'Genji Monogatari,'" pp. 48–58.

have thought anew about the Way of Poetry. Truly the distinction between right and wrong in poetry is like that between heaven and earth.[8]

This passage suggests that Nijō Tameyo was not particularly interested in religious allegoresis, and it was this lack of interest in a religious understanding of poetry rather than any perceived aesthetic differences that led Hanazono to prefer Tamekane as a teacher.

Later in the same text Hanazono repeated a conversation between Nijō Tamemoto (fl. 1313–50) and Tamekane to substantiate his argument about the important relationship between religious understanding and the interpreting (and writing) of profound waka poetry:

> Lord Tamemoto went on to say, "Lord Tamekane told me, 'Although I knew that His Majesty [Hanazono] had ability in poetry, it is remarkable that he has progressed so far in the inner meanings of the art, even though the secret teachings I entrusted him with at the time of my departure were not all that deep.' I replied, 'Although there is no such thing as a Buddhist sermon on poetry, his majesty's spirit has deepened with the study of the Dharma, so perhaps this is the reason for his progress.' To this Tamekane said, 'If this is so then he can never go wrong in his poetry, for there is no difference between the Dharma and the Way of Poetry.'" When I heard this, my faith was strengthened all the more. But there is nothing to be gained by writing further about this . . . the way to know poetry is through the understanding of the religious writings.[9]

The religious climate in the late thirteenth century and the desire of poets to legitimize their avocation in terms of Buddhism must have encouraged the development of esoteric commentaries. Tameaki's innovative use of etymological allegoresis was an essential part of this development, and it remained the dominant mode of literary analysis for about fifty years after his death. Even after the esoteric content of these commentaries fell out of favor, the strategy of etymological allegoresis continued to play an important role in literary pedagogy.

The attempt to make Heian secular literature fit medieval Buddhist discourse was reinforced by a contemporaneous move to homologize the native kami with Buddhist deities through the *honji suijaku* movement. Two other Buddhist concepts, expedient means and nondualism, were also crucial to these efforts.

---

8. Translation (modified) from Huey, *Kyōgoku Tamekane*, pp. 158–59.
9. Ibid., p. 159.

Expedient Means and the *Lotus Sutra*

Hōben (方便, Sk. *upāya*) is most often translated as "expedient means," but it could also be translated as "appropriate modes." The concept was widely promulgated in Japan through the popular canonization of the *Lotus Sutra*. The *Lotus Sutra* arose in the context of a struggle among various factions of Buddhism in India that came to a head around 100 B.C.E. By that time there were probably as many as twenty schools and sects of Buddhism led by professional priests who as specialists had become more and more dedicated to monasticism and were less and less interested in the role of Buddhism in secular life. Around the beginning of the Common Era, a group of lay Buddhists began a new movement, which they termed "Mahayana," or "great vehicle," Buddhism. They denigrated the monastic sects as "Hinayana," or "lesser vehicle," Buddhism. Hinayana Buddhism was said to include two types of Buddhists: the *śrāvaka*, who attempted to achieve enlightenment by listening to the Buddha's sermons, and the *pratyekabuddha*, who sought enlightenment through their own efforts to understand the impermanence of nature and life. The Mahayana was the path of the bodhisattva: one who brings the truth of enlightenment to the world in order to help other living beings attain it. Those Mahayana Buddhists who compassionately choose to work in the world to bring others to enlightenment, rather than hiding away in monasteries striving only for themselves, were said to follow the bodhisattva vehicle.

The *Lotus Sutra* was a Mahayana text developed specifically to harmonize the three vehicles (or modes) of salvation. The explanatory model the *Lotus Sutra* used to syncretize the conflicting theories was the concept of expedient means. In the *Lotus Sutra*, the Eternal Buddha, compassionately realizing that each person is at a different level of understanding, manifests himself in a variety of forms and uses whatever mode is appropriate to the individual:

> I know that living beings have various desires, attachments that are deeply implanted in their minds. Taking cognizance of this basic nature of theirs, I will therefore use various causes and conditions, words of simile and parable, and the power of expedient means and expound the Law for them. . . . I do this so that all of them may attain the one Buddha vehicle and wisdom embracing all species.[10]

The *Lotus Sutra*'s strategic deployment of the concept of expedient means to syncretize (rather than synthesize) competing worldviews is fundamentally

10. Watson, *The Lotus Sutra*, p. 32.

allegorical; as an interpretive strategy, it manages to "preserve the individual traits of the combining beliefs."[11] The concept of expedient means also promotes the use of parables and similes and thereby encourages the development of allegorical narratives.[12] As we saw from the examples of poems written as religious allegory in Chapter 2, in premodern Japan the *Lotus Sutra* was the main authoritative ground for texts written as allegories.

As Buddhism spread throughout Asia, it successfully used the concept of expedient means to assimilate local deities and rituals into Buddhism. In Japan it formed the rationalization for the idea that Buddhist deities "dimmed their radiance and mingled with the dust" (和光同塵 *wakō dōjin*) of this world by taking the form of kami. By this means older religious forms (native kami and shamanic rituals) were transformed and appropriated. Similarly, the idea of expedient means could be used to justify secular texts, such as the *Kokin shū* and *Ise monogatari*, whose original meaning had been problematized by changing religious values.

Expedient means understandably became the conceptual underpinning of the allegorical interpretive strategies developed by the Kamakura commentaries. One of these commentaries' most basic assumptions is that although the *Kokin shū* and *Ise monogatari* may superficially appear to be secular literature (*kyōgen kigo*) and lure the reader through the frivolous pleasure of reading, they prepare the reader for initiation into the true esoteric meaning of the texts. The *Kokin shū* and *Ise monogatari* become expedient means enticing people onto the path of enlightenment.

Nondualism, Waka as Dharani, and Poets as Bodhisattvas

The concept of nondualism developed within Mahayana Buddhism holds that the distinction between the terms of any binary opposition is merely a product of conventional perception; the enlightened mind transcends all such discriminatory thoughts. Within esoteric Buddhism some religious thinkers even argued that for the truly enlightened the passions are them-

11. Fletcher, "Allegory as Literary History," p. 43.

12. William LaFleur's extended discussion of the *Lotus Sutra* in *The Karma of Words* (see pp. 84–88) makes it clear that the *Lotus Sutra* is a powerfully allegorical text, although because he is working with a rather reduced and negative definition of allegory, he ends up claiming that it is not allegorical in the western sense.

selves enlightenment (*bonnō soku bodai* 煩悩即菩提) and that the cycle of birth and death is itself nirvana (*shōji soku nehan* 生死即涅槃). The same mode of thinking was used to argue that the distinction between secular waka poetry and Buddhist literature is meaningless as well: the Path of Poetry and the Path of Buddhism are one, nondual path to enlightenment. A direct corollary of this argument is that waka poetry and the Buddhist magical formulas called dharani (J. *darani* 陀羅尼, Sk. *dhāraṇī*) are ultimately nondual, as summed up in the phrase "waka are themselves dharani" (*waka soku darani* 和歌即陀羅尼).[13]

This idea was by no means marginal within medieval literary discourse. For example, in the biography of the Kegon priest Myōe Shōnin (1173–1232), we find the poet Saigyō (1118–90) discussing poetry as mantras with the young Myōe. Saigyō argues that poetry detached from appearances is a vehicle for enlightenment: "Such poetry is the true body of the Buddha, and therefore, composing a poem is the same as carving a statue of Buddha. Conceiving a verse is the same as reciting the esoteric True Words [Shingon]. Through this kind of poetry, I can understand the Dharma. If you fail to reach this stage, and if you study poetry without care, then it becomes a serious heresy."[14] Compare the following from the chapter "The Profound Reason for the Way of Poetry" in Mūjū Ichien's *Shaseki shū*:

> When we consider waka as a means to religious realization, we see that it has the virtue of serenity and peace, of putting to a stop the distractions and undisciplined movements of the mind. With a few words, it encompasses its sentiment. This is the very nature of mystic verses, or dharani. . . . Although dharani employ the ordinary language of India, when the words are maintained *as* dharani, they have the capacity to destroy wickedness and remove suffering. Japanese poetry also uses the ordinary words of the world; and when we use waka to convey religious intent, there

---

13. For a brief discussion of waka as dharani, see Yamada Shōzen, "Chūsei kōki ni okeru waka soku darani no jissen." In English, see Plutschow, *Chaos and Cosmos*, pp. 158–69.

14. From *Toganoo Myōe Shōnin denki*, a biography compiled by Myōe's disciple Girimbō Kikai; in *Myōe Shōnin shiryō* (Tōkyō Daigaku Shuppankai, 1971), vol. 1, pp. 302–3; translation from Plutschow, *Chaos and Cosmos*, p. 22. The conversation is probably apocryphal, since Myōe was only seventeen years old when Saigyō died. Saigyō certainly took the relationship of waka and the Buddhist Dharma seriously; it is possible that as a teenager Myōe attended a lecture by Saigyō and later reported his words. As part of the hagiographic process, the lecture might later have been transformed into a personal conversation. But given how well this comment corresponds with a similar statement by the thirteenth-century poet-priest Mūjū Ichien, it seems more likely to be a thirteenth-century addition.

will necessarily be a favorable response. When they embody the spirit of the Buddha's Law, there can be no doubt that they are dharani.

The words of India, China, and Japan differ, but their meanings are mutual and their results the same. Through them Buddhism spread, its doctrines were accepted, and the benefits have not been without avail. . . . The efficacy of Japanese poetry and the nature of mystic verses are in every respect to be understood as identical with dharani.[15]

This identification of waka and dharani, that a waka in and of itself can have magical efficacy if it embodies the spirit of the Buddhist Dharma, is a basic assumption in Tameaki's commentaries. Take, for example, the preface to *Waka chiken shū*:

In India there are the words (*kotoba* 言葉) of dharani. In China [dharani] were produced in the form of verses (*shi* 詩) and divided into six kinds. Among these six, the style of Japanese poetry has been continuously practiced in our country since the ancient age of the gods even unto this degenerate age. . . . Japanese poetry, combining diction (*kotoba*) and sentiment (*kokoro* 心), is "greatly harmonizing" 大和, and so it is called "greatly harmonizing poetry" (*Yamato uta* 大和歌).[16]

In other words, Japanese poetry (*Yamato uta*) is the "great harmonizer" and combines the essence of Sanskrit dharani and Chinese poetry. *Waka Kokin kanjō no maki* makes the point even more succinctly: "The words of Indian dharani are the words of our country of Yamato's poetry."[17] This work further argues for the chanting of certain waka as a powerfully efficacious Buddhist ritual and justifies this by revealing their esoteric links to Sanskrit seed syllables (J. *shūji* 種子, Sk. *bīja*) and Buddhist mantras. For example, *Waka Kokin kanjō no maki* claims that each line of the "Naniwazu" (Naniwa Bay) poem from the *Kokin shū* preface can be identified with a Sanskrit seed syllable (A, BI, RA, UN, and KEN) and that the poem as a whole thus functions as a mantra, whose recitation helps one better retain the true meaning of Shingon.[18] In commentaries such as these, far from being an impediment

15. Translation (modified) from Morrell, *Sand and Pebbles*, pp. 163–65.

16. Kunaichō *Waka chiken shū*, p. 97. Kushida Ryōko (*Zoku Shingon mikkyō seiritsu katei no kenkyū*, p. 524) cites a similar line from a Ryōbu Shinto text associated with the Hōbōtei-in, dated 1384: "Kōbō Daishi received this oracle from the Grand Shrine [at Ise] and recorded it as a secret matter. Dharani takes the form of Sanskrit poetry in India, Chinese poetry in China, and waka poetry in this country. Consider this deeply; it is a very profound secret."

17. *Waka Kokin kanjō no maki*, p. 467.

18. Ibid., p. 467.

to enlightenment, the "wild words and ornate phrases" of Japanese poetry are so efficacious that the simple act of chanting a poem leads to better understanding of the true meaning of esoteric Buddhism and is therefore to be treated as an important esoteric practice.

Honji suijaku

According to *honji suijaku,* Buddhist deities and kami are "not two, but identical in nature" (*funi dōtai* 不二胴体). Originally, this created a two-tiered effect: the kami were merely "phenomenal appearance," the expedient means by which the Japanese were prepared for the higher truth of Buddhist "Absolute Reality." However, by the Kamakura period, nondualism had been appropriated by Shinto apologists: if the kami and buddhas were like waves and water (i.e., inseparable aspects of the same reality), then neither took precedence.

The Kamakura commentaries argue that kami such as Sumiyoshi Daimyōjin and Tamatsushima Myōjin, who in the medieval period were worshipped as guardian deities of waka poetry, were *suijaku* manifestations whose true purpose was to transmit Buddhist enlightenment through poetry. They also argue that certain important human poets (most often Ariwara no Narihira and Kakinomoto no Hitomaro) were incarnations of kami and Buddhist deities who manifested themselves in human form to further the Path of Poetry as a path to enlightenment.

An example from *Gyokuden jinpi no maki* illustrates the three concepts of *honji suijaku,* expedient means, and nondualism at work: "The Buddhist Dharma and *Ise monogatari* differ only in name, not in substance. Narihira was incarnated and dwelt in this world; he hid the deep secrets of Shingon in a frivolous tale in order to benefit and enlighten each and every living being about the deep meaning of the profound Dharma. This tale is none other than an esoteric practice of Shingon."[19] Narihira, originally a Buddhist deity who chose to become temporarily incarnated in human form, wrote *Ise monogatari* as an expedient device. The commentary implicitly assumes that although at first *Ise monogatari* appears to be a secular text, properly initiated readers will understand it as a profoundly religious document: the Buddhist Dharma and *Ise monogatari* are "not two, but identical in nature."

---

19. *Gyokuden jinpi no maki,* pp. 536–37.

This interpretive strategy was also quite useful in resolving more mundane scholarly disputes. For example, *Kokin waka shū jo kikigaki* notes a disagreement between two important poetic scholars, Ki no Tsurayuki and Minamoto no Toshiyori (Shunrai), regarding which god originated the practice of poetry:

> Query: In Shunrai's diary we find "Japanese poetry was originated by Kunitokotachi no Mikoto." But in Tsurayuki's preface it says that it was originated by Izanagi no Mikoto. Please explain this discrepancy. Also in the *Nihon shoki* (Record of Japan) we find poems by Izanagi but not Kunitokotachi; why is this?
>
> Reply: Izanagi and Kunitokotachi . . . are one essential body with two names. Because they are in reality only one, Shunrai attributed Izanagi's poem to Kunitokotachi.[20]

The interpretation combines *honji suijaku* thinking with nondualism but with a new twist: the two kami who appear provisionally to be separate are actually one. This combination was a convenient and powerful interpretive tool for resolving discrepancies. The more heavily esoteric commentaries use it repeatedly.

Within Tameaki's commentaries the concepts of *honji suijaku*, nondualism, and expedient means both legitimate his use of etymological allegoresis and form the content of that allegoresis. Graphs are analyzed to reveal that certain poets were *suijaku* manifestations of kami and Buddhist deities as well as to prove the nonduality of waka and Buddhist formulas. Given the assumptions with which the interpreters started, these readings could have been predicted in advance. The question was not so much *what* interpretation they would reach, but *how* they would arrive at that pre-ordained reading. Jacqueline Stone makes a similar point about the use of etymological and numerological allegoresis (which she calls *kanjin*-style interpretation) in medieval Tendai secret oral transmissions (*kuden*):

> What all *kanjin*-style readings have in common is that, from a modern perspective, they are not *exegesis*, the "reading out" from a text to determine its meaning, though the medieval thinkers who produced them may often have understood what they were doing as uncovering the text's true purport. Rather they are a deliberate *eisegesis* or "reading in" that reconfigures the text in support of a prior insight or philosophical position—in this case, that of original enlightenment. It is this prior insight or position, not the text itself, that forms the basis of interpretation.[21]

---

20. *Kokin waka shū jo kikigaki*, p. 231.

21. Stone, *Original Enlightenment and the Transformation of Medieval Japanese Buddhism*, p. 158.

As Stone notes, in the case of the medieval Tendai *kuden* the *a priori* insight used to reconfigure the text is inevitably Original Enlightenment (*hongaku* 本学). As we shall see, in Tameaki's secret transmissions, each text is revealed to be an instance of a syncretic Shinto-Buddhist/Tachikawa understanding of *honji suijaku* and radical nondualism.

To understand the thinking behind etymological allegoresis, we need to discuss one more concept: the belief that language, when analyzed properly, has the potential to reveal the nature of both phenomenal reality and Absolute Reality.

The Magical Efficacy of Language and Early Uses of Paronomasia

Maureen Quilligan and Angus Fletcher agree, and it seems to hold in the Japanese context, that religious allegory and allegoresis presuppose at least a potential sacralizing power of language, a potency, a magic efficacy, that is rooted in a deeper-level unity with phenomenal reality. This is the faith that lies behind allegorical interpretation's punning paronomastic etymologies, its complex metonymies that give semantic force to proper names, and its reliance on analogical correspondences to unify microcosmos and macrocosmos. Correct interpretation of this system of correspondences reveals an "immanent logos" that ties language and phenomenal reality together. When language is believed to be empty of power and merely an arbitrary, transparent, neutral tool to be used as people see fit, allegory as narrative disappears.[22]

The idea that language has a magic phenomenality was certainly not particular to Buddhism: the notion of *kotodama* 言霊, that certain words (*koto* 言) have spirit (*tama* 霊) and therefore magical efficacy, has a long history within Japanese culture.[23] But the question remains: Where did the etymological and numerological allegoresis that came into widespread use in medieval Japan first arise?

According to Neil McMullin, etymological paronomasia was a factor in the creation of religious rituals beginning at least in the Nara period. In ana-

22. Quilligan (*Language of Allegory*, pp. 157–58) explains the seeming paradox of the reemergence of allegory in the twentieth century as the result of the current fascination with language; language may be "arbitrary," but it has once again become all-powerful in its ability to mediate reality at every level, conscious and unconscious.

23. See the discussion of *kotodama* in Plutschow, *Chaos and Cosmos*, pp. 75–87.

lyzing the development of the Gion Shrine cult of *goryō* (御霊, angry spirits who cause disease), he argues that paronomastic verbal association "played a key role in the development of cults."[24] Etymological paronomasia has two main strategies: graphic paronomasia resolves the written graph into its component parts and uses the parts as justification for the ritual usage or interpretation; homophonic paronomasia equates disparate entities through the aural resemblance of their names.

As an example of graphic paronomasia, McMullin cites a story in the *Bingo fudoki,* a topographical record of the Bingo province (modern Hiroshima prefecture) composed in the Nara period. The story explains the ritual use of a wreath of miscanthus reeds (*chi no wa*) to protect the wearer from disease. In his analysis of the relationship of the story to the development of the *goryō* ritual, McMullin notes that the graph used for *chi* (茅 miscanthus reed) in *chi no wa,* is composed of two parts. The upper part (艸) denotes grass (*kusa*), and the bottom part (矛) means spear or halberd (*hoko*), a long-handled weapon with a battle-ax at one end. The obvious explanation for the halberd in the ritual is that it is a symbol of "the power of the *goryō* ritual to destroy the effects of the activities of disease-causing divinities and departed spirits."[25] But McMullin also suspects that its use might be related to the fact that the graph for halberd appears in the graph for miscanthus. The reverse could be true, however: long, thin objects, including swords and halberds, were often used in shamanic rituals to entice spirits to possess the shaman. It may be that the miscanthus reed was seen as potentially protective because its long, thin shape makes it a "grass" form of "halberd."

A second method of producing ritual objects was based on homophonic paronomasia. McMullin notes the example of an amulet to ward off disease produced from eastward-protruding branches of willow trees. Eastward branches were probably chosen because east was the direction associated with disease and death. The willow branch, when bent to form a pentagonal star, was thought to have prophylactic powers. It seems likely that the pentagonal shape (*goryō* 五稜) was chosen because it was homophonic with the supposed cause of the illness: malevolent deceased spirits (*goryō* 御霊). As McMullin argues, "That the pentagonal star and the deceased spirit

24. McMullin, "On Placating the Gods and Pacifying the Populace: The Case of the Gion *Goryō* Cult," p. 275.

25. Ibid., p. 285.

ritual have the same pronunciation is, I suggest, neither accidental nor trivial, for such homophonous similarities constituted one major mechanism, probably the single most important mechanism, whereby early Japanese made identifications between otherwise seemingly disparate entities."[26]

In this early period, however, paronomastic analysis remains implicit rather than explicit. It is possible for a contemporary scholar such as McMullin to discern uses of paronomasia by early Japanese to produce rituals and ritual objects, but there are no examples of Japanese themselves performing this kind of interpretive analysis to justify such practices. It is not until the twelfth or thirteenth centuries that we begin to see conscious paronomastic interpretation and etymologizing by Japanese themselves. And when such examples do appear, they are used mainly to justify Taoist divination practices or *honji suijaku* identifications.

Paronomasia in Medieval Japanese Taoism

A long tradition within Taoism emphasizes written characters as talismans to be used in combination with spoken spells. The Taoist analysis of graphs to prophesy the future undoubtedly had a significant influence on the development of etymological paronomasia within Chinese and Japanese Buddhism.[27] Examples of etymological paronomasia used as an interpretive tool within Japanese Yin-Yang divination begin to appear around the twelfth century in texts such as Ōe no Masafusa's *Gōdan shō* (Selection of Ōe's conversations), a series of short essays transcribed from Masafusa's conversations by Fujiwara no Sanekane (1085–1112).[28] The text includes the following anecdote about a prophecy made in a dream to Fujiwara no Kaneie, who was known as the "Great Lay Priest," in which homophonic paronomasia played a role.

---

26. Ibid., p. 275.

27. Although it shows up again and again in the medieval Japanese Taoism, I have not had much luck in finding this kind of analysis in the scholarship on Chinese Taoist divination. Ch'en Hsiang-Ch'un ("Examples of Charm Against Epidemics with Short Explanations," pp. 37–38) analyzes fifteen Taoist talisman inscriptions and notes that "charm writers often resorted to play puns on words," but only one of his examples appears to involve punning.

28. Ōe no Masafusa (1041–1111) was an excellent scholar of Chinese; *Gōdan shō* is mainly a commentary on the *Wakan rōei shū*, with a few anecdotes such as this one, which eulogizes Masafusa's great-grandfather, Ōe no Masahira (952–1012).

When the Great Lay Priest was a major counselor he dreamt of crossing the Ōsaka Barrier in the falling snow. The barrier was completely white. He was greatly shocked by this dream, supposing that snow was an unlucky omen. He sent for a dream interpreter and related the dream. The man said, "Your dream was a most auspicious one. You have definitely nothing to worry about. Somebody is certain to offer you a mottled ox." Thereupon a man did indeed offer him a mottled ox, and Kaneie rewarded the dream interpreter. When Ōe no Masahira came to call, Kaneie related what had happened. Masahira was astonished. He urged Kaneie to take back the reward from the dream interpreter, and gave his own interpretation of the dream: "The Ōsaka Barrier contains the same character *kan* 関 as used in *kanpaku* 関白 [regent]. The snow is white, written with the character *haku* 白. It means that you are without question going to become the *kanpaku*." Kaneie was overcome with emotion. In the following year he was appointed as *kanpaku*.[29]

It is not clear how the first interpreter came to analyze the dream as foretelling the gift of a mottled ox, but he was probably working with the visual imagery of a barrier mottled with snow. The superior interpretation by Ōe no Masahira translates the visual images of the barrier (*kan* 関) and the whiteness of the snow (*haku* 白) into their written counterparts and then combines those graphs to create a new word, *kanpaku* (関白 regent), which forms the basis for the prophecy. Here we see the notion that the proper analysis of homophonic graphs not only can tell us about origins but can also illustrate the deeper connections between an object's essential nature and its phenomenal reality. When read correctly, through an etymological analysis that combines visual and verbal metaphors into a kind of prophetic synethesia, graphs have the power to reveal the future as well.

Another example of prophetic synethesia can be found in the didactic tale collection *Jikkin shō* (Selection of anecdotes illustrating ten moral principles; ca. 1252), but here the analysis is based on graphic paronomasia:

In the chamber of Empress Akiko[30] a dog gave birth to puppies. Since this was an unexpected good omen, the Empress was greatly excited and asked the scholar Ōe no Masahira its meaning. He replied, "This is a propitious occurrence. The character for dog consists of the character for 'big' with a short stroke written beside it (犬). If instead this short character should be written above the character, it becomes the character for 'heaven' 天. If written below, the character becomes that for

29. Ōe no Masafusa, *Gōdan shō*, pp. 37–38; translation from Keene, *Seeds in the Heart*, pp. 580–81. Although Fujiwara no Kaneie lived in the tenth century, there are no contemporaneous accounts of this event, and it is probably apocryphal.

30. Daughter of Fujiwara no Michinaga and consort of Emperor Ichijō (r. 986–1011).

'noble' 太. If the character for child 子 is written following either of these characters, the results are the combinations 'emperor' 天子 and 'prince' 太子, respectively. Therefore, you shall bear a prince, and he will surely become emperor."[31]

As Masahiro had predicted, Empress Akiko became pregnant with the future Emperor Go-Ichijō (r. 1016–36), but her labor was difficult and painful. Frantic with worry, her father, Fujiwara no Michinaga, raised a great commotion:

> Throwing open the partitions in front of him he ran outside crying, "What is to be done about this? The chanting of the sutras must be increased." Before he had even finished speaking, Fujiwara no Arikuni, who was still young at the time, said, "The delivery is now over. There is no need to increase the sutras." As he said this, a lady-in-waiting ran up and said, "The baby has been born."
>
> After things settled down, Arikuni was summoned and Michinaga inquired, "How on earth did you know that the baby had been born?" Arikuni replied, "Since the word for partition is written 'hindering a child' (障子) I knew the baby had been born."[32]

In the first part of the story, the components of the graph for dog (犬) are rearranged in various ways and then added to the graph for child (子). These manipulations are used to support an auspicious prophecy that Empress Akiko will bear a much-wished-for son. In the second part, the word for "partition" (障子 *shōji*) is analyzed into its component graphs 子 (child) and 障 (hindrance). When Michinaga threw open the partitions, Arikuni "saw" that the hindrances to the child had been overcome and that the baby had been safely delivered.[33]

The use of homophonic and graphic paronomasia in prophecies probably formed the background for the development of the etymological paronomasia used in esoteric Buddhism as a technique to syncretize native kami and Buddhist deities. The historical relationship remains very unclear, however. We know that by the twelfth century a lineage of scholarly monks had

---

31. Translation (modified) from Geddes, "A Partial Translation and Study of the *Jikkinshō*," p. 165.

32. Ibid., pp. 165–66.

33. Although Empress Akiko's pregnancy and labor are extensively described in *Eiga monogatari* (A tale of flowering fortunes; ca. 1092), the historical chronicle of Michinaga's time, neither of these incidents is mentioned. Once again the story is probably apocryphal, an indication that this kind of graphic analysis dates to a somewhat later period. See McCullough and McCullough, *A Tale of Flowering Fortune*, vol. 1, pp. 272–73.

emerged within Tendai Buddhism's syncretic cult of Sannō Shinto, which attempted to assimilate the Hie Shrines at the foot of Mount Hiei into the Tendai complex. This lineage was known as *kike* 記家, a name that combines the graphs for "record, chronicle" and "family, lineage." It may have been the *kike* who first used paronomasia as a consistent strategy.

Paronomasia and the Chroniclers of Mount Hiei

The Tendai *kike* specialized in the commentary, interpretation, and transmission of a mass of textual material collectively known as *kiroku* (記録, recorded documents). In an article on the development of the *kike*, Kuroda Toshio argues that not until the late thirteenth to early fourteenth century do we find evidence of any systematic attempts to organize the study of these documents or see a specific scholarly lineage being called *kike*.[34] For example, in the early fourteenth century Enkan (1281–1356) wrote in his autobiography that doctrinal study at Mount Hiei consisted of four fields in ascending order of importance: exoteric (*ken* 顕), esoteric (*mitsu* 密), discipline (*kai* 戒), and documents (*ki*[*roku*] 記[録]). The field of documents was further divided into six subjects of study: temples and sacred grounds, statues and paintings, miraculous manifestations in the form of kami, protection of the state, rituals, and practices of meditation. To judge from these remarks, the *kike* were firmly established on Mount Hiei by the late thirteenth century. However, since texts that fit Enkan's definition of "documents" were being produced as early as the twelfth century, we can assume that something like the *kike* were in existence at that time.[35]

According to Kuroda, the *kike* monks defined their mission as the study and mystical interpretation of the documents.[36] Their insights were passed on through oral transmissions (*kuden* 口伝). These oral transmissions, despite their name, did not exclude writing: "One of the peculiarities of oral

---

34. Kuroda Toshio, "Historical Consciousness and *Hon-jaku* philosophy in the Medieval Period on Mount Hiei," pp. 143–58. See also Stone, *Original Enlightenment and the Transformation of Medieval Japanese Buddhism*, pp. 123–30.

35. Hazama Jikō (*Nihon Bukkyō no kaiten to sono kichō*, pp. 245–66) argues that the *kike* probably originated in the late twelfth century, but that development and systematization began with Gigen at the close of the thirteenth century and ended with Kōsō in the first part of the fourteenth century. At that point the *kike* retroactively claimed that the founder of the lineage was Kenshin (1130–92).

36. Kuroda, "Historical Consciousness," p. 149.

transmission was its systematic recording of experiences, in-depth interpretations, or essential points of doctrine and practice."[37] The term *kuden* nevertheless implies that even in written form the text can be correctly understood only in the context of master-to-disciple teaching. Transmissions were written down to serve as a reminder for those who received them and also, undoubtedly, because simple possession served as a form of legitimating authority. Eventually such copies took the form of secret transmissions written on strips of paper (*kirigami* 切紙) as short sentences, verses, or episodic reminiscences. Over time they were annotated with addenda, revisions, and corrections. By the thirteenth century, transmission lineages (*kechimyakufu*) began to be attached to the *kirigami* as an added guarantee of their legitimacy and authority.

Each of Enkan's four fields also had its own initiation and ordination ceremony (*kanjō*). The *kanjō* for the field of documents was called the "initiation concerning dimming of radiance and mingling with dust to protect and benefit the national territory" (和光同塵利益国土灌頂 *wakō dōjin riyaku kokudo kanjō*). According to Kuroda, this name makes it clear that the ultimate duty of the *kike* was the study of the Shinto-Buddhist system of the Hie shrines, because that system held the key to the protection of the state. By carefully studying both contemporary and historical events at these shrines, the *kike* hoped to understand when and how buddhas and bodhisattvas manifested themselves as kami to protect the state. And the key to this was the study of documents.

Toward the end of the Heian period and throughout the Kamakura and Muromachi periods, a number of documents offering various rationales for syncretic identifications were composed on Mount Hiei, with the result that the associated kami and buddhas came to be seen as a single but complex, multilayered entity, to which the name Sannō 山王 was given. The *kike*'s primary goal was to show the ultimate identity of Shinto and Buddhism in the service of the state. In pursuit of this goal, new modes of rationalizing syncretization were developed, including the method that I have called "etymological allegoresis" because it uses etymological paronomasia as a means to syncretize native deities with Buddhism. This method of syncretization appears to have spread rapidly to Shingon Buddhism and then to other sects.

Alicia Matsunaga discusses an excellent example of etymological allegoresis used to rationalize the syncretization of the Sannō deity with Buddhist

37. Ibid., p. 147.

deities and principles. According to a medieval biography of the Tendai priest Gyōen (?–1047), the Sannō deity appeared to Gyōen and told him the following:

Do you know why I am called Sannō? I signify that three truths are one. The three [vertical] strokes of *san* 山 denote emptiness [*kū* 究], temporariness [*ke* 假], and the mean [*chū* 中]. The underlying stroke signifies oneness. *Oo* 王 consists of three [horizontal] strokes standing for the three truths while the center symbolizes oneness. So the two characters have three strokes and one common stroke. That is why I am called Sannō Myōjin. This means that all the underlying truths are in one mind and three thousand minds in one mind. Therefore I protect my Tendai and give peace to the country. There is no name without body and no body without name. There is no Dharma without name, and there is no name without Dharma. Body is Dharma—Dharma is name. This is called one vehicle. This is the meaning of my name.[38]

Gyōen's biography is found in a collection compiled in the early Edo period from a number of medieval sources, and it is difficult to date. It unlikely, however, that this kind of etymological analysis would have been produced during Gyōen's lifetime. The story's similarity to one in a text written by the Tendai monk Shinga (1329–?) makes it more probable that the story was produced in the Kamakura period, when the Sannō deity was widely worshipped on Mount Hiei and there would have been pressure to tie it to other aspects of Tendai Buddhism.[39] The graphs for Sannō are analyzed to reveal a hidden correspondence with the fundamental three-part Tendai doctrine of emptiness (all dharma are empty), temporariness (they appear to have provisional existence), and the middle path, which unites the other two. These three ways of viewing existence stand in a relation of conditional interdependence, a relation that is summed up in the phrase, *sandai ichijitsu* (三諦一実, three [relative] truths, one [absolute] truth). The two graphs in

38. Shiban, *Honchō kōsōden*, p. 680; translation from Matsunaga, *The Buddhist Philosophy of Assimilation*, pp. 190–91.

39. Shinga wrote: "The Buddha Śākyamuni now has manifested itself at the foot of Mt. Hiei as a divine entity known as Sannō. The purpose of this divine entity is to grant its protection to the practice of the Single-minded Threefold Contemplation. The divine entity revealed the following in an oracle to Abbot Kyōmyō: 'My name consists of a horizontal stroke striking three vertical strokes, and of one vertical stroke striking three horizontal strokes'" (Kojima and Fukuhara, "Tendai kuden hōmon no kyōdō kenkyū," p. 202; translation from Grapard, "Linguistic Cubism: A Singularity of Pluralism in the Sannō Cult," p. 226).

the name "Sannō" are made up of three parallel strokes with a fourth, unifying stroke, thus graphically symbolizing this relation.

The last part of the passage is particularly noteworthy, for it illustrates the philosophical basis for the persuasive authority of this kind of wordplay. The body, the dharma that make up that body, and the name attached to the body are indivisibly related; thus correct analysis of a name provides insight into the essence of what is named and, by extension, into the nature of reality. The discussion of the meaning of the title *Ise monogatari* in the Sanjōnishi lineage *Waka chiken shū* makes clear the commentary's assumption that names are not simply arbitrary: "The myriad things arise from their names, in accordance with the principle that the name is the result of the essential nature of the graph."[40] For the religious commentaries in particular, this principle is fundamental; their approach to textual analysis depends on a nonarbitrary relationship between words and both Absolute and phenomenal reality.

Once etymological allegoresis had been established as a means to assimilate kami into Buddhism, it began to be deployed as a strategy for syncretizing all aspects of Shinto ritual and associated practices. Take the following homophonic analysis of the term *miko* (usually written 巫女) from a thirteenth-century Tendai text, *Yōten ki* (Record of heavenly radiance):

> Shamanesses are called *miko*, a term written in this shrine with graphs meaning August Child 御子, because they serve the function of calling upon the compassion of Shakamuni Buddha and Yakushi,[41] who appeared originally as the Yin and Yang deities. Here is how this developed: in the past, a certain Jichi-in lived on the mountain. His knowledge had no boundaries. One day he gave the following instructions to a woman living in Kitsuji: "Go home and become a servant to Sannō. At the time of making offerings, you will begin an invocation with the catalpa bow that will enable you to guess the thoughts of someone without looking directly at that person. When you sound the string of the bow, Amida Buddha will come from the Pure Land, enter your mouth and tell you the thoughts and requests of those people." . . . The Original Ground of the Great Deity (daimyōjin) at the Grand Shrine is Shakamuni Buddha, who said "Everything in the three realms is mine. All living be-

---

40. Kunaichō *Waka chiken shū*, p. 117.

41. Yakushi (Medicine Master) is a popular buddha whose full name is Yakushi Rurikō Butsu (Master of Medicine Buddha of the Land of Emerald Light, Sk. Bhaiṣajyā-guru-vaiḍūryā-prabha). While a bodhisattva he made twelve vows, including a vow to cure beings of physical imperfections such as disease.

ings are my children." So the shamanesses who serve him when he appears in his Manifest Trace form as a kami should be referred to as his August Children.[42]

In this example of paronomasia, homophonic graphs (*ateji*) for *miko* that mean "august child" 御子 are substituted for the usual graphs. An etymological anecdote then appropriates the shamanic function of shrine priestesses into Buddhist rituals. The predicates of the "true" graphs for *miko* dictate the meaning and function of the real-world referent. The priority given to the written graph in passages like this makes it obvious that power inheres in the proper knowledge and interpretation of written signs: they are clues to the essential character of reality. The abundance of homophones in Japanese greatly expands the opportunities for such etymological play, and medieval Japanese scholars, both religious and literary, took full advantage of these opportunities.

An example of graphic paronomasia from *Yōten ki* also illustrates that the graph as signifier was thought to have an inherent, nonarbitrary relation to what it signified: "If you add the element meaning "tree" 木 to the left side of the graph usually read *kami* 神, it results in the graph read *sakaki* 榊. This explains why the *sakaki* tree is used in rituals and offerings on Mount Hiei."[43] The modern explanation of this character would be that when the Chinese writing system was introduced, the *sakaki* tree was the most important sacred tree in rituals involving the kami, and a graph that reflected that use was created. In the *Yōten ki*, however, the rationale is reversed: the *sakaki* tree was chosen for use in rituals because the graph used to write its name signaled that it was most appropriate for that purpose. Once again, we find the belief that since names and the graphs used to write them have a pre-existing relationship with their referent in the real world, correct analysis of the graph reveals those hidden sympathetic harmonies.

Kuroda divides the oral transmissions transmitted by the Tendai *kike* into two groups. One group tends to focus on esoteric texts and provides specific examples of magical formulas, theories and maxims, mystical apothegms, and poetry attributed to the patriarchal founders of Tendai. These fragments, supposedly taken from ancient documents, formed the basis for oral transmissions containing "poetry and formulas expressing the sacred and secret character of a mystical world."[44] The other group tends toward

---

42. *Yōten ki*, p. 619; translation (modified) from Grapard, "Linguistic Cubism," p. 218.
43. *Yōten ki*, pp. 612–14; translation (modified) from Grapard, "Linguistic Cubism," p. 219.
44. Kuroda, "Historical Consciousness," p. 154.

the anecdotal (*setsuwa-teki* 説話的), such as stories about manifestations of deities and miraculous occurrences involving historical figures. Kuroda describes this group as generally based in historical events and having a narrative bent; they tend toward fictionalized historicism. The contents seem quite similar, and probably overlap with, the origin stories of temple-shrine complexes and hagiographies of important religious figures that were popularized in the medieval period. This category of texts was probably considered somewhat more exoteric and was thus more widely disseminated. Kuroda also notes that a number of texts belonging to the first group deal with the Original Ground (*honji*, i.e., Buddhism), whereas texts belonging to the second group relate to matters pertaining to Manifest Traces (*suijaku*, i.e., Shinto).[45] To a certain extent, it is possible to categorize Fujiwara no Tameaki's commentaries in a similar way. Although there is a good deal of overlap in the contents of the two groupings, beginning and intermediate-level commentaries such as *Kokin waka shū jo kikigaki* are primarily anecdotal and historical; advanced-level commentaries such as *Gyokuden jinpi no maki* and *Waka Kokin kanjō no maki* are more esoteric and transcendent.

A few larger questions remain. Why did the *kike* lineage of scholarly monks come into existence, along with a mass of textual material transmitted secretly through *kanjō* initiations? And how did this culture of secret transmission move beyond the confines of shrine-temple complexes to become such a widespread feature of medieval Japanese culture generally?

The Culture of Secret Transmission in Medieval Japan

Within Japanese esoteric Buddhism at least as far back as Saichō (767–822), oral transmissions were used to transmit matters of faith and religious principle directly from master to disciple, but they were never a primary focus.[46] By the late thirteenth century, however, secret oral transmissions and initiations, backed by transmission lineage documents, had become the norm within both Tendai lineages and poetry families. And by the Muromachi period, secret transmission was the normative mode of transmitting knowledge in Japanese culture generally. It appeared in all schools of Buddhism,

45. Ibid.

46. For two examples of references to oral transmission in Saichō's works, see Stone, *Original Enlightenment*, p. 119. Stone cites Hazama Jikō in support of the position that there is no evidence that secret transmission played any important role in early Tendai.

Shugendō (mountain asceticism), Yin-Yang divination, and esoteric Shinto. It also spread to such other arts as Noh theater, calligraphy, landscape garden design, tea ceremony, sword making, and *biwa* recitation.[47]

Although concrete evidence is lacking, scholars generally acknowledge parallels between the culture of secret oral transmission within esoteric Buddhism and a similar emphasis on secret traditions among aristocratic poetry families. In fact, the timing of this development and similarities in content and method are striking enough that it is hard not to suppose that the development was encouraged by a number of shared determining factors.

One of the most important factors was simply that by the late Heian period, most of the high-ranking positions within the Tendai establishment on Mount Hiei were dominated by younger sons of the aristocracy. Neil McMullin notes that whereas in the early Heian period monks attained high monastic office primarily on the basis of character (virtue and intelligence) and seniority in Buddhist orders, this changed toward the end of the tenth century. The turning point came when the eighteenth head priest (*zasu* 座主) of Enryaku-ji, Ryōgen (912–85), adopted as his successor a younger son of Fujiwara no Morosuke (908–60), the head of the dominant Northern branch of the Fujiwara at the time. Whereas Ryōgen himself came from an obscure background and reached the heights of the sacerdotal elite through sheer intelligence and ambition, after his death, "blood took precedence over brains; it became much more important for a monk to have the proper family lineage than to have a profound knowledge of the sutras, a reputation for holiness, or seniority in orders."[48] The "aristocratization" of elite levels of the Tendai hierarchy became increasingly widespread until by the period 1070 to 1190 only 10 percent of monks who became the head priests of Enraku-ji or the chief abbots (*bettō* 別当) of Kōfuku-ji or who figured prominently in the annual court-sponsored lectures on the sutras came from a commoner (*shomin* 庶民) background.[49] This aristocratization meant

47. See, e.g., the discussion of the development of secret transmissions on landscape gardening in Slawson, *Secret Teachings in the Art of Japanese Gardens: Design Principles, Aesthetic Values*, pp. 46–53. Slawson notes that although Tachibana no Toshitsuna (1028–94) wrote a treatise on landscape gardening, *Sakuteiki* (Notes on garden making), it was not until the late thirteenth century (1289) that a colophon urging secrecy was added. Like me, he sees the economic decline of the aristocracy as an important factor behind the new emphasis on secrecy.

48. McMullin, "The *Lotus Sutra* and Politics in the Mid-Heian Period," p. 136.

49. See the statistics in Stone, *Original Enlightenment*, pp. 110–11; citing Hirata Toshiharu, *Sōhei to bushi*, pp. 105–8.

constant interactions and mutual influence between court families and the temple-shrine complex on Mount Hiei.

Concurrent political and economic changes were having a decisive effect on the aristocracy. Allan Grapard attributes the development of syncretic deities such as Sannō as well as the culture of secret transmission on Mount Hiei to late Heian political and economic insecurity. The aristocracy was gradually losing control of the country to warrior families. In addition, a series of natural disasters, graphically described in Kamo no Chōmei's *Hōjō ki* (Record of my hut; ca. 1212), were seen as evidence that the world had entered a "degenerate age" (*mappō*). Grapard argues that the shrines and temples of the cultic centers formalized systematic relations between the kami and Buddhist deities in order to stabilize their doctrinal, political, and economic position. By establishing strong relations between the kami and Buddhist deities, the shrine-temple multiplexes and the families affiliated with them hoped to gain enough strength to survive the crises befalling the country.[50]

Within the court proper, as discussed in Chapter 5, families such as the Rokujō and later the Mikohidari that had been pushed out of the higher levels of political power but who had strong poetic credentials could turn to their proprietary knowledge of obscure terms and poetic ritual to secure a place in the increasingly competitive court bureaucracy, as purveyors of such knowledge to would-be poets from emperors to samurai. In other words, the systematic development of pedagogies of secret initiation and transmission that could be used as cultural capital in either the religious or the secular sphere was an aristocratic response to the economic and political insecurity Grapard discusses.

A related factor was the problem of inheritance. Even on Mount Hiei, the *kike*, despite being clerics, often handed down secret traditions to their own sons (*shintei* 真弟, true disciples). The graph for *ke* (家 family) in *kike* 記家 thus functioned literally and not in the metaphorical sense of the term as "lineage," which is the more usual meaning in religious institutions. Because the master was often transmitting his knowledge not to his best and brightest disciple but to his son, some of the same difficulties that plagued poetry families at court appeared. The most obvious problem was dealing with incompetent offspring. In poetry families, the son was supposed to be

50. Grapard, *Protocols of the Gods: A Study of the Kasuga Cult in Japanese History*, p. 79.

capable of writing superlative poetry. In religious families, the son needed to be good at theorizing and disseminating religious doctrine. In both cases, any lack of aptitude could now be replaced, or at least supplemented, with a family tradition of secret knowledge that was resistant to more rationalized forms of theory. The claim was made that this secret tradition was based on knowledge gained through actual personal experience of historical events (passed down from antiquity within the family) or through mystical experiences (such as dream oracles from a deity). Because it was anecdotal and mystical, it could not be gained through the kind of logical deduction that informs theoretical treatises. It appealed to a different kind of authority, that of tradition, rather than persuasive logic. Armed with the superior authority of this tradition, even a mediocre son could assert his right to lead, whether within the religious hierarchy or in court poetry circles.

In analyzing medieval Tendai *kuden* lineages, Jacqueline Stone points to another factor in the development of the culture of secret transmission: an increasing emphasis on the correct performance of ritual, both religious and secular. According to Stone, the tenth-century prohibition on private sponsorship of rituals for the health of the emperor, fertility of imperial consorts, protection of the country, good harvests, and the like was mainly honored in the breach by the late Heian period. Sponsorship of esoteric rituals by individual nobles cemented ties between individual master-disciple lineages of esoteric ritual specialists and specific factions among the ruling elites and thereby played a role in the system of shifting alliances (*kenmon taisei* 権門体制) that formed the dominant power structure of the medieval period. As demand for these rituals grew and the competition among esoteric lineages for aristocratic patronage became fiercer, the rituals became more complex and more innovative. Stone argues that it was most likely this kind of competition that led lineages to emphasize the uniqueness of their own rites and to develop methods of secret transmission to protect that uniqueness.[51]

Stone suggests that with the increasing proliferation of rival lineages, each with its own secret knowledge of ritual form, the differences between lineages were no longer defined by doctrine:

> The differences among these schools were not chiefly [ones] of doctrine, but of concrete ritual forms (*jisō* 事相), such as mudras, mantras, and other secret formulas (*hihō* 秘法) used in esoteric rituals. What direction the altar should face, what deity

51. Stone, *Original Enlightenment*, p. 108.

should be enshrined as the object of worship (*honzon* 本尊) and what form it should take, what mantras or dharani should be recited and how many times, what offerings made, and so forth all came under the category of *jisō*; on their proper performance, the efficacy of the ritual was thought to depend. Such matters readily lent themselves to construction as secret knowledge and were kept hidden and transmitted orally and in private from master to disciple.[52]

Again, a similar argument could be made about the proliferation of poetic lineages. Although modern scholars focus mainly on stylistic differences between, say, the Reizei and the Nijō family adherents, at the time, the information considered most vital to the continuance of the family, and therefore most secret, was knowledge about the proper protocol for the various highly ritualized events involving waka poetry. Each poetry family warned its adherents that lacking its proprietary information on protocol, the beginning poet was prone to grave breaches of etiquette. Fujiwara no Tameaki may have gone to an extreme when he created an esoteric waka ceremony, along with specifications for the objects of worship, waka mantras, offerings, and so on. Nevertheless, in the poetry families generally, it was understood that poetic talent was ineffable and could not necessarily be taught; instead, what was taught were secret teachings specifying waka protocols that were transmitted as proprietary family secrets with warnings not to reveal them to outsiders.

One last point about the interaction of Tendai *kike* and court poetry families. The primary method used in oral transmissions (as in the example given above analyzing the graphs of Sannō) to rationalize and reinforce connections between shrines and temples was based on techniques that originated in poetic composition, particularly visual analogy and punning wordplay. According to Allan Grapard, the focus on associations based on resemblance may have been the result of the fact that the Japanese language was itself the result of systematic associations of indigenous and foreign streams, and thus the process of associating indigenous and foreign divinities was modeled on the process of assimilation found in language. Consequently, the associations between the divinities of a given cult obeyed linguistically grounded modes of combination such as association, metaphor, palindrome, anagram, and anagogy.[53]

Since the Tendai *kike* were also aristocrats, presumably well versed in the composition of waka poetry, it makes sense that they would employ poetic

52. Ibid., 108–9.

53. Grapard, *Protocols of the Gods*, pp. 81–82.

techniques that played with linguistic and visual metaphors. In other words, the aristocrats who by the late Heian period had taken over a majority of the important positions in the Buddhist hierarchy, especially the Shingon and Tendai sects, would have naturally used the poetic techniques of metaphor, association, and wordplay with which they were already so familiar.

Subsequently Tameaki took these techniques, which had been realigned through their immersion in esoteric Buddhist-Shinto syncretism, and reapplied them to secular poetry. As described in Chapter 2, he used three basic techniques of etymological and numerological allegoresis to transform relatively secular texts, the *Kokin shū* and *Ise monogatari*, into complex religious allegories. In doing so, he was finally able to finesse the problem of "wild words and ornate phrases" that so bedeviled medieval poets.

Shingon Tachikawa

Another important component in the development of Tameaki's commentaries was the Tachikawa sect of Shingon.[54] The standard explanation for the origin of Tachikawa is found in a polemical attack by the Shingon priest Yūkai Shōgon (1345–1416) in his *Hōkyō shō* (Compendium of the precious mirror; 1375):

Some speak of the disciple (and natural brother) of Assistant Archbishop Shōkaku [1057–1129] of Daigo-ji's Sanbō-in, a man called Ninkan Ajari (later known as Rennen).[55] Apparently this man was exiled to Izu because of some criminal affair. There he taught Shingon to women and laymen who ate meat and practiced other filthy

54. On Tachikawa, see Kushida Ryōkō, *Shingon mikkyō seiritsu katei no kenkyū*; Mizuhara Gyoei, *Jakyō Tachikawaryū no kenkyū*; Moriyama Shōshin, *Tachikawa jakyō to sono shakaiteki haikei no kenkyū*; and Sasama Yoshihiko, *Sei no shūkyō: Shingon Tachikawaryū to wa nanika*. In English, see Sanford, "The Abominable Tachikawa Skull Ritual"; Goepper, *Aizen-Myōō: The Esoteric King of Lust, An Iconographical Study*, pp. 102–13; and Faure, *The Red Thread: Buddhist Approaches to Sexuality*, which discusses issues of Buddhism and sexuality generally and includes a short section on Tachikawa (pp. 124–29). There is also a passing mention of Tachikawa in Yamasaki, *Shingon: Japanese Esoteric Buddhism*, p. 44. Since Sanford is working on a book of Tachikawa-related manuscripts, tentatively entitled "Not One, Not Two, Not Three: Reflections from a Shingon Mirror," the dearth of material in English should soon be rectified.

55. Ninkan (dates unknown) was the son of Minamoto no Toshifusa (1035–1131), a prominent political figure of the day. He appears to have changed his name to Rennen after his exile to Shūzen-ji on the Izu Peninsula. The following description of the early development of Tachikawa is indebted to James Sanford's unpublished manuscript, "Not One, Not Two, Not Three," particularly chap. 5, "The Emergence of Tachikawa-ryū."

acts and made them his disciples. At the same place there was a Yin-Yang master (*onmyōji* 陰陽師) from Tachikawa in Musashi province. This man studied Shingon with Ninkan and brought to it his own Yin-Yang practices. Truth and heresy were thus entangled. Inner and outer were all mixed together. The result was called the Tachikawa sect, and was held up as a branch of Shingon. This was the wellspring of a river of heresy.[56]

Yūkai's polemic has long been taken as a guide to the basic history of Tachikawa despite his antagonism. Ninkan, who was exiled in 1113 for being on the wrong side of an attempted *coup d'état* by Prince Sukehito against Emperor Toba and Retired Emperor Shirakawa and who is supposed to have committed suicide not long afterward, provided a convenient scapegoat for Yūkai.[57] In fact, the seeds of the Tachikawa sect probably developed within Shingon much earlier, around the beginning of the eleventh century, as a natural outgrowth of the powerful influence of Onmyōdō. Tachikawa took Shingon's emphasis on nonduality and combined it with Onmyōdō Yin-Yang theory, whose divinations and directional taboos had come to dominate the everyday life of the aristocracy. In fact, the tantric use of Yin/Yang, female/male sexual symbolism to express the ultimate nonduality of Shingon's numerous dualisms was not particularly unusual at the time. The Tachikawa sect's heterodoxy lay in the fact that it went a step further and literalized the metaphorical by promoting the practice of ritual sex as a path to enlightenment. Kūkai, the founder of Japanese Shingon, held out the promise of "acquiring Buddhahood in this very body" (*sokushin*

---

56. Yūkai, *Hōkyō shō*, *T.*, p. 848; *Hōkyō shō* is also published in Moriyama Shōshin, *Tachikawa jakyō to sono shakaiteki haikei no kenkyū*, pp. 572–81; and Pol Vanden Broucke, trans., *Hōkyōshō: Compendium of the Precious Mirror of the Monk Yūkai*, pp. 119–50. Translation (modified) from Sanford, "Compendium of the Precious Mirror," pp. 6–7. For alternative translations, see Vanden Broucke, *Hōkyōshō*, pp. 16–17; and the translated excerpt from *Hōkyō shō* in Tsunoda et al., *Sources of Japanese Tradition*, pp. 163–65.

57. Yūkai claims that Ninkan developed Tachikawa between his arrival in Izu and his reported suicide in the third month of 1114. This time frame is rather unlikely; as James Sanford ("Not One, Not Two, Not Three," pp. 12–13) points out, "He and his new friend had at most four months to meet, construct, proselytize and perhaps practice their hybrid ideology. . . . If Ninkan and company actually were in the midst of a creative outpouring of a whole system of exciting new ideas, what possible reason could he have had to throw himself off a cliff?" On the other hand, there is evidence from a diary by Nakamikado Munetada that in 1129 Ninkan was pardoned for his crimes and allowed to return to the capital. In that case, Ninkan would have had more than enough time to get a heresy going in the Kantō area.

jōbutsu 即身成仏); Tachikawa adherents apparently took this to mean that the body itself could be used as a means to enlightenment.

Tachikawa became increasingly popular throughout the twelfth and thirteenth centuries among both the aristocracy and the common people. Its growing popularity is attested by the appearance of tracts denouncing it, such as the following written around 1280 by Mujū Ichien in *Shaseki shū*:

> These persons lack true faith in Buddhism and do not aspire to celibacy, the first principle of monkhood. They cling to the forms of the secular world. They have such an unfortunate attitude that, when they attempt to practice Buddhism, they do not turn to suitable actions and books, but to strange aberrations . . . to such ideas as "the passions themselves are enlightenment," "the realm of *samsāra* [the cycle of life and death] is in and of itself Nirvana," "man and woman are the Twin Kongōkai [Diamond Realm] and Taizōkai [Womb-Storehouse Realm] mandalas," and "sexual intercourse is the union of Principle and Wisdom." They say these things just as if they were true, as if unclean acts were the inner practices of the esoteric schools.[58]

Mujū's attack points to radical nondualism, a fundamental Shingon tenet, as the source for the heterodoxies of Tachikawa. As James Sanford has pointed out, one can easily find precedents in orthodox Shingon texts for such claims as "the passions themselves are enlightenment" (*bonnō soku bodai*).[59] The problem, again, is that Tachikawa adherents literalized Shingon nondualism and argued that for a truly enlightened person provisional distinctions between passion and enlightenment, between sexual intercourse and sexual abstinence, were no longer pertinent. As we shall see, texts such as *Gyokuden jinpi no maki*, *Waka kokin kanjō no maki*, and *Ise monogatari zuinō* use the idea of radical nondualism to defend the practice of ritual sex as a means to enlightenment.

Tachikawa reached the height of its influence in the person of the priest Monkan (or Kōshin, 1278–1357), who was a close advisor to Emperor Go-Daigo (r. 1318–39).[60] In 1336, Go-Daigo fled Kyoto and established the

---

58. Mujū Ichien, *Shaseki shū*, pp. 496–97. Translation from Sanford, "The Abominable Tachikawa Skull Ritual," p. 3.

59. Sanford, "The Abominable Tachikawa Skull Ritual," p. 3*n*8.

60. Again, our basic information comes from Yūkai's *Hōkyō shō* (*T.*, pp. 849–50), which discusses the strong influence Monkan had on Go-Daigo's religious beliefs. According to Yūkai, Monkan started out as a Ritsu monk of Hokujō-ji, but then "snatched bits and pieces out of the holy teachings" of Shingon to create his own initiatory secrets and promoted rituals and incantations borrowed from Shugendō to promote magical effects. When Go-Daigo rewarded him by making him head of Daigo-ji and then Tō-ji, Shingon monks from Tō-ji and

southern dynasty in Yoshino, and Monkan was ousted from his position as head priest of Tō-ji. Thereafter Tachikawa appears to have gone into decline within court circles. In the 1370s Yūkai led an attack on all the elements within Shingon that he considered heterodox, including Tachikawa. Over the next hundred years, a large number of Tachikawa liturgical texts and documents were destroyed, and its practitioners were forced to leave the main Shingon centers. Although Tachikawa doctrines and rituals were suppressed in the main centers of Buddhist thought, they continued to percolate through the substratum of popular culture.[61]

I examine the Tachikawa content of the various commentaries in more detail in Chapters 10 and 11. Here, I focus on two of the most basic Tachikawa-influenced tenets of the Kamakura period commentaries.

First, the Path of Poetry (*waka no michi*) and the Path of Eroticism (*irogonomi no michi*) are inseparable. The "Akone no ura kuden" (Oral transmission of Akone Bay) section of *Gyokuden jinpi no maki*[62] describes how the primordial kami Izanami and Izanagi descended from heaven at Akone Bay. After each recited a poem, they had sexual relations and produced the islands of Japan.[63] This version of the creation myth conflates the cosmogonic procreative act with the origins of poetry and the origins of sexuality: from that time on, the Path of Eroticism and the Path of Poetry were intertwined as one. Sumiyoshi Daimyōjin, as a Manifest Trace of Izanagi, continues to protect and guide those who resolve to plumb the

---

Mount Koya protested with a strongly worded petition to the throne. See Vanden Broucke, *Hōkyōshō*, pp. 20–28, 132–43; Sanford, "Compendium of the Precious Mirror," pp. 11–16; Moriyama, *Tachikawa jakyō to sono shakaiteki haikei no kenkyū*, pp. 576–79.

61. Sanford ("The Abominable Tachikawa Skull Ritual," p. 4) lists a few Edo-period texts that include Tachikawa ideas: *Sangai isshin ki* (Record of the three realms' single heart), *Fudōson gu shō* (Humble selected notes on Lord Fudō), and *Konkō shō* (Selections on the primal cavity). Elements of Tachikawa also manifested in cultic practices associated with Aizen Myōō and the Dual Ganesha and in Tendai's Genshi Kimyōdan cult.

62. *Gyokuden jinpi no maki*, pp. 529–31. See also *Akone no ura kuden*, in Sasaki Nobutsuna, ed., *Nihon kagaku taikei*, vol. 4, p. 398.

63. In one version from the *Nihon shoki*, having decided to have sexual relations, the two kami proceeded separately around the pillar of Heaven (the jewel-spear previously used to stir the waters of the ocean). When they met on the other side, "The female deity spoke first and said: 'How pretty! A lovely youth!' The male deity then answered and said, 'How pretty! A lovely maiden!' Finally they became man and wife" (translation from Aston, *Nihongi*, p. 15). The *Kokin shū* commentary *Kokin waka shū kanjō kuden* (Katagiri, *Chūsei*, vol. 5, p. 486) specifically quotes this exchange as the origin of poetry in Japan.

protect and guide those who resolve to plumb the profound depths of these (non)dual paths.[64]

This basic explanation seems to have been used as a starting point for various etymological analyses, which generally incorporate Shingon's nondualistic dualisms. This content is justified by the Sumiyoshi Daimyōjin's Original Ground manifestations, especially that of Dainichi Nyorai, the central Buddha of Shingon.[65] Narihira, who was incarnated into a poetry family as an avatar of (among others) Izanagi, Sumiyoshi, and ultimately Dainichi Nyorai, hid within *Ise monogatari* profound esoteric truths. *Gyokuden jinpi no maki* notes one such truth: "The two graphs, *i* and *se*, are Yin and Yang. Yin and Yang are the origin of the manifold dharma. Thus, what is there that has escaped the benefits of these two graphs? In other words, all the manifold phenomena are the two characters *i* and *se*."[66]

Other sections of *Gyokuden jinpi no maki* spell out more explicitly the sexual meanings of the graphs *i* and *se*: "The graphs for *i* and *se* in the title *Ise monogatari* incorporate the Twin Realm mandalas (*ryōbu* 両部). The Womb and Diamond [Realm mandalas] are created through the Way of Men and Women [i.e., through sex]. '*I*' is 'womb' and 'woman.' '*Se*' is 'diamond' and 'man.'"[67] In the "Akone no ura kuden" sections of later texts such as *Ise monogatari zuinō*, these correspondences are pursued even further:

> "*I*" means female; "*se*" means male. Izanami is female and Izanagi is male. These two kami signify female and male. *I-se* refers to the aspects of female and male. "*I*" is called an "opened" graph (開字). It is the graph for the sound the mouth produces when it is open. "*Se*" is called a "joined together" graph (合の字). It is the graph for the sound produced just behind the teeth. As for the two aspects, "opened" and "joined together," the graph "joined together" is read *tsubomu* (to close up like a flower). Since the male's genitals are closed, they are referred to as "closed up." The graph for "opened" is read *hiraku* (to open up like a flower). Since the woman's geni-

64. Sometimes Sumiyoshi is identified as *both* Izanagi and Izanami (also referred to as the Kami of Yin and Yang [*in'yō no kami* 陰陽神]). Other times he is only identified as Izanagi, and various female kami such as Amaterasu Ōmikami, Toyouke Hime, or Tamatsushima Myōjin, are identified as *suijaku* (Manifest Traces) of Izanami.

65. The *honji* (Original Ground) of the third shrine at Sumiyoshi, Sokutsutsunoo no Mikoto, is Dainichi Nyorai. This may explain why Tameaki's commentaries consistently identify Sumiyoshi as "number three" (*daisan*); see *Gyokuden jinpi no maki*, pp. 526, 539.

66. Ibid., p. 536.

67. Ibid., p. 535. Note that the text says "*tai otoko*" (womb man), but this must be a transcription error.

tals are open, they are referred to as "the opened lotus flower." The male is a closed lotus flower; the female is an open lotus flower. These are referred to as the Diamond and Womb-Storehouse realms. In general, among the myriad plants, trees, rocks, rivers, and mountains under heaven, there is nothing that is other than, or external to, this *i-se*. All emerge out of *i-se* and do *i-se*. Although it might be thought that there are a myriad of *i-se*, all are really only the one *i-se*.[68]

The commentaries did not invent the idea of *i-se* as nondual duality. In esoteric Shingon, the phenomenal universe is believed to be the result of the interdependent interaction of the nondual duality represented by the Womb-Storehouse Realm (*Taizōkai*) and Diamond Realm (*Kongōkai*) mandalas. Those dualities are in turn seen as manifestations of Dainichi Nyorai as Absolute Reality (or True Thusness). These nondual dualisms easily lend themselves to identification by analogy with the Taoist principles of the feminine Yin and masculine Yang, whose primordial interaction created the universe. (As we shall see in the next section, there was also a strong connection to esoteric Buddhist-Shinto syncretism developing at the Ise shrines in the thirteenth century.)

As early as the *Nihon shoki* (Record of Japan; 720) the principles of Yin and Yang were associated with Izanami and Izanagi, the two kami whose primordial sexual relationship created the country. Ki no Tsurayuki alluded to this idea in one of the opening lines of the *Kokin shū* preface: "Poetry came into existence when heaven and earth were first separated" (*kono uta, ametsuchi hirake hajimarikeru toki yori idekinikeri*). Interpolated notes in the preface (which the commentaries assumed were also by Ki no Tsurayuki) specifically identify the birth of poetry with the marriage vows of Izanami and Izanagi beneath the bridge of heaven. The commentaries used this interpolated identification as justification for their conflation of the cosmogonic procreative act with the origins of poetry and sex.

Later in the *Kokin shū* preface, however, it becomes clear that Ki no Tsurayuki was not particularly well disposed to the idea of eroticism as the foundation for poetry. In fact, he criticized his contemporaries for writing poetry that was too personal in nature; specifically, he suggested that poetry had become eroticized to the point that it could be exchanged only in private, "a decaying log, buried in the houses of those devoted to eroticism, unknown to others." In the context of the Heian period, Tsurayuki was arguing for a

---

68. Kariya *Ise monogatari zuinō*, p. 434.

more public conception of waka poetry and attempting to give it a ceremonial function that would elevate its social status (and not coincidentally help elevate the status of lower-ranking poets like himself). As is often the case when a new conception is being argued, Tsurayuki resorted to an invented tradition. He claimed that in fact waka poetry was originally meant primarily to serve social functions (expressing wishes for a lord's long life, gratitude for favors received, and so on) or to smooth social relations by establishing a shared experience of beauty. According to Tsurayuki, this original, higher purpose had become trivialized and degraded by those who used poetry merely to pursue frivolous love affairs.

For Tameaki and his disciples, Tsurayuki's argument posed something of a problem. Tameaki therefore argued in *Kokin waka shū jo kikigaki* that Ki no Tsurayuki simply could not have meant what he appears at first glance to have said:

> The phrase "people's hearts today are fixated on eroticism [so their poetry has] become too flowery" (*ima no yo no naka iro ni tsuki hito no kokoro hana ni nari*) means that in the past, poets such as Hitomaro and Akahito used only true, meaningful words; there was nothing frivolous or meaningless. . . . The phrase "only in the houses of those devoted to eroticism" (*irogonomi no ie*) does not refer to actual houses where men and women have sexual relationships; it signifies the poetry families. Because poetry devoted to eroticism (*irogonomi no uta*) is taken as the origin, the poetry families are said to be "devoted to eroticism." The phrase "[poetry] has become like a decaying sunken log, unknown to others" means that the profound secrets of waka that have been transmitted within poetry families are not to be shown to anyone outside those families.[69]

Tsurayuki's criticism is thus neatly turned on its head. To be devoted to eroticism (*irogonomi*) is now synonymous with being a poet, since the way of eroticism is the very source of poetry. And the seemingly pejorative description of privately exchanged love poetry as a "decaying sunken log" turns out to be an affirmation of secret transmission.

Another basic tenet of the commentaries influenced by both the *honji suijaku* movement and Tachikawa Shingon is that Ariwara no Narihira was much more than the poet of eroticism *par excellence*. Narihira was an avatar who became mortal and wrote *Ise monogatari* as an expedient means to benefit and enlighten all living beings. He has been incarnated numerous times

---

69. *Kokin waka shū jo kikigaki*, p. 254.

throughout Japanese history, in the form of human beings as well as of native and Buddhist deities, including Izanami and Izanagi. As their manifestation, he has made love with numerous women in order to bring them enlightenment through sex.

The idea that Narihira slept with women to bring them to enlightenment was first voiced in texts associated with Tameaki such as the preface to the Sanjōnishi lineage version of *Waka chiken shū*: "Narihira is identified as two bodhisattvas: the Bodhisattva of Song and Dance in Paradise and the Horse-Headed Kannon. Seeing the plight of humanity . . . he was born as a human into this world . . . and eventually brought consolation to 3,733 suffering women. He recorded his activities in *Ise monogatari* in order to explain to later generations the [esoteric] meaning of eroticism (*irogonomi*)."[70] At first the interlocutor strongly objects: "Every scripture says that to approach a female is the ultimate karmic act; thus all buddhas warn about this in particular, calling it either 'fixing the mind on boundless kalpas' or 'one cause leading to five hundred births.' What kind of bodhisattva is it who tries to encourage escape from suffering by urging people to take the path of which others have made such dire warning? This is strange indeed."[71] The interlocutor is eventually won over by the Tachikawa argument that in this degenerate world humanity has become bored with good intentions and finds it difficult to follow the Buddhist precepts; so the buddhas have devised a way known as the "Dharma of the Harmonious Union Between the Two Fluids of Womb and Egg." This path of enlightened sex was devised as an expedient means by Narihira as bodhisattva. It is an adaptation to human propensities that allows those people who would otherwise wander in endless darkness to be guided to a state of buddhahood in this very existence.

Ryōbu Shinto

The syncretic Shinto-Buddhist movements of Ryōbu Shinto and Sannō Shinto were developed by esoteric Buddhist monks in conjunction with Shinto priests. Ryōbu Shinto is associated mainly with Shingon, and Sannō Shinto with Tendai. According to Mark Teeuwen, however, the evidence points to Ryōbu Shinto originating at the Tendai temple of Onjōji (Miidera), and it makes more sense to distinguish Ryōbu and Sannō Shinto by

70. Kunaichō *Waka chiken shū*, p. 108.

71. Ibid., pp. 108–9; translation (modified) from Bowring, "The *Ise monogatari*," p. 36.

subject matter (Ryōbu Shinto focusing on the Ise Shrines, and Sannō Shinto on the Hie/Hiei complex) than on sectarian origins.[72] I have already discussed the development of the interpretive strategy of etymological and numerological allegoresis by the *kike* on Mount Hiei involved in Sannō Shinto, an interpretive strategy that was also employed by Ryōbu Shinto and was borrowed by Tameaki for use in his commentaries. In terms of the actual content of the commentaries, however, Ryōbu Shinto appears to have been more influential for Tameaki. The fact that Tameaki's commentaries might be influenced by Ryōbu Shinto is not surprising since Tameaki was a Shingon priest. And as discussed in Chapter 6, we know from the transmission lineages of the *Kingyoku sōgi* variant of *Gyokuden jinpi no maki* that Tameaki had contact with another Shingon priest, Ichijō Yoshimoto, who was situated in Ise.

The name Ryōbu Shinto literally means "Shinto of the Twin Realm Mandalas." The two mandalas referred to are, of course, the central mandalas of Shingon Buddhism: the Womb-Storehouse Realm and the Diamond Realm. They are visualizations, respectively, of the compassion (or reality-principle; *ri* 理) and wisdom (*chi* 智) aspects of Dainichi Nyorai. Referred to jointly as the Ryōbu mandalas, they express the truth that compassion and wisdom are nondual in Dainichi (*richi funi* 理智不二). The main focus of monks involved in the development of Ryōbu Shinto was to establish identifications between the central teachings of Shingon, expressed in the *Dainichi Sutra* (*Dainichi kyō; Mahāvairocana Sutra*) and the *Diamond Peak Sutra* (*Kongōchō kyō*) and the Ryōbu mandalas associated with those sutras, and the Ise Shrines. And so in Ryōbu Shinto, the sun goddess Amaterasu, deity of the Inner Shrine (Naikū) at Ise, was identified with the Womb-Storehouse Realm mandala, with the compassion aspect *ri*, and with sun and fire. The fertility goddess Toyouke, deity of the Outer Shrine (Gekū), was identified with the Diamond Realm mandala, with the wisdom aspect *chi*, and with the moon and water. And just as the Womb-Storehouse Realm and Diamond Realm mandalas were understood as ultimately nondual, the Inner and Outer Shrines were also understood as ultimately one in essence.[73]

Amaterasu as the Great Sun Deity (Ōhirume 大日霊) had been identified much earlier with Dainichi Nyorai (大日如來), whose name also

72. Teeuwen, *Watarai Shintō: An Intellectual History of the Outer Shrine in Ise*, p. 51.
73. Ibid., pp. 53, 232.

means "Great Sun."[74] With the addition of Toyouke, a whole series of non-dual dualities could be symbolically assigned to the layout and architecture of the Inner and Outer Ise shrines, and by the late thirteenth century, such identifications begin to appear in popularly disseminated texts such as Mūjū Ichien's *Shaseki shū*. In the opening to that work, Mūjū described a pilgrimage he took to the Ise Shrines during the Kōchō period (1261–64) in which he met a shrine priest who enumerated how various design features of the Ise Shrine could be identified with Shingon theory:

> The Great Sun Buddha (Dainichi Nyorai) came forth from this capital of Inner Realization to assume local manifestations in the land of the sun [Japan]. Thus, the deity of the Inner Shrine at Ise [Amaterasu] is the Great Sun of the Womb-Storehouse Realm; and patterned after the Four-Enclosure mandala are the several shrine fences: *tamagaki* 玉垣, *mizugaki* 瑞垣, *aragaki* 荒垣, and so on.[75] Likewise, there are nine logs (*katsuogi* 鰹木) on the roof of the main hall of the Inner Shrine, symbolizing the nine Holy Ones of the Womb-Storehouse Realm. We are accustomed to identifying the deity of the Outer Shrine [Toyouke] with the Great Sun Buddha of the Diamond World and also with Amida. It is doubtless to symbolize the Five Wisdoms of the Diamond World that its design consists of five moon-circles. When the Ryōbu mandala is viewed in the light of Yin-Yang teaching, wherein the Yin is female and the Yang male, the eight petals of the Womb-Storehouse parallel the shrine's Eight Maidens; and it is because the Five Wisdoms of the Diamond World are represented by male divinities that there are a group of five male shrine dancers.[76]

By the early 1260s such metonymic identifications were apparently accepted by the priests at the Ise Shrines and may have even been widely known and accepted outside the shrines. Mūjū strongly opposed dogmatic exclusivity with regard to the path to enlightenment and was obviously open to an esoteric reading of Ise Shinto. As we have seen, however, his championing of a mapping of identifications between the Ise Shrines and Shingon did not mean that he approved of the more Tachikawa-influenced readings of the Twin Realm mandalas and the Inner and Outer Shrines. Nevertheless, to

---

74. Traditionally the identification is first attributed to Gyōgi (668–749), but the oldest written sources date to the late Heian period. See the more detailed discussion in ibid., pp. 52–53.

75. The mandala is formed by a series of concentric squares; the Inner Shrine fences are constructed in the same way, starting with innermost *mizu gaki*, inner and outer *tamagaki*, then outermost *aragaki*.

76. Translation (modified) from Morrell, *Sand and Pebbles*, p. 74.

judge from *Shaseki shū* the syncretism behind Ryōbu Shinto was already seen as orthodox by the mid- to late thirteenth century, when Tameaki was actively producing commentaries. And Tachikawa had become popular enough that Mūjū thought it necessary to attack it as a heterodox form of such syncretism.

Although Ryōbu Shinto is thought to have developed during the thirteenth century, the earliest authenticated written records that explicitly state the associations date from the 1280s on (*Shaseki shū* is one of the earliest). This means that the real push to create secret Ryōbu Shinto–influenced *kuden*, transmission lineages, and esoteric Shinto *kanjō* occurred at the same time that Tameaki was at his most productive. Tameaki's commentaries employ the same etymological and numerological allegoresis used by Ryōbu Shinto to make *honji suijaku* identifications between Dainichi Nyorai and kami such as Amaterasu and Toyouke and include similar (albeit Tachikawa-influenced) content. Consider, for example, this passage from *Gyokuden jinpi no maki*:

> The graphs for *i* and *se* in the title *Ise monogatari* incorporate the Twin Realm mandalas. The Womb and Diamond [Realm mandalas] are created through the Way of Men and Women [i.e., through sex]. "*I*" signifies the Womb Realm. "*I*" signifies that the manifold dharma are gathered together as one essential substance.[77] Therefore the more than seven hundred deities gathered in the Womb-Storehouse are as one essential substance. Therefore "*I*" is read "to gather." "*Se*" is the Diamond Realm. "*Se*" is read "to plant a seed." Accordingly, the Diamond Realm's symbolic attribute is the *bīja* seed syllable.[78] The Diamond Realm takes the seed [syllable] and impregnates the Womb Realm. What this means is that the Twin Diamond and Womb realms are created through the two graphs *i* and *se*.[79]

Here *Gyokuden jinpi no maki* makes a series of correlations between the graphs for *i* and *se* and the Twin Realm mandalas and ultimately argues that the graphs precede the Womb-Storehouse and Diamond Realm mandalas and are their source. In other words, the graphs are the source for all of exis-

77. *Ichinyo* 一如 is the essential substance of all existence and is equivalent to *shinnyo* (真如), True Thusness or Absolute Reality.

78. *Sanmaya no katachi* 三魔耶の形: the symbolic attribute identified with a buddha or bodhisattva that expresses his true inner nature (for example, the lotus held by Kannon). Here the seed syllable is the symbol that expresses the true inner nature of the Diamond Realm.

79. I have used the corrected version in Arai Eizo, "*Kokin shū* kanjō hisho to Bukkyō kyōri: *Kokin* denjushi shikō," p. 6; cf. *Gyokuden jinpi no maki*, p. 535.

tence. It seems likely that the thinking that underlies this and other such passages was developed within Ryōbu Shinto.

Watarai Shinto, developed by the Outer Shrine priests at Ise, was an adaptation and expansion made possible by the initial Ryōbu Shinto equation of the Inner and Outer Shrines ("one not two"). This form of Shinto, which was created through the production of secret oral transmissions claiming oracular revelation and legitimized through spurious transmission lineages, was utilized by Outer Shrine priests to further redefine and elevate the status of their shrine and their shrine deity, Toyouke Hime, over and against the Inner Shrine and Amaterasu. Mark Teeuwen argues that the five secret books of Watarai Shinto, drawing on material that may date to the ninth and tenth centuries, were probably written over an extended period of time. They were, however, given their final form in the last decades of the thirteenth century (1266–95), probably by the Outer Shrine priest Watarai Yukitada (1236–1305).[80] I do not believe it coincidental that the period in which the five secret books emerged as "works of unrivaled antiquity and sanctity" corresponds almost exactly with Tameaki's period of activity (1265–95). The reasons for the development of Watarai Shinto and the spurious secret commentaries and initiations supporting it were both religious (the flourishing of Buddhism and widespread movement toward greater syncretism) and economic (a crisis caused by declining revenues from the imperial court); they thus strongly parallel the reasons for Tameaki's development of the secret commentaries.

Although there is a fair amount of material in the commentaries associated with Tameaki that is obviously related to Ryōbu Shinto, direct references to material that might be correlated with Watarai Shinto are far fewer. The main possible connection is simply that Toyouke is mentioned when one would expect Amaterasu. For example, according to both *Gyokuden jinpi no maki* and *Kokin waka shū jo kikigaki*, Narihira took a collection of secret commentaries on waka poetry called "Gyokuden" with him when he was sent as an envoy to the Ise Shrine (episode 69). He dedicated his copy to the shrine for safekeeping. Five reigns later, Emperor Daigo sent Fujiwara no Kanetaka to Ise Shrine, where he received the "Gyokuden" after dreaming of it. He gave it to Emperor Daigo, who was so impressed that he had Ki no Tsurayuki use it as a basis for compiling the first imperial anthology, the

80. Teeuwen, *Watarai Shintō*, pp. 11–17; see also idem, "Attaining Union with the Gods: The Secret Books of Watarai Shintō," pp. 225–27.

Kokin shū. Gyokuden jinpi no maki specifies that it was presented first to the Outer Shrine of Toyouke Hime, who appeared to Narihira in a dream vision and recited a poem. Next Narihira presented the text to the Inner Shrine, where a red-robed acolyte appeared to recite a poem for Amaterasu. The fact that both the Inner and the Outer shrines are mentioned would at least indicate that the author was attempting to be evenhanded and give each shrine its due.[81] A bit further in the text, however, there is a brief entry (perhaps an interpolation) that specifies only Toyouke as the transmitter of "Gyokuden":

> These two fascicles were given to Narihira by Sumiyoshi. The "Gyokuden" was presented to Toyouke of Yamada no Hara 山田原の豊受. Narihira transmitted the other scroll, "Akone no ura kuden," to [his son] Shigeharu. . . . Also, it is said that the transmission lineage from the Sumiyoshi deity was transmitted to Toyouke, who in turn transmitted it the Engi Mikado [Emperor Daigo].[82]

This passage would seem to be promoting Toyouke and the Inner Shrine above Amaterasu and the Outer Shrine.

Another, somewhat confusing, section in *Gyokuden jinpi no maki* correlates Amaterasu and Toyouke with Izanagi, Izanami, and Sumiyoshi:

> In fact, the conjugal relationship of Sumiyoshi and Toyouke is written of in this text ["Gyokuden"]. . . . There is a secret about Amaterasu Ōmikami. The shrine at Isuzu River is known as the Inner Shrine. This is the sun (Yang 陽) kami. The embodiments of her Original Ground are the deities Izanagi and Izanami. Toyouke is enshrined in the Outer Shrine at Yamada no Hara. She is the same substance as Izanami, while Sumiyoshi is the same substance as Izanagi. . . . Long ago they were husband and wife.[83]

In this case we seem to have an overabundance of identifications. Izanagi and Izanami are embodiments of Amaterasu; in turn Toyouke is identified as Izanami and Sumiyoshi as Izanagi. But their conjugal relationship would explain why the oracular revelations from Sumiyoshi would be transmitted through Toyouke.

Other sections of *Gyokuden junpi no maki* appear to go against Watarai Shinto's promotion of Toyouke: "Above there is Amaterasu Ōmikami. Amaterasu subsumes the two kami identified with the Inner and Outer shrines at Ise. The Inner Shrine is Yang, the Outer is Yin. Similarly Dai-

81. *Gyokuden jinpi no maki*, pp. 524–25.

82. Ibid., p. 526.

83. Ibid., p. 527.

nichi Nyorai subsumes the Womb and Diamond realms. Amaterasu is the Manifest Trace manifestation of Dainichi."[84] Here the text seems to imply that Amaterasu, as *suijaku* manifestation of Dainichi Nyorai, is the *honji* for the incarnate deities of both the Inner and Outer shrines and so superior to them both, a position that the priests of Watarai Shinto would have rejected.

Since transmission lineages identify Tameaki's disciple, Yoshimoto, as a Shingon priest living in Ise, it would be nice if the texts transmitted to him (*Kokin waka shū jo kikigaki* and the *Kingyoku sōgi* variant of *Gyokuden jinpi no maki*) mentioned Toyouke; this would provide a possible link. However, both texts simply say that Narihira transmitted *Gyokuden* to the (Ise) Grand Shrine (Daijingū), and that it was in turn transmitted to Emperor Daigo. *Kingyoku sōgi*'s transmission lineage for the *Gyokuden* transmission of *Kokin shū*–related secrets does claim that Narihira presented *Gyokuden* to "Ise Toyouke Amaterasu Ōmikami" 伊勢豊受天照大神 on the eleventh day, sixth month, thirteenth year of Jogan (871).[85] But this is not much support for Watarai Shinto. The much more specific references to Toyouke are found in the *Gyokuden jinpi no maki* transmitted to Tameaki's disciple Shinsui. Although it seems likely that Shinsui was a Shingon priest, since he received the transmission the same day as Yoshimoto, we cannot locate him firmly in the Ise area. So in the end we have no real evidence that Tameaki was involved with the Outer Shrine priests who were developing, at precisely the same time, spurious commentaries based on oracular revelation, filled with etymological and numerological allegoresis, and supported by spurious transmission lineages. The simultaneous development may simply be a coincidental effect of similar determining factors (economic, political, and religious), but the coincidence strikes one as suspicious. The problem awaits further research.

By employing Ryōbu Shinto and Tachikawa–influenced ideas such as these in conjunction with the Mahayana concept of nondualism, the *honji suijaku* theory of hypostasis, and a belief in the magical efficacy of language, Tameaki was able to achieve one of the ultimate feats of medieval syncreticism. In commentaries such as *Gyokuden jinpi no maki*, he transformed the completely secular *Ise monogatari* and the amatory exploits of Narihira as the Man of Old into a deeply esoteric text. In *Kokin waka shū jo kikigaki* and *Waka Kokin kanjō no maki*, he managed to perform a similar feat for the secu-

---

84. Ibid., p. 233.

85. Ishigami Hideaki, "Kunaichō Shoryōbu-zō *Kingyoku sōgi*," pt. I, p. 48.

lar poetry of the *Kokin shū*. Tameaki provided his audience what it wanted: a solution to the problem of "wild words and ornate phrases" that would allow poets to produce poetry in good conscience. One problem remained, however. The medieval literary establishment tended to value only those commentaries that had the proper family pedigree. Thus Tameaki had to legitimate commentaries that he had manufactured himself. As we shall see, he devised a number of ingenious ways to enlist the full authority of the Mikohidari poetry house for his commentaries.

8

Problems of Authority

During the Kamakura period, the problem of legitimating the secret transmissions became paramount. Since the commentaries claimed to reveal hidden truths about historical events that had happened a couple centuries earlier, the question of how a particular family came to have access to those secrets was crucial: the authority of the text depended on it. A second major problem was to justify allegorical interpretation. That is, the proponents of the secret transmissions had to prove that *Ise monogatari* and the *Kokin shū* were allegories, that one needed a "key" to read them correctly, and that that key had been transmitted secretly within one's own poetry family.

Fujiwara no Tameaki addressed these problems of authority in a number of ways. First, he developed a waka initiation ceremony modeled on the *kanjō* ordination and initiation ceremony of esoteric Buddhism. During these waka *kanjō*, the initiates received secret commentaries along with genealogical transmission lineages (*kechimyakufu* 血脈譜), which verified that these secrets had indeed been handed down in an unbroken line from generation to generation. Second, the commentaries were filled with allusions to Chinese and Japanese historical and literary sources that appeared to support the interpretations. Third, Tameaki produced an etiology[1] that explained

1. I use "etiology" in the sense of "an account of the origins of a phenomenon." In *The Spencer Encyclopedia*, K. K. Ruthven ("Etiological Tales," p. 255) gives this definition of "etiology": "The sort of myths we call etiological attempt to explain, in satisfying ways, the cause (*aitia*) of something whose origin worries people. For example, the knowledge that everybody

that the commentaries transmitted during the waka *kanjō* had originally been received by Ariwara no Narihira through an oracular revelation from Sumiyoshi Daimyōjin, and he showed how the content of these commentaries came to form the basis for both the *Kokin shū* and *Ise monogatari*.

In regard to Tameaki's etiology, three questions are important for understanding the basis for the commentaries' authority. First, why was Sumiyoshi Daimyōjin chosen as the oracular source for the commentaries? In order to answer this question, I examine the development of both Sumiyoshi Daimyōjin and Tamatsushima Myōjin as patron deities of waka poetry. Second, how did Narihira come to be identified as an avatar of Sumiyoshi Daimyōjin? And third, since no historical record credited Narihira with an esoteric religious affiliation, how did the commentaries explain Narihira's profound grasp of Shingon Buddhism?

The Development of the Waka *Kanjō* Ceremony

All sects of Buddhism in Japan have ceremonies in which a candidate, after an appropriate period of preparation, becomes a priest or nun by cutting off his or her hair, receiving the precepts, and donning clerical vestments. However, only esoteric Buddhism performs the *kanjō* ordination and initiation ceremony.[2] According to Adrian Snodgrass:

> The initiation (Sk. *abhiṣeka*) rituals derive from the coronation ceremonies of kings in ancient India, where water from the four seas was sprinkled on the head of the new monarch to symbolize his power over the worlds in the four directions. . . . [In esoteric Buddhism] the *abhiṣeka* is a ritual of consecration and initiation that marks the entry of the sādhaka into a new plane of spiritual awareness. The Japanese translation of *abhiṣeka, kanjō* (灌頂 literally, "head sprinkling"), for all practical purposes is synonymous with "initiation."[3]

---

in the world has been produced from the sexual conjunction of male and female prompts speculation about the origin of the 'first' male and female, and related questions such as whether one of the sexes came first, and if so, which." The stories about the origin of poetry and sex provided in *Gyokuden jinpi no maki* certainly fit this usage.

2. The description of the *kanjō* ceremony given here is indebted to Yamasaki, *Shingon*, pp. 175–81; and Snodgrass, *The Matrix and Diamond World Mandalas in Shingon Buddhism*, vol. 2, pp. 732–34. See also Ryūichi Abé's extended description in *The Weaving of Mantra: Kūkai and the Construction of Esoteric Buddhist Discourse*, pp. 132–41.

3. Snodgrass, *The Matrix and Diamond World Mandalas*, vol. 2, p. 732.

The first known use of the word *kanjō* in relation to poetry appears in a commentary by Rokujō Akisue's grandson Kiyosuke. A special appendix to the fourth "extra" fascicle of *Ōgi shō* (Poetic profundities; ca. 1130s) states that only a "kanjō no hito" (an initiated person) should be allowed to peruse its secrets: "This fascicle enumerates the very heart of waka. It should not be shown to an uninitiated person. The person to be initiated should be selected by age and talent. Tamatsushima Myōjin gives divine protection to this fascicle."[4] A number of ideas can be discerned in this quotation. First, there are poetic secrets, placed in specially designated sections of texts, that must be hidden from anyone outside the poetry family. Second, teachers initiate students in these secrets, and those accepted as disciples must evidence the proper poetic qualifications. Third, the Path of Poetry is under the protection of a kami, Tamatsushima Myōjin.

To judge from this passage, by the mid-twelfth century esoteric Buddhism's *kanjō* system was being used as a way of warning recipients of a text to keep it hidden from those outside their own poetic school. Another clue that the Rokujō family may have been involved in developing the waka *kanjō* is found in a description of an initiation ceremony in Tameaki's *Waka kanjō den*: "The format of this *kanjō* ceremony was transmitted from [Rokujō] Kiyosuke's family."[5] These two statements hint that Rokujō Kiyosuke might have taken the Hitomaro memorial ceremony (Hitomaro *eigu*), which his grandfather Akisue first performed in 1118, and transformed it into something approximating a *kanjō* ceremony. A number of Ietaka school commentaries dating from the 1260s and 1270s contain the word *kanjō* in their titles. As noted in Chapter 6, by that time the Rokujō family had apparently joined forces with the Ietaka school. So it is possible that the Ietaka school was performing some form of waka *kanjō* that it had borrowed from the Rokujō, and Tameaki then appropriated the ceremony from the Ietaka school through his links with Tsumori Kunisuke, who had married Ietaka's granddaughter.

Miwa Masatane, however, argues that in Rokujō Kiyosuke's use of the term *kanjō no hito*, *kanjō* is used figuratively, without reference to specific rites, and implies only admission to an esoteric course of study. Miwa argues that it was only with Fujiwara no Tameaki that the *kanjō* pedagogy began to be

---

4. As quoted in Miwa, *Kagaku hiden no kenkyū*, p. 11. See also Miwa Masatane, "Hisho no seiritsu ni kakawaru mondai," pp. 137–59.

5. As quoted in Miwa, *Kagaku hiden no kenkyū*, p. 34.

used systematically as a model for teaching the poetic tradition.[6] As Miwa points out, we have no records of the performance of *kanjō* ceremonies by either the Rokujō or the Ietaka school, and Ietaka school commentaries contain no descriptions of ceremonies similar to those found in Tameaki's treatises. There is, however, a direct connection between Tameaki's *kanjō* and the Rokujō Hitomaro memorial ceremony: Tameaki incorporated the eulogy to Hitomaro written for the first Hitomaro memorial ceremony into his description of a waka *kanjō* ceremony in *Waka Kokin kanjō no maki*.[7] When we consider this in conjunction with the *Waka kanjō den*'s assertion that the format for the *kanjō* ceremony was transmitted from Rokujō Kiyosuke, it seems likely that Tameaki portrayed the Hitomaru memorial ceremony as a *kanjō* initiation ceremony in order to establish a venerable tradition for his own waka *kanjō*. Until scholars are able to figure out who influenced whom, however, it will not be possible to claim absolutely that Tameaki invented the form.

Whoever originated the waka *kanjō*, it is clear that Tameaki developed it into a much more sophisticated pedagogical system. Texts closely connected with Tameaki such as *Waka kanjō den* and *Waka Kokin kanjō no maki* contain explicit explanations of how the waka pedagogical system was integrally related to the Shingon *kanjō* system, as well as detailed descriptions of *kanjō* rituals. It is clear that by the early fourteenth century the institution of secret literary transmissions had become standard for both the Nijō and the Reizei. In order to understand this development, we need to look more closely at what the *kanjō* ceremony meant within esoteric Buddhism.

Esoteric Buddhist Initiation Ceremonies and the *Waka Kanjō*

There are at least five levels of initiation ceremonies in Shingon Buddhism. The fourth level, Transmission of the Dharma Initiation (*denpo kanjō* 伝法灌頂), which signifies the initiate's formal acceptance into the Shingon lineage, is considered a prerequisite for more advanced practice. In this ceremony, the disciple, who has met certain standards of character and personal devotion and performed a rigorous course of study and preparation, ritually enters the path that leads to becoming a Dharma master (*ajari*). During the

6. Miwa Masatane, "Chūsei kadō ni okeru kanjō denju ni tsuite."
7. *Waka Kokin kanjō no maki*, p. 460.

initiation, the disciple receives the nominal title of Dharma master, thus marking his or her potential to reach that exalted status; instruction in meditative practices, including secret mantras and mudras; and the transmission lineage attesting the unbroken continuity of generations of Shingon masters leading up to the present.

According to James Sanford, the *kanjō* ceremony in esoteric Buddhism has two main functions.[8] First, simply by undergoing the *kanjō*, the initiate is empowered with latent knowledge that is meant to slowly awaken his or her understanding of the secret materials transmitted. Second, it places the initiate in the lineage of those who have already received the secrets and privileges being transmitted. It certifies one's status as a recipient and, eventually, as a potential teacher and transmitter. For this purpose, the reception of the transmission lineage document is fundamental. Within Shingon, the transmission lineage signifies a direct link to the buddhas and founding patriarchs; receiving the transmission lineage ritually symbolizes the recipient's potential to achieve the same level of enlightenment.

From the descriptions of the waka *kanjō* ceremony scattered throughout the Kamakura commentaries, we can see the ways that the waka *kanjō* borrowed these esoteric trappings. First, there is nearly always an admonition that the material should be transmitted only to someone who has demonstrated the proper qualifications—a fervent devotion to poetry and an appropriate level of talent. Whereas in Shingon, the goal is to become a Dharma master, in the esoteric world of poetry, the goal is to become a sage of poetry (*kasen* 歌仙). Thus the title conferred is *kasen* rather than *ajari*. And rather than instruction in secret meditative practices, the initiate receives esoteric oral transmissions on poetry, such as *Kokin shū* 409 ("Honobono to") or the "Naniwazu" poem, which are to be read as mantras.

Tameaki's *Waka kanjō den* provides an excellent description of the waka *kanjō* ceremony:

I will transmit whatever is not harmful to those whose performance on this Path demonstrates they seek with deep resolve.[9] During the *kanjō* ceremony a list of the waka that have been transmitted within the house is taught to the initiate. The names of those poems are given in the section on ritual protocol. This *kanjō* is similar to that

8. James Sanford, pers. comm., 1996.

9. Since *Waka kanjō den* is an entry-level text, one interpretation of this line might be that Tameaki has agreed to reveal only preliminary secrets to someone who is outside his family but has demonstrated enthusiasm for pursuing the Path of Poetry as a path to enlightenment.

> of the Shingon school. When the audience, the emperor, and the crown prince are ready, water from the four seas is taken and sprinkled on the crown prince's head to signify that he has been appointed to succeed to the emperorship. That is why it is called the "kanjō" 灌頂 (head-sprinkling) ceremony. When someone is to be established as a sage of poetry, one follows this format for the ceremony. A sage of poetry is someone who has excelled in this tradition. Although there are so many gods as to be numberless, to begin with, you need to establish the Five Buddhas of Waka: Kakinomoto no Hitomaro, Yamabe no Akahito, Sarumaro no Dayū, Ono no Komachi, and Ariwara no Narihira. These were all Buddhist incarnations who took to the upper limit their mastery of the Path of Poetry. Images of Sumiyoshi Daimyōjin's triune form and Shōtoku Taishi, who both act as guarantees of waka's truth, are also hung. The rest of the gods of poetry may be added as you think best.[10]

Tameaki begins by asserting the main qualification needed by the initiate: excellence as a poet demonstrated by dedication to the Path of Poetry. He explicitly identifies the ceremony as Shingon and explains the term *kanjō* through its literal meaning of "head-sprinkling."[11] In addition, the *kanjō* ceremony is linked to an installation ceremony used to anoint the crown prince. The anointing of a potential sage of poetry becomes the equivalent of anointing a crown prince, the potential emperor. By implying a connection with the installation ceremony, Tameaki enlists the prestige of an imperial ceremony. In the Shingon initiation ceremonies, as Taikō Yamasaki points out, the master enacts Dainichi Nyorai's transmission of truth to the initiate with the sprinkling of water on the crown of the head: "In a state of mutual empowerment with Dainichi Nyorai, the master sprinkles the water while reciting a mantra of the Five Buddhas, the initiate performing the mudras and mantras of related bodhisattvas. In this way the essence of the esoteric teaching is expected to enter the initiate, opening channels to the source of enlightenment."[12] In the waka *kanjō*, the master is probably enacting the transmission of secret poetic truths from Sumiyoshi Daimyōjin to Hitomaro, Narihira, and other sages of poetry. And it may be that given the identification of five of the Six Sages of Poetry with the Five Wisdom Buddhas of the Diamond mandala, the mantra of the Five Wisdom Buddhas was employed in the waka *kanjō*.

---

10. As quoted in Miwa, *Kagaku hiden no kenkyū*, p. 34.

11. The etymology of "head-sprinkling" comes directly from the *Dainichi Sutra*, which was used by Kūkai as the scriptural basis for his creation of the Shingon *kanjō* ceremony. See Ryūichi Abé, *Weaving of Mantra*, pp. 135–36.

12. Yamasaki, *Shingon*, p. 180.

Although a transmission lineage is not mentioned here, a variant of *Gyokuden jinpi no maki* explicitly states what material is to be transmitted: "the transmission lineage, 'Gyokuden' (Jeweled transmission), 'Akone no ura kuden,' and other transmissions. Also appropriate material from the *Kokin shū* and *Ise monogatari*."[13] Apparently these transmission lineages served a function parallel to that of the Shingon *kanjō*: they provided a direct link to the deities and sages of poetry by placing the initiate in a long line of masters and, by the act of bestowal itself, signified that the initiate had demonstrated both poetic excellence and sincere devotion to the Path of Poetry as a path to enlightenment. In addition (and perhaps most important), the transmission lineage, with a date and representative poem for each person on the list, validated that the secrets being transmitted derived from some great originating figure and had been passed down in an unbroken line to the present. Like Dainichi Nyorai in esoteric Buddhism, Sumiyoshi Daimyōjin functioned as the originating ground: his revelations initiated the transmission lineage. For this reason, although the images to be hung in the initiation hall differ slightly from text to text, Sumiyoshi Daimyōjin is always a central image of worship.

Besides a picture of Sumiyoshi, *Waka kanjō den* also mentions images of Shōtoku Taishi, Hitomaro, Akahito, Sarumaro, Komachi, and Narihira. The function of these portraits of the founding "fathers and mothers" of the Path of Poetry was similar to that of the *chinsō* (or *chinzō* 頂相), an image of the Dharma master, within Muromachi period Zen transmissions. In *The Rhetoric of Immediacy* Bernard Faure explains the *chinsō* as a device

> that allowed the ritual transmission of the master's charisma to take place and that provided access to it, thereby linking magically the possessor of the *chinsō* to the mainstream of the tradition perpetuated by his master. The *chinsō* thus lays the ritual ground on which the rarefaction of legitimate authority through succession documents (*shisho* 嗣書) could take place as a specific case.[14]

Hitomaro, Narihira, and other poetic sages were revered as the founders of a Path of Poetry that had been transmitted in an unbroken line through the ages, and their portraits clearly were a kind of "proto-*chinsō*" in the sense that Faure describes.

---

13. As quoted in Miwa, *Kagaku hiden no kenkyū*, p. 39.
14. Faure, *Rhetoric of Immediacy*, pp. 174–75.

A passage from Tachibana no Narisue's *Kokon chomon jū*, previously quoted in Chapter 5, reveals how the portrait was used as a guarantee of the Rokujō lineage's authority:

Rokujō Akisue, who was among the emperor's intimates, requested that he be allowed to copy [the Hitomaro portrait], but he initially was refused. He persisted until at last he got permission. His eldest two sons, Nagazane and Ieyasu, were not particularly talented at poetry, so he gave it to his third son, Akisuke.

As for Kanefusa's original, the Ono Grand Empress asked to borrow it. Most unfortunately, while she had it in her possession it was burned in the same fire that destroyed a copy of the *Kokin shū* in Ki no Tsurayuki's own hand. So Akisuke's copy is all that remains of the original. It is rumored that there is a pledge to the gods (*kishomon*) attached that you not transmit it or allow it to be copied by anyone who is not a talented poet, even if he or she is your own child.

Since a Hitomaro memorial ceremony could be performed only with the proper portrait, its authenticity and transmission were of some concern to the Rokujō. This concern appears in the form of a sacred warning, which stresses that the portrait be transmitted only to a poet of talent, regardless of blood lineage. The implication is that if there were no talented poets in the Rokujō family, the transmission would go to someone outside the family. The fact that Akisue passed over his first and second sons and transmitted the portrait to his third son appears to validate this stricture. The warning is, however, merely nominal. It transforms the transmission of the portrait into a form of poetic legitimation of the Rokujō family in general and Akisuke in particular. Being allowed to copy the picture or receiving it signifies that you are talented; Akisuke is thus, *ipso facto*, talented. The portrait functions as a form of cultural capital, whose possession gives the house authority and creates a symbolic center for the family-lineage. This function is also expressed quite clearly in *Ise monogatari zuinō*, a commentary in which Narihira is treated as the founding patriarch of the esoteric sect of I-Se. His portrait becomes a *chinsō* that guarantees the authority and authenticity of the sect's teachings: "Those people within our lineage who are to transmit the secrets of *Ise monogatari* must above all preserve the image of Narihira as he appeared on his death bed, wearing the *eboshi* court cap and a blue silk courtier's robe."[15] Here the portrait of Narihira replaces that of Hitomaro as the main image displayed in the initiation hall to lend its authority to the initia-

15. Kariya *Ise monogatari zuinō*, p. 428.

tion ritual. The transmission of the portrait, carefully preserved within the lineage, is treated as a sign that the initiate has mastered the Path of Poetry.[16]

In line with the *honji suijaku* tendencies of these commentaries, poetic sages such as Narihira and Hitomaro are also treated as incarnations of Sumiyoshi Daimyōjin and various Buddhist deities. As kami-buddhas incarnate, the portraits of these poets appear to function both as *chinsō* and as *honzon* (本尊 objects of worship) within the waka *kanjō*, a move that redoubles their poetic authority. This kind of redoubling is especially evident in the production of the so-called waka mandala popular at the time. An abbreviated description in the *Kingyoku sōgi* variant of *Gyokuden jinpi no maki* indicates that a waka mandala was displayed in Tameaki's waka *kanjō*:

> Waka altar:
> left: waka mandala
> right: Thirty-six Sages of Poetry
> center: Sumiyoshi, Amaterasu, Hitomaro
> Ritual implements for the images: 20 lamps, 12 altars.
> Whatever else seems appropriate at the time.
> Banners hung in the four corners of the room.[17]

The earliest mention of a waka mandala is found in Tachibana no Narisue's *Kokon chomon jū*:

> Because Sensai loved poetry, he often composed it and held poetry meetings. He drew a waka mandala that included the Seven Past Buddhas and the names of the Thirty-six Sages of Poetry. . . . Although this mandala was an important treasure of the main temple, somehow or other it ended up at Ise Shrine. . . . In the ninth month of 1249, when they were transferring the deity to the Outer Shrine at Ise, I was present when they brought out the mandala for inspection.[18]

Sensai (?–1127) was a Tendai priest well versed in poetry active at the beginning of the twelfth century. He appears to have drawn the waka mandala for use during poetry meetings held at his home.

---

16. There is a possibility that the emphasis on Narihira's robe indicates that his robe was being transmitted as a sign of legitimation as well. For a discussion of robes as coveted relics embodying the charisma of their original owners, see Faure, *Rhetoric of Immediacy*, pp. 165–66.

17. As quoted in Miwa, *Kagaku hiden no kenkyū*, pp. 38–39.

18. As quoted in ibid., p. 40.

In the poetry collection *Shoku Shika waka shū* (Collection of verbal flowers continued; ca. 1165), Rokujō Kiyosuke noted that his father, Akisuke, had also produced a waka mandala: "The governor of Sakyō, Akisuke, drew a waka mandala, and on the day of the [Hitomaro?] memorial ceremony people composed poems on the *Lotus Sutra*."[19] The mention of a waka mandala, as well as poems on the *Lotus Sutra*, hints that the Hitomaro memorial ceremony as performed by Akisuke had a Buddhist coloration. It seems likely that a waka mandala was transmitted within the Rokujō house, for use in the Hitomaro ceremony and other later ceremonies that combined Buddhism and the composition of poetry.

Although we do not have a description of the waka mandala mentioned in the *Kingyoku sōgi* variant of *Gyokuden jinpi no maki*, it seems likely Sumiyoshi would have been the central image (probably in his Original Ground form as the bodhisattva Kōkitokuō), perhaps with the Five Sages of Poetry as the Five Wisdom Buddhas of the Diamond Realm mandala or even all Thirty-six Sages of Poetry. It may also have included the Heavenly and Earthly Kami who guard poetry, starting with Kunitokotachi no Mikoto, Izanagi, and Izanami.

Only a few extant passages suggest concrete details of what happened in the waka *kanjō*. In addition to the abbreviated description of the layout of the initiation hall from *Kingyoku sōgi* quoted above, a passage from Tameaki's *Chikuen shō* describes the preparations for a waka lecture ceremony (*koshiki*). The layout was probably similar to that used for the waka *kanjō*:

> Ordinarily, for the lecture, five matters must be done. Before the audience gathers at the meeting site, the seating must be arranged. First, the images of Hitomaro and Sumiyoshi Daimyōjin should be hung to the right and left, respectively. If there are other images, they can be hung to the right and left in order of their official ranking. Next, in front of Hitomaro and Sumiyoshi the lectern should be placed as usual. Flowers should be arranged in vases, and incense should be burning. The altar should also be as usual. Along the left side of the lectern, which is in front of the flower vases, place a round cushion for the lector. To the right of the lectern, place another round cushion for the marshal. To the left and right [of the cushions], spread tatami mats for the high-ranking participants. Next the seats of the musicians and the *gāthā* master. The scribe's seat is not predetermined. No matter where [the ceremony takes place], things are to be arranged in this manner.[20]

---

19. As quoted in ibid.
20. *Chikuen shō* (*NKT*), pp. 424–25.

Tameaki's *Waka kokin kanjō no maki* gives a more in-depth view of what happens at the ceremony:

Those who aspire to the Path of Poetry follow in the footsteps of the forerunners. There is a ritual for this, called the *kanjō* ritual. The person who desires to perform a *kanjō* designates the place. After the place is purified, the portraits of the Thirty-six Sages of Poetry are installed. Flowers are arranged for presentation, incense is burnt, everything is prepared to give a sense of magnificent beauty.

The teacher enters the initiation hall first and explains the format and reasons for this ceremony. Then he stands and calls in the initiate. The initiate enters respectfully and sits to the left of the teacher. The teacher bows three times and moves to the main platform. Next, the three foundational poems [*honka* 本歌] are transmitted secretly: "Yakumo tatsu," "Naniwazu ni," and "Honobono to" are each recited three times.[21] Flower petals are sprinkled on the initiate's head, and then the initiate bows three times and moves up to the main platform, where he recites the three poems himself. Now both the initiate and the teacher recite one of their own poems. The initiate bows again and is given a theme; when he presents the poem, he does so kneeling. The teacher takes the poem and reads it aloud. Next, [Kiyosuke's eulogy on Hitomaro is intoned]. . . . The teacher leaves his seat and recites the three founding poems three more times each. Then the initiate leaves his seat and bows to the teacher three times and, kneeling again, asks for the *kanjō* initiation [*kanjō no sahō* 灌頂の作法]. When he receives it, the teacher says, "This *kanjō* ceremony contains the deep meaning of waka. To acknowledge that you do not take this lightly, you should place your forehead on this text three times, and make sure you learn each of these matters well."[22]

There then follows a list of secrets that are to be transmitted to the initiate.

Another description comes from "The Protocol for a *Kokin shū* Transmission Ceremony" ("*Kokin waka shū* denju no shidai") in *Kokin waka shū hiji* (Secret matters of the *Kokin waka shū*). This passage makes it quite clear how lucrative these waka *kanjō* ceremonies could be:

First purify the space; next hang the main images (*honzon*).
Order of images: Sumiyoshi Daimyōjin, Amaterasu, Hitomaro
Six "denju" sweet rice cakes: three red, three white.

In front of the images should be placed: gold coins (nine *mon*), other coinage (ten *kan*), five dyed goods, five *kosode* robes, ten rolls of silk, five *obi* silk belts, one long

21. All three poems are mentioned in the *Kokin shū* preface.
22. *Waka Kokin kanjō no maki*, p. 460.

sword, one short sword, fine crepe paper (ten quires), thick paper (thirty quires), miscellaneous paper (fifty quires), three fans.

In front of the teacher should be placed: gold coins (five *kan*), three dyed goods, two *kosode* robes, five rolls of silk, one long sword, one short sword, one horse,[23] thick paper (ten quires), miscellaneous paper (thirty quires).

Three white *obi* belts: one each in front of the images, the teacher, and the initiate.[24]

Given this kind of economic exchange, it is not surprising that *kanjō* ceremonies quickly became popular among both the Nijō and the Reizei schools. And although by the late fourteenth century, the form of the poetry initiation had changed from the Shingon-influenced *kanjō* to a *kirigami* initiation borrowed from Sōtō Zen, the poetry initiation itself continued to support the Nijō and Reizei families both economically and politically.[25]

Tameaki and the Imperial Enthronement *Kanjō*

We have a good deal of concrete evidence that Tameaki was behind the development of the waka *kanjō*; it is also possible that Tameaki was involved in the creation of a ceremony for the imperial enthronement (*sokui kanjō* 即位灌頂) in which a secret mudra and dharani mantra (or several mudras and dharanis) were transmitted to the emperor by the regent (*kanpaku* or *sesshō*). The new emperor would subsequently perform the secret mudra and mantra on his way to the enthronement platform on the day of his accession to the throne. This initiation ceremony, which became popular in the fourteenth century and continued to be performed until the end of the Edo period, was known as the *sokui in'myō denju* (即位印明伝授), the conferring

23. It seems likely that some kind of a representation of a horse is meant here.

24. As quoted in Miwa, *Kagaku hiden no kenkyū*, pp. 43–44. There is a nearly identical list in *Kokin waka shū kanjō kuden*, p. 498.

25. *Kirigami* (or *kirikami* 切紙) were single sheets of paper on which oral transmissions were transcribed; their use flourished in the late medieval period within the Sōtō Zen and Pure Land schools. They mainly described techniques and protocols for secret rituals (funerals, consecrations, Dharma transmissions, precept initiations, and so on). As with Shingon *kanjō* oral transmissions and transmission lineages, mere possession of *kirigami* was considered a guarantee of authority, and it is clear that the idea for *kirigami* originated in esoteric Buddhism. For a short discussion in English, see Bodiford, *Sōtō Zen in Medieval Japan*, pp. 155–57.

of the mudra and dharani of the enthronement audience.[26] Kamikawa Michio has outlined the possible historical development of the *sokui in'myō denju*.[27] Although there is some earlier evidence of the influence of the structure and symbolism of the esoteric Buddhist *kanjō* on the enthronement ceremony,[28] the first reliable recorded instance of the *sokui in'myō denju* is for the enthronement of Emperor Fushimi in 1288. According to an entry in Emperor Fushimi's diary (*Fushimi tennō nikki*) for the thirteenth day of the third month of Shōō 1 (1288): "This evening the *kanpaku* [Nijō Morotada], during the accession, conferred the secret mudra and such matters. This was done properly according to established standards."[29] During the emperor's procession to the enthronement hall two days later, he performed the mudra and dharani he had learned from Morotada.[30]

The content of the 1288 ritual is not known, and a variety of versions of the ceremony are preserved in subsequent ritual manuals. In the more elaborate versions, three mudra and two dharani are performed by the emperor on the day of his enthronement, including the mudra of "Rule over the Four Seas" (*shikai ryōshō-in* 四海領掌印), the "Wisdom Fist" mudra (*chiken-in* 智拳印), and the dharani ritual of Dakini (*Dakiniten-hō* 荼吉尼転法).[31] The appropriateness of the mudra of Rule over the Four Seas is obvious. Dakini, who was the central deity of the ritual, was identified as the Original Ground of Amaterasu Ōmikami and an incarnation of Dainichi Nyorai. The identification of Amaterasu, the ancestor of the imperial line, with the central deity would have been politically essential in an enthronement ceremony. The Wisdom Fist mudra was often paired with the Dakini dharani.

Mark Teeuwen, in a discussion of the *sokui kanjō*, notes that "a striking aspect of the Dakini mantra in this imperial ritual is its sexual connota-

---

26. The last performance was in 1847, for Emperor Kōmei's enthronement ceremony. The enthronement ceremonies for his successor, Emperor Meiji, were completely purged of Buddhism, and a new "invented tradition" based on a "purified" Shinto ideology was constructed.

27. Kamikawa Michio, "Accession Rituals and Buddhism in Medieval Japan," p. 251. This article is a translation of Kamikawa Michio, "Chūsei no sokui girei to bukkyō."

28. See Ryūichi Abé's discussion of the *sokui kanjō* in *Weaving of Mantra*, pp. 359–67. Abé is concerned with the symbolic "buddhisization" of the emperor as *tenrin shōō* (転輪聖王), the universal monarch described in Buddhist scriptures, through the *sokui kanjō*.

29. Kamikawa, "Accession Rituals," p. 251.

30. Ibid. See also Mark Teeuwen, "The Kami in Esoteric Buddhist Thought and Practice," p. 114*n*40.

31. Kamikawa, "Accession Rituals," pp. 259–60.

tion."[32] According to *kirigami* associated with the ritual, the mantra represents the unity of the Womb-Storehouse Realm and Diamond Realm mandalas (*ryōbu funi* 両部不二), which express not only the union of Dainichi's aspects of compassion and wisdom but also the joining of Dainichi's female and male aspects. "The Dakini mantra, then, was explained to express the sexual union of the emperor (embodying the male, Kongōkai [金剛界 Diamond Realm] aspect of Dainichi) and the empress (embodying the female, Taizōkai [台蔵界 Womb-Storehouse Realm] aspect of Dainichi)."[33] In addition, the Wisdom Fist mudra is quite sexually suggestive: it is formed by wrapping the fingers of the right hand around the upright index finger of the left hand. This mudra, Teeuwen points out, makes "a perfect companion to the Dakini mantra expressing the union of the emperor and empress (or Kongōkai and Taizōkai)."[34] And although Teeuwen suggests that such tantric symbolism was ubiquitous within Shingon in the late thirteenth century, the Dakini dharani was in fact a central ritual of the Tachikawa sect.

It seems unlikely that the Regent Nijō Morotada would have had the knowledge of tantric Buddhism required to create such an initiation ceremony; in that case, who did? One possibility is Morotada's younger brother Dōgen, the head priest (*zasu*) of the Tendai temple-shrine complex on Mount Hiei. Kamikawa Michio quotes a section from *Sokui kanjō in'myō yurai no koto* (On the origin of the mudra and dharani of the *sokui kanjō*; 1500) that he believes indicates this was the case: "According to reports, during the accession of the Retired Emperor Fushimi on the third month, fifteenth day of Kōan 11 (1288), the minister to the empress, Jūraku-in Dōgen (son of the regent Nijō Yoshizane), argued and cajoled [his brother] the current regent [Nijō Morotada] into conferring (the *in'myō kanjō*) for the sake of the lord."[35]

Two main lineages of *sokui kanjō* protocols were transmitted in the medieval period, one that claimed only the Nijō family of regents should confer the mudra and mantra, the other claiming that right for the Tendai head abbots.

---

32. Teeuwen, "The Kami in Esoteric Buddhist Thought and Practice," p. 106.

33. Ibid., p. 107. Note that Teeuwen's much more detailed analysis of the *sokui kanjō* includes other elements of esoteric Shinto and Tachikawa content besides those mentioned here. See also the translations of a *sokui kanjō* protocol in Kamikawa, "Accession Rituals," pp. 259–61; and Ryūichi Abé, *Weaving of Mantra*, pp. 361–62.

34. Teeuwen, "The Kami in Esoteric Buddhist Thought and Practice," pp. 107–8.

35. The syntax is unclear, but given Fushimi's diary entry above, it seems most likely that although Dōgen was promoting the *in'myō kanjō*, Morotada actually conferred it. Kamikawa, "Chūsei no sokui girei to Bukkyō," *Nihonshi kenkyū*, no. 300 (Aug. 1987), p. 51.

This would seem to point to two transmissions: one from Nijō Morotada to his son Kanemoto and one via Morotada's brother Dōgen. Nevertheless, the "Tendai" protocol is primarily Shingon-related, with a very strong Tachikawa flavor, and I would argue that Fujiwara no Tameaki is the most likely source of such content. Tameaki was the father-in-law of Morotada's son Kanemoto; Morotada's grandson, the future regent Michihira, was born in 1287, and we can be sure that Tameaki and Morotada were in contact. In addition, we know from an exchange of poems discussed in Chapter 6 that Tameaki was on terms of easy acquaintance with Dōgen. Although there is no proof that Tameaki was instrumental in the development of this new enthronement initiation ceremony, his close marital ties with Morotada and Dōgen, plus the fact that he was a Shingon priest who dabbled in Tachikawa and already had a good deal of experience with the creation of secret *kanjō* initiations, make him a likely candidate as a source of the content of the ceremony as well as a spurious transmission lineage tracing it back to Kūkai, the founder of Shingon. In addition, according to Itō Masayoshi, the idea of the *sokui kanjō* dharani appears to have been widely disseminated within popular culture, forming the basis for Muromachi period Buddhist tales known as *Jidō setsuwa* 児童説話 (Tales of Jidō) and related Noh plays (*Makura Jidō* and *Kiku Jidō*).[36] This kind of dissemination into popular forms of literature occurred with other secret transmissions associated with Tameaki.

As noted above, the conferral of the mudra and dharani for the *sokui kanjō* became a secret transmission within the Nijō family of regents. Emperors Hanazono and Go-Daigo indicated a strong interest in the *sokui in'myō denju*, but apparently neither actually received it. According to his diary, Hanazono received the mudra from Archbishop Zōki in 1317, almost ten years after his accession ceremony. Go-Daigo's religious advisor, the notorious Tachikawa adept Monkan, wrote about the enthronement protocol in a postscript to his *Himitsu gentei kuketsu* (Oral transmission of the innermost secrets; 1338),[37] and the *Hōkyō shō* claims that he performed the Dakini dharani on Go-Daigo's behalf. According to Amino Yoshihiko, in the 1320s Go-Daigo himself performed the Dakini dharani ritual in an attempt to overthrow the Kamakura shogunate.[38] Tameaki's grandson Michihira had served

---

36. Itō Masayoshi, "Jidō setsuwa kō."

37. Kamikawa, "Accession Rituals," p. 253.

38. Amino Yoshihiko, *Igyō no ōken* (Heibonsha, 1986), as cited in Kamikawa, "Accession Rituals," p. 263; see also Goble, *Kenmu: Go-Daigo's Revolution*, pp. 96–97.

as Go-Daigo's tutor while he was crown prince; however, when Go-Daigo became emperor in 1318, for reasons of political expediency he removed Michihira as regent and replaced him with Ichijō Uchitsune (1290–1325). Michihira eventually became one of Go-Daigo's most trusted ministers and installed one of his daughters (Eishi) as junior consort (*nyōgo* 女御).[39] But at the crucial time of Go-Daigo's enthronement, Michihira was not the regent and so would not have conferred the *sokui in'myō denju*.

It is likely, however, that Michihira received instructions on the *sokui in'myō denju* from his father or grandfather, since his son Nijō Yoshimoto conferred the mudra and dharani on the infant Emperor Go-Komatsu (r. 1392–1412) in 1382 and perhaps on four previous emperors as well (Kōmyō [r. 1337–48], Sukō [r. 1349–51], Go-Kōgon [r. 1353–71], and Go-En'yū [r. 1374–82]). According to a transmission lineage in the *Sokui kanjō in'myō yurai no koto*, Yoshimoto's grandson Ichijō Kaneyoshi also received the transmission. This is corroborated by Kaneyoshi's *Tōka zuiyo* (Leaves from the Peach Blossom Court; 1480), in which Kaneyoshi listed the *sokui kanjō in'myō* as the first of twelve "family transmissions."[40] If Tameaki did have a hand in the creation of the *sokui kanjō*, he may have seen it as a way to give his new in-laws and especially his grandson Michihira a political edge. Tameaki's great-grandson Nijō Yoshimoto did indeed use it that way: to confirm the legitimacy of the northern dynasty of emperors.

During the northern dynasty two of the three imperial regalia were missing: the sacred sword, which was lost during the battle of Dan no Ura, and the sacred seal, which was in the hands of the southern dynasty. Kamikawa, in analyzing the correlation of religious symbolism and political ideology in

---

39. From 1323 to 1331, Michihira was the imperial document examiner (*nairan*), a function previously associated only with regents. And according to *Masu kagami* (The clear mirror; ca. 1376), when Go-Daigo returned from exile in 1333, "The capital buzzed with the news of Emperor Go-Daigo's return from Hōki. His Majesty stopped first at the Tō-ji Temple in order to make necessary decisions, and the Nijō Former Minister of State Michihira presented himself there by imperial command. . . . Since there was to be no regent, Michihira was simply named head of the Fujiwara clan, with jurisdiction over affairs in the capital. His delighted relatives took this to mean his power would extend throughout the land" (translation from Perkins, *The Clear Mirror*, p. 219). Note that *Masu kagami* has been attributed to Nijō Yoshimoto. For Michihira's relationship with Go-Daigo, see also Goble, *Kenmu*, pp. 41, 180–81. Although there is no evidence that Michihira was involved in Tachikawa practices, given Go-Daigo's strong interest in Tachikawa, it is possible that having Tameaki as a grandfather was at the very least politically useful to Michihira.

40. Kamikawa, "Accession Rituals," p. 255.

the *sokui in'myō denju,* suggests that Yoshimoto may have used the Wisdom Fist mudra and Dakini dharani as symbolic substitutes in the enthronement ceremony to guarantee the legitimacy and authority of the northern dynasty of emperors.[41] The Dakini dharani in particular has a strong association with Tachikawa, and Kamikawa notes *Jidō setsuwa* connected to the *sokui kanjō* in which "abnormal" sexual activity is used "to reverse a disrupted imperial order and bring about a new sacred order."[42] Given this kind of symbolic understanding, the performance of the Dakini dharani ritual by Monkan and Go-Daigo can be seen as one more tactic in Go-Daigo's attempt to destroy the Kamakura shogunate and re-establish imperial authority and power.[43] Yoshimoto, as regent for the northern dynasty of emperors, would have been in a similar situation and attempting to establish the legitimacy of the northern dynasty over and against the southern dynasty of "usurpers." And the fact that the Nijō family of regents alone knew the secret mudra and dharani mantra, as well as the proper protocol for the *sokui kanjō,* would have placed them in a position of authority that Yoshimoto could use to his political advantage. Such manipulation of cultural capital for political power was something Tameaki understood very well.

Although the mudra and mantra were performed during the enthronement *kanjō,* the transmission of the mudra and dharani itself did not function as a *kanjō.* That is, the conferral of the mudra and dharani on the emperor does not seem to have implied that the emperor was to be initiated into a lineage relationship of master and disciple; nor did the emperor-to-be assume a new Buddhist religious status, such as *ajari* (Dharma master), through the ceremony. Kamikawa argues that if the conferral of the mudra and dharani had been a true *kanjō,* it would have established a master-disciple relationship and incorporated the emperor into one of the factions of the temple social structure. This would have been inimical to the religious ideology inherent in the *sokui kanjō* itself, which is meant to produce an emperor at the apex of both the religious and the political world order, an ideal Buddhist monarch outside of and unaligned with those very factions.[44]

---

41. See Teeuwen, "The Kami in Esoteric Buddhist Thought and Practice," pp. 105–9, for a discussion of the correlation of religious symbolism and political ideology, mainly focusing on the multiple meanings of Dakini's "wish fulfilling gem," which symbolizes "the unlimited powers that can be acquired by those who have mastered the ritual of *Dakiniten-hō.*"

42. Kamikawa, "Accession Rituals," p. 263.

43. Vanden Broucke, *Hōkyōshō,* p. 22.

44. Kamikawa, "Accession Rituals," pp. 269–70.

There is another way of looking at it, however. From the point of view of someone like Tameaki or Nijō Morotada, initiating the emperor into a master-disciple relationship would have contravened the whole purpose of developing the *sokui in'myō denju* as a Nijō family secret. If the emperor, as initiate, could transmit the mudra and dharani to his successor himself, what role would there be for the next Nijō regent? Instead, the master-disciple relationship needed to be constructed within the Nijō family, from father to son. That this was in fact what happened can be seen in the transmission lineage received by Ichijō Kaneyoshi. With the enthronement of each new emperor, the transmission of the secret mudra and dharani could be used to reinforce the relationship of the Nijō family to the emperor.

One last point: in his description of a waka *kanjō* in *Waka kanjō den* (quoted above), Tameaki argued that the ultimate source of the waka *kanjō* is a Shingon installation ceremony used to anoint a crown prince. By implying a connection to a ceremony for the installation of a crown prince, Tameaki supplemented the esoteric aura of the waka *kanjō* with the prestige of an imperial ceremony. *Waka kanjō den* is one of Tameaki's earliest works (dated to around 1265), and at the time Tameaki could have had no inkling that he would one day be intimately involved in the political power structure through his daughter's marriage into the Nijō family of regents. Although we have no proof (Tameaki appears to have been a master of effacement when it comes to claiming authorship), one can imagine that he would have jumped at the chance to help create an imperial *kanjō* that would aid his descendents.

Authoritative Sources for the Commentaries

Another way that the commentaries attempted to reinforce their authority was by alluding to Chinese and Japanese historical and literary sources at every possible opportunity. The authorities quoted in the Reizei school *Ise monogatari shō* include Po Chü-i's poetry collection (plus a number of other Chinese poetry collections); the Confucian *Analects* and the Five Classics; Sima Qian's history (*Shih chi*); an otherwise unknown commentary referred to as the *In'yō ki* (The record of Yin and Yang); various Buddhist works such as *Jizo jurin kyō* (The sutra of the ten rings of Jizo), *Tendaisan fu* (Topics regarding Mount Tendai), and Kūkai's *Sangyō shiki*; personal diaries (most often the diary of the Heian poet Fujiwara no Nagayoshi); Japanese histories such as the *Nihon shoki*; and poetry collections from the *Man'yō shū* (ninth century) through *Goshūi waka shū*. *Kokin waka shū jo kikigaki* also quotes from a number of Japanese sources, including *Man'yō shū*, *Nihon shoki*, and the personal diaries of Nagayoshi and Minamoto no Toshiyori.

As the eminent scholar Ichijō Kaneyoshi pointed out in the mid-Muromachi period, many of these sources are highly dubious: "Upon close examination not a single one of the Japanese or Chinese sources turns out to be authentic."[45] Although some of the texts quoted still exist today, the passages quoted in the secret transmissions are almost invariably not to be found in the current recensions of those texts. And when one does locate the quotation, as Otsu Yūichi managed to do for *Ise monogatari zuinō*'s citations from a text referred to as *Yotsugi no homon*, it turns out that the passage cited was probably interpolated into the text by Tameaki or his disciples.[46] It seems certain that a number of these texts are completely spurious.

Suzaku-in zuinō (a commentary on *Ise monogatari* Retired Emperor Suzaku [r. 930–46] supposedly commissioned from Fujiwara no Nagayoshi and Minamoto no Michinari) and Nagayoshi's diary are good examples of spurious texts used as substantiating evidence for material in the commentaries. References to both are sprinkled throughout the Reizei school *Ise monogatari shō*.[47] Despite the fact that neither Nagayoshi nor Michinari were contemporaries of Emperor Suzaku,[48] the story that they wrote a commentary on *Ise monogatari* for him seems to have been quite widespread in the Kamakura period.

For example, in the Reizei school *Ise monogatari shō*, a reference to *Suzaku-in zuinō* occurs as part of the discussion of the historical development of the variant texts. A nearly identical anecdote appears in a Reizei commentary in the Imperial Household Agency Library entitled *Ise monogatari chū kenmon shō* (Selected commentary on *Ise monogatari* from oral and written sources). According to *Kenmon shō*, Fujiwara no Nagayoshi and Minamoto no Michinari

---

45. Katagiri, *Ise monogatari no kenkyū (shiryōhen)*, p. 505.

46. *Yotsugi* 世継 is the generic name for the narrator in historical tales; the term is used as an abbreviation for *yotsugi no monogatari*. Otsu Yūichi (*Ise monogatari kochūshaku no kenkyū*, pp. 30–31) identifies *Yotsugi no honmon* specifically as the Maeda family lineage of the twelfth-century historical chronicle *Mizu kagami* (The water mirror; late twelfth century). See also Katagiri Yōichi, [Tesshinsai bunko] *Ise monogatari kochūshaku sōkan*, vol. 2, pp. 496–98, 503.

47. For a discussion of *Suzaku-in zuinō* and Nagayoshi's diary, as well as the arguments for and against the possibility of either of them having existed, see Otsu, *Ise monogatari kochūshaku no kenkyū*, pp. 37–41.

48. Suzaku reigned 930–46; Nagayoshi is thought to have been born in 938 or 949; Michinari's birth date is unknown, but he died in 1019, making him a contemporary of Nagayoshi.

received an imperial edict to write a commentary (*chū* 注), a summary of essential points (*zuinō* 髄脳), and an inventory (*mokuroku* 目録) of *Ise monogatari*. It was placed in a storeroom (*nurigome* 塗籠) and therefore is called the "Nurigome Manuscript" (塗籠本). Later, during the reign of Retired Emperor Go-Toba, this text was placed in the care of Fujiwara no Teika.[49]

In both the Reizei school *Ise monogatari shō* and *Ise monogatari chū kenmon sho*, it is clear that the reference to Nagayoshi and Michinari's commentary functions as a link in a lineage of transmission that gives authority to both the commentary tradition and Teika's recension of *Ise monogatari*.

Ise monogatari zuinō also refers to the *Suzaku-in zuinō* in its "Akone no ura kuden" (Oral Transmission on Akone Bay): "This matter is not mentioned in the historical chronicle *Yotsugi*. It is a personal secret of Narihira, so it is not written of in *Suzaku-in zuinō* either. Only in the Narihira family anthology is it written down for posterity."[50] Here, the *lack* of corroborating evidence is, rather neatly, turned into an asset. *Ise monogatari zuinō* uses references to two texts supposedly written by scholars outside the Ariwara family, as part of its claim to be an Ariwara family document.

On the other hand, the author of *Ise monogatari zuinō* had no qualms about quoting from Nagayoshi's diary (*Nagayoshi shiki*) in order to substantiate certain "public" events. Both *Gyokuden jinpi no maki* and *Ise monogatari zuinō* quote a passage from Nagayoshi's diary describing Narihira's visit to the Sumiyoshi shrine, where he is supposed to have received the revelations that resulted in these texts. Nagayoshi's diary also quotes the eulogy for Narihira supposedly given by his second son, Shigeharu (d. 905?). The problem with this use of Nagayoshi's diary is, of course, that the medieval commentators seem to have seriously misdated Nagayoshi's life span: Narihira died in 880, and the earliest date suggested for Nagayoshi's birth is 938.

Both *Suzaku-in zuinō* and Nagayoshi's diary are also used in the commentaries as substantiating evidence for the tantric reading of *i-se* as signifying Izanagi and Izanami, the Kami of Yin and Yang whose sexual union originally created Japan, as well as signifying female and male human beings, whose sexual union continues the Path of Procreation. For example, in the Kariya text of *Ise monogatari zuinō* we find: "According to the *Suzaku-in zuinō*, when sexual relations occur between man and wife, the sexual fluids congeal

---

49. Otsu, *Ise monogatari kochūshaku no kenkyū*, p. 38.
50. Kariya *Ise monogatari zuinō*, p. 433.

and form into a female or male."[51] Here the likely aim is to prove that a Tachikawa-influenced reading of *Ise monogatari* existed in the Heian period.

Nagayoshi's diary appears on Reizei Tamesuke's library inventory of 1317, mixed in among sections from *Gyokuden jinpi no maki*; it thus seems likely that some version of it was created specifically to substantiate the commentaries. However, according to Otsu Yūichi, there are no currently extant texts that correspond, even in part, to the afore-mentioned citations scattered throughout the commentaries.[52]

The production of spurious sources to provide legitimating authority for dubious interpretations was not limited to Kamakura literary commentaries. Jacqueline Stone and Paul Groner have noted that at about the same time, Tendai oral transmission texts were routinely citing fictitious sutras and commentaries or attributing passages to existing works that they do not in fact contain. Stone argues that such an interpretive approach "was by no means the result of ignorance of source materials; nor does the modern idea of forgery, with its connotation of deliberate deceit, seem to apply here. It was simply that the compilers of such texts were guided by a hermeneutical principle of fidelity, not to a received body of classic texts, but to a particular premise or insight."[53] In the case of Tendai oral transmission texts, that premise was Original Enlightenment. One could make a similar argument for Tameaki's commentaries by substituting content informed by Tachikawa Shingon and esoteric Shinto as the premise. And as we have seen, a similar process of manufacturing spurious authenticating texts was occurring within Watarai Shinto, as the Outer Shrine priests at Ise attempted to substantiate their position vis-à-vis the Inner Shrine. However, whereas religious scholars such as Stone and Mark Teeuwen are willing to give Tendai and Watarai Shinto commentaries that employ such tactics the benefit of the doubt, literary scholars have dismissed such works out of hand and assumed the worst about the authors' motives.

51. Ibid., p. 435.

52. There is an early Edo manuscript entitled *Suzaku-in zuinō*, but it does not seem to correspond in any way with the commentary citations; in addition, Otsu (*Ise monogatari ko-chūshaku no kenkyū*, pp. 41–47) argues that the style and content indicate that it is, in fact, not an esoteric commentary at all.

53. Stone, *Original Enlightenment*, p. 159. See also Paul Groner, "A Medieval Japanese Reading of the *Mo-ho chih-kuan*."

An Etiology for Tameaki's Commentaries

Both the transmission lineages and the quotation of various texts such as Nagayoshi's diary helped legitimate Tameaki's interpretations, but neither really addressed the question of whether *Ise monogatari* and the *Kokin shū* were written as allegories. This was an extremely important point, since in order for Tameaki's allegorical readings to be justified, there had to be some kind of corroboration that the texts were, indeed, written as allegories. Tameaki appears to have come up with an influential solution to this particular problem by means of an ingenious reading of episode 117 in *Ise monogatari*. The fact that this reading appears again and again not only in texts affiliated with Tameaki but in nearly every other Kamakura period secret commentary, from the Reizei school *Ise monogatari shō* to the Nijō school *Ise monogatari zuinō*, demonstrates its usefulness as substantiation for the allegorical interpretations that formed the basis of the waka *kanjō* system.

Episode 117 from *Ise monogatari* describes how an anonymous emperor visited Sumiyoshi Shrine and exchanged poems with the Daimyōjin:

Once in the past an emperor journeyed to Sumiyoshi.

> *ware mite mo / hisashiku narinu / Sumiyoshi no*
> *kishi no himematsu / ikuyo henuran*
>
> It's been ages since I first saw the princess pine along the shore at Sumiyoshi; how many reigns must it have seen go by?[54]

The [Sumiyoshi] Kami manifested itself and replied:

> *mutsumashi to / kimi wa shiranami / mizugaki no*
> *hisashiki yo yori / iwaisometeki*
>
> Don't you know of our intimate relation? This wave-washed shrine fence has protected you since time immemorial.[55]

Although in Teika's recension of *Ise monogatari* the "ware mite mo" poem appears to be by an emperor, the idea that Narihira was present on this occasion appeared quite early in the reception history of *Ise monogatari*, since in some versions of *Ise monogatari* the text continues:

---

54. *Kokin shū* 905, anonymous.

55. *Shin Kokin shū* 1857, with the following foretext: "According to *Ise monogatari*, during an imperial visit to the Sumiyoshi Shrine, the Kami manifested itself and transmitted this."

Hearing this, Narihira, who was in attendance, composed the following:

> *Sumiyoshi no / kishi no himematsu / hito naraba*
> *ikuyo ka heshi to / towamashi mono o*
>
> Princess Pine on the shore of Sumiyoshi, if only you were human,
> I would ask how many reigns you have seen.[56]

When he recited this, a badly dressed old man (*okina*) appeared and replied:

> *koromo dani / futatsu ariseba / Akahada no*
> *yama ni hitotsu wa / kasamashi mono o*
>
> If only I had two robes,
> I'd lend one to Stark Naked Mountain (Akahada no yama).[57]

According to Tameaki school texts such as *Gyokuden jinpi no maki*, *Kokin waka shū jo kikigaki*, and *Shinsen teisetsu shū*, as well as Tameaki-influenced texts such as *Ise monogatari zuinō* and the Reizei school *Ise monogatari shō*, not only was Narihira in attendance at the shrine, but it was he (not the emperor) who recited the "ware mite mo" poem. This is the moment when Narihira's special relationship to Sumiyoshi Daimyōjin is revealed for the first time:

On the twenty-eighth day of the first month of Ten'an 1 [857], Emperor Montoku [r. 850–58] went on a pilgrimage to Sumiyoshi Shrine with Narihira in attendance. At that time a beneficent breeze purified Narihira, and he was possessed by the kami. Everyone watched in amazement, staring at the kami's altar. Narihira bowed low before the altar and recited the following poem:

> It's been ages since I first saw the princess pine along the shore
> at Sumiyoshi;
> how many reigns must it have seen go by?[58]

At that moment the earth shook, and the wind rustled through the pines. Next, when Narihira approached the jeweled altar, pushed it open, and looked inside, a young child dressed in a red robe appeared and replied:

> Don't you know of our intimate relation? This wave-washed shrine fence
> has protected you since time immemorial.[59]

---

56. *Kokin shū* 906. It seems probable that this section was added because an unknown editor wanted to link *Kokin shū* 905 and 906 in one episode.

57. Both the Koshikibu Naishi variant and Tameuji variant include this material. For an analysis of the variants of this episode, see Kobayashi Shigeyoshi, "Sumiyoshi no okina no monogatari," p. 3.

58. *Kokin shū* 905, anonymous.

> The meaning of this poem is: "you are me: why have you forgotten your Original Ground (*honji*)? In the shadow of this pine, I have spent years as a Manifest Trace (*suijaku*). During that time how much have I benefited living beings? To benefit and save the multitude of living beings, I have been provisionally born in a human body."[60]

The relationship between Narihira and Sumiyoshi implied here is made quite explicit at a number of later points in *Gyokuden jinpi no maki*: for example, "the myōjin and Narihira are not two, but identical in nature (*funi dōtai* 不二同体)."[61] It was on this occasion as well that the Daimyōjin revealed the most profound secrets of poetry to Narihira: the "Akone no ura kuden" and the "Gyokuden."

> At this time two fascicles of texts were given to Narihira. Narihira transmitted [one] text to his second son, Shigeharu. These matters are discussed in Nagayoshi's diary: "[Narihira's] son Shigeharu added the material [in *Ise monogatari*] that comes after the Serikawa Imperial Progress. He did this to transmit the inner meaning of waka, the Path of Eroticism." However, only "Akone no ura kuden" was transmitted to Shigeharu, "Gyokuden" was not. Narihira offered "Gyokuden" to Amaterasu Ōmikami. It was not heard of for five imperial reigns. The five reigns were those of Seiwa, Yōzei, Kōkō, Uda, and Daigo. During the Engi era [901–23], Middle Counselor Kanetaka was sent as an imperial messenger to the Ise Grand Shrine. In a dream Kanetaka saw something wrapped up come from the shrine. When he woke up and looked around, he found [a scroll] wrapped in brocade. He took this and presented it to Emperor Daigo. This was "Gyokuden."[62]

According to *Kokin waka shū jo kikigaki* when "Gyokuden" was presented to Emperor Daigo in Engi 3 (903), he was so impressed that he immediately

---

59. *Shin Kokin shū* 1857.

60. *Gyokuden jinpi no maki*, pp. 545–46.

61. Ibid., p. 538. This identification, which occurs in the "Naidō ron" section, takes place in the context of an explication of the poem from *Ise monogatari* episode 106 (*Kokin shū* 294, Narihira). *Gyokuden jinpi no maki* claims that the poem was composed by Tatsuta Daimyōjin, but since Tatsuta Daimyōjin and Sumiyoshi Daimyōjin are the same deity, and Narihira is an avatar (*kegen* 化現) of Sumiyoshi, the poem was attributed to Narihira. The identification of Narihira with Sumiyoshi is also essential to *Gyokuden jinpi no maki* explications of "Tsuki ya aranu" (*Ise monogatari* episode 4), p. 539; and "Mizu mo arazu" (*Ise monogatari* episode 99), p. 541.

62. I have used the *Kokin waka shū jo kikigaki* (pp. 229–30) version of the story here because it is more condensed and easier to follow than the version in *Gyokuden jinpi no maki*. The version in the Reizei school *Ise monogatari shō* is substantially the same; however, *Shinsen teisetsu shū* differs somewhat in that it seems to indicate that both texts were transmitted to the Ise Shrine.

ordered the compilation of the *Kokin shū*: "When the emperor saw this text, he understood the deep meaning of waka. From this time he began to revere this path and asked that the *Kokin shū* be compiled. Thus Narihira's 'ware mite mo' poem is the origin of the imperial anthologies of the eight reigns."[63] In other words, Narihira kept "Akone no ura kuden" and transmitted it to his son Shigeharu; the implication is that Narihira used it as the basis for writing *Ise monogatari* and then transmitted it to his son so that later generations of his family would be able to correctly interpret *Ise monogatari*'s esoteric meaning.

According to a transmission lineage in the *Kingyoku sōgi* variant of *Gyokuden jinpi no maki*, the texts that explained the true meaning of *Ise monogatari* were transmitted through Shigeharu to a series of not particularly famous descendents of Narihira. By the eleventh century, however, the transmission crossed over to more important poets such as Fujiwara no Toshitada, Shunzei, Teika, Tameie, and finally Tameaki.[64]

According to *Gyokuden jinpi no maki*, the second text, "Gyokuden," was not transmitted to Shigeharu, but was offered along with a transmission lineage to the Outer Shrine at Ise.[65] In most versions of *Gyokuden jinpi no maki* there is a *Kokin shū* lineage document that corroborates this transmission account.[66] It traces the transmission of *Kokin shū* commentaries from

---

63. *Kokin waka shū jo kikigaki*, p. 230.

64. "*Ise monogatari* shishi sōshō kechimyakufu," in Ishigami Hideaki, "*Kingyoku sōgi*," pt. II, pp. 45–46.

65. The version given in *Kikigaki* states that "Gyokuden" was presented to Amaterasu, whereas the *Gyokuden jinpi maki* version of this story specifies that it was presented not to the Inner Shrine of Amaterasu, but to the Outer Shrine of Toyouke no Hime; see Katagiri, *Chūsei*, vol. 5, pp. 524–25, 526. As discussed in Chapter 7, this may hint that Tameaki had some kind of contact with the Outer Shrine priests who were developing, at precisely this same time, spurious commentaries to support Watarai Shinto, a newly created form of Ryōbu Shinto. A lineage document in the *Kingyoku sōgi* version of *Gyokuden jinpi no maki* indicates that one of Tameaki's most important disciples, a Shingon priest named Ichijō Yoshimoto, lived in Ise province; this may have been a connection. See Ishigami Hideaki, "*Kingyoku sōgi*," pt. I, p. 48.

66. The *Kingyoku sōgi* version of *Gyokuden jinpi no maki* includes two transmission lineages for the *Kokin shū*: "Kechimyaku nengo okugaki dai to hiuta" and "*Kokin* waka shishi sōden kechimyakufu" (ibid., pp. 47–48). *Gyokuden jinpi no maki* only includes one: "Kechimyaku nengo okugaki" (Katagiri, *Chūsei*, vol. 5, pp. 531–35). See also the listing of the contents of all the variants of *Gyokuden jinpi no maki* in Ishigami Hidemi, "*Gyokuden jinpi no maki* kaidai kō." (Ishigami Hidemi and Ishigami Hideaki are the same person; Ishigami changed his name to Hideaki for a short time.)

Narihira to Ise Shrine and from there to Emperor Daigo, Tsurayuki, Minamoto no Shitagō, Nagaie, Minamoto no Tsunenobu, Minamoto no Toshiyori, Shunzei, Teika, Tameie, and finally, Tameaki. Thus the origin stories for the two most important secret texts transmitted within the *kanjō* ceremony claim that "Akone no ura kuden" and "Gyokuden" formed the bases for *Ise monogatari* and the *Kokin shū*, respectively. This meant, of course, that those with access to "Akone no ura kuden" and "Gyokuden" could read *Ise monogatari* and *Kokin shū* as they were meant to be read, as esoteric Buddhist allegories. The origin stories' self-authenticating transmission lineages completed the hermeneutic circle of authority.

For the etiology outlined above to be persuasive, both "Akone no ura kuden" and "Gyokuden" had to be revelations from Sumiyoshi Daimyōjin, the guardian deity of waka poetry. How did Sumiyoshi Daimyōjin become the central figure of sacred poetic authority? Moreover, Narihira had to be an avatar of Sumiyoshi Daimyōjin and thus uniquely qualified to receive and transmit those revelations. How and why was it accepted that a poet could be an avatar of a kami? How did Narihira specifically become associated with Sumiyoshi Daimyōjin? Finally, given the esoteric and often Tachikawa content of the commentaries, Narihira had to have been trained in Shingon Buddhism.

Sumiyoshi Daimyōjin as the Deity of Waka Poetry

The deities who collectively became known as the Sumiyoshi Daimyōjin began as guardians, not of poetry, but of fishermen and others who made their living by the sea.[67] Suminoe was a port thought to have been established in Naniwa sometime in the fourth century during the reign of Emperor Nintoku (r. 313–99). Later the sea receded, and the area came to be called Sumiyoshi. In the Nara and early Heian period, sailors prayed for safe passage and good fishing to the kami at Suminoe Shrine. The three masculine kami were known as Sokozutsunoo no Mikoto, Nakazutsunoo no Mikoto and Uhazutsunoo no Mikoto. According to the *Koji ki* (Record of ancient matters; 712) and the *Nihon shoki*, they were born when Izanagi purified himself

67. The following discussion relies in good part on Nishimoto Yutaka's (*Sumiyoshi Taisha*, pp. 105–14) discussion of Sumiyoshi as *okina* (sacred old man) and Miwa Masatane's ("*Chikuen shō* karon no seisei to hatten: kashin toshite no Sumiyoshi myōjin o megutte") analysis of the development of the Sumiyoshi Daimyōjin as the guardian deity of waka poetry. In English, see Ponsonby-Fane, *Suminoe no Ohokami*.

after his trip to the underworld.[68] These were the three deities who possessed Empress Jingū and directed her campaign against Korea.[69] Probably because of this association, sometime later Empress Jingū came to be enshrined as a fourth deity at Sumiyoshi.

According to Nishimoto Yutaka, by the Nara period the combined deities of Sumiyoshi were thought to appear in human form.[70] In the *Koji ki* story about the two brothers who had the luck of the sea and luck of the mountains, it is thought that the sea-brine deity, Shiotsuchi no Kami, who appears to the younger brother, Hoori no Mikoto, and gives him good advice about how to deal with his older brother, is related to Sumiyoshi. In the *Nihon shoki*, Shiotsuchi is described as Shiotsutsu no Oji (Old Man of the Sea). Nishomoto argues that this Old Man of the Sea is the same as the triune of masculine deities associated with Sumiyoshi.[71] This is the guise of Sumiyoshi Daimyōjin described in the "Akashi" chapter of *Genji monogatari*, in which Genji calls on Sumiyoshi Daimyōjin as the deity of the sea for protection from a tremendous storm, and receives an oracle from the deity in a dream directing him to leave Suma Bay and travel to Akashi.[72]

The Sumiyoshi deity's appearance in *Genji monogatari* leads us to the second step in the development of Sumiyoshi Daimyōjin: the association of the Sumiyoshi area with literature. By the late Heian period, Sumiyoshi was famous for its picturesque scenery. For example, *Sarashina nikki* (Sarashina diary; eleventh century) contains this description:

> On the following evening we reached the Bay of Sumiyoshi just as the sun was sinking over the mountaintop. I have never seen a painting to equal the beauty of this scene—the pine branches and the sky all shrouded with mist, the surface of the sea, the waves breaking on the beach,

---

68. Phillipi, *Kojiki*, p. 70; Aston, *Nihongi*, p. 27.

69. Phillipi, *Kojiki*, pp. 259–63; Aston, *Nihongi*, pp. 226–38. The fourteenth-century scholar Kitabatake Chikafusa describes the same events; see Varley, *A Chronicle of Gods and Sovereigns: Jinnō Shōtōki of Kitabatake Chikafusa*, p. 101–2. According to Phillipi, the three masculine deities appear to have been ancestor deities of the Azumi clan, seafarers and traders who may have played an important role in Jingū's expedition to Korea.

70. Early appearances of Sumiyoshi in human form (i.e., as an *arahitogami* 現人神) are mentioned in *Settsu kuni fudo ki* and *Harima kuni fudo ki* as quoted in *Shoku Nihon ki*, as well as in a *Man'yō shū* poem; see Nishimoto, *Sumiyoshi Taisha*, pp. 105–6.

71. Nishimoto, *Sumiyoshi Taisha*, p. 107.

72. Seidensticker, *The Tale of Genji*, p. 246–52.

How shall I describe it,
to what shall I compare it—
this Bay of Sumiyoshi on an autumn eve?[73]

Sumiyoshi with its pine trees was considered a poetic place-name (*uta makura* 歌枕) quite early on; it is listed by Nōin in *Nōin uta makura* under "Sumiyoshi in the province of Settsu."[74] The name was also used as a pivot word in waka poetry, playing on the literal meaning of Sumiyoshi as "living well." For example, *Kokin shū* 917:

Sumiyoshi to / ama wa tsugu tomo / nagai su na
hito wasuregusa / ou to iu nari

Though fisherfolk say Sumiyoshi is a good place to live, don't
stay there long,
for it's said that grasses of forgetfulness thrive there too.[75]

According to Miwa Masatane, the literary and the religious aspects of Sumiyoshi begin to be integrated in the late Heian period. Miwa suggests that the gradual shift of Sumiyoshi Daimyōjin's popular image from a seafaring deity to the guardian deity of waka poetry began when Emperor Shirakawa established the twenty-two shrines that were to receive official recognition. Sumiyoshi Shrine was included in the central seven and became a popular stopping place on the pilgrimage route to Kumano. It is from around this time that we start to see the dedication of sets of poems at Sumiyoshi Shrine.[76]

The preface to such a set of poems by Sensai, the Tendai priest who drew a waka mandala to use in poetry meetings, provides one of the earliest explicit associations of the Sumiyoshi deity with poetry. Sensai organized poetry contests that included poets such as Fujiwara no Mototoshi and Minamoto no Toshiyori. In 1106 he made a pilgrimage to Sumiyoshi Shrine, arriving on the thirteenth day of the ninth month in order to confess, along the lines of Po Chü-i, his poetic sin of "wild words and ornate phrases." At the shrine he painted a portrait of the Daimyōjin and presented it along with the following "confession," which served as a preface to a set of poems:

---

73. Morris, *As I Crossed a Bridge of Dreams*, p. 15.

74. Nōin, *Nōin uta makura*, p. 92.

75. In ibid. (p. 74), Sumiyoshi is associated with "forgetting grass" because of *Kokin shū* 917.

76. Miwa, *Kagaku hiden no kenkyū*, p. 21.

Poetry arose long ago with the separation of Yin and Yang and the formation of mountains and rivers. The feelings inspired by the illustrious kami caused [humans] to compose poetry. Sumiyoshi left metaphors as Manifest Traces, and later generations of poets have followed those few examples he left in the dust and grime of this world. If one inquires into Sumiyoshi's Original Ground, the deity is none other than the bodhisattva Kōkitokuō, who gathered up the sutras when the Buddha died in the Sala Forest and later gave sermons on them. The language of the sutras is simple and easy; it has only one meaning that is true. I have often composed poems in an impromptu fashion. On a spring morning, I have playfully pointed to the cherry blossoms and called them clouds. On autumn evenings, I have taken the moonlight for snow. I cannot avoid the criticism of having used illusory language. What good can come of an excess of flowery language? Therefore I have painted an image of the Bodhisattva and intoned a sutra while facing the image in order to do recompense for my sins. And I ask that all the wild words of my entire lifetime be a link to my enlightenment. That is all.[77]

Sensai's identification of Sumiyoshi with the bodhisattva Kōkitokuō was undoubtedly no accident. According to the *Nirvana Sutra*, Kōkitokuō is the bodhisattva who copied down the Buddha's sermons. These lecture notes then supposedly served as the source for a number of sutras. By claiming that Sumiyoshi is an incarnation of Kōkitokuō, Sensai sets up the argument that waka poetry is the Japanese equivalent of sutras or, at the very least, an effective expedient device used by buddhas and bodhisattvas in their Manifest Trace guise as Japanese deities.

In 1128 the first poetry contest held at Sumiyoshi Shrine took place. This contest was said to have been prompted by the Sumiyoshi Daimyōjin's appearance in a number of different people's dreams, an indication that he was angry and jealous that a poetry contest had not yet been held at his shrine. The next Sumiyoshi poetry contest, organized by the lay priest Dōin (1090–1179?) and judged by Fujiwara no Shunzei, took place in 1170. An anecdote from Tachibana no Narisue's *Kokon chomon jū* gives us a sense of the contemporary attitude toward Sumiyoshi Daimyōjin:

On the ninth day of the tenth month of 1170, Priest Dōin gathered a number of people together at Sumiyoshi Shrine to hold a poetry contest. . . . Fujiwara no Sanesada [then 32] composed the following poem on the theme "Shrine Moon":

---

77. Sensai, *Ungō-ji seinen zan kyōgen kigo waka jo*, p. 236. For a discussion of Sensai and a somewhat different translation of this same section, see Plutschow, *Chaos and Cosmos*, p. 161.

> *furinikeru / matsu mono iwaba / toite mashi*
> *mukashi mo kaku ya / Suminoe no tsuki*
>
> If this aged pine could talk, I'd ask whether
> the moon over Suminoe shone as radiantly in the distant past
> as it does tonight.

Shunzei, who was judging, was very impressed with this poem, and everyone else gave it high marks as well. Not long after this, Sanesada was traveling by boat through Settsu province with the yearly tribute from his family's domain in Tsukushi, when an evil wind came up and the waves threatened to overrun the boat. Suddenly an old man (*okina*) appeared out of nowhere and managed to avert the crisis by helping out with the rowing. The boatmen were awestruck. The old man told them: "An old man who lives in the area has come because he was so impressed with the poem, 'If this aged pine could talk.' Please report this." So saying, he disappeared. The Sumiyoshi deity must have been so moved by the poem that he appeared in person. This is a very mysterious story.[78]

Here we have a nice illustration of how, by the late twelfth century, all of Sumiyoshi's attributes had been assimilated into one package. In this anecdote Sumiyoshi as *okina* appears in his guise of a kami who guards the waterways and protects those who travel across them, but he does so because he was impressed by a poem composed at his shrine.

According to Kamo no Chōmei's *Mumyō shō*, Dōin believed that devotion to Sumiyoshi would improve his poetry: "The Lay Priest Dōin's fervent devotion to poetry. In his deep devotion to the discipline of poetry, Dōin was unparalleled. Even into his eighties he traveled from Kamo to Sumiyoshi monthly, praying that he might compose fine poems. He deserves praise for this."[79] It seems likely that Dōin organized the Sumiyoshi poetry contest because of this fervent devotion, which he wished to spread to others. From this and the previous anecdote, it appears that a link between poetry and devotion to Sumiyoshi Daimyōjin had been firmly established by the 1170s.

There are a number of indications that the Mikohidari house (including Shunzei, Teika, and Tameie) venerated Sumiyoshi as the guardian of waka poetry. First, Shunzei served as a judge for the 1170 Sumiyoshi poetry contest. Second, Shunzei's *Gosha hyakushu* (Hundred-poem sequence dedicated at five shrines) followed the example of Sensai in dedicating a set of poems

78. Tachibana Narisue, *Kokon chomonjū*, pp. 216–17.

79. Kamo no Chōmei, *Mumyō shō*, p. 90. For a slightly different translation, see Hilda Katō, "The *Mumyōshō*," p. 396.

as a confession of "wild words and ornate phrases." Third, Shunzei invoked both Sumiyoshi Daimyōjin and Tamatsushima Myōjin as guardian deities of poetry in his preface to *Senzai waka shū* (Collection of Japanese poems of a thousand years, ca. 1187). And *Shōtetsu monogatari* has the following story:

In his old age Lord Shunzei continued as always to compose poetry day and night and did nothing about religious preparations for the world to come. Worried about what might become of him in the next life, he undertook a retreat of seven days at the Sumiyoshi Shrine. He appealed to the god, vowing, "If poetry is a useless activity, I will give up this art from now on and devote myself wholeheartedly to religious preparations for the life to come." On the seventh night of his retreat, the deity appeared to him in a dream and said, "Japanese poetry and the Way of the Buddha are one whole not two." Concluding from this that he should not seek the path of the Buddha apart from this art, he devoted himself to poetry more fervently than ever, it is said.

Teika, too, made a retreat at Sumiyoshi, timing it so that the thirteenth night of the ninth month would correspond to the seventh night of his stay, and making the same appeal to the god as Shunzei had done. On the thirteenth night of the ninth month, the deity appeared to him and said, "For you the moon is radiant." So he decided that the art of poetry was indeed as the god said. The work in which these and other matters are recorded is called *Record of the Radiant Moon* (*Meigetsu ki*).[80]

There are some doubts about the veracity of this account, particularly the story about Teika. It seems to have been lifted from *Maigetsu shō* (Monthly notes; 1219), which some scholars have argued is at least partially spurious. Compare the pertinent passage from *Maigetsu shō*:

Some time ago, during the Genkyū era [1204–1206], when I made a retreat at Sumiyoshi, I had a wonderful dream inspired by the god, in which I was told, "For you the moon is radiant." Because of this I wrote my *Record of the Radiant Moon*, so as to contribute to the poetic traditions of my house—although it was, I realize, a far greater task than I was worthy to perform.[81]

The problem is that *Meigetsu ki*, which from the description would seem to be a compilation of Teika's poetic insights, is in fact the name now given to Teika's *kanbun* diary. There is no mention in this diary of any visit to Sumiyoshi during the Genkyū era. I will not go into the arguments here, but most scholars now feel that the contents of *Maigetsu shō* as a whole conform well

80. Translation (modified) from Brower, *Conversations with Shōtetsu*, pp. 89–90.

81. Fujiwara no Teika, *Maigetsu shō* (*NKBT*), p. 527; translation (modified) from Brower, "Fujiwara Teika's *Maigetsushō*," p. 422.

enough to Teika's opinions stated elsewhere to be taken as Teika's work, and that this particular passage might have been interpolated into the text in the late thirteenth or early fourteenth century.[82] If, as Robert Brower has suggested, the Reizei family had initial possession of the text, it would make some sense that this kind of interpolation about Sumiyoshi was made, since so many of the Reizei commentaries influenced by the Tameaki school involved Sumiyoshi Daimyōjin. An anecdote in which Teika was himself granted a vision of Sumiyoshi would have given added authority to the Reizei school *Ise monogatari shō*, which incorporated the origin story of the "Akone no ura kuden" and "Gyokuden."

Another interesting point here involves dating. In *Maigetsu shō*, no specific dates are given for Teika's trip; in *Shōtetsu monogatari*, however, we are told that Teika went in the ninth month and timed his visit so that the seventh day of his visit would coincide with the nearly full moon on the thirteenth. The moon of the thirteenth day of the ninth month was generally considered the second most beautiful moon of the year (after the fifteenth of the eighth month) and so was called *meigetsu* (明月 radiant moon).[83] During the medieval period, there was also a large festival at the shrine on that day with horse races, sumo wrestling, and various dances to *gagaku* 雅楽 orchestral music.[84] It is possible that Sensai set a precedent when he chose this day to present his set of confessional poems; besides Teika, Minamoto no Tsunenobu in *Waka chiken shū* and the Noh playwright Komparu Zenchiku in *Meishuku shō* received dream visions on this night.[85] I doubt these dates are coincidental. It would seem that by the mid-Kamakura period, an artist

---

82. For a discussion of how the lines in question pertain to the problem of *Maigetsu shō*'s authenticity, see Brower, "Fujiwara Teika's *Maigetsushō*," pp. 404–5.

83. This may be another reason why Shōtetsu referred to the text that recounts the story about Teika's visit to Sumiyoshi as *Meigetsu ki*.

84. For a description of the medieval records of this festival, see Nishimoto, *Sumiyoshi Taisha*, pp. 178–82.

85. Minamoto no Tsunenobu is known to have written a Chinese poem praising the radiant moon of the ninth month:

> The clear, round moon lights that darkness;
> In the splendid hall we start a banquet—the night grows old.
> With vigour we discuss the shining beauty of this evening;
> It is even more gorgeous than the rays on the fifteenth of mid-autumn.

Translation from Smits, *The Pursuit of Loneliness*, p. 70. Smits (ibid., p. 124*n*75) notes Kojima Noriyuki's suggestion that in the Heian period the thirteenth of the ninth month may have actually been more popular for poetry gatherings than the fifteenth of the eighth month.

seeking a reassuring revelation from Sumiyoshi that his artistic practice had Buddhist value went on the thirteenth night of the ninth month.

Texts more reliably attributable to Teika also indicate his veneration of Sumiyoshi. In Teika's *Gotoba-in Kumano gokō ki* (Record of the imperial progress to Kumano by Retired Emperor Go-Toba; 1201), Go-Toba composed the following poem when the imperial procession stopped at Sumiyoshi on the way to Kumano Shrine:

> *aioi no / hisashiki iro mo / toki wa nite*
> *kimi ga dai mamoru / Sumiyoshi no matsu*
>
> The ancient twin pine at Sumiyoshi whose color remains evergreen
> protects this age of our sovereign.

Teika's reply:

> *kakute nao / kawarazu mamore / yo yo o hete*
> *kono michi terasu / Sumiyoshi no kami*
>
> Sumiyoshi Kami, who has enlightened this path through the ages,
> please give it your unchanging protection.[86]

In Teika's poem, "this path" (*kono michi*) apparently refers to the Path of Poetry. More generally, however, these poems focus on the benevolent protection of the kami and its efficacy as an image of verdant long life.

Two other poems by Teika make a more direct correlation between Sumiyoshi and poetry:

> *kata bakari / ware wa tsutaeshi / waga michi no*
> *tae ya hatenuru / Sumiyoshi no kami*
>
> My small efforts at transmitting the path;
> Sumiyoshi Kami, have they all come to nothing?[87]
>
> *tsure mo naku / nao Suminoe ni / tamuke kusa*
> *hikisuteraruru / michi no kuchiba o*
>
> Although I should have been dead long ago, I'm still alive;
> here at Suminoe I dedicate these withered leaves discarded
> on the roadside.[88]

86. As quoted in Miwa, "*Chikuen shō* karon . . . Sumiyoshi myōjin o megutte," p. 50.

87. *Shūi gusō* 1195.

88. Ibid., 2895. As quoted in Miwa, "*Chikuen shō* karon . . . Sumiyoshi myōjin o megutte," p. 50.

Both poems clearly assume a strong connection between Sumiyoshi and poetry, especially the deity's protection for the Path of Poetry. The second poem implies a comparison between the evergreen needles of the Sumiyoshi pine and Teika's own withered "leaves" of poetry, for which he hopes to gain immortality by dedicating them to Sumiyoshi Shrine.

Finally, Tameie's *Shichisha hyakushu* (Hundred-poem sequence dedicated at seven shrines), which emulates his grandfather Shunzei's *Gosha hyakushu*, has this poem about Sumiyoshi:

> *Shikishima no / Yamato koto no ha / kimi ni aite*
> *man'yo mamore / Sumiyoshi no kami*
> Sumiyoshi Kami, with our sovereign, please protect the poetry
> of these scattered islands of Yamato through ten thousand ages.[89]

The poem puns on *man'yo*, which in one sense means "ten thousand generations" (万代) but also alludes to the *Man'yō shū* (万葉集 Collection of ten thousand leaves). Like an emperor who commissions poetry anthologies, Sumiyoshi protects and promotes the poetry of Japan. Although there is more than a hint of self-interest here (Tameie was commissioned to compile two imperial anthologies), it is clear that Tameie, like his father, Teika, and grandfather Shunzei, venerated Sumiyoshi as the deity of waka poetry. It is not surprising then, that his son Tameaki's commentaries would use Sumiyoshi Daimyōjin as the authoritative source for the esoteric secrets of waka.

Tamatsushima Myōjin as the Female Deity of Waka Poetry

The rise of Sumiyoshi Daimyōjin as the deity of waka poetry is probably not unrelated to the number of excellent poets in the Tsumori family, the hereditary shrine administrators at Sumiyoshi from the late twelfth century onward. They undoubtedly encouraged poetry contests at their shrine, as well as the notion that worship of Sumiyoshi would move one forward on the Path of Poetry. We do not, however, have any direct evidence for their participation in the development of Sumiyoshi Daimyōjin as the guardian deity of waka poetry, except for poems such as the following by Tameaki's friend, Tsumori Kunisuke:

89. As quoted in Miwa, "*Chikuen shō* karon . . . Sumiyoshi myōjin o megutte," p. 50.

Shikishima no / michi mamorikeru / kami o shimo
waga kamigaki to / omou ureshisa

What joy to think that my shrine fence
is that of the kami who protects this Path of Poetry.[90]

On the other hand, we do have such evidence for the development of Tamatsushima Myōjin as Sumiyoshi's female counterpart. It is worth digressing here to discuss that development, both because Tamatsushima is often mentioned in the commentaries and because it sheds light on the process by which a deity takes on new functions.

The Tamatsushima Shrine is located on a small island, now called Imoseyama, in what used to be called Waka no Ura (和歌浦 Waka Bay) in Wakayama prefecture. Waka Hirume no Mikoto (稚日女尊) was enshrined there originally, and then, perhaps because Empress Jingū venerated her, Empress Jingū was enshrined there as well. Probably because of the shrine's location on Waka Bay and because one of Tamatsushima's aspects was named Waka Hirume no Mikoto (although written with different graphs), Tamatsushima Myōjin came to be associated with waka poetry. This association in turn led to the enshrinement of Sotoori Hime, a consort of Emperor Ingyō (r. 411–53), who was traditionally considered the first of the great female poets. In both the Japanese and the Chinese prefaces to the *Kokin shū*, Sotoori Hime is honored as the poetic ancestor of Ono no Komachi. It was probably because of this association that Sotoori Hime was added to make up the triune of female deities.[91]

In a section from the third fascicle of *Ōgi shō*, Rokujō Kiyosuke noted the connection of Sotoori Hime and Tamatsushima with Sumiyoshi:

Regarding the "Sotoori Hime" mentioned in the *Kokin shū* preface: according to the *Nihon shoki* she was the daughter of the second lineage Crown Prince Wakanuna. In the eighth year of his reign, Emperor Ingyō went to Fujiwara in the spring, during the second month, and secretly watched Sotoori Hime's behavior.[92] That night, Sotoori Hime was alone, longing for the emperor. Unaware that he was already there, she composed the following poem:

---

90. *Shin Gosen shū* 742.

91. Katagiri, "Waka no ura," in idem, *Uta makura, uta kotoba jiten*, pp. 441–43.

92. According to the story in the *Nihon shoki*, Sotoori Hime was the younger sister of Emperor Ingyō's main wife. Because of this wife's jealousy, he kept Sotoori Hime tucked away at Fujiwara near Asuka and was not able to visit her very often (Aston, *Nihongi*, pp. 318–21).

waga seko ga / kubeki yoi nari / sasagani no
kumo no furumai / kanete shirushi mo

The spider spinning his web is a sign that this night
my beloved will surely come.[93]

Sumiyoshi has four shrines; the southern shrine is dedicated to Sotoori Hime. According to Tsumori Kunimoto, she is called Tamatsushima Myōjin.[94]

Kunimoto was head shrine administrator of Sumiyoshi, the thirty-ninth generation of the Tsumori family to hold that post. He was an excellent poet and part of a literary circle surrounding Emperor Shirakawa that included Kiyosuke's grandfather Akisue.

Both Tsumori Kunimoto's (1023–1102) personal poetry collection and Kiyosuke's *Fukurozōshi* present a more complete version of the story of how Tamatsushima and Sumiyoshi were associated:

In order to get the stone for the altar of one of the shrines, I [Kunimoto] went to the province of Kii, where there is a shrine on the island of Tamatsushima in Waka Bay. Inquiring about it, I was told that the deity Sotoori Hime, finding the place attractive, became a kami there and that the people who cross over to the island present poems. So I composed the following:

toshi furedo / oimosezushite / Waka no ura ni
ikuyo ni narinu / Tamatsushima hime

Although the years go by, she is always young.
For how many generations has Tamatsushima Hime gone down
to Waka Bay?

The night I presented this poem, I had a dream in which the altar door opened, and twelve court ladies appeared wearing Chinese-style robes. Expressing their pleasure, they gave instructions on which stone I should take. When I searched as instructed, there was a stone that fit the dream oracle. When the stone was worked upon, one blow caused it to break into twelve pieces [equivalent to the twelve court ladies], and it was perfect for the altar.[95]

---

93. *Nihon shoki* (*Kokka taikan* 65); *Kokin shū* 1110. The *Nihon shoki* poem differs slightly; Kiyosuke follows the *Kokin shū* version. See Edwin Cranston's translation of the *Nihon shoki* poem in *A Waka Anthology*, p. 85. Kiyosuke appears to have combined the story from *Nihon shoki* with the poem from the *Kokin shū*. In China and Japan it was thought that a spider spinning a web on your robe was a sign that the one you await will come.

94. Rokujō Kiyosuke, *Ōgi shō*, pp. 349–50.

95. Quoted in Miwa, *Kagaku hiden no kenkyū*, pp. 21–22. See also Rokujō Kiyosuke's version in *Fukurozōshi*, p. 158. There is a pivot on "waka" meaning "poetry" (和歌) and "young"

It seems likely that in this story we are seeing the Tsumori family's incorporation of Tamatsushima into Sumiyoshi as one of a triune of female deities worshipped at the fourth shrine. This incorporation would have been given further support by the fact that Empress Jingū was an aspect of both Sumiyoshi and Tamatsushima; the shrine selected to house Tamatsushima at Sumiyoshi already enshrined Empress Jingū. Kunimoto's story indicates that prior to Tamatsushima's incorporation into Sumiyoshi, the deity as Sotoori Hime was being presented with poems as a form of worship. Like Sumiyoshi, she appeared to respond best to prayers in the form of poems. Kunimoto's own poem, which alludes to Waka Bay, explicitly connects Tamatsushima and waka, and the deity responds favorably.

A poem from the personal collection of Fujiwara no Mototoshi, a contemporary of Kunimoto's, further corroborates the popularity of the worship of Tamatsushima as a deity of waka:

Upon hearing that someone on the way to Kumano had composed a poem at Waka Bay:

> *Waka no ura ni / kimi ga iioku / koto no ha o*
> *ika ni kikiken / Tamatsushima hime*
>
> The poem you leave at Waka Bay for Tamatsushima Hime—
> what does she think of it?[96]

Mototoshi seems ambivalent about Tamatsushima Myōjin's power to answer prayers in the form of waka. His poem nevertheless indicates the presence at the time of a widespread belief that if someone fervently desires something, especially something involving poetry, Tamatsushima Myōjin will respond.

Tamatsushima's triune of female deities quickly became linked with the triune of male deities at Sumiyoshi. This led to the two often being presented together as the mother and father of waka poetry. As noted above, Fujiwara no Shunzei, who was a disciple of Mototoshi, invoked the pair in his preface to *Senzai shū*: "This collection . . . will be transmitted for as long as the breeze blows through the pines at Sumiyoshi, the peaceful waves lap at Tamatsushima, across thousands upon thousands of springs and autumns,

---

(若). In Kiyosuke's version, Waka Bay is written with the graphs 若浦 rather than 和歌浦, which underscores the pun.

96. *Mototoshi shū* 178; quoted in Miwa, *Kagaku hiden no kenkyū*, p. 22.

through reign upon reign layered like frost upon stars."[97] Thus, by the late twelfth century, it was taken as a poetic commonplace that Tamatsushima and Sumiyoshi were two of the three guardian deities of waka, along with Kakinomoto no Hitomaro.

Late thirteenth-century texts such as Tameaki's *Kokin waka shū jo kikigaki* and *Gyokuden jinpi no maki* made a concerted effort to explain the relationship of Tamatsushima and Sotoori Hime to give temporal precedence to Tamatsushima's position as the female deity of waka poetry. For example, *Kokin waka shū jo kikigaki* reverses the probable development of the Tamatsushima deities in the course of its discussion of the line from the *Kokin shū* preface that relates Ono no Komachi and Sotoori Hime:

The line "Ono no Komachi is in the lineage (*nagare/ryū* 流) of Sotoori Hime of old" does not mean that she was a descendant of Sotoori Hime; it means that she received the lineage of Sotoori Hime's teachings on poetry. Ono no Komachi was the granddaughter of Middle Counselor Yoshizane, the daughter of the governor of Dewa, Ono no Tsunetaka. Sotoori Hime was the granddaughter of Emperor Ōjin [r. 270–310], the daughter of the second lineage Crown Prince Wakanuna, and the consort of Emperor Ingyō. In the various schools this person [Sotoori Hime] is called Tamatsushima. This identification is not without some logic. According to the teaching in our school, when Emperor Kōkō was ill and various prayers were being performed on his behalf, a court lady dressed in a red skirt appeared by his pillow at dawn and recited this poem:

> *tachikaeri / mata mo kono yo ni / ato taren*
> *kono na ureshiki / Waka no ura nami*
>
> I want to return once again, to leave my traces in this world
> like the waves returning to the shores of Waka Bay, whose name
> so delights me.

In his dream the emperor asked "Who are you?" and the woman replied, "Sotoori Hime." In accordance with the dream, in Ninna 3 [887] on the thirteenth day of the ninth month, the emperor sent Major Controller of the Right Minamoto no Takayuki as an imperial emissary to build Tamatsushima Shrine in Waka Bay. When Shinpen Shōnin petitioned her, she appeared in her Original Ground form as Shōkannon, and he worshipped her [in that form]. The idea of her leaving her Manifest Traces at Waka Bay derives from the idea of "returning waves" in the poem. Sotoori Hime manifested herself as a kami at Waka Bay by means of the

---

97. Quoted in Miwa, *Kagaku hiden no kenkyū*, p. 20.

poem about the returning waves. It is said that since the name "Waka Bay" was especially auspicious, she decided to manifest her traces there.[98]

Given this origin story's relatively late date (1280s), it is of rather doubtful authenticity, but it contains some noteworthy points. First, when Ki no Tsurayuki said in the *Kokin shū* preface that Ono no Komachi's poetry was in Sotoori Hime's *nagare* (stream or current), he was undoubtedly simply making the point that Ono no Komachi's passionate love poetry was in the style of Sotoori Hime. By the time of Tameaki's *Kokin waka shū jo kikigaki*, however, the graph for *nagare* (流) was read as "lineage" or "school" (*ryū*), and Ono no Komachi was understood to have literally received Sotoori Hime's secret teachings on poetry. Second, the origin of Tamatsushima Shrine is directly related to the dream oracle recitation of a poem that incorporates the name "Waka Bay." The emperor takes the line "the very name of Waka Bay is delightful" (*sono na ureshiki Waka no ura*) as a sign that Tamatsushima in her aspect as the poet Sotoori Hime has found the name Waka Bay delightful, and so desires to have a shrine built for her there. The connection between poetry and the creation of the shrine is absolutely fundamental, and naturally Tamatsushima should be worshipped as a guardian deity of poetry. Third, the date of the thirteenth day of the ninth month ties this story to Sumiyoshi as the guardian deity of waka poetry, since, as we have seen, this is the pre-eminent night for dream oracles relating poetry and Buddhism. Fourth, the identification of Tamatsushima's Original Ground as Shōkannon fits Ono no Komachi's common identification in the commentaries as one of the six forms of Kannon that save living beings in the Six Paths of Reincarnation (六道 *rokudō*).[99] This identification lent further

---

98. *Kokin waka shū jo kikigaki*, pp. 280–81.

99. Shōkannon is the most common of the six forms of Kannon. Ono no Komachi is also often identified as Nyoirin Kannon, who appears with a jewel or pearl (玉 *tama*), which symbolizes that all prayers will be fulfilled. It seems likely that this identification came about because of *Kokin shū* 557 in which Ono no Komachi plays on the *Lotus Sutra* parable of the priceless jewel that a man sews into the robe of his sleeping friend. The play on jewel (*tama*) in this poem would have provided a further link to Tamatsushima 玉津島. By the Muromachi period Komachi and Tamatsushima were firmly linked in the popular imagination: according to Zeami's *Sarugaku dangi* (Reflections on Noh; 1430), in an earlier version of the Noh play *Sotoba Komachi* (Komachi on the stupa), Komachi travels to Tamatsushima Shrine to make an offering and is rewarded by the appearance of an intermediary deity. See Rimer and Yamasaki, *On the Art of Nō Drama: The Major Treatises of Zeami*, p. 215; for a brief discussion of how Zeami's elimination of Komachi's connection to the deity affects the play, see

support to the idea that Ono no Komachi was an incarnation of Tamatsushima, a reincarnation of Sotoori Hime, and a fitting counterpart to Narihira as the kami of Yin and Yang.

Narihira as *Okina*

The next step is to identify the process that made it possible for Tameaki to identify Narihira as an avatar of Sumiyoshi in his commentary on episode 117 of *Ise monogatari.*

First, in some of the later episodes of *Ise monogatari*, the "Man of Old" is identified as *okina* or *katai okina* (かたゐ翁 humble old man).[100] Originally, this probably meant little more than that the character had become old.[101] As we have seen, however, in some versions of episode 117 Sumiyoshi Daimyōjin manifests himself as an *okina.* The first impulse toward identifying Sumiyoshi Daimyōjin and Narihira as *okina* would have been the tendency among some readers of *Ise monogatari* to consider repetition of a generic title or descriptive phrase as a sign that two seemingly separate characters were to be identified as one.

Tameaki's identification of the Narihira *okina* and Sumiyoshi Daimyōjin *okina* as one figure who could serve as the source for oracular revelation in his commentaries would have been encouraged by a number of other factors as well. The first, of course, was the rise of Sumiyoshi Daimyōjin as the guardian deity of waka poetry. The choice of Sumiyoshi Daimyōjin as the source of

---

Yokota-Murakami, *The Formation of the Canon of Nō: The Literary Tradition of Divine Authority*, pp. 27–28.

100. The designation of the Man of Old as *okina* occurs in episodes 76, 77, 79, 81, 83, and 97. (Episode 114, which also mentions an old man, was generally understood to refer to Ariwara no Yukihira.) In a number of these episodes the character is further identified with Narihira by his position: officer in the Imperial Guards (76), middle captain (97), or director of the Right Horse Bureau (77, 83). Itō Masayoshi ("Yōkyoku *Takasago* zakkō," p. 118) notes that in one version of *Ise monogatari* (*Jingū Bunko-bon*) episode 117 includes the phrase *okina no nariayashiki* (the supernatural splendor of *okina*). However, this probably indicates a retroactive equation of Sumiyoshi-Narihira-*okina* because of the influence of the Kamakura commentaries.

101. Katagiri Yōichi (*Ise monogatari no shinkenkyū*, pp. 26–29) argues that this *okina* persona is the implied narrator. Katagiri suggests that *Ise monogatari* as a whole is structured like *mugen* (dream) Noh, in the sense that Narihira, who died in 880, returns to life as an old man and relates stories of his youth in the distant past, a world of courtly elegance that can never be recovered. Katagiri attributes this idea to Origuchi Shinobu. Although the idea is very appealing, it seems to me that there may be an ahistorical projection going on here in terms of the possible meanings that *okina* could have had in the Heian period.

revelation in Tameaki's commentaries was probably not unrelated to Tameaki's friendship with Tsumori Kunisuke. As mentioned in Chapter 7, Kunisuke was married to the granddaughter of Ietaka and may well have been involved in writing the Ietaka school version of *Waka chiken shū*, the first commentary to attribute its insights to oracles from Sumiyoshi Daimyōjin.

Second, *honji suijaku* thinking, which used puns and repetition to create identifications between the Original Ground of buddhas and bodhisattvas and kami as their Manifest Traces, was also used to identify famous poets, scholars, and important historical figures with kami and bodhisattvas. The identification of Narihira as a manifestation of Sumiyoshi makes a great deal of sense since it redoubles the poetic authority of the text. Not only is the sacred authority of Sumiyoshi brought into play, but if Narihira is none other than Sumiyoshi, the reader is getting the facts straight from the horse's mouth, so to speak—Who would know better than Narihira himself the secrets hidden in *Ise monogatari*?

Third, Tameaki may have wanted to make Narihira into an object of devotion comparable to Hitomaro in the Rokujō family. The central focus of Tameaki's commentaries is, after all, Narihira rather than Hitomaro. The problem with this last hypothesis is that all the descriptions of waka ceremonies in Tameaki-affiliated texts continue to give Hitomaro's image the pre-eminent place in the initiation chamber, along with Sumiyoshi Daimyōjin.[102] Perhaps, since Narihira was supposed to be Hitomaro reborn, it was not thought necessary to make Narihira the ritual focus, despite his importance as the vehicle for Sumiyoshi's revelations. As we shall see, however, in Nijō Tameakira's *Ise monogatari zuinō*, Narihira clearly takes on this function, which may indicate that Tameakira was attempting to develop a ceremony for the Nijō house that would be the equivalent of the Rokujō Hitomaro memorial ceremony.

Narihira's Esoteric Education

One last question that arises in conjunction with the commentaries is how Narihira come by such a profound understanding of esoteric Buddhism. The amount of Shingon Tachikawa content in the commentaries made it vital to explain how Narihira, who according to the historical record had little

102. See, e.g., the diagrammatic illustration of the physical arrangements for a waka lecture ceremony in *Chikuen shō* (*NKT*), p. 425.

or no formal religious training, was capable of even understanding, much less transmitting, that esoteric content. The obvious answer was to claim that Narihira had studied at a temple at some point in his youth. Given the importance of transmission lineages in legitimating the commentaries, it makes sense that the temple would be Tō-ji, the head temple for Shingon, and the priest he studied with would be Shinga (783–879), the younger brother of Kūkai and one of his foremost disciples. Shinga became the head of Tō-ji temple and the fourth grand archbishop (*daisōjō*) of the Shingon school.

Shinga's name appears in Tameaki's *Gyokuden jinpi no maki* as part of an explanation of a poem from episode 124 in *Ise monogatari*:

> *omou koto / iwade tada ni ya / yaminubeshi*
> *ware to hitoshiki / hito nakereba*[103]
>
> Since there is no like-minded person here,
> I'll just keep my thoughts to myself and say nothing.

Now as for Narihira's true intent and conception lying behind this poem, it signifies that he would not speak of how *Ise monogatari* was created or of the Path of Intercourse between men and women. When Narihira was fourteen, he became a disciple of Grand Archbishop Shinga, and from the age of sixteen to twenty-eight, he studied the inner secrets of Shingon. In the various transmission lineages, his Buddhist name is given as Kōken (好賢 Loving-Wisdom). Although he was a lay person, he took a Buddhist name. Thus the phrase "I'll just keep my thoughts to myself and say nothing" (*omou koto iwade*) means "remain silent and do not reveal the deep secrets of Shingon." Because Narihira was especially steeped in passion, Shinga transmitted the true meaning of Shingon, keeping nothing back.[104]

In the Nijō school *Kokin waka shū kanjō kuden*, this story is slightly altered and amplified by an anecdote indicating a miraculous birth:

Three days before his birth, in a dream, the four types of lotus flowers were scattered in the four directions from his mother's womb. A light shown from out of the womb, and from within the light the two characters 喟 and 嘥 appeared. Then two buddhas, Shakamuni and Tahō, sat and explained the principle of the non-arising seed syllable A. . . . After he was born, in accordance with his understanding of the superior vehicle of Shingon, he was called "Mandara-maru." When Narihira was

---

103. There is a slight discrepancy between the *Gyokuden jinpi no maki* version of this poem and the standard version found in episode 124 of *Ise monogatari*. The first three lines in *Ise monogatari* run: "omou koto / iwade zo tada ni / yaminubeki." The difference has little effect on the meaning.

104. *Gyokuden jinpi no maki*, p. 535.

eleven, he went to study with Grand Archibishop Shinga, the head priest at Jōgan-ji and Kōbō Daishi's disciple.[105]

As Arai Eizō has pointed out, there are a number of reasons why Shinga would have been chosen as Narihira's preceptor. First, it was necessary that the teacher be of the highest ranking, preferably a grand archbishop. Given Narihira's life dates, this meant Shinga, who was in approximately the right place at the right time to make a relationship with Narihira possible. Arai presents a biography of Shinga constructed from various documents:[106]

801: Birth. The younger brother of Kūkai by about 30 years.

806: Kūkai's return from China: Shinga begins training and progresses through levels of initiation.

833: Receives Shingon "secret seal" initiation. Is placed in charge of various temples.

850: Works with Fujiwara no Yoshifusa designing Kajō-ji in celebration of Yoshifusa's grandson's birth (the future Emperor Seiwa). From this time forward he serves the crown prince.

852: Supervises the moving of Emperor Ninmyō's (r. 833–90) Seiryōden palace, which becomes the basis of Kajō-ji temple. He builds a Western Hall and Empress Junshi builds an Eastern Hall for Yoshifusa's Shakamuni Buddha Hall (Shakadō).

861: Becomes the fourth head of Tō-ji temple (the main Shingon temple in Kyoto).

862: Builds Jōgan-ji in the back garden of Kajō-ji.

879: Death.

According to *Gyokuden jinpi no maki*, Narihira, born in 825, met Shinga in 838, studying with him from 840 to 852.[107] In 838 Shinga would have already been ordained to teach for five years. In 852, Shinga became active in the building of Kajō-ji and, one would suppose, too busy to continue supervising

105. *Kokin waka shū kanjō kuden*, p. 505. See also Arai Eizo, "*Kokin shū* kanjō hisho to Bukkyō kyōri," p. 7. The Reizei school *Ise monogatari shō* (p. 293) also includes a brief reference to Shinga: "From the time that he was eleven Narihira studied with Archbishop Shinga at Tō-ji. When he was sixteen, on the second day, third month of Shōwa 14 [847] he underwent the coming-of-age ceremony at Emperor Ninmyō's palace. His childhood name was 'Mandara.'" Since according to the traditional Japanese system for counting age (*kazoedoshi*) Narihira was sixteen in Shōwa 7 (840), this may be a transcription error.

106. Arai, "*Kokin shū* kanjō hisho to Bukkyō kyōri," p. 9.

107. Note that ages are figured according to the traditional *kazoedoshi* system.

Narihira's training. There are thus no glaring historical discrepancies that would preclude Shinga from being Narihira's preceptor.

A second reason that Shinga was an appropriate choice as teacher for Narihira is his strong political connections to Regent Fujiwara no Yoshifusa and his sister the Empress of the Fifth Ward, Junshi. Despite Narihira's convoluted relationship to the dominant Fujiwara court faction led by Yoshifusa, the Kamakura commentaries, most of which were written by members of the Fujiwara family, generally downplayed any implicit subversion or criticism of their ancestors.[108] The Reizei school *Ise monogatari shō* and the Nijō school Bishamondō *Kokin shū chū*, for example, claim that when Narihira was exiled, Yoshifusa took pity on him and let him stay in his villa in Higashiyama.[109] Fujiwara no Junshi is also portrayed in a sympathetic light. According to commentaries on episode 5, Junshi was the owner of the Fifth Ward mansion in which Takako and Narihira secretly met. Although initially resistant to their secret trysts, she eventually relented and allowed them to meet. In this view Junshi, who like Yoshifusa should have been adamantly opposed to Narihira's relationship with Takako since it was so clearly disruptive of their political plans for the girl, is strangely supportive. Given the attitude of the commentaries, Shinga's political and social connections to Yoshifusa, Junshi, and Seiwa would have made him even more attractive as a possible teacher of Narihira.

Another reason Shinga was chosen as Narihira's preceptor is that Tachikawa transmission documents nearly always name Shinga in their transmission lineages. For example, the Tachikawa text *Juhō yōshin shō* (On the circumspect maintenance of Dharma) states: "Among the numberless disciples of Kōbō Daishi there were ten disciples of the *kanjō* level. These were all at a high level of wisdom, practice, and virtue. Among these Jichie and Shinga were especially praised by Kōbō Daishi. Therefore he left behind an order . . . that when Jichie passed on, Shinga was to become the head of Shingon."[110] *Gyokuden jinpi no maki* clearly implies that Shinga was involved in Tachikawa: "Because Narihira was especially steeped in passion, Shinga transmitted the

108. For discussions of Narihira as a figure of resistance to the Fujiwara, see Okada, *Figures of Resistance*, pp. 131–56; and Marra, *The Aesthetics of Discontent*, pp. 35–53.

109. See Bishamondō *Kokin shū chū*, p. 11; and Reizeike-ryū *Ise monogatari shō*, pp. 305, 308. See also the Nijō school *Kokin waka shū kanjō kuden*, pp. 512–13, which claims that it was Fujiwara no Takako's brother Mototsune who aided Narihira.

110. Cited in Arai, "*Kokin shū* kanjō hisho to Bukkyō kyōri," pp. 10–11.

true meaning of Shingon, keeping nothing back." Narihira's natural aptitude for tantric sex was apparently already obvious at the age of fourteen. Finally, the line "In the various transmission lineages his Buddhist name is given as Kōken (Loving-Wisdom)," makes it seem likely that at some point there existed a transmission document that contained the names of both Shinga and Kōken-Narihira.

The commentaries also connect Narihira with Tachikawa lineages through a story about a monk named Jōkai at the Tō-ji temple who fell in love with Narihira. This passage is from a commentary on *Kokin shū* 641 in *Kōan jū nen Kokin shū kachū* (Kōan 10 commentary on *Kokin shū* poems):

> *hototogisu / yume ka utsutsu ka / asa tsuyu no*
> *okite wakareshi / akatsuki no koe*
>
> O nightingale, was I awake or in dreams when first I heard dawn's song,
> that dew-drenched morning I awoke and parted from him?

> As a child, when Narihira attended an enthronement ceremony in Saikō 3 [856] during Emperor Montoku's reign, he was seen by the priest Jōkai, who fell in love with him and began visiting him secretly. Afterward, when one of them heard the nightingale at dawn, remembering the tryst he composed this poem and sent it. Jōkai was Prince Shinnyō's son. Mandara was Prince Abo's son. So they were cousins. Mandara was Narihira's childhood name. One should inquire into whether this poem was by Narihira or Jōkai.[111]

Although the story may seem plausible given Narihira's reputation and the common medieval practice of sexual relationships between acolytes and priests, the dates are all wrong.[112] Nevertheless, the connection is interesting for two reasons. First, it is the only example I have found in the commentaries that asserts Narihira had a homosexual relationship. Perhaps as the kami of Yin and Yang he was automatically predisposed to relationships with

---

111. *Kōan jū nen Kokin shū kachū*, p. 400.

112. Saikō 3 (856) was in Montoku's reign, but the enthronement ceremony was in 851. And since in 856 Narihira was 32 years old, he was not a "young boy." Prince Shinnyō (dates unknown) was the Buddhist name of Emperor Heizei's son Takaoka. In 810 he was named the crown prince under Emperor Saga (r. 809–23), but he was later deposed in a political struggle. He then took orders in Shingon and studied under Kūkai. Whether Prince Shinnyō had a son named Jōkai is unverified, but the historical affiliation of Narihira's uncle with Shingon would have provided further support for Narihira's supposed esoteric training. See Arai, "*Kokin shū* kanjō hisho to Bukkyō kyōri," p. 12; for a short biography of Prince Shinnyō in English, see Yamasaki, *Shingon*, pp. 219–20*n*8.

women. In the all-male context of his study at a Buddhist temple, however, his reputation would demand that he make do with what was available.

Second, according to Arai Eizō, the name Jōkai shows up in at least two Tachikawa-related texts: *Sengen menju* (Direct transmission from Sengen) and *Hōkyō shō*.[113] It seems likely that the commentaries incorporated the name Jōkai from Tachikawa lineages in an attempt to insert Narihira into Tachikawa transmission lineages and thus give the commentary's Tachikawa content more authority.

Although Fujiwara no Tameaki was a son of Fujiwara no Tameie and a grandson of Teika, he appears to have been excluded from the Mikohidari poetic legacy. This should have been a serious handicap in the competitive poetic circles of the late thirteenth century, in which the backing of one's family tradition counted more than innate poetic talent. As we have seen, however, Tameaki managed to come up with a number of ingenious strategies to give his commentaries authority and legitimacy. To judge from the subsequent infiltration of these strategies into the Nijō and Reizei school commentaries, it seems they were quite successful. In the next three chapters, we will examine the contents of those commentaries in much greater detail.

113. Arai, "*Kokin shū* kanjō hisho to Bukkyō kyōri," p. 13. Since Arai does not supply footnotes, I was unable to locate *Sengen menju* 纂元面受 (and my translation of *Sengen* as a name is thus very tentative; *menju* means "face-to-face transmission"). In *Hōkyō shō*, the name Jōkai is mentioned twice, but in both cases the name refers to a monk who lived from 1074 to 1149 and was a disciple of Shōkaku (the founder of Sanbo-in and the older brother of Ninkan, the alleged founder of Tachikawa). Given this lineage, it would not be surprising that Jōkai would appear in Tachikawa lineages. See Yūkai, *Hōkyō shō*, *T.*, p. 848; and Vanden Broucke, *Hōkyō-shō*, pp. 15, 125–26.

9

Tameaki-Affiliated Commentaries (Part I)

The six commentaries analyzed in the next three chapters are either directly associated with Fujiwara no Tameaki or use the method of etymological and numerological allegoresis he developed. These chapters provide an overview of the development of Tameaki's allegorical method, as well as the direction it took in the thirty years after his death. Four of the commentaries are thought either to be by Tameaki or to have been borrowed by Tameaki from the Ietaka school but revised extensively. Of these Tameaki-affiliated commentaries the earliest is *Waka chiken shū* (Collection of revealed knowledge of waka), a commentary on *Ise monogatari* with a colophon dated 1265. *Kokin waka shū jo kikigaki* (Lecture notes on the preface to the *Kokin waka shū*) probably dates from the 1270s. In terms of the waka initiation, *Waka chiken shū* was probably aimed at introductory students, and *Kokin waka shū jo kikigaki* for intermediate students. *Gyokuden jinpi no maki* (Jeweled transmission of deep secrets) and *Waka Kokin kanjō no maki* (Initiation on waka of the *Kokin shū*), both dating from the 1280s, involve much more complex religious allegoresis and appear to have been meant for higher-level initiates (these two texts are discussed in Chapter 10).

The other two commentaries (discussed in Chapter 11) were produced after Tameaki's death. One is a compendium of texts known collectively as the

Reizei school *Ise monogatari shō* (Selected comments on *Ise monogatari*), the core of which was probably developed by Reizei Tamesuke early in the fourteenth century, but which continued to be supplemented in the Muromachi and transmitted during the Edo period. Although it employs occasional religious allegoresis, for the most part it uses etymological and numerological allegoresis to read *Ise monogatari* as political allegory. This secularized use of allegoresis may have laid the groundwork for the *Kokin denju*, which employed etymological and numerological allegoresis to read the *Kokin shū* but emptied that reading of most esoteric Buddhist content. The other commentary I consider, *Ise monogatari zuinō* (The essence of *Ise monogatari*), was probably created by Nijō Tameakira (1295–1364) in the 1320s or 1330s. *Ise monogatari zuinō* continues to employ the methods of religious allegoresis developed by Tameaki, but to some rather surprising ends.

Waka chiken shū

Waka chiken shū is probably the earliest of the secret Kamakura period commentaries on *Ise monogatari*. The inner colophon indicates that it was written by Minamoto no Tsunenobu (1016–97),[1] but this attribution is believed to be spurious.[2] The manuscript thought to be the earliest surviving copy contains a colophon with a transmission date of 1265, and if this date can be taken seriously, the first version of *Waka chiken shū* most likely came into existence around that time.[3]

---

1. Minamoto no Tsunenobu was a successful courtier and poet of the late Heian period. He achieved senior second rank in 1077, the position of major counselor (*dainagon*) in 1091, and he died as vice governor-general (*gon no sochi*) of Dazaifu (present-day Kyushu). He was active as a poet in both Chinese and Japanese. Although both he and his son Minamoto no Toshiyori (or Shunrai) were considered eccentric poets in their own time, Tsunenobu's style of descriptive nature poetry was increasingly appreciated by the more innovative poets, and his poems were often included in later imperial poetry anthologies. For more detailed information on Tsunenobu's life and poetry, see Smits, *The Pursuit of Loneliness: Chinese and Japanese Nature Poetry in Medieval Japan, Ca. 1050–1150*, pp. 100–157.

2. The simplest reason to believe the attribution spurious is that the text is clearly based on the version of *Ise monogatari* collated by Fujiwara no Teika and so must postdate him.

3. There are three published texts that date to the Kamakura period, two of them in the Sanjōnishi lineage. The Kunaichō Shoryōbu den Tameuji hitsu *Waka chiken shū* has a colophon that indicates the text was transmitted in 1265 (supposedly from Tameie) and then again in 1292. Katagiri (*Ise monogatari no kenkyū [shiryōhen]*, p. 475) admits that since the attribution to Tsunenobu is spurious, the dating may also be problematic, but he believes that the first *Waka chiken shū* was probably produced in the 1260s.

As we shall see, the two main lineages of *Waka chiken shū* are associated with the Tameaki school (referred to as the Sanjōnishi lineage) and the Ietaka school (the *Zoku Gunsho ruijū* lineage).[4] The Sanjōnishi lineage of texts is associated with Tameaki because ideas specific to it recur frequently in later Tameaki-affiliated texts; the *Zoku Gunsho ruijū* lineage is associated with the Ietaka school because those texts generally claim a transmission lineage that includes Fujiwara no Ietaka. On the whole, the Sanjōnishi lineage seems to have been much more widely disseminated. The Noh plays and *otogizōshi* (short prose tales) that employ imagery and ideas from *Waka chiken shū* generally used the Sanjōnishi lineage of texts. And when the Muromachi poet-scholar Ichijō Kaneyoshi attacked *Waka chiken shū* as written "by someone obsessed with the erotic who spuriously used Minamoto no Tsunenobu's name," he quoted particulars that make it clear that he was referring to a Sanjōnishi lineage text.[5]

Although there are significant differences in detail between the two lineages, their fundamental approach to textual interpretation is much the same. Both focus most of their interpretive energy on identifying the "real" names of the anonymous men and women of the stories and providing precise historical dates for events. Since the basic contents are almost identical, most

---

4. Otsu Yūichi designated the two lineages Sanjōnishi and *Zoku Gunsho ruijū*. He chose the "Sanjōnishi" designation because the main text in that lineage was transmitted by Sanjōnishi Sanekata. Katagiri Yōichi refers to the Sanjōnishi lineage as the "Shoryōbu" lineage after the text published in his *Ise monogatari no kenkyū (shiryōhen)*. Both Otsu and Katagiri refer to the second lineage as the *Zoku Gunsho ruijū* lineage because that Edo period compendium was the first place a *Waka chiken shū* in this lineage was published (*Zoku Gunsho ruijū*, vol. 18, pt. I, pp. 442–535). Katagiri Yōichi has published texts from both lineages in *Ise monogatari no kenkyū (shiryōhen)*. The Sanjōnishi lineage Kunaichō Shoryōbu den Tameuji hitsu *Waka chiken shū* can be found on pp. 96–195; the *Zoku Gunsho ruijū* lineage Shimabara Kominkan Matsuhira Bunko *Waka chiken shū* can be found on pp. 198–286. Another text in the *Zoku Gunsho ruijū* lineage has been published in two parts in Fujishima Aya, "Kyūshū Daigaku Otonashi Bunko zō *Waka chiken shū*"; this version contains a number of sections missing from the version printed in Katagiri. For a comparison of the two texts, see Fujishima Aya, "Kyūshū Daigaku *Waka chiken shū* ni tsuite." There is a third lineage based on the Hosaka *Waka chiken shū*, which also dates to the Kamakura period, but this fragmented text is useful only for dating purposes. For a detailed discussion of the three lineages, see Otsu, *Ise monogatari kochūshaku no kenkyū*, pp. 49–74; for a brief synopsis, see Miwa Masatane, "Ietaka gisho no sakusha," p. 123.

5. For example, in Kaneyoshi's *Guken shō* we find, "According to this *Waka chiken shū*, Narihira is the avatar of the Horse-headed Kannon, and Ono no Komachi is the avatar of Nyoirin Kannon." This attribution is found only in the Sanjōnishi lineage of *Waka chiken shū*; see Ichijō Kaneyoshi, *Ise monogatari guken shō*, p. 505.

scholars assume that both lineages originated in the same source. Miwa Masatane has argued that soon after Tameaki produced the founding text of the Sanjōnishi lineage *Waka chiken shū*, the Ietaka school used it to produce its own version.[6] There are, however, good reasons to question this sequence. Before we get into the issue of antecedents, however, let us examine the form and content of the texts themselves.

Both lineages begin with an introductory "preface" that deals with general questions such as the origin and development of waka as the Buddhist Dharma. As in the *Kokin shū* preface, Susanoo no Mikoto's "Yakumo tatsu" (Manifold clouds rising) marriage poem from the *Nihon shoki* is deemed the first example of regularized thirty-one-syllable poetry. The commentary then uses numerological allegoresis to identify homologies between various Buddhist concepts and rhetorical conventions in waka. The convention of thirty-one syllables is explained in terms of the thirty-two signifying marks of the Tathāgata.[7] Next, the Three Poetic Essentials[8] are correlated with the three bodies of the Tathāgata (Nyorai): the Dharma Body (*hosshin* 法心), the Reward/Enjoyment Body (*hōjin* 報身), and the Accommodative Body (*ōjin* 應身). They are also correlated with the three manifestations of the Tathāgata as Emptiness (*kū* 空), Phenomenal Appearance (*ke* 假), and the Middle Way (*chū* 中). The preface then discusses the Six Poetic Modes presented in the *Kokin shū* preface and correlates them with the Six Virtuous Practices (*ropparamitsu* 六波羅密) that lead to enlightenment.[9] These virtuous practices are in turn linked to the Six Forms of Poetry (*rokutai* 六体): *tanka, chōka, sedōka, konponka, kaibunka,* and *haikai*. The basis of true poetry is found to be the thirty-one syllable, five-line tanka: "If none of the five lines lacks heart (*kokoro*), then you will create a Buddha of the Five Roots, Five Powers; and of course if you compose one hundred waka, you will create one hundred buddhas; a thousand waka, one thousand buddhas."[10] Next, the Six Forms of Poetry are aligned with the Six Paths of Reincarna-

---

6. Miwa, *Kagaku hiden no kenkyū*, pp. 209–20.

7. See the discussion of this passage in Chapter 2, pp. 39–40.

8. I.e., the three ways that the essential meaning (*kokoro*) of a poem may be expressed: the topic is felt deeply but not expressed in words; the topic is expressed in words but not felt deeply; the topic is both felt deeply and expressed in words.

9. The six virtuous practices are charity (*fuse*), observing precepts (*jikai*), perseverance (*ninniku*), energy (*shōjin*), meditation (*zenjō*), and wisdom (*chie*).

10. Kunaichō *Waka chiken shū*, p. 99. Translation (modified) from Bowring, "The *Ise monogatari*," p. 42. Compare a similar passage in *Waka Kokin kanjō no maki*, p. 462.

tion; the tanka and haikai, with their established form of thirty-one syllables, are associated with the paths to heaven and hell. Whereas a tanka leads to the Buddha's grace and the release of enlightenment, a haikai (comic or unorthodox poem) represents sin and the hell of reincarnation. The Eight Poetic Illnesses are then correlated to the Eight Buddhist Sufferings: birth, illness, old age, death, separation, meeting someone you hate, not getting what you desire, and the pain accompanying the growth of your body. The introductory preface concludes by strongly stressing the importance of *Waka chiken shū* as a secret transmission; it is not to be revealed casually to unqualified outsiders.

The next fascicle, entitled "Important Matters Regarding *Ise monogatari*" ("*Ise monogatari* daiji") in the Sanjōnishi lineage, begins to address the major questions about *Ise monogatari* (the work's authorship, textual development, and the meaning of its name). This section opens by relating the writer's (Minamoto no Tsunenobu) pilgrimage to Sumiyoshi Shrine and his meeting on the thirteenth night of the ninth month of an old man (*okina*), a manifestation of Sumiyoshi Daimyōjin. After much hemming and hawing, the old man agrees to reveal the secrets of *Ise monogatari* to Tsunenobu. From this point, the work follows a question-and-answer format, with Tsunenobu asking the questions and Sumiyoshi Daimyōjin (as the *okina*) giving the answers. The Daimyōjin begins by discussing the authorship and textual development of *Ise monogatari*.[11]

Although the author of *Waka chiken shū* thought that the basic material for *Ise monogatari* was written by Narihira, he or she knew that there were sections that both predated and postdated Narihira's lifetime and that at least one other author/editor was involved in the creation of the text. There was also the problem of textual variants: although the writer of *Waka chiken shū* used Fujiwara no Teika's recension, he had to account for the major *Ise monogatari* variant, the "Imperial Huntsman" text, which begins with episode 69. The answer given in *Waka chiken shū* is that Narihira wrote the core of the text while he was living in Nagaoka under house arrest in 865 but did not finish it until fifteen years later, just before his death.[12] For the most part,

---

11. The following summary follows the Kunaichō *Waka chiken shū*, pp. 103–8. I have tried to point out places where the other textual lineage differs. For another summary of the same section of the Kunaichō Shoryōbu text, see Bowring, "The *Ise monogatari*," pp. 29–30.

12. The Shimabara *Waka chiken shū* does not specify that Narihira was at Nagaoka when he wrote *Ise monogatari*; see Katagiri, *Ise monogatari no kenkyū (shiryōhen)*, p. 210.

he used incidents from his own life, but combined them with older stories. He wrote out a fair copy of a final draft by 879.

Realizing that he was dying, he entrusted the text to his wife at the time, the poet Ise. He directed her to make it public under the name of *Ise monogatari* but not to let people know that it was his work. He died soon after. Although at first Ise was prostrate with grief, eventually she returned to court and entered the service of Emperor Uda's (r. 887–97) consort, Shichijō no Kisaki (Onshi). As a lady-in-waiting, she came to the attention of Emperor Uda and soon became a favorite. Time passed, and she forgot all about the manuscript. One day something came up that reminded her of it, and she discovered a text with "Ise monogatari" written on it in an old box. This manuscript was the "Imperial Huntsman" text. Finding that it contained a number of intimate details about her life with Narihira, she decided to remove all references to herself.

According to *Waka chiken shū*, Ise replaced the sixteen episodes that mentioned her with other, similar stories (this explains why there are episodes that "postdate" Narihira). She then added the last two episodes (124 and 125), which describe Narihira's deathbed scene. (She is supposed to have added these to his personal poem collection as well, when she edited that volume.) She made the revised text public in 891; although no author's name was attached to it, people generally assumed that Ise had written it. A year or two later, on the anniversary of Narihira's death, she secretly returned to the village where they had once lived together. There she found another manuscript entitled "Ise monogatari." This turned out to be the text that begins with Narihira's coming-of-age ceremony (the first episode in the Teika recension). Since this text was better organized, she realized that it was the real final draft. She revised this text in the same way she had the "Imperial Huntsman" version and asked people to destroy the earlier version (but, of course, at least one copy survived).

Waka chiken shū's account explains the inclusion of incidents that postdate Narihira's lifetime as well as the existence of variant texts, questions extremely vexing to medieval scholars.[13] For modern scholars, of course, the *Waka chiken shū* explanation does not hold water: Ise was probably less than years old when Narihira died, and a relationship between them is extremely unlikely. Nevertheless, this commentary makes Ise central to the rewriting

13. Richard Bowring makes the same point in "The *Ise monogatari*," pp. 30–32.

and editing of the text; some scholars now argue that this may in fact have been the case.[14]

At this point there is an interpolation unique to the Sanjōnishi lineage, which was discussed in the section on Tachikawa in Chapter 7. Narihira is identified as the incarnation of two bodhisattvas, the Bodhisattva of Song and Dance and the Horse-headed Kannon. He slept with 3,733 women as an expedient means and wrote *Ise monogatari* as a record of these activities. The *Zoku Gunsho ruijū* lineage omits this Tachikawa-influenced material.

The next interpolated item in the Sanjōnishi lineage *Waka chiken shū* is a list of the "twelve most important women" in *Ise monogatari*, followed by a detailed description of each of them giving their family background and rank and identifying the most important episodes in which they appear. Sometimes an analysis of poems associated with them is also given. At the end is a list of nearly all the episodes specifying the woman associated with each. Each woman is supplied an epithet, most often based on a place-name but sometimes based on an important element of the story, and then her "real" name is given. Identifications are given even for episodes not discussed in the main body of the *Waka chiken shū* text.[15] Again, all this information is omitted in the *Zoku Gunsho ruijū* lineage of texts.

In both lineages, the *okina* then turns to the question of the title of *Ise monogatari* and proposes three possible explanations (these explanations continued to be the main ones entertained throughout the medieval period). The first is that the title derives from Narihira's affair with the Ise Priestess in episode 69. This is rejected on the grounds that when a tale (*monogatari*) is named after a place, all the events in the story generally occur there; if it is named after a character in the story, that character is central. The affair with the Ise Priestess, although unprecedented and outrageous, occupies two or three episodes at the most; the affair with Fujiwara no Takako is much more important.

The second explanation is that it was named after the poet Ise because of her work on the text. This explanation is rejected on the grounds that

14. Both Richard Okada (*Figures of Resistance*, pp. 114–16) and Richard Bowring ("The *Ise monogatari*," pp. 9–14) suggest that Ise may have had a hand in shaping the urtext of *Ise monogatari*.

15. A number of episodes are omitted from the episode-by-episode analysis; some of these may have been lost, others, especially the later, less important episodes, were probably intentionally omitted. See Katagiri, *Ise monogatari no kenkyū (kenkyūhen)*, pp. 485–86.

monogatari are not named after their authors. The example cited is *Genji monogatari*, which, the writer points out, was not entitled *Murasaki monogatari* after its author, Murasaki Shikibu.

The third explanation is that the title was taken from a story about two men, one from Ise and the other from Hyuga, who died on the same night. One died before his time, but since his body had already been cremated, he was brought back to life in the body of the other man, causing much consternation and confusion among the two men's families. From this story the phrase "Ise or Hyuga" had come to stand for anything confusing, mixed up, topsy-turvy. In writing *Ise monogatari*, Narihira and Lady Ise had deliberately distorted historical events, substituting "a man" and "a woman" for the names of the people involved, changing place-names, and rearranging historical chronology, all because they wanted to refer to events that would otherwise have been too politically delicate to mention openly. According to the Sanjōnishi lineage *Waka chiken shū*:

> The sequence of this story is disordered; what should be at the beginning comes later, what should come later is placed at the beginning; matters from the past are written as though happening to someone in the present, things that are happening in the present are written as though they happened in the distant past. Incidents in the capital are transposed to the countryside and vice versa. This *monogatari* was purposefully written in a chaotic, disordered manner, and so, in accordance with the saying, "Ise or Hyuga," it was called *Ise monogatari*.[16]

As Richard Bowring has pointed out, this explanation is clearly self-serving because it not only establishes a reason for the incoherencies of the text but practically demands that the commentator step in to "re-create" a coherent original that has purposefully been obfuscated.[17]

After the basic questions about authorship and title have been settled, the interpretation of specific episodes begins. The "man" and "woman" of each episode are carefully identified with "real" people, and specific dates are assigned. If the location of the episode is unclear or problematic in any way, that, too, is explained.

Besides basic differences in content, the two lineages of texts exhibit stylistic and formal differences. The Sanjōnishi lineage variants seem to be written in the first person, as though Minamoto no Tsunenobu were re-

16. Kunaichō *Waka chiken shū*, p. 119.
17. Bowring, "The *Ise monogatari*," p. 32.

counting his encounter with the deity at Sumiyoshi. The *Zoku Gunsho ruijū* lineage, on the other hand, is written from what would be the classical Japanese equivalent of third person, with no first-person personal pronouns and no direct addressing of the reader.[18] In addition, the two lineages are formatted somewhat differently. The Sanjōnishi lineage *Waka chiken shū* is divided into six fascicles; the *Zoku Gunsho ruijū* lineage *Waka chiken shū* into four. Both use a question-and-answer format, but the Sanjōnishi lineage uses the graphs for "bird" 鳥 to indicate "question" and "wind" 風 for "answer." These minor differences in format are significant because of a reference to *Waka chiken shū* in the Tameaki school's *Kokin waka shū jo kikigaki* that mentions such identifying details.

Miwa and Katagiri connect the Sanjōnishi lineage of *Waka chiken shū* texts to Tameaki because certain sections of the introduction unique to that lineage are clearly influenced by Tachikawa and resemble later Tameaki texts such as *Waka Kokin kanjō no maki* and *Gyokuden jinpi no maki.*[19] They also point out that there appears to be a direct allusion to *Waka chiken shū* in *Kokin waka shū jo kikigaki,* which is firmly established as a text affiliated with Tameaki written in the 1270s:

Major Counselor Minamoto no Tsunenobu went to Sumiyoshi to pray to the Daimyōjin to reveal the secrets of waka. He spent three full weeks there; the last night there was a cloudless moon over Suminoe Bay. An old man appeared and asked Tsunenobu, "What are you praying for?" Tsunenobu replied "Emperor Toba has asked me about the seven important secrets regarding waka. Since I could not ask the representatives of the various poetic families, I have prayed to Sumiyoshi to reveal those secrets to me." The old man said "What do you want to know about these important matters?" Tsunenobu then asked about the secrets one by one. The old man listened and said "Those are easy. You don't have to wait for the Daimyōjin's oracle," and he revealed the secrets over the course of seven nights.

---

18. For example, in the Sanjōnishi lineage Kunaichō *Waka chiken shū,* when Tsunenobu speaks, the phrase used is *konata yori iwaku* (I said), whereas in the Shimabara *Waka chiken shū,* the phrase is *dainagon no iwaku* (the major counselor said). Katagiri (*Ise monogatari no kenkyū [kenkyūhen],* p. 484) argues that the *Zoku Gunsho ruijū* lineage Shimabara *Waka chiken shū* is written as though Ietaka were transmitting Tsunenobu's words.

19. For a comparison of *Waka chiken shū* and *Waka Kokin kanjō no maki,* see Miwa, *Kagaku hiden no kenkyū,* pp. 151–52. Miwa argues that because in places the content of the two texts is so similar, they must be in the same lineage, if not by the same author. He also argues that *Waka Kokin kanjō no maki* is the basis for the Sanjōnishi lineage *Waka chiken shū* preface. In terms of dating alone, however, this seems problematic.

Tsunenobu wrote these answers down in twelve fascicles. Six fascicles were entitled *Chōfu mondō shinto fuden* (The kami's transmission of the exchange between the bird and wind); these six fascicles are now called *Chiken* (Knowledge revealed).[20] The old man was the [Sumiyoshi] Myōjin's manifestation. It seems that because Ietaka wanted to differ from Teika, he did not inquire into this transmission but instead created a new school by altering Teika's interpretations and readings of characters. However, because Ietaka did not receive the authentic transmission lineage passed down from Tsunenobu, our school regards Ietaka's lineage as a subordinate branch of our own.[21]

There are six relevant points here. First, there is a text called *Chiken,* and second, it is attributed to Minamoto no Tsunenobu. The text is based on revelations from Sumiyoshi Daimyōjin who appeared to Tsunenobu as a venerable old man (*okina*). Fourth, it is recorded in six fascicles. Fifth, given its original title, it probably follows a question-and-answer format ("the bird inquires X; the wind replies Y"). Finally, Ietaka changed the names and the readings of the characters and created his own version, but the "Teika" version is the authentic one.

Both lineages of the text agree on the first three points. Only the Sanjōnishi lineage of *Waka chiken shū,* however, is structured in six fascicles and uses the form "the bird inquires; the wind replies." And clearly, the last point is used to explain the existence of two competing versions of *Waka chiken shū* and to discredit the version associated with Ietaka. This tells us that both lineages of *Waka chiken shū* were in existence by the 1270s, when *Kokin waka shū jo kikigaki* developed. Who, then, was the first to develop this text, Tameaki or the Ietaka poetry faction?

---

20. Nakagawa Shinnichi ("*Ise monogatari* chūshakusho toshite *Gyokuden jinpi no maki* no ichi," pp. 24–25) interprets the meaning of this sentence differently: that there were two texts, each consisting of six fascicles, one entitled "The Kami's Transmission of the Exchange Between the Bird and Wind" and the other "Knowledge Revealed." He uses this interpretation to support his argument that *Kikigaki* is not necessarily referring to *Waka chiken shū* and hence *Waka chiken shū* is not necessarily by Tameaki. However, if one argues that in *Kikigaki* Tameaki is attempting to legitimate his revised version of the Ietaka school *Waka chiken shū,* it makes more sense to interpret the text as I do.

21. *Kokin waka shū jo kikigaki,* pp. 223–24. Here the term *matsu* 末 (subordinate branch) is probably being used in a delegitimizing sense of "later and inferior in status." See, e.g., the passage in *Hōkyō shō* (*T.*, p. 849) in which the Shingon priest Yūkai attacks the Tachikawa adept Monkan for not receiving the orthodox teachings of Kūkai (see also Vanden Broucke, *Hōkyōshō*, pp. 21, 133).

This is an important question because a number of the ideas presented in the preface to *Waka chiken shū* about the relationship of the form of waka with Buddhist concepts are treated as fundamental secrets in later Tameaki-affiliated texts. Perhaps because of this, Miwa suggests that Tameaki wrote the first *Waka chiken shū* text in the 1260s and within ten years or so the Ietaka school had produced its own version and attached a transmission lineage that included Ietaka.[22] There are, however, a few problems with this position. As Nakagawa Shinnichi has pointed out, an episode-by-episode comparison of the interpretations of the Sanjōnishi lineage *Waka chiken shū* and the sections on *Ise monogatari* in *Gyokuden jinpi no maki* (which is more securely attributed to Tameaki) reveals virtually no overlap between the two commentaries.[23] A more important point from my perspective is the disjunction between the preface and the episode-by-episode analyses that follow in the Sanjōnishi lineage texts. Whereas the preface resorts to extensive use of numerological allegoresis, identifies *honji suijaku* manifestations of Narihira such as the Horse-headed Kannon and the Bodhisattva of Song and Dance, and explains Narihira's erotic relations with various women as expedient devices to lead them to enlightenment, the episode-by-episode analysis does not employ religious allegoresis as an interpretive strategy.

For example, compare the Sanjōnishi lineage *Waka chiken shū* analysis of episode 4 with *Gyokuden jinpi no maki*'s analysis. The comments in the Sanjōnishi lineage *Waka chiken shū* treat the episode as relatively straightforward and unproblematic:

> This episode has no hidden meaning. The poem means [that the author is in a state of] confusion: "Is this moon not the moon of last year? Is this spring not the spring of last year? The days and months of last year are counted up, and although I feel that my body is the same, everything appears to have mysteriously changed." Or it might be, "The moon is last year's moon, the spring has not changed from last year's spring, my body alone has changed from last year. Last year's Kisaki is not here, and I long for her." Or again, "All alone and longing for her, I cannot recapture last year's feeling. I feel as in the old days when I hadn't yet met her."[24]

In contrast, the *Gyokuden jinpi no maki* sees episode 4 as filled with hidden meanings:

---

22. Miwa, *Kagaku hiden no kenkyū*, pp. 119–21.
23. Nakagawa Shinnichi, "*Ise monogatari* chūshakusho," p. 27.
24. Kunaichō *Waka chiken shū*, p. 140.

The moon (*tsuki*) in "Tsuki ya aranu" refers to Nijō no Kisaki. The emperor is referred to as "sun"; the consort is referred to as the "moon." Thus "is this not the moon?" means "is this not Nijō no Kisaki?" Nijō no Kisaki is the manifestation (*keshō* 化生) of Empress Jingū, the transformation body (*keshin* 化身) of the deity of the third shrine at Sumiyoshi. Narihira is the transformation body of Sumiyoshi. Thus the phrase means "Has the consort of old forgotten the ancient age of the gods?" "Haru ya mukashi no haru naranu" means "Have you forgotten that long ago you and I, as the two kami [Izanagi and Izanami], ruled this country?" "Wagami hitotsu wa moto no mi nishite" means "My body alone is Sumiyoshi. Have you forgotten my Original Ground?"[25]

Waka chiken shū's orthodox analysis of the possible meanings of the "Tsuki ya aranu" poem of episode 4 is fairly close to those a modern scholar might argue. *Gyokuden jinpi no maki*, on the other hand, reads the episode in terms of the *honji suijaku* understanding of Nijō no Kisaki and Narihira as various kami.

A comparison of *Waka chiken shū* with Tameaki-affiliated texts reveals an even more striking point: although *Waka chiken shū* is supposed to be a revelation from Sumiyoshi Daimyōjin, Narihira is not identified as a *honji suijaku* manifestation of Sumiyoshi. As we saw in the preceding chapter, this identification, which is made by virtually all the texts associated with Tameaki, is based on a unique interpretation of the story in episode 117 in which an unidentified emperor visits the Sumiyoshi Shrine and exchanges poems with the deity. Tameaki-affiliated commentaries claim that Narihira accompanied Emperor Montoku on a visit to the shrine and that the exchange of poems in the episode is an exchange between the Daimyōjin and Narihira. The Daimyōjin's poem, when analyzed correctly, reveals that Narihira is his avatar and thus worthy of receiving the most profound secrets of poetry, the "Akone no ura kuden" and the "Gyokuden." The first becomes the source for *Ise monogatari*; the second for the *Kokin shū*.

The *Waka chiken shū* analysis of episode 117 identifies the emperor as Heizei and makes no mention of Narihira. Sumiyoshi Daimyōjin simply possesses a shrine priestess (*miko*) and through her recites the poem. As we saw in the last chapter, the story about Narihira receiving the "Akone no ura

25. *Gyokuden jinpi no maki*, p. 539. As discussed in Chapter 8, Empress Jingū was enshrined at Sumiyoshi as part of the triune of deities that make up Tamatsushima Myōjin. One implication of this passage is therefore that Nijō no Kisaki, Tamatsushima Myōjin, and Izanami no Mikoto form a feminine triune as counterpart to Narihira, Sumiyoshi Daimyōjin, and Izanagi no Mikoto.

kuden" and "Gyokuden" was absolutely fundamental to substantiating Tameaki's allegorical interpretive approach to *Ise monogatari* and the *Kokin shū*. The fact that no version of *Waka chiken shū* mentions it therefore is quite suspicious.

If we assume that *Waka chiken shū* originated with Tameaki in the 1260s, then we have to explain the fact that within ten years his position on a number of major interpretations of *Ise monogatari* had changed radically. This seems unlikely. Nakagawa Shinnichi sees this as conclusive proof that *Waka chiken shū* was not authored by Tameaki.[26] However, Nakagawa does not offer an alternative poetry house as the source of the Sanjōnishi lineage of *Waka chiken shū*, nor does he account for the Tachikawa-influenced sections of the Sanjōnishi lineage *Waka chiken shū* introduction or similar analyses in later Tameaki texts. Moreover, he does not address why Tameaki felt it necessary to try to legitimate the "Teika" version of *Waka chiken shū* in his *Kokin waka shū jo kikigaki*.

The most likely scenario is that quite early in his career Tameaki acquired an Ietaka school *Ise monogatari* commentary. After making some simple changes in style and format (dividing it into six fascicles rather than four and adding "bird" and "wind" to the question-and-answer format) and interpolating esoteric material into the introduction, he appropriated it as a "Teika" family text. Supporting this hypothesis is another text, *Waka kanjō shidai himitsu shō*, with two lineages, one associated with the Ietaka school and one with the Tameaki school. Miwa argues that Tameaki took an Ietaka school text and, by supplementing it with additional commentary, made it his own.[27] If Tameaki did this with one text, it makes sense to assume that he did the same with another. In addition, the hypothesis would explain

26. Nakagawa, "*Ise monogatari* chūshakusho," pp. 26–27.

27. Miwa (*Kagaku hiden no kenkyū*, p. 220) resolves the problem of influence going one way in the case of *Waka kanjō shidai himitsu shō* (from Ietaka school to Tameaki school) but the other way in *Waka chiken shū* (from Tameaki school to Ietaka school) by arguing that Tameaki composed *Waka kanjō shidai himitsu shō* early on while he still needed to ingratiate himself with the Ietaka school, whereas *Waka chiken shū* was written after Tameaki had already acquired a good deal of power, and it would have been the Ietaka school that wanted to ingratiate themselves. One difficulty here is that the Tameaki school version of *Waka chiken shū* is generally dated earlier than the Tameaki school version of *Waka kanjō shidai himitsu shō* because the latter includes numerous bits and pieces taken from Tameaki school texts dating from the 1270s, such as *Kokin waka shū jo kikigaki*.

why the episode-by-episode analysis of *Waka chiken shū* displays no interest in allegorizing *Ise monogatari*.

This lack of interest in allegorization is particularly noteworthy, since, like the Reizei school *Ise monogatari shō*, the Sanjōnishi lineage *Waka chiken shū* claims that Narihira never went to Azuma. Nevertheless, it still treats the Azuma episodes (7–15) as if the incidents described had actually happened; there is no attempt to allegorize the names of places that Narihira visited or to read the poems for hidden meanings.[28] Another important point is that *Waka chiken shū* allows for the possibility that both old stories and new stories are mixed together in *Ise monogatari*; not every episode has to be about Narihira. When we consider the Reizei school *Ise monogatari shō* in Chapter 11, we will see a very different textual approach taking shape.

Waka chiken shū's systematic episode-by-episode analysis in which the "historical truth" behind each episode's fictional veneer is revealed had a strong influence on later Tameaki commentaries on *Ise monogatari*. Although there is little allegoresis in the main body of the text, the preface's *honji suijaku* identifications of Narihira as the Horse-headed Kannon and the

---

28. The Sanjōnishi lineage *Waka chiken shū* argues that Narihira did not go to Azuma but was kept under house arrest at his mother's mansion in Nagaoka, a ruse abetted by Nijō no Kisaki's brother, the Horikawa Regent Fujiwara no Mototsune. The introduction to the *Zoku Gunsho ruijū* lineage *Waka chiken shū* suggests instead that Narihira wrote *Ise monogatari* during the period he was supposedly involved with the poet Ise (according to the commentary they "married" when he was 52 and she was 25). However, in the analysis of episode 7 we find the following:

> Question: It is said that once, a man, going to Azuma, traveled along beside the ocean between Ise and Owari. Did he really go there?
>
> Answer: As mentioned in the preface, he did not actually go there. It was just a story invented to make people think he had gone to the countryside. It was just a cover story.

Since there is no copy of a *Zoku Gunsho ruijū* lineage text earlier than the Edo period, this textual discrepancy may indicate that at some point the editor of this lineage of texts removed the more allegorical and Tachikawa-influenced sections in the introduction but failed to correct the commentary on episode 7. Since episode 7 of the Sanjōnishi lineage *Waka chiken shū* is missing from the version published in Katagiri's *Ise monogatari no kenkyū*, we cannot check the two against each other. Since other commentaries associated with the Ietaka school contain a good deal of Tachikawa-influenced material, and since in the analysis of the first episode in the Reizei school *Ise monogatari shō* the Ietaka school is specifically identified as one source for *irogonomi* readings of *Ise monogatari*, the idea that those sections were edited out seems plausible. This would mean, of course, that Tameaki's Tachikawa leanings may have initially developed from contact with the Ietaka school. See Reizeike-ryū *Ise monogatari shō*, p. 293.

Bodhisattva of Song and Dance, as well as the extensive use of Buddhist numerological homologies, are greatly expanded on in later texts. A number of the basic identifications of historical characters in *Ise monogatari* were first made in *Waka chiken shū*, and it continued to be an important source for such identifications, as can be seen in Noh plays related to *Ise monogatari* such as *Izutsu* (The well-curb) and *Unrin'in* (Unrin temple).

Kokin waka shū jo kikigaki

Kokin waka shū jo kikigaki: san ryū shō (Lecture notes on the *Kokin shū* preface: from the Three Schools) is one of the earliest medieval commentaries on the *Kokin shū* preface.[29] It is assumed to be by Tameaki, because the colophon contains a transmission date of Koan 9 (1286) to his disciple Ichijō Yoshimoto. Its question-and-answer format, with occasional moments of rather colloquial digression ("that reminds me . . . "), reflects its origin as lecture notes (*kikigaki*). Perhaps because of this more informal, anecdotal presentation, and because it was an intermediate-level text that did not include the abstruse esoteric content of higher-level texts such as *Gyokuden jinpi no maki* and *Waka Kokin kanjō no maki*, *Kikigaki* was one of the most widely disseminated commentaries on the *Kokin shū*. Its anecdotes formed the basis for numerous Noh plays and *otogizōshi*, and its analysis of the Six Poetic Modes from the *Kokin shū* preface had a strong influence on the Noh playwright Zeami's understanding of the rhetorical structure of poetic imagery.

Kokin waka shū jo kikigaki was not the first anecdotal commentary. To a certain extent, it was probably modeled on Rokujō Kiyosuke's *Fukurozōshi*, which contains numerous anecdotes about the origins of poetic imagery. It may have also been influenced by the waka section of Tachibana no Narisue's *Kokon chomon jū*, which was produced about twenty years earlier. *Kikigaki* was, however, the first systematic attempt to read and interpret the *Kokin shū* preface line by line. In this, it was probably influenced by the *Waka chiken shū*'s episode-by-episode reading of *Ise monogatari*; *Kikigaki*'s interest in establishing the historical circumstances behind otherwise unidentified poems also follows the interpretive path first laid down by *Waka chiken shū*. This supposition is supported by the direct reference to *Waka chiken shū*

29. There are sixteen known texts in four lineages. See Katagiri, *Chūsei*, vol. 2, pp. 29–58; and Miwa, *Kagaku hiden no kenkyū*, pp. 122–49, for further discussion of authorship, dating, and variant texts.

in the opening passage of *Kikigaki.* Unlike *Waka chiken shū,* however, *Kikigaki* uses etymological allegoresis to support its interpretations.

Methodically working its way through the kana preface, *Kikigaki* begins by identifying allusions to historical chronicles and/or poems; once the allusion is established, it identifies the author (his or her rank, parentage, and so forth). It also gives the "true" circumstances under which the poem was written and occasionally uses that information to explicate the poem allegorically to show hidden meanings that hint at (and thus tautologically substantiate) the "history" the commentator has presented. It also explicates difficult and obscure words, with a particular focus on pillow words (*makura kotoba*) such as *hisakata* and *chihayaburu* that by the Kamakura period were already considered puzzlingly archaic and were the object of much etymological speculation. For these words, the etymological analysis is often substantiated by anecdotal evidence about the circumstances of the word's first usage. *Kikigaki* also deals with any factual or cultural contradictions and almost invariably resolves them via some form of allegoresis.

As *Kikigaki* makes its way through the preface, explanations are most often triggered by obscure phrases and the desire to identify the historical episodes behind Tsurayuki's comments. *Kikigaki* begins with an etymological discussion of the very first phrase of the *Kokin shū,* "Yamato uta." "Yamato" was originally a name for the Kansai region in which the clan who founded the imperial lineage lived. By the medieval period, it had become a metonym for "Japan" or "Japanese," and "Yamato uta" was generally understood to mean "Japanese poetry." The question being addressed here is why "Yamato" should be written with the graphs 大和, which literally mean "greatly gentled" or "greatly harmonizing." *Kikigaki* gives two reasons. First, as poetry moved from India to China to Japan, it was softened and disciplined by the deployment of the theory of the Six Poetic Modes, and hence Japanese poetry is known as "greatly gentled poetry." Second, as mentioned in the *Kokin shū* preface, Japanese poetry has the power to gentle the hearts of fierce warriors, demons, and kami and thus is known as "greatly gentling."

Kikigaki has a field day when it reaches the section of the *Kokin shū* preface that enumerates the wide variety of ways that a poet can express meaning through natural images. It provides for each image an origin in a specific poem and then identifies the circumstances of that poem's composition and its author, date, place of composition, and so on. In this way *Kikigaki* provides a "historical" basis for metaphors that by the Kamakura period had become highly conventionalized. A good example is the commentary on a plant name, *ominaeshi* (damsel flower), and a place-name, Otokoyama (Man Mountain):

With regard to the line, "otokoyama no mukashi o omoiidete, ominaeshi no hitotoki o kuneru," both the *Nihon shoki* and *Genji monogatari* commentaries say that in the era of Emperor Heizei, there was a man named Ono no Yorikaze. He lived in Yawata but loved a woman from the capital; so both of them traveled back and forth to visit. One time, when he visited the woman, he promised before leaving that he would definitely come on a certain day at a certain time. The woman waited for him, but since he did not come, she went to his house in Yawata to find out what happened to him. A servant in the house told her that just recently he had started seeing another woman and was visiting her. The woman, bitterly angry, went to the Yawata river; taking off her robe decorated with yellow mountain roses (*yamabuki*), she threw herself into the river and died.

When the man returned to his house, the servant told him that the woman from the capital had visited and then left. He chased after her and found the robe with the mountain rose decorations on the riverbank. He realized this was the robe she wore every day. Then to his dismay, he saw her lifeless body floating in the river. He gathered up her body and the robe and returned home, where he performed a memorial service. Because he spent some time in the capital in service at the palace, he thought he might like to have the robe with him as a memento, and so he sent for it, but it had decayed into the ground and become damsel flowers.[30] When the messenger told him of this, Yorikaze went to see and found a riot of damsel flowers blooming. When he drew near, the flowers appeared to feel bitter anger and bent away (*kuneru*) from him. When he moved away, they returned to normal. The line "ominaeshi no hitotoki o kuneru" refers to this incident. It was from this that the flower got the name "damsel flower." The man felt as though the woman had come back to life and expressed her bitter resentment. Thinking that she had thrown her life away for him, he decided he would do the same for her, in the hope that they might be reborn together. He threw himself into the same river and drowned. Because the man had lived in the Yawata mountains, that place became known as Otokoyama (Man Mountain). The site where the woman was buried is the Woman's Grave Mound. The river at Yawata is called the River of Tears (Namidagawa). In a poem:

ika bakari imose / no naka o uramiken
yukina nagaruru / Namidagawa kana

How great is the bitterness between man and wife?
The scandal spreads as a river of tears.

---

30. He seems to have left it on top of the gravesite, where as it decayed, it turned into damsel flowers.

The poem tells of the bitterness between this man and woman. From this poem the river became known as the River of Tears.[31]

There are four main etymological foci to this story in the *Kikigaki* text: how the flower got the name "damsel flower" and its distinctive yellow coloring; how the mountain near the Hachiman Shrine in Yawata got the name "Man Mountain"; how a river that flows near the shrine got the name "River of Tears"; and why Tsurayuki used the unusual word *kuneru* in the line about the damsel flower. The first three questions are answered straightforwardly by supplying the love triangle that formed the historical origin of the names.

The answer to the fourth question is more convoluted. In the medieval period people were not clear on what Tsurayuki meant by *kuneru*. Usually *kuneru* means "to twist, bend, or be curved"; in addition, it seems to have a feminine, sexual connotation. In the *Kokin shū* preface, however, it is hard to see how "bend" or "be curved" could work. The meaning of *kuneru* is problematic even today: the editors of the Iwanami *Kokin shū* text gloss it as "to complain" (*guchi o iu* 愚痴を言ふ), and the *Iwanami kogo jiten* cites this line in support of its definition of "to take ironically" (*hiniku o toraeru* 皮肉をとらえる). *Kikigaki* takes a different approach: it uses the usual definition of the word *kuneru* as the keystone in a story about a damsel flower who "turns away" (*kuneru*) from her former lover (*hito*) because of her bitter resentment. And this extremely feminine movement of twisting away and hiding her face from the man in anger and resentment explains why the flower is called a "damsel" flower. The obscurity of Tsurayuki's unusual use of the word *kuneru* is transformed into a clue to the reader, an intentional hint of the true story behind the phrase, a story that *Kikigaki* provides. The obscurity of the phrase thus paradoxically becomes a tautological proof of the story's authenticity.

A second example from *Kikigaki*'s analysis of this section of the *Kokin shū* preface shows how *Kikigaki* used allegorical analysis to resolve geographical discrepancies. The problematic phrase is "thinking of the twin pines at Takasago and Suminoe[32] growing together" (*Takasago Suminoe no matsu mo aioi no yō ni oboe*). The difficulty hinges on the interpretation of *aioi* (相生), since originally *aioi* meant "twin pines" in the sense of two trees growing from a single root:

---

31. *Kokin waka shū jo kikigaki*, pp. 262–63.

32. Suminoe is the name of a small inlet below the Sumiyoshi Shrine; the two names are used nearly interchangeably.

There are two meanings to the phrase "the twin pines of Takasago and Sumiyoshi grow together." One is that both Takasago and Sumiyoshi are famous for their pines. As the pines in both places grow together (*oiai* 生合), so this path [of poetry] will flourish.

Question: But Takasago is in Harima and Sumiyoshi in Settsu province. They are three days travel apart. How can they "grow together"?

Answer: Actually, this phrase is not to be taken literally. The preface at this point is to be understood as fabrication; this is a convention taught by poetry families. Takasago signifies the ancient age of Emperors Kanmu and Heizei, who ordered the compilation of the *Man'yō shū* so that the Path of Poetry would flourish. Suminoe signifies the age of Emperor Daigo, who ordered Ōshikōchi Mitsune and Ki no Tsurayuki among others to compile the *Kokin shū*, so that the Path of Poetry would flourish. As for the pines, they signify that poetry shall be as long-lasting as the needles of the pine tree.[33]

Here we see again the implication that a discrepancy in the literal meaning of the text is a signal to those properly trained within one of the poetry families that there is a hidden, "true" meaning.

As noted above, one possible audience for this kind of commentary was the provincial samurai poet who wanted the inside scoop, so to speak, on what must otherwise have been a frustratingly opaque court tradition of poetry. *Kikigaki*'s emphasis on anecdotes would have made it appealing to a wide variety of people, an appeal that may also explain why the stories presented in this text quickly begin turning up in popular tales such as *Soga monogatari* and *Arokassen monogatari*, as well as becoming favorite sources for the Noh. The story of the damsel flower and Man Mountain was used as the basis for the Noh play *Ominameshi*, and the explanation of the true significance of the Takasago and Sumiyoshi pines is alluded to in one of Zeami's most famous plays, *Takasago*.

Kikigaki's discussion of the Six Modes by which poetry expresses meaning was also widely influential. The explanations basically repeat those provided in Tameaki's earlier *Chikuen shō* but are somewhat amplified. For example, Tameaki explicates the first kind of poetic meaning, the *soe uta* (風歌 or 諷歌), as an implicit metaphor:

The essential meaning (*kokoro*) is hidden in a natural image. . . . Like the colorless, formless wind that can nevertheless be discerned when it brushes something, the essential meaning of this kind of poem is expressed via implicit metaphor; that is why

33. *Kokin waka shū jo kikigaki*, in Katagiri, *Chūsei*, vol. 2, pp. 261–62.

it is called "wind poem" 風歌. An example of this is the "Naniwa Bay" poem. The hidden meaning of the poem is about Emperor Nintoku, but it is expressed on the surface through the image of the plum blossoms.[34]

Besides identifying how meaning is presented in *soe uta,* the passage also explains why the graph for "wind" is used to represent "soe." Since Tsurayuki had simply borrowed the graphs from the "Major Preface" to the *Book of Songs,* their use was not transparent to Heian and Kamakura period readers.[35] *Kikigaki* provides a rationalization based on an analogy between the invisible wind whose effects we can discern in natural phenomena and the invisible (implicit) meaning that we can discern in poetic images.

One of the distinctive traits of Tameaki's approach to the Six Poetic Modes is that his analysis is grounded in the rhetorical structure of the poems Tsurayuki provides as examples. For *soe uta* Tsurayuki chose the "Naniwa Bay" poem:

> *Naniwazu ni/saku ya kono hana/fuyu komori*
> *ima wa harube to/saku ya kono hana*
>
> At Naniwa Bay, they've blossomed! The winter-shrouded trees
> are dressed in blossoms,
> telling us that spring has come.

According to Tsurayuki, this poem was written to celebrate the beginning of Emperor Nintoku's reign. The interpolated notes add that for three years, when Emperor Nintoku was in Naniwa and still a prince, both he and the crown prince ceded their rank and refused to take the throne. Because of this a Korean scholar, Wani, composed this poem urging that Nintoku take the throne. *Kikigaki* begins its analysis by adding even more detail to the bare bones of this story and identifies not just the crown prince but Nintoku's two other brothers as well.

The Naniwa poem was implicitly read as an allegory in the *Kokin shū* preface. In both *Kikigaki* and *Chikuen shō,* this allegorical reading is made quite explicit. *Chikuen shō* explains this in some detail:

"Naniwa" is the name of Nintoku's palace. The meaning of the phrase, "at Naniwa Bay they've blossomed! The winter-shrouded trees are dressed in blossoms" means that although it is still winter and there are no blossoms yet, the nobility look like

---

34. Ibid., p. 249.
35. On this point, see Wixted, "Chinese Influences on the *Kokin shū* Prefaces," pp. 393–94.

flowers [in their festive robes]. The phrase "telling us that spring has come" means "now is the time for flowery show." On the surface of this poem one can see nothing about Emperor Nintoku; however, Nintoku's enthronement is the meaning hidden beneath. This kind of poem is called *soe uta*. The character *fu* 風 means *fu* 諷 (hint, insinuation, satire).[36] This *fu* is metaphorical. Like the wind that has no form, yet we know it when it touches various things, in a "wind poem" the sentiment is revealed by touching on a different thing.[37]

Here *Chikuen shō* demonstrates that there is nothing in the imagery of the "Naniwa Bay" poem itself that explicitly refers to this political context. It is only through our knowledge of the context for the poem that we can read the "winter-shrouded trees" as an allusion to political instability and the blossoms heralding spring as courtiers dressed in flowery robes to herald the new reign. Thus the imagery functions as an implicit metaphor whose true meaning can be understood only by correlating it with an extrinsic discursive context. In other words, *Chikuen shō* and *Kikigaki* see *soe uta* as an allegorical trope. This definition utilizes the strongest possible precedent, Tsurayuki's *Kokin shū* preface, for reading other poems allegorically, even (or especially) those that at first glance do not appear to have an allegorical meaning.

Kikigaki continues through the rest of the modes explaining the remaining ways that poems present meaning to the reader. This explication was later used by Zeami to formulate his own theory of the Six Poetic Modes for Noh:

Borrowing these six terms [the Six Poetic Modes] should prove useful for the path of learning the performance arts. However, on this path we divide plays into nine levels. I will try to make clear how each level relates to the Six Poetic Modes.

Soe uta: This is the level of the style of marvelous flower. As it says in a commentary on the *Kokin shū* (*Kokin chū*), it is "like a wind whose color and form are invisible, but which can be discerned when it brushes something."[38]

The *Kokin shū* commentary cited here is clearly a text in the lineage of *Kikigaki*; it appears that Tameaki's conception of how poetry expresses meaning influenced Zeami's conception of how a Noh play does so.

Although obscure phrases and a rage to identify are the main motivating triggers for commentary in *Kikigaki*, moments of cultural dissonance between the Heian and Kamakura periods become paradigmatic triggers as

---

36. Note that the term *fūyu* 諷諭 is understood to mean allegory.

37. *Chikuen shō* (NKT), pp. 415–16. Compare the explanation in *Kokin waka shū jo kikigaki*, p. 247.

38. Zeami, *Rikugi*, p. 180.

well. For example, in the very first section, the line "When we hear the song of the warbler in the flowers, the voice of the frog dwelling in the waters, we realize that every living being recites poetry" (*hana ni naku uguisu, mizu ni sumu kawazu no koe o kikeba iki toshi ikeru mono, izure ka uta o yomazarikeru*) triggers a response because of differences between Heian and Kamakura religious assumptions.[39]

Kikigaki's analysis begins with the point that the warbler was the first of all birds, the frog, the first of all insects/reptiles (*mushi* 虫), and that they thus represent all birds and insects. However, Ki no Tsurayuki did not mean literally that all fauna recite poetry. He was alluding to two unusual stories (supposedly from the *Nihon shoki*). In the first, a young disciple is reincarnated as a warbler who sings a poem for his master; in the second, a young woman is reincarnated as a frog and leaves a poem in her tracks.[40] According to *Kikigaki*, instances in which human beings become fauna and in that form recite poetry are, in fact, surprisingly numerous. This, according to *Kikigaki*, was the point Tsurayuki was trying to make. The analysis thus begins quite typically by revealing the poetic anecdotes that the commentary asserts were Tsurayuki's allusive subtext.

Kikigaki then takes an interesting turn: it re-emphasizes that "iki toshi ikeru mono" does not mean that all living beings literally recite poetry. Instead, it refers to the fact that the bodies of all living beings consist of the Five Modalities (wood, fire, metal, earth, and water), and so their voices echo these five elements. Each of the five lines of waka is matched with one of the Five Modalities. Therefore the voices of living beings are waka. The questioner then points out that not only living beings but also nonsentient grasses and trees, dust and sand, are made from the Five Modalities. Why does Tsurayuki not mention them as well?

According to Nagayoshi's diary, "Waka is the essential body (躰) of the Five Modalities; to write the words (*kotoba*) is the essential body, to understand their sentiment (*kokoro*) is the virtuous derivative activity (徳).[41] The rustling of the eastern

39. *Kokin waka shū jo kikigaki*, pp. 225–28.

40. These two stories (along with the pertinent lines from the *Kokin shū*) appear in a slightly abbreviated form in the Muromachi prose tales *Soga monogatari* and *Hioke no soshi* (Tale of the brazier); see Cogan, *The Tale of the Soga Brothers*, pp. 146–47; Skord, *Tales of Tears and Laughter*, p. 103.

41. The poetic concepts of *kotoba* (words, diction) and *kokoro* (essential meaning, content) are here related to the Buddhist concepts of the essential body or substance (*tai* 躰) and its derivative function or activity (*toku* 徳).

breezes in the spring forest, the crying of the insects in autumn's northern frosts, all of these are manifestations of poetry. They are the essential body of waka." Thus the voices of both sentient and nonsentient beings are manifestations of poetry. Why then does [Tsurayuki] say only the voices of living beings are waka?[42]

The answer is that the phrase "all living beings" is an all-inclusive category under which the nonsentient can also be found; therefore Tsurayuki did not need to mention the nonsentient specifically.

Here we see an attempt to resolve an important difference in the basic religious assumptions of the Heian and Kamakura periods. Although the concept of buddhahood for the nonsentient (*sōmoku jōbutsu* 草木成仏, "the grasses and trees become Buddha") was formulated by the tenth century, it took a century or two for it to take hold in the popular imagination. Thus the question of whether nonsentient beings could recite poetry would not have seemed an important issue to Ki no Tsurayuki. It was clearly an issue for the Kamakura commentators, however, and in Muromachi Noh, the concept of buddhahood for the nonsentient becomes a major theme.[43]

Kikigaki illustrates the medieval desire to understand the historical basis of metaphors and metonymies as well as the etymological origins of poetic place-names (*uta makura*) and the names of flora and fauna. It also illustrates how changes in religious and cultural values triggered the need for commentary that could resolve contradictions between the Heian and Kamakura worldviews. In addition, through comparisons to other schools, as well as allusions to other Tameaki-affiliated commentaries, *Kikigaki* reinforces the authority of the Tameaki school as a whole as well as its own place as an intermediate-level text in the *kanjō* pedagogical system.

Kikigaki opens by identifying its major competition: "There are three schools of *Kokin shū* commentary. The first is Teika's, the second is Ietaka's,

---

42. *Kokin waka shū jo kikigaki*, p. 227.

43. It is possible that Tsurayuki was aware of this doctrinal debate between the older Hossō school, which held that only certain beings (even excluding some categories of human beings) possess the Buddha nature, and the newer Tendai school, which followed the ninth patriarch, Chan-jan (711–82), in arguing that all matter possesses the Buddha nature, and therefore even nonsentient grasses and trees can become Buddha. However, it was not until 963 that a debate was held on this subject between Ryōgen (912–85), who later became head priest of Enraku-ji on Mount Hiei, and representatives of the Hossō school from Nara. Ryōgen triumphed over his adversaries, and subsequently the Tendai position was accepted by all the prominent sects of the Muromachi period. See Donald Shively, "Buddhahood for the Nonsentient: A Theme in Nō Plays," pp. 139–41.

and the third is [Rokujō] Yukiie's."[44] Although Rokujō Yukiie figures prominently in this first passage, he is subsequently mentioned again only once.[45] Instead the main interpretive contest is always between an "Ietaka" and "Teika" explanation, and invariably Teika's position (identified with "our house") is found to be correct. The Ietaka school is treated as a kind of illegitimate offspring of the Teika school:

> Query: Ietaka was a disciple of Shunzei, and Shunzei was Teika's father. Why should Ietaka's school be separate?
>
> Answer: After Shunzei's death, Teika and Ietaka were like left and right wings. However, because Ietaka received only the secondary (末) teachings from Teika, he was not able to get the full interpretation.[46]

To prove its point that the Ietaka school has less legitimacy, *Kikigaki*, in a passage quoted in full above (pp. 219–20), describes how two variant texts of *Chiken shū*, transmitted to Minamoto no Tsunenobu by Sumiyoshi Daimyōjin, came into existence: "It seems that because Ietaka wanted to differ from Teika, he did not inquire into this transmission but instead created a new school by altering Teika's interpretations and readings of characters."[47]

Thus, according to *Kikigaki*, Ietaka received the correct interpretations from Shunzei but then willfully altered them so that he could establish his own poetry house. Here authority stems not from Teika's superior understanding of poetry, but from the fact that he alone received the authentic transmission lineage originating with Tsunenobu. This attitude toward "authority" is directly related to the growing emphasis on family tradition over poetic talent. It is ironic that Tameaki, who was for the most part shut out of his family's poetic legacy, should have done so much to promote traditional authority through his development of the waka *kanjō*.[48]

---

44. *Kokin waka shū jo kikigaki*, p. 223.

45. Ibid., p. 266.

46. Ibid., p. 223. Here again the term is *matsu* 末 (branch, subordinate), indicating that the lineage is secondary and possibly illegitimate.

47. As noted in the previous section, *Chiken shū* probably refers to the Ietaka and Tameaki school variants of *Waka chiken shū*. See ibid., p. 24.

48. And Tameaki may be identifying with the figure of Minamoto no Tsunenobu, who according to *Waka chiken shū* was excluded from the knowledge possessed by the major poetry families and so was forced to pray to Sumiyoshi Daimyōjin for direct mystical revelation of those secrets.

Kikigaki includes other sections that encourage a belief in the oracular authority of Sumiyoshi Daimyōjin as the guardian deity of waka poetry and so support the waka *kanjō* system. In its discussion of the line "[Japanese poetry] causes invisible demons and kami to be emotionally moved" (*me ni mienu oni kami o mo, aware to omowase*), *Kikigaki* argues that because the kami love poetry, they will be moved to grant petitions in the form of waka. An example of this from the *Nihon shoki* is cited, and then there is a digression that begins, "There are numerous examples proving that poetry is loved by kami; just at the moment, *Ise monogatari* comes to mind."[49] This serves to introduce the etiological commentary on episode 117, in which Narihira accompanies Emperor Montoku to Sumiyoshi Shrine and while there exchanges poetry with the Daimyōjin and receives two secret transmissions on poetry. By providing only the etiology and not the actual contents of these secret transmissions, *Kikigaki* would have whetted the appetite of disciples for higher-level initiation texts such as *Gyokuden jinpi no maki* and encouraged disciples to continue their studies so that they could acquire those esoteric transmissions.

49. *Kokin waka shū jo kikigaki*, p. 229.

10

Tameaki-Affiliated Commentaries (Part II)

Gyokuden jinpi no maki

Gyokuden jinpi no maki (Jeweled transmission of deep secrets) interprets both the *Kokin shū* and *Ise monogatari* as revelations of the profound secrets of Shingon esoteric Buddhism. Although all the sections in this work are unified by this interpretive stance, they appear to have been written as separate oral transmissions and then collected into one manuscript. *Gyokuden jinpi no maki* was probably a collection of special transmissions for higher-level initiates. This has led to a great deal of variation between textual lineages, and a certain amount of contradiction among sections even within one variant. A number of shorter spinoff texts also contain material found in *Gyokuden jinpi no maki.*[1] Miwa Masatane attributes *Gyokuden jinpi no maki* to Fujiwara no

1. Spinoff texts include *Gyokuden shū waka saichō* (Collection of highest-level jeweled transmission on waka), *Jinpi kushō* (Nine fascicles of deep secrets), and *Akone no ura kuden* (Oral transmission of Akone Bay), all three of which are published in vol. 4 of *Nihon kagaku taikei*, pp. 391–98. *Gyokuden shū waka saichō* correlates with the first two sections of *Gyokuden jinpi no maki* (Katagiri, *Chūsei*, vol. 5, pp. 522–24); *Jinpi kushō* correlates with "Kushō mitsuden" (Katagiri, *Chūsei*, vol. 5, p. 567); and *Akone no ura kuden* correlates with a section of the same name (Katagiri, *Chūsei*, vol. 5, pp. 529–30). Another spinoff text, *Ise monogatari engi* (Commentary on *Ise monogatari*), is a selection of six oral transmissions from *Gyokuden jinpi no maki* that relate specifically to *Ise monogatari* ("Kuchū shingi," "Naidō ron," "Niji gi," "Shichigatsu

Tameaki for two reasons. First, there are similarities between it and the two poetic treatises *Chikuen shō* and *Tameie kuden*, which are thought to be by Tameaki. Second, the transmission lineages of all variants of *Gyokuden jinpi no maki* include Tameaki's name.[2]

There are two main lineages of *Gyokuden jinpi no maki* texts: one transmitted through a disciple of Tameaki known as Shinsui and the other through the Yoshimoto discussed in Chapter 6, who also figures in the transmission lineages for *Kokin waka shū jo kikigaki* and *Chikuen shō*. The first lineage came to be called *Gyokuden jinpi no maki* because that is the title of its first section; for the same reason, the second lineage came to be called *Kingyoku sōgi* (Twin meanings of gold and jewels). About two-thirds of the material in the two lineages overlaps, an indication that they are variants rather than different texts. In addition, the transmission dates for the two are very close. According to the colophons, Shinsui received *Gyokuden jinpi no maki* from Tameaki on the twelfth day of the twelfth month of 1278.[3] Yoshimoto received the material relating to *Kokin shū* on the eleventh and that relating to the *Ise monogatari* on the twenty-eighth.[4]

The textual organization of the two lineages differs in important ways, and these differences provide additional hints about Tameaki's attempts to legitimate his commentaries. The Shinsui lineage texts mix commentaries on the *Kokin shū* and *Ise monogatari* in no particular order, and its two transmis-

---

nanoka taeiru koto," "Tsuki ya aranu," "Mikawa gi," and "Kaigō onna inmei no koto"). It is published in Katagiri, *Ise monogatari no kenkyū (kenkyūhen)*, pp. 579–82. *Waka entei hishō* (Selected comments on the secret depths of waka) correlates with the sections in *Gyokuden jinpi no maki* that discuss close and distant linking (Katagiri, *Chūsei*, vol. 5, pp. 563–67). It is also connected to *Chikuen shō*'s discussion on that topic (*NKT*, pp. 414–15). Sections 2, 5, 7, 8, and 11 of *Kakinomoto no Hitomaro no koto* (The matter of Kakinomoto no Hitomaro; published in Miwa, *Kagaku hiden no kenkyū*, pp. 486–500) contain material that also appears in the *Gyokuden jinpi no maki* discussion of Hitomaro and Akahito (Katagiri, *Chūsei*, vol. 5, pp. 554–62). Finally, there are different versions of *Iwami no jo shiki* (Record of the wife from Iwami) with varying amounts of material; see the discussion in Miwa, *Kagaku hiden no kenkyū*, pp. 108–15. The variant published in *Nihon kagaku taikei* basically consists of the opening and closing sections of *Gyokuden jinpi no maki* plus material from an earlier commentary (*Kisen shiki* [Record of Kisen], late tenth century) on the four poetic illnesses. It concludes with an abbreviated version of the etiology based on *Ise monogatari* episode 117 and claims that it is the "Gyokuden" transmitted by Sumiyoshi Daimyōjin to Narihira in Ten'an 1 (*NKT*, vol. 1, pp. 31–34).

2. See Miwa Masatane, "*Chikuen shō* karon no seisei to hatten: *Gyokuden shū*, *Akone no ura kuden* ni tsuite"; and idem, "*Chikuen shō* no seiritsu ni kansuru futatsu, mitsu no mondai."

3. *Gyokuden jinpi no maki*, p. 534.

4. *Kingyoku sōgi* (sections 26–27), pt. I, pp. 47–48; (section 60), pt. II, p. 46.

sion lineages are placed somewhat haphazardly. The first, entitled "Order of Transmission" ("Kechimyaku no shidai"), traces the transmission as Nobumitsu → Toshitaka → Teika → Tameie → Tameaki → Shinsui. Then there is a note: "A colophon listing the same transmission lineage with dates" ("onajiku kechimyaku nengo okugaki"). However, the list that follows is quite different. It starts with Sumiyoshi Daimyōjin and continues Hitomaro → Narihira → Emperor Tenmu → Amaterasu Ōmikami → Emperor Daigo → Tsurayuki → Tokibumi → Shitagō → Nagaie → Tsunenobu → Toshiyori → Shunzei → Teika → Tameie → Tameaki → Shinsui → Seisoku.[5] Until the *Kingyoku sōgi* variant was published in the early 1990s, scholars were puzzled by the two transmission lineages.

Kingyoku sōgi is better organized than the Shinsui *Gyokuden jinpi no maki*. This organization clearly links the text to the story of the origins of *Ise monogatari* episode 117, which was used to legitimize the allegorical interpretive strategy employed in Tameaki-affiliated commentaries. It does so by neatly grouping all the material on the *Kokin shū* separately from the comments on *Ise monogatari* and by providing appropriate transmission lineages for each section. It is clear from the two transmission lineages for the *Kokin shū* material and the one transmission lineage for the *Ise monogatari* material that they were carefully devised to substantiate the story of Narihira's receiving the two secret transmissions on poetry, "Gyokuden" and "Akone no ura kuden," from Sumiyoshi Daimyōjin and their subsequent transmission to Tameaki.

To recapitulate the etiology based on episode 117, Narihira used the "Akone no ura kuden" to write *Ise monogatari* and then transmitted it to his son Shigeharu so that a select few in later generations would be able to understand its esoteric secrets. He took "Gyokuden" with him when he was sent as an envoy to the Ise Shrine and left his copy at the shrine for safekeeping. Five reigns later, Emperor Daigo sent Fujiwara no Kanetaka to the shrine, where he received the "Gyokuden" after dreaming of it. He gave it to

5. *Gyokuden jinpi no maki*, pp. 531–34. It is not clear why Hitomaro and Emperor Tenmu are in the lineage, since they interfere with the chronology, but note that Hitomaro, Tenmu, and Amaterasu are not provided with transmission dates. In the *Kingyoku sōgi* lineage, Hitomaro is identified as an incarnation (*keshin*) of Sumiyoshi Daimyōjin, and both Narihira and Ki no Tsurayuku are identified as "Hitomaro reborn" (Ishigami Hideaki, "Kunaichō Shoryōbu-zō *Kingyoku sōgi*," pt. 1, p. 47). Since there are a number of secret transmissions about Hitomaro, it may be that inserting Hitomaro and an emperor contemporaneous to Hitomaro was meant to legitimize those transmissions.

Emperor Daigo, who was so impressed that he had Ki no Tsurayuki use it as a basis for compiling the first imperial anthology, the *Kokin shū*.

In line with this story, at the end of the *Kokin shū* material there are two almost identical transmission lineages. "Transmission Lineage with Colophon Dates, Reign Names, and Secret Poems" ("Kechimyaku nengo okugaki dai to hika") supplies names, dates of transmission, and one poem for each poet on the list. "Transmission Lineage of Masters to Disciples on Waka in the *Kokin shū*" ("*Kokin* waka shishi sōden kechimyakufu") gives names, dates, and some biographical information about each poet.[6] Both of these transmission lineages are basically the same: Sumiyoshi Daimyōjin → Narihira (1/28/857) → Amaterasu Ōmikami (871) → Emperor Daigo (903) → Tsurayuki (919)[7] → Tokibumi (no date) → Shitagō (949) → Nagaie (949) → Tsunenobu (995) → Toshiyori (1184) → Shunzei (1204) → Teika (1220) → Tameie (1249) → Tameaki (3/13/1273) → Yoshimoto (12/11/1273) → Kaishō (7/25/1286) → Suōmaro (4/10/1299).[8] This transmission lineage with its official-looking dates, proof poems, and signatures was meant to guarantee the historicity of the Narihira story and simultaneously substantiate the truth-value of the secret transmissions. There are, however, numerous problems with these dates, the most common being a transmission date either before the birth or after the death of the poet named.[9] This may indi-

6. Ishigami Hideaki, "Kunaichō Shoryōbu-zō *Kingyoku sōgi*," pt. 1, pp. 47–48.

7. This transmission date would seem to be too late for Tsurayuki to have used the secret transmission from Emperor Daigo to compile the *Kokin shū*. None of the other transmission lineages, including the other *Kokin shū* transmission lineage in *Kingyoku sōgi*, has a date for this. It may have been omitted from the other lineages because someone realized that it did not work.

8. After Tameie, the "*Kokin* waka shishi sōden kechimyakufu" interpolates Tameuji and Tameyo, and then returns to Tameaki → Yoshimoto → Kaishō → Suōmaro. This interpolation may indicate that the text became part of the Nijō transmission, and it was thought necessary to add the founders of the Nijō school to make the transmission look more legitimate (Ishigami Hideaki, "Kunaichō Shoryōbu-zō *Kingyoku sōgi*," pt. 1, p. 48).

9. For example, Fujiwara no Nagaie is supposed to have received the transmission from Shitagō in 949; Nagaie was not born until 1005, 22 years after Shitagō's death. Similarly, Minamoto no Tsunenobu (1016–97) is supposed to have received the transmission from Nagaie in 995; neither Nagaie nor Tsunenobu was born yet. Toshiyori's dates are 1055?–1129?, yet he is supposed to have received the transmission from Tsunenobu in 1184 and transmitted the *Kokin shū* material to Shunzei in 1204. Shunzei receives the transmission in the year of his death, 1204, and it is hard to understand how he was able to transmit the material to Teika in 1220. The fact that all the variants have practically the same dates indicates that the problems are probably not due to miscopying.

cate Tameaki's lack of access to official histories that gave approximate biographical dates. Or perhaps he did not care about accuracy, since the recipients of the transmission, mainly provincial samurai and poet priests in the Kantō region, would have had little or no opportunity to check the dates against a more authoritative source.

At the end of the material on *Ise monogatari*, the *Kingyoku sōgi* presents another list, "Transmission Lineage from Masters to Disciples on *Ise monogatari*" ("*Ise monogatari* shishi sōshō kechimyakufu"). This transmission corroborates the claims that Narihira transmitted the *Ise monogatari* material to his son Shigeharu: Sumiyoshi Daimyōjin → Narihira (1/28/857) → Shigeharu (880) → Motokata (888) → Motokiyo (no date) → Korezumi (889) → Narimasa (890) → Muneie (898) → Tomoyuki (903) → Kimiyuki (905) → Mikuni (1184) → Toshitada (1185) → Shunzei (1188) → Teika (1219) → Tameie (1221) → Tameuji (1264) → Tameyo (no date) → Tameaki (5/11/1267) → Yoshimoto (12/28/1278)→ Kaishō (7/25/1287) → Suōmaro (4/10/1299).[10] In the first part of the lineage, the transmission is not to well-known poets, as it was in the *Kokin shū* lineage, but to descendents of Narihira.[11] In order to legitimate the transmission to the Mikohidari family, the lineage says that Toshitada adopted Takahashi no Mikuni as his disciple.[12] In this way the "Gyokuden" transmission on the *Kokin shū* and the "Akone no ura kuden" transmission on *Ise monogatari* were reunited in the person of Shunzei, who received the first from his teacher Toshiyori and the second from his father, Toshitada. It is interesting that this transmission lineage remains attached only to the *Ise monogatari* material in the *Kingyoku sōgi* variant; perhaps the large number of non-poets and the somewhat odd grouping of dates were seen as problematic.[13]

---

10. Ishigami Hideaki, "Kunaichō Shoryōbu-zō *Kingyoku sōgi*," pt. II, pp. 45–46.

11. I have not been able to trace the genealogy of Ariwara no Narihira's descendants to see if the genealogy presented here is historically valid. Note, however, the gap between 905 and 1184. There is a similarly inexplicable gap (995–1184) in the *Kokin shū* transmission lineage.

12. Under Mikuni, the transmission lineage says: "Takahashi no Ason Mikuni, Junior Third Rank. Kimiyuki's fourth son. Adopted by Middle Counselor Fujiwara no Toshitada and so changed his name to Fujiwara. Received the transmission on 1/13/1184 (Genryaku 1)." Having been adopted by Toshitada, Mikuni transmitted the *Ise monogatari* material to him the following year. See Ishigami Hideaki, "Kunaichō Shoryōbu-zō *Kingyoku sōgi*," pt. II, p. 45.

13. Here again Tameuji and Tameyo have been interpolated into the lineage between Tameie and Tameaki, a sign that the text was transmitted within the Nijō family.

The third transmission lineage in *Kingyoku sōgi* matches the perplexing transmission lineage beginning with Minamoto no Nobumitsu (926–76) found in the Shinsui variant of *Gyokuden jinpi no maki*.[14] In both texts the transmission lineage is preceded by a section analyzing the meaning of the phrase "daimyōjin." The section in *Gyokuden jinpi no maki* is untitled; in *Kingyoku sōgi* it is called "The Meaning of *Daimyōjin*" ("Daimyōjin no gi") and is accompanied by the note "Middle Counselor Nobumitsu's dream." Apparently the lineage beginning with Nobumitsu was meant specifically for the transmission on the meaning of "daimyōjin" alone. A transcriber of *Gyokuden jinpi no maki*, not realizing what had been intended, simply joined the two lineages.

Although the transmission lineages for the *Kokin shū* and *Ise monogatari* material would at first seem to indicate that all the material was transmitted to Narihira by Sumiyoshi Daimyōjin in 857, a number of individual oral transmissions are attributed to others. In *Kingyoku sōgi* these include Ariwara no Shigeharu's "Record of the Middle Captain's Entrance into Nirvana" ("Chūjō nyūmetsu no ki") which records Narihira's deathbed scene; Minamoto no Nobumitsu's "The Meaning of *Daimyōjin*" ("Daimyōjin no gi"); Minamoto no Tsunenobu's "Transmission of the Golden Tablet" ("Kinsatsu den"), "The Matter of the Twelve Avatars" ("Jūninin no keshin no koto"), and "Record of the *Kanjō* Ritual for Waka Transmission" ("Waka denju kanjō shiki"). An oral transmission is even attributed to Teika: "The Theory of the Inner Path" ("Naidō ron"). Including a number of important poets as sources for the secrets would have made the transmission as a whole look fuller and more substantial.

Although the inclusion of Tameuji and Tameyo in the transmission lineages of *Kingyoku sōgi* indicates that the text was transmitted within the Nijō school, there seems to be an equally strong connection between *Gyokuden jinpi no maki* and the Reizei school. First, a number of the sections now in *Gyokuden jinpi no maki* are listed separately in Tamesuke's library catalogue of 1317.[15] Second, references to material from *Gyokuden jinpi no maki* occasionally appear in the Reizei commentaries on *Ise monogatari*. For example, the preface to the Reizei school *Ise monogatari shō* contains a direct reference to

14. As in *Gyokuden jinpi no maki*, the lineage runs from Nobumitsu to Tameaki, but then continues Yoshimoto → Kaishō → Suōmaro. Ishigami Hideaki, "Kunaichō Shoryōbu-zō *Kingyoku sōgi*," pt. I, p. 45.

15. This is another reason to suspect that *Gyokuden jinpi no maki* is a miscellaneous collection of semirelated transmissions; see Katagiri, *Ise monogatari no kenkyū (kenkyūhen)*, p. 576–77.

such material.[16] And it seems likely that the Reizei explanation of the "true" meaning of the graphs *i-se* as representing the kami of Yin and Yang, Izanami and Izanagi, was also borrowed from *Gyokuden jinpi no maki*. Third, in the last section of *Kingyoku sōgi* there is a series of explanations of *Ise monogatari* episodes found nowhere else; these have strong connections to the Reizei school *Ise monogatari shō* commentary on those episodes.[17] Since these sections appear at the end of *Kingyoku sōgi*, it is not clear whether they were originally part of the text or were added later. The text was published only in 1992, and the research necessary to determine whether the Reizei school *Ise monogatari shō* is based on these sections remains to be done.

In terms of content, the following section from *Gyokuden jinpi no maki* gives a good sense of the character of the commentary as a whole. It addresses Narihira's poem from episode 124:

> *omou koto / iwade tada ni ya / yaminubeshi*
> *ware to hitoshiki / hito shi nakereba*
>
> Since there is no like-minded person here,
> I'll just keep my thoughts to myself and say nothing.

Now as for Narihira's true intent and conception lying behind this poem, it signifies that he would not speak of how *Ise monogatari* was created out of the Path of Intercourse between men and women.[18]

Gyokuden jinpi no maki is to be understood as containing precisely those "thoughts" of Narihira's that would not be understood by ordinary folk but should be transmitted only to "like-minded" people: "The phrase 'I'll just keep my thoughts to myself' (*omou koto iwade*) means 'remain silent and do not reveal the deep secrets of Shingon.'"[19] These profound secrets were to be carefully preserved and transmitted only to those who had been specially initiated into that poetry school.

Like *Waka chiken shū* and *Kokin waka shū jo kikigaki*, *Gyokuden jinpi no maki* attempts to reveal the "true reality" beneath the "phenomenal appearance" of the text it analyzes. However, whereas those texts concentrated mainly on revealing the hidden historical subtexts of *Ise monogatari* and the *Kokin shū*

---

16. "The Profound Meaning of the Two Graphs" ("Niji no shingi") and "The Theory of the Inner Path" ("Naidō ron"), in Reizeike-ryū *Ise monogatari shō*, p. 292; cf. *Gyokuden jinpi no maki*, "Waka no niji shingi," p. 550, and "Naidō ron," pp. 536–37.

17. Ishigami Hideaki, "Kunaichō Shoryōbu-zō *Kingyoku sōgi*," pt. III, pp. 54–62.

18. *Gyokuden jinpi no maki*, p. 535. See also note 103 to Chapter 8, p. 206.

19. *Gyokuden jinpi no maki*, p. 535.

preface, *Gyokuden jinpi no maki* concentrates on revealing the hidden religious subtext. It does so through an extensive use of *honji suijaku* identifications, reinforced by the concepts of expedient means and nondualism, and by various forms of etymological allegoresis. The content thus revealed turns out to be heavily influenced by Tachikawa's syncretic mix of Shingon, Taoist Yin-Yang theory, and Ryōbu Shinto.

The difference between the approach of *Gyokuden jinpi no maki* and *Waka chiken shū* is clear in their commentaries on the first episode of *Ise monogatari*, in which the Man of Old undergoes a coming-of-age ceremony (having the courtier's cap ritually placed on his head for the first time) and goes hunting in Kasuga Village in the old capital of Nara. *Waka chiken shū* concentrates on explaining obscure terms and providing "historical" names and dates. It identifies the Man of Old as Narihira and the two young women he meets in Kasuga village as Ki no Aritsune's daughters, gives the exact date for his coming-of-age ceremony, and explains the meaning of various difficult phrases. *Gyokuden jinpi no maki* also concentrates on naming names and explaining difficult phrases, but it reveals them to be hiding, not a historical subtext, but a transcendent layer of religious meaning:

> [In the opening line] the phrase "mukashi otoko" (the Man of Old) means "wagami" (my body). It is an indication that [Narihira is] Sumiyoshi's avatar.[20] Sumiyoshi's Original Ground (*honji*) is Kannon. Because Kannon is the eternal buddha who has no beginning or end, Narihira is referred to as "mukashi" (昔, old or ancient). "Otoko" (man) refers to the Diamond Realm of Dainichi [Nyorai], which is understood as male. The women are Aritsune's daughters, [who represent the female] deity of the Womb-Storehouse Realm. The line "he went to the capital at Nara" means "for the purpose of aiding and transforming all living beings by bestowing an expedient device for their benefit, he took an ordinary human form and came into this corrupt world, forming a karmic link to humanity." . . . In this way, the essential purpose of this tale is to help us grasp the profound meaning of Shingon.[21]

Here as elsewhere *Gyokuden jinpi no maki* applies etymological allegoresis of names in order to reveal the "profound meaning of Shingon." By analyzing the graphs for "the Man of Old," *Gyokuden jinpi no maki* is able to prove that Nari-

20. This may be referring to the "Tsuki ya aranu" poem from episode 4, which ends "wagami hitotsu moto no mi ni shite" (my body alone remains as it was originally), a phrase that *Gyokuden jinpi no maki* (pp. 552–53) took to indicate that Narihira was an incarnation of Sumiyoshi Daimyōjin and ultimately Dainichi Nyorai.

21. Ibid., p. 536.

hira is an avatar of both Sumiyoshi Daimyōjin and Kannon and that he represents the male aspect of the Dainichi Nyorai's Diamond Realm, identified with Toyouke Hime of the Outer Shrine at Ise. He took on human form as Narihira in order to write *Ise monogatari*, which with proper interpretation serves as an expedient means to enlighten humanity. And his eroticized relationship with the two sisters is transformed by their identification with Dainichi's Womb-Storehouse Realm into a model of enlightened sex.

In fact, in most explications of *Ise monogatari* in *Gyokuden jinpi no maki*, the analysis inevitably reveals that Narihira is an avatar teaching the way of conjugal relationships as an expedient means to enlightenment. In these analyses, Narihira is identified not only with Sumiyoshi Daimyōjin and Izanagi no Mikoto but also with the Tatsuta and Kasuga Daimyōjin (although both of these are seen, in turn, as alter egos for Sumiyoshi). And as in the passage quoted above, Narihira is not the only one identified with various kami; a number of the women with whom he sleeps are also revealed to have been avatars. Ki no Aritsune's daughter is elsewhere identified with Izanami no Mikoto, Nijō no Kisaki is a manifestation of the kami of the third shrine at Sumiyoshi (Tamatsushima Myōjin), and Somedono no Naishi is Hotōmi no Mikoto.[22] Ultimately each of these female deities is aligned with Dainichi Nyorai's Womb-Storehouse Realm. This identification proves that Narihira's lovers appeared in this world to help him provide a model of sexual enlightenment for all living beings.

The Elusive "Gyokuden" and "Akone no ura kuden"

Since so much of *Gyokuden jinpi no maki* is devoted to providing the details of Narihira's reception of the two secret transmissions "Gyokuden" and "Akone no ura kuden," as well as the transmission lineages for those texts, one would naturally expect these two transmissions to be included in *Gyokuden jinpi no maki*. It is not at all clear, however, which of the sections or groups of sections correspond to those secret transmissions. Spin-offs of *Gyokuden jinpi no maki* include sections entitled "Gyokuden" and "Akone no ura kuden," but the contents are not always the same as the sections in *Gyokuden jinpi no maki* with those titles. It may well be that "Gyokuden" was an empty rubric for esoteric secrets related to the *Kokin shū* and "Akone no

22. Ibid., pp. 544, 539, 541.

ura kuden" for *Ise monogatari*. If so, Tameaki had complete discretion to select whatever secrets he thought appropriate for transmission to a particular disciple. Since the disciples were enjoined not to show the text to anyone, the differences in transmission from one initiate to another would not be immediately evident. Tameaki was creating a web of interconnecting, mutually authenticating texts, but because they were going to different people at different levels of initiation, the fit did not need to be perfect.

We can, nevertheless, make some tentative guesses about the likely content of the "Akone no ura kuden" and "Gyokuden" transmissions. Let us start with "Akone no ura kuden." The etiological story for both transmissions is itself sometimes called "Akone no ura kuden" and sometimes "Akone no ura kuden nikki" (A diary of the oral transmission of Akone Bay). It can be found in roughly the same form in *Shinsen teisetsu shū* and *Kokin waka shū jo kikigaki*. In both of those texts, it is used as an enticement for the next level of initiation, in which the initiate would actually receive the secret transmissions. The etiological story is given in more detail in *Gyokuden jinpi no maki* (sections 3–4, 31), in *Kingyoku sōgi* (section 48), and in a very abbreviated form in *Iwami no jo shiki* (Record of the wife from Iwami), a spin-off of *Gyokuden jinpi no maki.*[23]

It would not make sense, however, for the etiology to be the secret itself. The most likely candidate is "Akone no ura kuden" (section 8) of *Gyokuden jinpi no maki.*[24] This section describes how Izanami and Izanagi descended from the High Plain of Heaven to the coast off Akone (near Ise Shrine). After each recited a poem, they had sexual relations, thereby producing the islands of Japan. This version of the creation myth conflates the cosmogonic procreative act with the origins of poetry and the origins of sex: from that time on, the Path of Eroticism (*irogonomi no michi*) and the Path of Poetry (*uta no michi*) have been intertwined as one. *Gyokuden jinpi no maki* identifies this primordial sexual event, which took place at Ise, as "the pledge of I-Se" in a poem:

---

23. *Shinsen teisetsu shū* is quoted in Miwa, *Kagaku hiden no kenkyū*, pp. 82–83; *Kokin waka shū jo kikigaki*, in Katagiri, *Chūsei*, vol. 2, pp. 229–30; *Gyokuden jinpi no maki*, in Katagiri, *Chūsei*, vol. 5, pp. 524–26, 545–46; *Kingyoku sōgi*, in Ishigami, "Kunaichō Shoryōbu-zo *Kingyoku sōgi*," p. 41; *Iwami jō shiki*, in *Nihon kagaku taikei*, vol. 1, p. 34.

24. Katagiri, *Chūsei*, vol. 5, pp. 529–31; see also sections 49 and 50 in Ishigami Hideaki, "Kunaichō Shoryōbu-zo *Kingyoku sōgi*," pt. II, pp. 41–42. A somewhat different "Akone no ura kuden" is published in *Nihon kagaku taikei*, vol. 4, p. 398. This version is presented in the first person, as though spoken directly by Sumiyoshi Daimyōjin.

ima koso wa / Ise no chigiri mo / hajimetsure
Ise no chigiri wa / sue hisashikere

Even now the pledge of I-Se begins again;
the pledge of I-Se that has no ending.[25]

This reading assumes the reader's familiarity with points made elsewhere in *Gyokuden jinpi no maki*, that the graphs for Ise 伊勢 are identified with Izanami and Izanagi, as well as the Womb-Storehouse and Diamond Realm mandalas.

The *Gyokuden jinpi no maki* "Akone no ura kuden" concludes by analyzing the graphs for Akone no ura 阿古根浦:

Query: So what kind of place is this Akone no ura?

Reply: The phrase "Akone" 阿古根 has two meanings. One meaning refers to the Akone district near the Ise Grand Shrine. The second [etymological meaning is as follows:] "*a*" means "not born/arising." [i.e., it is the Sanskrit seed syllable A]. It signifies that Amaterasu Ōmikami, as the sovereign of the land, governs all the myriad kami. The graph "*a*" (阿) means "impartiality" (*muhen* 無遍). "*Ko*" [古 read as *mukashi*] refers to the ancient past, when the sun deity hid herself in the celestial cave and bore three males and one female, and when the pledge of husband and wife occurred. "*Ne*" [根 read as origin, foundation] refers to the birth of the original deities of Japan, when all the myriad things were first produced. "Ura" [浦 bay] is a name for Japan. The oral transmission of Akone is an inquiry into the true names of the [two] sun kami, Amaterasu Ōmikami and Sumiyoshi Daimyōjin. Because these [two] sun kami brought forth the kami of the Five Modalities, they are called the mother and father. In reality, the sun kami are two deities, but the same in essence. This must be kept very, very secret. Now this "Akone no ura kuden" was transmitted to Narihira by the greatly revered Daimyōin and became a treasured secret of the Nijō family. It is not to be revealed to other houses. We are grateful to hear this innermost matter.[26]

Here Sumiyoshi Daimyōjin is identified with Amaterasu Ōmikami. As noted above, in the *Nihon shoki* the three kami that later collectively become Sumiyoshi are relatively minor deities. This transmission may indicate an attempt to aggrandize Sumiyoshi by making him not only the male counterpart to Amaterasu but also, via nondualism, ultimately her equivalent, "identical in nature." Sumiyoshi Daimyōjin, as a Manifest Trace manifestation of Izanagi, continues to protect and guide those who resolve to plumb the pro-

25. *Gyokuden jinpi no maki*, p. 529.
26. Ibid., pp. 530–31.

found depths of the nondual paths of eroticism and poetry.[27] Identifications such as these reinforce the etiology of the transmissions by creating a tightly woven tapestry of identifications between Narihira, Sumiyoshi, Ise, Amaterasu, and Izanami and Izanagi. As such, this "Akone no ura kuden" would make an appropriate source for *Ise monogatari* written as an allegory of Tachikawa secrets.

The content of the "Gyokuden" transmission is also difficult to identify precisely. *Gyokuden jinpi no maki* states: "Regarding the term *gyokuden* we can derive certain meanings. If it refers to an open place [i.e., the vagina], it is written 'jeweled gate' 玉門 or the 'opening for a child' 子門穴. If it is closed [i.e., the penis], it is written 'jeweled stalk' 玉茎."[28] This etymological analysis might lead one to think that the contents of "Gyokuden" involve a Tachikawa-influenced reading similar to that given above for the "Akone no ura kuden." However, in Tameaki's intermediate-level commentary, *Shinsen teisetsu shū*, "Gyokuden" is identified as a group of teachings about close and distant linking.[29] This seems a surprisingly prosaic source for a tantric reading of *Kokin shū*.

A more likely candidate is the first section of *Gyokuden jinpi no maki*, which is entitled "Gyokuden jinpi."[30] In this section, a waka poem's upper

---

27. Sometimes Sumiyoshi is identified as both Izanagi and Izanami (also referred to as the Kami of Yin and Yang [*in'yō no kami*]). Other times he is only identified as Izanagi, and other kami such as Amaterasu Ōmikami, Toyouke Hime, or Tamatsushima Myōjin, are identified as *suijaku* of Izanami.

28. *Gyokuden jinpi no maki*, p. 527.

29. This identification correlates with sections 52–59 of *Gyokuden jinpi no maki*, section 63 of *Kingyoku sōgi*. There is also a spinoff text entitled *Waka entei hishō* that has not yet been published. *Gyokuden jinpi no maki*, pp. 563–67; Ishigami Hideaki, "Kunaichō Shoryōbu-zo *Kingyoku sōgi*," pt. III, pp. 51–53.

30. Section 1 of *Gyokuden jinpi no maki*, pp. 522–24. "Iwami no jō shiki" combines sections 19–21 of *Kingyoku sōgi* (equivalent to the first and last sections of *Gyokuden jinpi no maki*). Sections 20–21 are a listing of thirty-one guardian kami and their shrines, which are identified with the thirty-one syllables of a waka poem. Thus, simply by reciting a poem the poet receives the protection of these guardian kami. The colophon implies that "Iwami no jō shiki" is the *Gyokuden* transmission, a treasure of the Nijō house that is not to be shown to anyone outside the school. This claim supports the idea that the first section in *Gyokuden jinpi no maki* (section 19 of *Kingyoku sōgi*) is the "Gyokuden" transmission. For "Iwami no jō shiki," see Sasaki, *Nihon kagaku taikei*, vol. 1, pp. 32–34. Kushida Ryōko (*Zoku Shingon mikkyō seiritsu katei no kenkyū*, pp. 525–27) quotes a text associated with Hōbōtei-in entitled *Gyokuden waka hishō* (Selected secret comments on the jeweled transmission on waka), which is similar to the "Gyokuden jinpi" section, with a Nijō transmission lineage dated 1455 that includes Tameie, Tameuji, and

three phrases (5–7–5) and lower two phrases (7–7) are identified with the nondual dualities of heaven and earth, Yin and Yang, and the Womb-Storehouse and Diamond Realms. In addition, each phrase is identified with one of the Five Modalities, the Five Confucian Virtues, four seasons (plus eulogies appropriate for any season), four directions (plus the center), five kami (the Sun Kami, Hiruko no Mikoto, Susanoo no Mikoto, Amaterasu Ōmikami, the Moon Kami), the Five Wisdom Buddhas of the Diamond Realm mandala, and the Five Stages of Enlightenment. An exemplary poem is given for each phrase.[31] The transmission also includes ritual directions for the practitioner. The poet is to face the four cardinal directions and the center, composing a seasonal poem to entertain (*hōraku*) each of the kami and confessing his or her sins to each of the buddhas. By doing so the poet destroys delusion and achieves buddhahood.

Given the parallels between this description and the mandala of the Five Wisdom Buddhas of the Diamond Realm (the directions, modalities, and other identities correspond well), it seems likely that this passage is a description of a waka mandala as well as directions for ritual performance.[32] Dainichi Nyorai, identified with Amaterasu Ōmikami, is placed at the center of the mandala, and the other four Wisdom Buddhas and their Manifest Trace kami are arranged in the four corners (equal to the four directions). Oddly enough, although "Gyokuden" was supposed to have been transmitted by Sumiyoshi Daimyōjin, he does not appear in this waka mandala. Nevertheless, the material in this section, which advises that poetry be composed in a syncretic ritual context and in correspondence with complex numerological allegoresis, would have provided a suitable key for allegorical readings of the *Kokin shū*. It is probably the best candidate for the elusive "Gyokuden."

Scholars find *Gyokuden jinpi no maki* interesting because its shows the extensive influence of the heterodox Tachikawa sect of Shingon in the late thir-

---

Tameyo but omits Tameaki. Kushida also believes this is the "Gyokuden" mentioned in the "Akone no ura kuden."

31. Although there is no explanation for how each poem relates to the identifications, the poem illustrating spring contains "spring" in the first phrase, the second poem contains "summer" in the second phrase, and so on; the fourth poem illustrating the "center" contains "Amateru kami" in the fourth phrase.

32. Kushida Ryōko (*Zoku Shingon mikkyō seiritsu katei no kenkyū*, pp. 525–26) also argues that the *Gyokuden* manuscript he analyzes is a performative version of a waka mandala.

teenth century. In section after section *Gyokuden jinpi no maki* employs etymological allegoresis to reveal a Tachikawa-influenced syncretic Buddhist-Shinto poetics. A related text, *Waka Kokin kanjō no maki*, however, takes etymological allegoresis to new lengths. Every poetic technique discussed, every poem interpreted, is shown to have profound esoteric meaning.

Waka Kokin kanjō no maki

Waka Kokin kanjō no maki (Initiation on waka from the *Kokin shū*) organizes and consolidates material found in earlier texts, bringing the reading of poems as allegories of Tachikawa and Ryōbu Shinto secrets to its highest development. There is only one copy extant, a manuscript dating from 1656 with a colophon that claims an origin with Hitomaro, then transmits via Tsunenobu → Shunzei → Teika → Tameie → Tameaki → Tamekiyo. The last transmission is dated 1306; since Tameaki's latest appearance in the historical record is in 1295, this transmission date is unlikely, but scholars agree that the commentary was probably written by Tameaki in the 1280s. Of all Tameaki's commentaries, it is the most strongly esoteric Buddhist reading of poetic principles and so was presumably considered appropriate only for the highest level of initiates, which may explain why it was not disseminated more widely. Miwa Masatane sees this text as one of the founding texts of the *kanjō* style of poetic initiation borrowed from esoteric Shingon Buddhism, which became the foundation for the pedagogical method used by both the Reizei for their *Ise monogatari* commentaries and the Nijō *Kokin denju*.[33]

As discussed in Chapter 8, the first fascicle of *Waka Kokin kanjō no maki* opens with a description of a waka *kanjō* ceremony. Unlike other commentaries, which refer to the waka *kanjō* but do not give much detail, the protocol presented in this text would enable the recipient to produce his or her own waka *kanjō* ceremony; consequently this work must have been considered valuable. At the end of the description is a list of seven secrets that are to be transmitted in the ceremony. The obvious inference would be that the

---

33. *Waka Kokin kanjō no maki* is thought to be related to *Waka kanjō shidai himitsu shō* (associated with the Ietaka school) and to form the basis for *Kokin waka shū kanjō no maki* (spuriously attributed to Shunzei; the colophons of variant texts include either Kyōgoku Tamekane or Reizei Tamesuke). The content also connects it to both lineages of *Waka chiken shū*, both variants of *Gyokuden jinpi no maki*, and to Nijō Tameyo's *Etsumoku shō*. See Miwa, *Kagaku hiden no kenkyū*, pp. 150–53; and Arai Eizo, "*Kokin shū* kanjō hisho to Bukkyō kyōri."

rest of the *Waka Kokin kanjō no maki* transmits those secrets, but the text does not appear to include all of them (it is not that easy to tell from the titles, which are somewhat obscure, perhaps purposefully so). The first fascicle, however, does include the first three secrets listed. The discussion of the first secret, "Yamato uta," includes an etymological allegoresis of the graphs for waka (和謌) very similar to that of the "The Profound Meaning of the Two Graphs for Waka" ("Waka no niji shingi") in *Gyokuden jinpi no maki*,[34] but in even greater detail. The second secret, "The Six Poetic Modes and the Six Forms of Poetry" ("Rikugi rokutai"), is an explanation of the Six Forms of Poetry (*rokutai*) listed in the Chinese preface to the *Kokin shū* (*tanka*, *chōka*, *sedōka*, and so on) in terms of number of lines and syllable count. Each is then correlated with one of the Six Paths of Reincarnation (*rokudō*). This section has strong parallels to the preface of *Waka chiken shū* and makes a similar argument that whereas composing tanka leads to reincarnation in heaven, indulging in haikai leads to reincarnation in hell, and that by composing excellent tanka, one creates "a Buddha of the Five Roots, Five Powers."[35]

The third section, "Three Tones" (*San kyoku*), identifies the *kokoro* (meaning), *kotoba* (diction), and *sugata* (form) of waka poetry with various groups of three, including three Sanskrit *bīja* seed syllables (A, BAN, and UN); the Womb-Storehouse Realm, Diamond Realm, and Dainichi; and the three bodies of the Tathāgata (Nyorai), the Dharma Body (*hosshin* 法心), the Reward/Enjoyment Body (*hōjin* 報身), and the Accommodative Body (*ōjin* 應身). They are also correlated with the three truths of the Tathāgata as Emptiness/Void (*kū* 空), Phenomenal Appearance (*ke* 假), and the Middle Way (*chū* 中). Again, a similar passage can be found in the preface of *Waka chiken shū*, but the more complex version in *Waka Kokin kanjō no maki* features intricate diagrams that spell out the various identifications.[36]

---

34. *Gyokuden jinpi no maki*, p. 550; cf. the first section of *Kingyoku sōgi*, in Ishigami, "Kunaichō Shoryōbu-zō *Kingyoku sōgi*," pt. I, p. 42. A reference to the title "The Profound Meaning of the Two Graphs" also appears in the preface to the Reizeike-ryū *Ise monogatari shō*; see Chapter 11, p. 269.

35. For a comparison of the two texts, see Miwa, *Kagaku hiden no kenkyū*, p. 152; *Waka Kokin kanjō no maki*, pp. 462–63; Kunaichō *Waka chiken shū*, pp. 98–100; Shimabara *Waka chiken shū*, pp. 200–202.

36. *Waka Kokin kanjō no maki*, pp. 464–66; Kunaichō *Waka chiken shū*, p. 98; Shimabara *Waka chiken shū*, p. 200.

The second fascicle opens with a history of the origins of Japanese poetry, which is basically the same as that given in the opening lines of the *Waka chiken shū* but written in *kanbun* (the variety of written Chinese then current in Japan): poetry emerged as Sanskrit dharani in India and as verse in China; in Japan it originated in the Age of the Gods and has continued until the present; the first example of regularized thirty-one-syllable verse was composed by Susanoo no Mikoto.[37] The commentary then turns to an analysis that might correlate with the eighth secret, "The Two Mother and Father Poems" ("Chichi haha futatsu uta"). The poems designated as the "mother and father" of waka poetry in the *Kokin shū* preface are the "Naniwa Bay" ("Naniwazu ni") poem and the "Asaka Mountain" ("Asaka yama") poem; "Naniwa Bay" is also given as an example of *soe uta* (風哥 implicit allegory), the first of the Six Poetic Modes. *Waka Kokin kanjō no maki* omits the "Asaka Mountain" poem and concentrates on the "Naniwa Bay" poem, which it argues is by itself both mother and father. The commentary identifies each line with a *bīja* seed syllable to make its case that the poem allegorizes the procreative origin of all existence. The following section analyzes a poem, "Opening Blossoms" ("Saku hana ni"), which is given in the *Kokin shū* preface as an example of a *kazoe uta* (数え歌 enumerative poem). The "Opening Blossoms" poem is subjected to a diagrammatic allegoresis that identifies each line with a stage of enlightenment, a stage of life, the seasons, and so on. Following the analysis of the poems is a section that claims that the name Hitomaro actually designates four different people and/or deities.[38] This may correlate with the fifth secret transmitted in the waka *kanjō*, "The Ordering of Hitomaro" ("Hitomaro no shidai"). Among the four is an "*okina* Hitomaro" identified with the Sumiyoshi *okina* who appeared to Minamoto no Tsunenobu on the thirteenth day of the ninth month in *Waka chiken shū*. The description given of the Hitomaro *okina* closely resembles that given for the Sumiyoshi *okina* in *Waka chiken shū*; again we can see how *Waka Kokin kanjō no maki* links itself to earlier texts. The last part of the second fascicle presents three heavily esoteric interpretations of the "Honobono to" poem, popularly attributed to Hitomaro. The third, and last, fascicle goes back

37. See Miwa, *Kagaku hiden no kenkyū*, p. 151; *Waka Kokin kanjō no maki*, p. 467; Kunaichō *Waka chiken shū*, p. 97; Shimabara *Waka chiken shū*, p. 199.

38. The third section of *Kingyoku sōgi* is titled "The Matter of the Four Hitomaros" ("Yonin Hitomaro no koto"), but the details are different. See Ishigami Hideaki, "Kunaichō Shoryōbu-zō *Kingyoku sōgi*," pt. I, p. 42.

over much of the same ground as the first two fascicles, emending and supplementing some explanations.[39]

A detailed description of one of the interpretations of the "Honobono to" poem in the second fascicle will serve to give a flavor of the commentary as a whole. "A Diagram (or Mandala) of the True Meaning of the Poem 'Honobono to'" ("'Honobono to' uta no jitsugi zu [mata wa mandara to unnun]") employs a Tachikawa theory that James Sanford has called "spiritual embryology" or "fetal Buddhahood" to develop a system of correspondences between the five phrases of *Kokin shū* 409 and the five stages of fetal development.[40]

As Sanford notes with regard to the development of spiritual embryology, since one of the major tenets of Buddhism is the endless cycle of reincarnation, "the symbolic ramifications of birth, death, and spiritual transformation take on forms that would not be expected in a Western setting."[41] Spiritual embryology appears to have developed specifically out of concern with and speculation about the nature and duration of the gap between one lifetime and the next. This concern tends to focus on two periods: the period between the physiological death of one body and the biological conception of the next; and the subsequent interval between conception and actual birth, particularly during the first five weeks when the fetus develops from a "dot" to something approximating a human form with arms and legs.[42] Spiritual embryology attempts to correlate the two periods with esoteric Buddhist concepts such as Original Enlightenment (*hongaku*) and acquiring Buddhahood in this very body (*sokushin jōbutsu*).

Original Enlightenment is the idea that everything (sentient and nonsentient) is, in principle, innately enlightened. All things are composed of the material Five Great Elements (*godai* 五大) plus an immaterial mind/consciousness (*kokoro*). This material body and immaterial mind are nothing other than manifestations of the enlightened Dharma Body and Dharma

---

39. This fascicle is clearly related to *Kokin waka shū kanjō no maki*; see the comparison in Miwa, *Kagaku hiden no kenkyū*, p. 156.

40. See Sanford, "Spiritual Embryology in Shingon Buddhism"; and idem, "Wind, Waters, Stupas, Mandalas." The following summary of the basic tenets of spiritual embryology has also benefited from personal discussions with Sanford.

41. Sanford, "Wind, Waters, Stupas, Mandalas," p. 1.

42. As Sanford (ibid., p. 3*n*3) notes, Japanese sources exhibit considerable confusion about whether a locution like "four seven day" means the fourth-seven-days (i.e., the fourth week), the fourth month's seventh day, or the forty-seventh day. For convenience sake, I have assumed five one-week intervals are meant.

Mind of the Cosmic Buddha, Dainichi Nyorai. Given that all things exist as microcosmic manifestations of the macrocosmic Dharma Body and Dharma Mind, all things must be innately enlightened.

At birth, however, delusion and ignorance occlude the memory living beings have of their Original Enlightenment. According to Shingon doctrine, this functional loss of buddhahood can be remedied only by the three practices of esoteric Buddhism. By repeating mantras, performing mudras, and meditating, the body/mind complex achieves an enlightened state of *musō munen* (無相無念, being without the object of perception or discriminative thought) identical with the Dharma Body and Dharma Mind of the Cosmic Buddha and thus re-accesses the previously occluded Original Enlightenment. This enlightened state is *sokushin jōbutsu*, "acquiring Buddhahood in this very body."

Waka Kokin kanjō no maki gives a concrete explication of the process by which human beings come to be "originally enlightened" in the womb.[43] The five stages of fetal development are shown to be analogous to the Five Stages of Enlightenment: Awakening Consciousness, Practice, Enlightenment, Entering Nirvana, and Expedient Means as Ultimate Goal. Thus, in the fifth week, when the fetus has taken on a fully human form, it has attained full enlightenment.

In "Diagram (or Mandala) of the True Meaning of the Poem 'Honobono to,'" allegoresis of *Kokin shū* 409 is used to illustrate these ideas.[44]

> *honobono to / Akashi no ura no / asagiri ni*
> *shima gakure yuku / fune o shi zo omou*
> In the faint glimmering of the dawn at Akashi Bay,
> my thoughts go with the boat that disappears among the islands
> into the morning mist.

The commentary is abbreviated, consisting mainly of marginalia around pictures of the five stages. Clearly there would have been much more extensive oral explanations by the teacher. I can make only limited guesses at those explanations by analogy with other parts of the same commentary, as well as other spiritual embryology texts.

---

43. Cf. the similar section in *Kokin waka shū kanjō no maki*, in Kondō Yoshihiro, ed., *Chūsei shinbutsu setsuwa (zoku)*, pp. 171–73. This manuscript has a colophon signed by Reizei Tamesuke and dated 1323.

44. See *Waka Kokin kanjō no maki*, pp. 473–75. Cf. the *Kokin waka shū kanjō kuden*'s analysis of this same poem given in Chapter 2, p. 34.

The first two or three lines are assigned relatively detailed associations: a Sanskrit *bīja* seed syllable, a stage of enlightenment, one of the Five Wisdom Buddhas of the Diamond Realm mandala identified with five aspects of the Tathāgata's all-inclusive knowledge, and the direction at which each of these Buddhas is stationed within the mandala. Last, and most important, each line is associated with a stage of the development of the fetus in the womb.[45] As the text continues, however, the format breaks down somewhat, perhaps because the author felt that it was not necessary to elaborate all the associations in written form.

In the first line, "Honobono to [akashi]" (faintly [glimmering]), the image of the dawn's first faint light is associated with the east and with the first stage of enlightenment, Awakening Consciousness (*hosshin* 発心). "Honobono" is written with the graphs 若若 (very young), which underscores that this is the very beginning of life. "Honobono to" is also associated with the Sanskrit seed syllable *A*, the "earth" syllable seen as the ultimate origin of everything. Finally, it is associated with the Wisdom Buddha Ashuku, who stands for Great Perfect Mirror Wisdom. This is the first stage of fetal development, when the red essence of the mother (menstrual blood) and the white essence of the father (semen) combine to create a fetus that is innately enlightened.[46] This stage is understood as a dot, illustrated as a circle containing a red Sanskrit *A* with a mirror image *A* in white. These two *bīja* seed syllables represent the female and male "seeds" necessary for conception:

> The red-colored *A* seed syllable is the mother's essence, which becomes the flesh of living beings. The white-colored *A* seed syllable is the father's essence, which becomes the bones of living beings. These two seed syllables colored white and red represent the karmic seeds of the buddhahood of Dainichi Nyorai's Diamond and

---

45. Note that Tameaki's diagram of the development of the fetus is almost identical to one found in a later Tachikawa spiritual embryology text, the *A-Un jigi* (The meaning of the syllables *A* and *UN*). James Sanford hypothesizes that the *A-Un jigi* text dates to the Edo period because of its Confucian elements, but the fact that nearly identical diagrams and identifications appear in Tameaki's commentary indicates that the basic elements of the *A-Un jigi* text were already in existence in the thirteenth century. The connection between the two texts is another reason why *Waka Kokin kanjō no maki* is an invaluable text for religious scholars. For the *A-Un jigi*, see Mizuhara Gyoei, *Jakyō Tachikawaryū no kenkyū*, pp. 33–34. For a discussion of this text, see Sanford, "Wind, Waters, Stupas, Mandalas," pp. 17–21.

46. This first stage is usually called "Kalalaṃ" (J. *kararan* 羯刺藍) in spiritual embryology texts. For a listing of the five stages, see Sanford, "Wind, Waters, Stupas, Mandalas," p. 3.

Womb-Storehouse mandalas. When a living being's fleshly body is the Twin Realms (*ryōbu*) of Dainichi, buddhahood in this very body occurs (*sokushin jōbutsu*).[47]

In other words, by uniting the dual aspects of the Womb-Storehouse and Diamond realms, the conception process itself leads to buddhahood in this very body. The moment of conception is the initial moment of the awakening consciousness and is signified in the poem by the first line, "faintly glimmering."

In the second line of the poem, "Akashi no ura," Akashi is read as *akashin* (明心, pure heart) and *ura* (浦 bay) as signifying "depths" (底): "the inner depths of a pure heart."[48] It is associated with the seed syllable *BI*, the "water" syllable, an appropriate association considering the literal meaning of "Akashi Bay," as well as with south, the second stage of enlightenment, that of Practice (*shugyō* 修行), and the Wisdom Buddha Hōshō, who stands for the Wisdom of Understanding the Ultimate Equality of All Things. In this second stage of fetal development, the fetus looks like a three-day-old crescent moon: "At the second-week stage, it takes on this form, becoming the seed of the Twin Realm Dainichi, which is signified by the two upper ends of the crescent moon. It is also said that this is the start of meditation and wisdom."[49] In other words, during this stage, the fetal seed is no longer a spot but a segment with two nodes, which will become the left and right shoulders. One node is identified with Meditation and the Womb-Storehouse Realm, the other with Wisdom and the Diamond Realm.

In the third and fourth lines, "asagiri ni / shimagakure yuku" (disappearing behind the islands in the morning mist), *shimagakure yuku* (島隠れ行く hidden behind the islands) is understood as *shi ma ongyō* (四魔隠行 the practice of hiding the four evils). The thin morning mist (*asagiri* 朝霧 read 浅霧) helps to hide the four evils and thus (in the fifth line) enables the "boat" to reach the "other shore" of Nirvana. The third line (*asagiri ni*) is associated with the direction west and the Wisdom Buddha Muryōju (another name for Amida Buddha, who saves sentient beings by taking them to his Western Paradise), as well as the stage of Enlightenment (*bodai* 菩提). Muryōjū signifies the Wisdom of Wondrous Observation; here, it would seem that the wisdom of knowing when not to see is the key to gaining

47. *Waka Kokin kanjō no maki*, pp. 473–74.
48. *Ura* 浦 (bay) is probably being read as *ura* 裏 (inner).
49. *Waka Kokin kanjō no maki*, p. 474.

enlightenment. It is also associated with the seed syllable *RA*, the "fire" syllable, perhaps appropriate if mist is thought of as similar to smoke. The third stage of fetal development is pictured as a half moon with a pointed projection in the middle and is described as follows: "During the third-week stage, the fetus takes this form. The bones begin to harden; the head and the left and right shoulders appear. This is like the upper half of a three-pointed vajra, which represents the Three Mysteries, the Three Stages of Awakening Bodhicitta, the Three [Dharma] Bodies, the Three Latent Forms of the Three Mysteries."[50]

After these detailed explanations, the associations begin breaking down. Perhaps having come this far, it was not felt necessary to spell out all the associations: logically the fourth line should be associated with the north, the Wisdom Buddha Fukūjōju, who stands for the Wisdom of the Perfection of Action, the stage of Entering Nirvana (*nyū nehan* 入涅槃), and the Sanskrit seed syllable *UN* (the "wind" syllable). The text instead pictures a five-layered stupa (*gorin* 五輪) surrounded by: "During the fourth-week stage, the fetus takes this form. The form represents the originally enlightened Tathāgata; the Five Innately Awakened Thathāgatas [here, the Five Wisdom Buddhas of the Diamond Realm mandala].[51] Therefore waka has five phrases and thirty-one syllables."[52] Taken together Dainichi Nyorai and the other four buddhas signify the nonduality of Oneness and Diversity. Here they may also serve as referents to the beginning of the development of the five main body parts (head, arms, and legs). The five phrases of waka appear to be homologous with the Five Wisdom Buddhas, and the thirty-one syllables homologous to the central buddha, Dainichi Nyorai. The homology of the thirty-one syllables makes sense, given the explanation in the *Waka chiken shū*'s preface that the thirty-one syllables are equivalent to the thirty-two signifying marks of the Tathāgata (the invisible "meaning" of the poem is the thirty-second syllable).[53]

The fifth and final picture is of a fully formed human body. Written in the margin is: "[The fetus] becomes the Buddha of Fully Ripened Buddha-

---

50. Ibid.

51. *Hongaku Nyorai* (the Tathāgata of Primordial Enlightenment) would be Dainichi; *hōnen jigaku gobu nyorai* (the Five Innately Awakened Tathāgatas) would be Dainichi plus the Wisdom Buddhas.

52. *Waka Kokin kanjō no maki*, p. 475.

53. Kunaichō *Waka chiken shū*, p. 97.

hood absorbed in meditation on the Aspiration to Wisdom,[54] and dwelling in the stage of Non-attachment. The form in the mother's womb becomes the Buddha Completely Satisfied with the Five Wisdoms."[55] Logically, the fifth line should be associated with the center, Dainichi Nyorai, the Wisdom of the Essence of the Dharma Realm, the seed syllable *KEN* (space/emptiness), and the stage of Expedient Means as Ultimate Goal (*hōben kyūkyō* 方便究竟). This last stage occurs when we achieve enlightenment as to the nonduality of expedient means and Absolute Truth, an enlightenment that leads to a bodhisattva's return to this world to save sentient beings by expedient means.

In the "Honobono to" poem, *fune o shizo omou* (船をしぞ思ふ my thoughts go with the boat) is treated as *fune oshiso omou* (船惜しそ念ふ), "the (passionate) thought of longing for the boat." The marginalia explain further that Dainichi Nyorai, "the Dharma-Realm Body of Essential Nature and Wisdom, the Buddha of Satisfaction in the Myriad Dharma, is also called 'the raft.'" In other words, the fifth phrase of the poem refers to Dainichi Nyorai's becoming a bodhisattva to save sentient beings caught in the current of passion by serving as a boat to Nirvana. However, it must be remembered that Dainichi Nyorai is none other than the fetus itself (the young, pure awakening heart/consciousness). According to an Edo spiritual embryology text, *Sangai isshin ki* (Record of the three realms' single heart), "It is the heart's desire of all bodhisattvas to enter the world in bodily form. . . . In truth, the womb is the sacred precinct of the first arrival [in this world] of all kami, buddhas, and bodhisattvas."[56] In other words, when the fetus takes on a fully human form, it has also achieved the fifth stage of enlightenment. The process of birth is thus understood as the means by which a bodhisattva returns to this world. From this perspective, the poem as a whole can be taken as a description of how, in the fetal awakening consciousness, the desire for enlightenment arises. This desire in turn leads to rebirth in this world as a bodhisattva, signified as a boat that will carry sentient beings through the thin mists that veil the four evils, to reach the far shore of Nirvana.

---

54. *Jōgu bodai kannen* 上求菩提観念: meditation on the wisdom aspect of the bodhisattva aspiration.

55. *Waka Kokin kanjō no maki*, p. 475.

56. Translation from Sanford, "Wind, Waters, Stupas, Mandalas," p. 29.

The highly compressed and elliptical fashion in which this interpretation of the "Honobono to" poem is presented is typical of the *Waka Kokin kanjō no maki* commentary as a whole. It clearly was used in conjunction with oral teachings that fully explicated the relationship between Tachikawa spiritual embryology and waka poetry. And, I would argue, the references and amplified explanations of material found in other lower-level texts, such as *Waka chiken shū* and *Gyokuden jinpi no maki*, show that it was meant to fit into a graduated program of instruction. The ceremony described at the start of the commentary is said to be the "third" waka *kanjō (Yamato uta san kanjō)*, which suggests that this text was transmitted as part of a higher-level initiation. The level of difficulty makes it obvious why it was not disseminated the way *Waka chiken shū* and *Kokin waka shū jo kikigaki* were. Nevertheless, although its influence on Muromachi popular culture was slight, it is a remarkable example of the lengths to which medieval poets were willing to go in their attempts to homologize Buddhism and waka poetry. And as one of the earliest examples of spiritual embryology, it is an important text for scholars interested in the development of Tachikawa Shingon. In the next chapter, we will see a slightly different take on spiritual embryology in Nijō Tameakira's *Ise monogatari zuinō*.

11

Reizei and Nijō Commentaries After Tameaki

The Development of Historical Allegoresis

By the late thirteenth century, Tameaki's esoteric commentaries had firmly established the literary use of etymological allegoresis. In the early fourteenth century, the Reizei school began to introduce secularized forms of etymological allegoresis into its more historical commentaries on *Ise monogatari*. These historical commentaries continued the process of identifying names, dates, and places begun in the Heian period but much more systematically. An important factor in this development was undoubtedly the Reizei school's position that virtually all the episodes could be related to events in Narihira's life. Given the number of episodes that fail to conform to the Narihira persona, etymological allegoresis practically became a necessity.

Waka chiken shū also pursued an episode-by-episode analysis aimed at uncovering a historical substratum beneath *Ise monogatari*'s fictional veneer. Its author(s) did not feel compelled, however, to make every episode conform to the contours of the Narihira persona; some episodes were considered to be old tales mixed in with the new. For example, episode 23 tells the story of two young people whose parents oppose their marriage. The young boy is a child of "a person who wanders the countryside" (*inaka wataraishikeru hito*), a somewhat obscure phrase, now usually understood to mean a peddler. Obviously this phrase does not apply to Narihira, the grandson of two emperors. For this reason, *Waka chiken shū* identified the episode as an "old story." The Reizei school *Ise monogatari shō*, however, claimed that the boy and girl were Narihira and Ki no Aritsune's daughter. Both of their fathers, Prince Abo and Ki no Aritsune, had land in the village of Kasuga in Nara. Although they lived in the capital, they occasionally traveled to Kasuga to survey their land. The enigmatic phrase "a person who wanders the countryside" was carefully placed in the episode to hint at this "fact."[1]

If every episode was to be treated as dealing with Narihira, an allegorical reading strategy was almost inevitable. One can see an initial impulse toward allegoresis in the interpolated commentary at the end of episode 6, which identified the "one-gulp demon" as Fujiwara no Takako's brothers. The commentary explicitly treats the episode as having two layers of meaning and identifies the anonymous characters. However, it is not until the Reizei school commentaries that one begins to see hidden puns in the text used as tautological evidence for the commentary's historical reading.

The Reizei school *Ise monogatari shō* uses historical etymological allegoresis to analyze the opening line of *Ise monogatari*: "In the past, a man who had gone through the 'first cap' ceremony, went hunting on his estate at Kasuga village, near the Nara capital" (*Mukashi, otoko uikōburi shite, Nara no kyō, Kasuga no sato ni shiru yoshite, kari ni inikeri*). The Reizei commentary explains this in almost obsessive detail. An imperial envoy was needed for a festival at Kasuga Shrine in Nara, which was to take place on the third day of the second month of Jowa 14 (847). Since no one was available who met the stipulated conditions (a fifth-rank member of the aristocracy, of pleasing countenance), Narihira underwent the capping ceremony and was installed in that rank the day before (the second day of the second month). However, since a son of an imperial prince would ordinarily not have been used as an envoy, Narihira was only "provisionally" (*kari ni*) assigned to serve because of his exceptional looks.[2]

The commentary goes to great lengths to give exact dates and fill in as much background detail as possible (how, where, and why the event took place). At first glance, the basic approach in this episode would appear to be identical with that of *Waka chiken shū*. The focus on the wordplay on *kari ni* (taken to mean both "provisionally" 仮に and "to go hunting" 狩に) signals,

---

1. Reizeike-ryū *Ise monogatari shō*, p. 294.
2. Ibid.

however, one of the main interpretive differences between the two. The Reizei commentary appropriates the allegorical technique developed in Tameaki's religious commentaries; it posits the deliberate insertion of puns and wordplays as a means of building "hidden" layers of meaning into the text. Here *kari ni* is assumed to be an intentional signal to the initiated reader; it corroborates the commentary's explication. In addition, the position of the pun on *kari ni* in the first episode allows it to stand as a trope for the interpretive process of the Reizei commentaries generally: that is, taking the "phenomenal appearance" of the text to be merely "provisional."

The Nijō school's *Ise monogatari zuinō*, which was probably written by Nijō Tameakira in the 1320–30s, is another example of the continued use of etymological allegoresis even after the *honji suijaku* thinking on which it was based had been discarded. *Ise monogatari zuinō* employs all three forms of etymological allegoresis but argues against *honji suijaku* thinking. Thus, although it is a heavily Tachikawa-influenced text, it lays the groundwork for later literary commentaries that dispensed with the syncretic esoteric content while continuing to use an interpretive technique that developed out of syncretic esotericism.

The Reizei school *Ise monogatari shō*'s and the Nijō school *Ise monogatari zuinō*'s use of etymological allegoresis without the *honji suijaku* content represents a new development. It presaged the creation of more secularized forms of commentary, particularly the Nijō school's *Kokin denju*, in which etymological allegoresis continued to be used, but the content was influenced more by Neo-Confucianism.

The Reizei School *Ise monogatari shō*

The most representative Reizei school commentary on *Ise monogatari* is generally considered to be Reizeike-ryū *Ise monogatari shō* (Selected comments on *Ise monogatari* of the Reizei family lineage). The work is a Muromachi compendium of at least three sources. Katagiri Yōichi argues that the core text was called *Senkin bakuden* (Not to be transmitted for a thousand gold pieces) and thinks it was produced by Reizei Tamesuke.[3] A text by that name appears in

3. The following discussion summarizes Katagiri's argument in *Ise monogatari no kenkyū (kenkyūhen)*, pp. 538–40. The phrase "senkin bakuden" was commonly found in the texts and colophons of secret commentaries; for example, a similar phrase appears in the preface to the Shimabara *Waka chiken shū* (p. 205) and in *Kingyoku sōgi* (see Ishigami Hideaki, "Kunaichō Shoryōbu-zō *Kingyoku sōgi*," pt. I, p. 42).

Tamesuke's library catalogue of 1317;[4] so the core text was probably in existence by that date.[5] A second source is Fujiwara no Teika's annotation of a *Kokin shū* commentary by Kenshō, *Kenchū mikkan* (Secret annotations of Kenshō's commentary on the *Kokin shū*).[6] The final source is notes on the lectures of the Reizei school poet Imagawa Ryōshun (1326–1417?) taken by his students, Shōtetsu (1381–1459) and Reizei Mochitame (1401–54).[7]

Since all extant manuscripts of Reizei commentaries on *Ise monogatari* are in the form of lecture notes (*kikigaki*), there are considerable differences between texts.[8] There are also numerous contradictions and inconsistencies within *Ise monogatari shō*, particularly between the preface and the analyses of the individual episodes. This is not surprising since the version of *Ise monogatari shō* we have today seems to be a pastiche of quotations from a wide variety of older commentaries, developed over the course of at least a hundred years. Despite these problems, Katagiri argues that *Ise monogatari shō* is representative of the Reizei interpretive approach to *Ise monogatari*, and that this approach, in turn, became the most common approach of historical commentaries to *Ise monogatari* in the late Kamakura period and also, on a popular level, in the Muromachi.

Reizei Tamesuke probably developed *Senkin bakuden* between 1300 and 1317 (when it appears in his library catalogue), basing his approach in part on earlier esoteric commentaries such as *Gyokuden jinpi no maki*.[9] Quite a few of

---

4. For a discussion of the Reizei school library catalogue (*sōshi mokuroku*) of 1317, see Katagiri, *Ise monogatari no kenkyū (kenkyūhen)*, pp. 576–92.

5. An extant commentary bearing that name is probably related; it is a collection of notes taken from the lectures of the early Muromachi poet Imagawa Ryōshun, who was part of the Reizei school.

6. Kenshō was Rokujō Kiyosuke's brother by adoption and, like his brother, had a high reputation for scholarly learning. There is a manuscript of *Kenchū mikkan* that includes a date of 1221 in a transmission lineage from Fujiwara no Mototoshi to Shunzei (Teika's father). In *Ise monogatari shō*, *Kenchū mikkan* is cited to substantiate points with regard to poems that are included in both the *Kokin shū* and *Ise monogatari*. See also Chapter 5, p. 91.

7. As the adopted grandson of Nijō Tamekuni and the head of the Reizei family, Mochitame inherited both families' poetic documents from his grandfather Reizei Tamekuni (fl. 1401–9), who was adopted by Nijō Tameakira.

8. Variants include *Ise monogatari chū*, *Ise monogatari nurigome shō*, and Teika-ryū *Ise monogatari chū*; see Katagiri, *Ise monogatari no kenkyū (kenkyūhen)*, p. 532.

9. Note also that the sections on *Ise monogatari* at the end of *Kingyoku sōgi* are apparently strongly connected to *Ise monogatari shō*. See Ishigami Hideaki, "Kunaichō Shoryōbu-zō *Kingyoku sōgi*," pt. III, pp. 54–62.

the titles of sections in *Gyokuden jinpi no maki* appear in Tamesuke's library catalogue, and at various points *Ise monogatari shō* refers to "separate oral transmissions" (*bechi kuden* 別口伝) that correlate well with sections in *Gyokuden jinpi no maki*. In a comparison of the two texts, Nakagawa Shinnichi has pointed out a few examples of this phenomenon.[10] For example, the Reizei school commentary on episode 65 notes in regard to the term *kannagi* (巫, shrine medium or shaman): "There is an oral transmission on this" (*kuden ari*).[11] The "Mitarashi River" ("Mitarashi gawa") section of *Gyokuden jinpi no maki* explicates the term.[12] In the discussion of the phrase "in the light of the moon" (*tsuki no oboro naru ni*) in episode 69, the Reizei commentary states: "This matter is a secret matter. There is a separate oral transmission."[13] "The Ise Priestess Episode" ("Saigū dan") section of *Gyokuden jinpi no maki* deals with this line.[14] Another example is the Reizei commentary on episode 124 in which Narihira opines in a poem, "Since there is no like-minded person here, I'll just keep my thoughts to myself and say nothing." The *Ise monogatari shō* explicates the poem's meaning as "Since there is no one who could share my thoughts about the deep secrets of erotic poetry, I intend to say nothing." It then goes on to state that "There are three secret matters within this poem. . . . These secret matters are transmitted separately."[15] This may be a reference to "The Middle-Level Oral Teaching on the Profound Meaning" ("Kuchū shinson gi") in *Gyokuden jinpi no maki*.[16]

The most important correlation with Tameaki's commentaries occurs in the *Ise monogatari shō*'s explication of episode 117:

On the twenty-eighth day of the first month of Ten'an 1 [857], Emperor Montoku went on a retreat to Sumiyoshi. Narihira accompanied him, and it was Narihira who recited "Ware mite mo" [Since I first saw . . .]. The deity manifested himself, taking

10. Nakagawa, "*Ise monogatari* chūshakusho toshite *Gyokuden jinpi no maki* no ichi," pp. 28–30.

11. Reizeike-ryū *Ise monogatari shō*, p. 360.

12. *Gyokuden jinpi no maki*, p. 538.

13. Reizeike-ryū *Ise monogatari shō*, p. 363.

14. *Gyokuden jinpi no maki*, pp. 538–39.

15. Reizeike-ryū *Ise monogatari shō*, p. 398.

16. As discussed in Chapter 8, this section explains how Narihira studied with the Shingon Grand Archbishop Shinga as a boy and pledged not to reveal openly the deep secrets of Tachikawa Shingon. These secrets include homologies between the graphs of "i" and "se," female and male, and the Womb-Storehouse and Diamond Realm mandalas of Shingon; see *Gyokuden jinpi no maki*, pp. 535–36.

possession of a shrine medium (*kannagi*) to give the reply poem. This is the most central episode in *Ise monogatari*. This is one of the three secret matters of *Ise monogatari*.[17]

This abbreviated version of the all-important origin story for the "Akone no ura kuden" strongly links *Ise monogatari shō* with *Gyokuden jinpi no maki*.

Since numerous sections from *Gyokuden jinpi no maki* appear on Reizei Tamesuke's library catalogue and *Ise monogatari shō* correlates well with those sections, it seems likely that Reizei Tamesuke used the two in conjunction with a *kanjō*-style pedagogical system of initiation. The core text of *Ise monogatari shō* would have been an intermediate-level commentary containing only fairly low-level esoteric content. By alluding to the higher-level oral transmissions included in *Gyokuden jinpi no maki*, it would have whetted the appetite of the initiate for more instruction. Perhaps because it contained relatively little esoteric material, *Ise monogatari shō*'s new, more historical approach to the use of etymological allegoresis was widely disseminated and continued to be influential long after Tachikawa Shingon and the *kanjō* commentaries it produced had been discarded.

An Analysis of Content

The preface of *Ise monogatari shō* attempts to deal with the larger issues of *Ise monogatari*: the development of the text (including why there are so many variants), the origin and authority of the commentary itself, and the problem of the title. The text proper analyzes each episode using the methods of etymological allegoresis.

The preface begins with a discussion of the numerous variant texts of *Ise monogatari*.[18] This discussion shows how *Ise monogatari shō* attempts to authenticate both the "Teika" manuscript, passed down to heirs of the Mikohidari house such as Reizei Tamesuke, and *Ise monogatari shō* itself. According to *Ise monogatari shō*, *Ise monogatari* survives in several variants: (1) Narihira's holograph, (2) Prince Tomohira's manuscript, (3) Abe no Moroyasu's manuscript, (4) Kamo no Naishi's manuscript, (5) the Nun Kō Nii's manuscript, (6) the poet Ise's edited (*nakagaki*) manuscript, and (7) Fujiwara no Nagayoshi's Imperial Huntsman manuscript. Narihira's holograph

17. It seems likely that here the three essential secrets to be transmitted are those named in *Waka Kokin kanjō maki*: "Akone no ura kuden," "Gyokuden," and either "Kushō" or the transmission lineages.

18. The following summarizes Reizeike-ryū *Ise monogatari shō*, pp. 290–92.

and the last two manuscripts receive the most attention in the subsequent discussion.[19]

As in *Waka chiken shū*, Narihira is said to have written two drafts, both of which his wife the poet Ise edited. In the *Ise monogatari shō* version of these events, Narihira wrote a first draft while living with Ise in Nagaoka. After Narihira's death, when Ise was serving at court, Emperor Uda requested a copy; because there were seventeen episodes about her relationship with Narihira, Ise revised them and substituted poems from the *Man'yō shū* for those written by Narihira. This variant, known as Lady Ise's edited manuscript, was passed down in the Ietaka school.

According to *Ise monogatari shō*, "Narihira's" holograph postdates the draft by Ise. It begins with the episode in which Narihira receives the "first cap" of manhood and travels to Kasuga. It was transmitted to Narihira's second son, Shigeharu, along with the "Akone no ura kuden" revelation from Sumiyoshi Daimyōjin. In the time of Narihira's grandson, Motokiyo, Retired Emperor Suzaku requested the Narihira holograph. Motokiyo added two other scrolls from the Daimyōjin, and Suzaku then commanded Fujiwara no Nagayoshi and Minamoto no Michinari to write a commentary on *Ise monogatari* based on that text. They wrote a twenty-scroll commentary (later referred to as *Suzaku-in zuinō*) that included the three scrolls of revelations from the Daimyōjin as well as the Narihira holograph. Because this manuscript was placed in a storehouse (*nurigome*, literally "lacquered chamber"), it is also known as the Nurigome manuscript. When Narihira's text was made

19. It is difficult to determine whether any of these texts still exists today. According to *Ise monogatari shō*, Prince Tomohira's manuscript had extra poems and stories in it and was transmitted in the Rokujō family. (Today the text usually associated with the Rokujō family is the *Kari no tsukai bon* [Imperial Huntsman text] that begins with episode 69. A version of it is thought to have been collated by Kenshō.) Abe no Moroyasu's text started with episode 23. The Kamo no Naishi manuscript had no episode about the Ise Priestess. According to one source, this text was identical to Abe no Moroyasu's manuscript, but it was partially damaged in a fire, and stories and poems were added to replace the lost parts. It ended with the Serikawa Imperial progress. The Nun Kō Nii, a fourth-generation descendent of Narihira, was Koresumi's daughter. This text was transmitted within Narihira's lineage, but this text, too, was partially burned, and only the parts that the nun had memorized were rewritten. It had fewer poems than the other versions, and the nun replaced some of the missing episodes with poem-stories from her own life. See Katagiri, *Ise monogatari no kenkyū (shiryōhen)*, p. 290. Note that this history of variant texts takes for granted that until the late Heian period, at least, the various owners of *Ise monogatari* manuscripts felt little compunction about adding or subtracting episodes.

available to Nagayoshi and Michinari, other people gained access to it as well, and that was how textual variants two through five came into existence. All these variants, like the Nurigome manuscript, begin with the episode in which Narihira receives the first cap,[20] but according to *Ise monogatari shō* only the Nurigome manuscript is truly faithful to Narihira's holograph. Several generations later, Retired Emperor Horikawa (r. 1086–1107) gave a copy of the Nurigome text to Fujiwara no Toshitada (Teika's grandfather) for safekeeping. However, at that time two of the three scrolls with the revelations from the Daimyōjin were not passed along. Takahashi no Mikuni, a seventh-generation descendant of Narihira, was adopted by Toshitada and became a Fujiwara. Toshitada requested the material given to Suzaku, and Mikuni transmitted the other two scrolls to him. This was the text that Fujiwara no Teika inherited.

Ise monogatari shō claims that Nagayoshi and Michinari wanted to disseminate *Ise monogatari* widely, and they secretly made a copy of the Nurigome manuscript from the storehouse. They revised it so that it began with the episode in which Narihira visits the Ise Priestess as an imperial huntsman (episode 69 in the Teika recension). This is why the text is known as the Imperial Huntsman manuscript (*Kari no tsukai bon*). This history correlates with what is known of Kenshō's recension, passed down within the Rokujō family.

This is a convoluted and at points contradictory lineage indeed—the *Waka chiken shū* explanation is much simpler and more to the point. Of course, *Ise monogatari shō* is attempting to deal with many more variant texts than *Waka chiken shū*, which mentions only the Teika and the Rokujō family's Imperial Huntsman recensions. Overall, it would appear that *Ise monogatari shō* is attempting to account for three main variant lineages: Lady Ise's edited manuscript (Ietaka lineage), Narihira's holograph (Teika lineage), and the Imperial Huntsman text (Rokujō lineage). The Ietaka lineage manuscript is discredited as a rough draft edited by Lady Ise, and the Imperial Huntsman text as being the result of editing by Fujiwara no Nagayoshi and Minamoto no Michinari. The Teika lineage recension is the only true text: it is Narihira's final version, passed down within the Ariwara family, relatively free of meddling editors, and then transmitted to Toshitada, Teika's grandfather.

---

20. Here *Ise monogatari shō* appears to contradict itself; previously the text stated that Abe no Moroyasu's text began with episode 23.

Ise monogatari shō's explanation leaves a number of points unresolved. *Waka chiken shū*, for example, explains the presence of stories that predate and postdate Narihira as the result of Lady Ise's two revisions. Here, however, Lady Ise's text is seen as only a minor variant; this leaves unresolved the problem of the episodes that are not about Narihira. It may be that the writers and editors of *Ise monogatari shō* simply did not consider this an important problem, since every episode is, willy-nilly, forced to fit into Narihira's life by imaginative allegoresis. What was of concern to them was establishing an authoritative lineage for Teika's recension. They were also establishing the provenance of the commentary traditions that formed the basis for the Reizei school interpretation of *Ise monogatari*, specifically, Nagayoshi's commentary *Suzaku-in zuinō*, which supposedly included three scrolls from Sumiyoshi Daimyōjin, one of which was entitled "Akone no ura kuden."

The description of "Akone no ura kuden" and the story detailed in *Ise monogatari shō* about its transmission follows very closely that given in the *Kingyoku sōgi* variant of *Gyokuden jinpi no maki*: Sumiyoshi Daimyōjin → Narihira (1/28/857) → Shigeharu (880) → Motokata (888) → Motokiyo (?) → Korezumi (889) → Narimasa (890) → Muneie (898) → Tomoyuki (903) → Kimiyuki (905) → Mikuni (1184) → Toshitada (1185) → Shunzei (1188) → Teika (1219).[21] As in the *Kingyoku sōgi* transmission lineage, Narihira transmits "Akone no ura kuden" to his son Shigeharu along with his holograph of *Ise monogatari*. When we reach Narihira's grandson Motokiyo, however, the story takes a slightly different twist to account for *Suzaku-in zuinō*, which *Ise monogatari shō* claims was written by Nagayoshi and Michinari at the request of Retired Emperor Suzaku and which includes "Akone no ura kuden" as well as two other revelations from Sumiyoshi Daimyōjin. *Suzaku-in zuinō* is often cited in *Ise monogatari shō* to corroborate "historical" events, as well as the more tantric readings of *Ise monogatari*.[22]

The later transmission of *Suzaku-in zuinō* skips the next five descendents of Narihira given in the *Kingyoku sōgi* transmission lineage by having Retired Emperor Horikawa give a copy of *Suzaku-in zuinō* and Narihira's holograph to Fujiwara no Toshitada. This omission makes sense, since the names (Korezumi → Narimasa → Muneie → Tomoyuki → Kimiyuki) are otherwise obscure, and the close grouping of transmission dates (889, 890, 898,

21. Ishigami Hideaki, "Kunaichō Shoryōbu-zō *Kingyoku sōgi*," pt. II, pp. 45–46.

22. As in *Gyokuden jinpi no maki*, Nagayoshi's diary is also frequently cited as supporting evidence. Neither text appears to be extant today.

903, 905) followed by a 180-year gap is somewhat problematic. However, *Ise monogatari shō* manages to bring the *Kingyoku sōgi* lineage back into the picture by claiming that two of the revelations were separately transmitted to Toshitada when he adopted Takahashi no Mikuni. The idea that Toshitada adopted Mikuni comes directly from notes in the *Kingyoku sōgi* transmission lineage. From this it appears that Reizei Tamesuke had access to some version of the *Kingyoku sōgi* variant of *Gyokuden jinpi no maki*, and that *Ise monogatari shō*'s preface is an attempt to align the two so that each could reinforce the authority of the other.

Another point of contact between *Kingyoku sōgi* and *Ise monogatari shō* is the title *Suzaku-in zuinō* itself. Although *Suzaku-in zuinō* is not mentioned in *Gyokuden jinpi no maki* or any other Tameaki commentary, it does appear in the group of oral transmissions on *Ise monogatari* given at the end of *Kingyoku sōgi*. According to *Kingyoku sōgi*, the name "Nurigome" was given to one version of *Ise monogatari* because Retired Emperor Suzaku commissioned Minamoto no Nōakira, Fujiwara no Atsutada, and others to compile a recension of *Ise monogatari*, and this recension was stored in a secret *nurigome* storehouse.[23] Although the names of the compilers differ, *Ise monogatari shō*'s claim that Suzaku was involved in the Nurigome manuscript and creation of the *Suzaku-in zuinō* may have its basis in *Kingyoku sōgi*. However, since the dating of the last sections of *Kingyoku sōgi* has not been established, this remains speculation.

Ise monogatari shō's preface turns next to the problem of the title. Five explanations are provided, for the most part duplicating those found in *Waka chiken shū*, along with possible rebuttals. First, it is suggested that *Ise monogatari* was named after Lady Ise, who had a hand in editing the text. This possibility is not rebutted. Since Lady Ise's text was considered only a minor variant, perhaps a rebuttal was not considered necessary. The second suggestion is that it was named after the Ise Priestess (*Saigū*), because Narihira's affair with her was unprecedented and of central importance to the tale as a whole. The text rebuts this suggestion by arguing that it should then have been called the *Saigū monogatari* (Tales of the Ise Priestess). Why name it after the place rather than the person? The third explanation is the "Ise or Hyuga" anecdote. *Ise monogatari*, like the people in the "Ise or Hyuga" story,

---

23. Ishigami Hideaki, "Kunaichō Shoryōbu-zō *Kingyoku sōgi*," pt. III, p. 54.

is not what it seems: although the surface plot of *Ise monogatari* appears to be about worldly passion, its inner truth is the Buddhist Dharma. When one understands this story, one may realize Buddhahood in this very body. This is rebutted in the same way as the Ise Princess suggestion: Why is it not then called *Ise ya Hyuga monogatari* (Tales of Ise or Hyuga)? This erroneous idea is attributed to the Ietaka school.

The fourth explanation is based on the idea that in the *Nihon shoki* the characters for *i* and *se* signify female and male, respectively. This reading is further substantiated by reference to the *Kegon Sutra* and the *In'yō ki*.[24] The preface points out that Narihira must not be an ordinary person since his violation of the Ise Priestess went unpunished by the gods and explains his true purpose in writing *Ise monogatari*:

> *Ise monogatari* does not simply tell of relations between men and women. It was written in order to explain the ineffable: how the Kami emerged from Yin and Yang, heaven and earth, and how poetry came to be the custom of Japan. *I* signifies Izanami no Mikoto; *se* signifies Izanagi no Mikoto. This tale explains how these two kami, as the gods of Yin and Yang, were the first to have sexual relations, and so created the Path of Eroticism. The heavenly kami are *se*; the earthly kami are *i*. . . . These matters are explained in more detail in "The Profound Meaning of the Two Graphs" ("Niji no shingi") and "The Theory of the Inner Path" ("Naidō ron").[25]

There follows an extended description of Izanami and Izanagi's conjugal creation of the islands of Japan, the sun, moon, plants, trees, mountains and rivers, and then "one female, three males": the Sun kami (Amaterasu Ōmikami at Ise Shrine), the Moon kami, Hiruko no Mikoto, and Susanoo no Mikoto. The title *Ise monogatari* came about because the title "one female, three males" would have been too unwieldy; so just the "one female" (Amaterasu as the "Ise" kami) was used.

This passage follows the same train of Tachikawa thought, discussed in Chapter 7, that appears in the preface to the Sanjōnishi lineage *Waka chiken shū*, as well as *Gyokuden jinpi no maki*, *Waka Kokin kanjō no maki*, and *Ise monogatari zuinō*. The last line refers to two oral transmissions in *Gyokuden jinpi no maki*: "The Profound Meaning of the Two Graphs of Waka" ("Waka

---

24. I have not been able to ascertain whether the *Kegon Sutra* offers this reading (it is rather doubtful); the *In'yō ki*, quoted a number of times in the commentary, is otherwise unknown.

25. Reizeike-ryū *Ise monogatari shō*, p. 292.

no niji shingi") and "The Theory of the Inner Path."[26] Both of these use etymological allegoresis to explicate the tantric meanings of *i* and *se*. Here we have another clue that *Ise monogatari shō* was written by someone with access to a version of *Gyokuden jinpi no maki*.

Ise monogatari shō next proceeds to an episode-by-episode analysis using etymological allegoresis to align any seemingly anomalous points with the Narihira persona. This method of interpretive allegoresis is most evident in episodes 7–15, which deal with Narihira's putative "exile to the Eastern Provinces" (*Azuma kudari*). As discussed in Chapter 4, one trigger for this interpretive allegoresis was the internal contradiction between these episodes and episode 65, which also treats Narihira's affair with the young Fujiwara no Takako. In episodes 7–15, the man is exiled to the Eastern Provinces, whereas in episode 65 he is exiled to a place near enough to the capital that he can return each night to play the flute outside the storehouse where Takako is being kept. A second trigger would have been the geographical discrepancies in these episodes, which would have undercut the medieval reader's trust in the work's historical accuracy. To explain away these contradictions, *Ise monogatari shō*, like the Sanjōnishi lineage of *Waka chiken shū*, suggests that in reality Narihira did not go to the Eastern Provinces.

The Sanjōnishi lineage *Waka chiken shū* maintains that Narihira spent his exile in Nagaoka, where he wrote his first draft of *Ise monogatari*. *Ise monogatari shō* agrees: at some point Narihira lived in Nagaoka and wrote *Ise monogatari* while living there with the poet Ise. It argues, however, that during his supposed exile to the Eastern Provinces he was living under house arrest in Regent Fujiwara no Yoshifusa's palace in the Eastern Hills.

Although the same triggers probably underlie both *Ise monogatari shō*'s and *Waka chiken shū*'s claims, the disparity in his "true" destination signals a significant difference in the two commentaries' interpretive approach. In the case of *Waka chiken shū*, Nagaoka was chosen as Narihira's destination because of episode 58, which begins, "Sometime in the past a man who was a great gallant built himself a house at Nagaoka and took up residence there." This episode includes a poem attributed to Ise in the poetry anthology *Kokin waka rokujō* (ca. 976–87),[27] and so it supplied a basis for the idea that Narihira lived in exile at Nagaoka with her. In addition, in episode 84 we are told

26. *Gyokuden jinpi no maki*, "Waka no niji shingi," p. 550, and "Naidō ron," pp. 536–37. See also *Waka Kokin kanjō no maki*, pp. 460–61.

27. *Kokin shū* 984, anon.; *Kokin waka rokujō*, Ise.

that "once in the past, there was a man of rather low rank whose mother was an imperial princess. The mother lived at Nagaoka." This information suggested that Narihira built the house for his mother in Nagaoka and spent his exile on his mother's estate.[28]

For *Ise monogatari shō*, the choice of the Eastern Hills as Narihira's destination was probably initially motivated by the prose foretext to episode 59:

> Sometime in the past, a man got the idea to live in the Eastern Hills. (What do you suppose he was thinking about the capital?) He wrote this poem:
>
> *sumiwabinu / ima wa kagiri to / yamazato ni*
> *mi o kakusubeki / yado motometen*
>
> I've had enough of living in misery;
> I'll seek out shelter in some mountain village where
> I can hide myself away.
>
> Thus he left the capital.

Thematically this episode could easily be linked to the exile to the Eastern Provinces in which the man leaves the capital because of "certain circumstances that made life difficult for him." The Eastern Hills also had the virtue of being close enough to the capital that it would be possible for him to return each night, as indicated in episode 65. The clinching argument, however, depends on the Reizei allegorical reading strategy: the fact that Narihira is said to have been exiled to the *Eastern* Provinces was a deliberate hint that Narihira had actually been kept under house arrest in Yoshifusa's villa in the *Eastern* Hills.

Having shown that the "exile to the East" originated in a wordplay, the Reizei commentary proceeds to interpret each of the "exile to the Eastern Provinces" episodes through the allegorical technique of reading both the foretext and the waka for puns, clues to the hidden "historical" truth behind the fictionalized facade. As Narihira traveled from place to place in the east, he composed poems in response to the beauties of the natural scenery. For example, in episode 7, we are told that the man traveled along the Eastern

---

28. Note that although the Shimabara *Waka chiken shū* asserts that Narihira built a mansion on his mother's estate in Nagaoka, it does not specifically maintain that Narihira spent his exile there. The commentary on episode 58 identifies the woman involved as the Ise Priestess, now relieved of her duties and living in a nearby mansion. See Katagiri, *Ise monogatari no kenkyū (shiryōhen)*, pp. 262–63.

Sea road between Ise and Owari (*Azuma ni ikikeru ni Ise, Owari no awai no umizura o yuku ni*). According to *Ise monogatari shō*:

The phrase "Where Ise meets Owari" (*Ise Owari no awai* 伊勢尾張のあわひ) signifies the final meeting (*owari no awai* 終の交) of the tryst between the Consort [Nijō no Kisaki] and Narihira. The graphs for *i* and *se* signify Yin and Yang. The phrase "final" (*owari*) was used because as a man and woman they had reached the end of their love tryst.[29]

Here a phrase that appears to be simply a description of a geographical location is transformed into a secret allusion to the ending of Narihira's affair with Nijō no Kisaki. Since Narihira never went to the Eastern Provinces, all such geographical locations are prime targets for allegorization.

Ise monogatari shō even manages to transform poems that appear to be responses to natural phenomena into allegories. For example, in episode 8, Narihira composes a poem on first seeing Mount Asama, at that time a live volcano:

Shinano naru / Asama no take ni / tatsu kemuri
ochikochi bito / mi yawa togamenu

From Shinano's Asama Peak smoke rises;
how could people near and far see it and not be awed?[30]

Ise monogatari shō treats the rising smoke as a trope for Narihira's burning love:

The phrase *Shinano no kuni* (信濃の国 Shinano province) is read *shina no ku* (品の苦 the pain of Narihira's low station). . . . *Asama no take* (浅間の嶽 Asama Peak) signifies "he wretchedly (*asamashiku* 浅ましく) pondered how he had gotten to this state." . . . *Asama no keburi* (浅間の煙 the smoke from Asama) signifies "the flames of my passion."[31]

The Reizei interpretation of the poem in sum: "Since it is my fate to meet with such wretched sufferings, people near and far, even if you see the smoldering of my burning passion, please do not criticize me for it."[32] The commentary transforms the poem into a complex allegory of Narihira's suffering.

---

29. Ibid., p. 305.
30. *Shin Kokin shū* 903, Ariwara no Narihira.
31. Reizeike-ryū *Ise monogatari shō*, p. 306.
32. Ibid., p. 307.

In episode 9, the man reaches the province of Mikawa (Three Rivers) near Yatsuhashi (Eight Bridges). The "three rivers" of Mikawa are identified as "the three women that Narihira truly loved": Nijō no Kisaki, Somedono no Kisaki, and Shijō no Kisaki. The "eight bridges" of Yatsuhashi are identified as "the eight women he could never bring himself to abandon": Sanjō no Machi, Ki no Aritsune's daughter, Lady Ise, Ono no Komachi, Tadabumi's daughter, the "young grass woman" (*waka kusa no onna*, Narihira's younger sister), Masazumi's daughter, and the Ise Priestess.

The Reizei commentators systematically read the "Exile to the Eastern Provinces" episodes via puns and wordplays as signaling hidden historical truths. Although there are moments when *Ise monogatari shō* reads *Ise monogatari* as a religious allegory, overall the general tendency is toward a more secularized, "political" reading of *Ise monogatari*. These more politically inclined readings were most influential for later critics in the Muromachi and Edo periods (and even today). In the Nijō-affiliated *Ise monogatari zuinō* on the other hand, the tantric reading of *Ise monogatari* continued to dominate, but as we shall see, the contents of that reading changed in some surprising ways.

Ise monogatari zuinō

Ise monogatari zuinō rivals *Waka Kokin kanjō no maki* in its tantric allegoresis of a secular text and employs spiritual embryology to transform *Ise monogatari* into a complex philosophical argument for ritual sex as a path to enlightenment. The text was undoubtedly written by a Tachikawa adept, but scholars disagree on whether this adept was Fujiwara no Tameaki or a later writer.[33]

The dating and attributions of authorship of *Ise monogatari zuinō*, like most of the Kamakura secret commentaries, are speculative since they are based on lineage documents that are complete fabrications and on scholars' guesses about the "influence" of one text on another. Although *Zuinō* certainly contains much material relating to Tameaki-affiliated commentaries, including oral transmissions on the pillow word *chihayaburu* ("Chihayaburu to iu koto") and Akone Bay ("Akone no ura kuden"), Tameaki's name does not appear in the colophons for either of the two main lineages of *Ise monoga-*

33. Material from this section previously appeared in my "Allegories of Desire"; see also my "*Ise monogatari zuinō*: An Annotated Translation."

tari zuinō, as it usually does for texts written by him or one of his direct disciples.[34] So it is not surprising that there should be considerable disagreement among scholars as to whether Tameaki was involved in this text.

Based on similarity of content, Miwa Masatane follows Otsu Yūichi in arguing that *Zuinō* should be grouped with Fujiwara no Tameaki's other texts and sees no reason to doubt the date of 1282 (Kōan 5) found in the colophon of the earliest known manuscript (in the Tesshinsai Bunko). Briefly put, Otsu and Miwa argue that other Tameaki texts (especially *Waka Kokin kanjō no maki*) are strongly influenced by Tachikawa, and *Zuinō* shares at least one secret teaching, the "Oral Transmission of Akone Bay" ("Akone no ura kuden"), with other Tameaki-affiliated texts such as *Gyokuden jinpi no maki*.[35]

Katagiri Yōichi, on the other hand, contends that it is a later text, probably from the 1220s or 1230s. Katagiri points out that in contrast to nearly all the other Tameaki-affiliated texts, the name *Ise monogatari zuinō* does not appear in Reizei Tamesuke's 1317 library catalogue of the family manuscripts, and so was probably not yet in existence.[36] He suggests instead that the author of *Zuinō* may have been someone under the influence of Emperor Go-Daigo's notorious spiritual advisor, Monkan. Given the strong textual connections to works thought to be by Fujiwara no Tameaki, it seems likely

34. There are two basic lineages of *Zuinō* texts: those corresponding to the Jingu Bunko shozō Hayashizaki Bunko kyūzō manuscript (hereafter referred to as "Hayashizaki") and those following the Kariya Chōritsu Toshokan zō and Jingu Bunko shozō Miyazaki Bunko manuscripts (hereafter referred to as "Kariya" and "Miyazaki"). Texts in both lineages contain a general introduction, seven fascicles of "deep secrets," and two oral transmissions: "The Matter of *Chihayaburu*" ("Chihayaburu to iu koto") and "The Two Gates of Ise (Selections from the *Kanjō* Ceremony of the Ultimate Principle): The Oral Transmission on Akone Bay" ("Ise no nimon [gokuri kanjō sen]: Akone no ura kuden"). Texts in the Miyazaki/Kariya lineage contain extra material as part of the "Oral Transmission of Akone Bay," and one text in this lineage, the Tesshinsai Bunko manuscript (hereafter referred to as "Tesshinsai"), contains an additional oral transmission and transmission lineage found in no other *Zuinō* text. The Tesshinsai text, which dates from the late Muromachi period but contains a colophon with the date Kōan 5 (1282), is the earliest known manuscript of *Zuinō*. For a brief discussion of the two textual lineages, see Katagiri, *Ise monogatari no kenkyū (shiryōhen)*, pp. 880–81. Kushida Ryōko (*Zoku Shingon mikkyō seiritsu katei no kenkyū*, pp. 528–530) discusses a text entitled *Zuinō Ariwara no Narihira den*, which is clearly a variant of *Zuinō*, in his discussion on waka *kanjō*.

35. See Otsu, *Ise monogatari kochūshaku no kenkyū*, pp. 26–37; Miwa, *Kagaku hiden no kenkyū*, pp. 92–96.

36. See the Reizei library catalogue in Katagiri, *Ise monogatari no kenkyū (kenkyūhen)*, pp. 576–77.

that the author was also one of his disciples or at least someone with access to his commentaries.[37]

Although *Zuinō* is clearly indebted to material in Tameaki-affiliated texts, on the whole I agree with Katagiri that the text dates to the 1320s or 1330s, but for reasons of content and interpretation that Katagiri does not raise. First, although one finds sections analyzing the graphs used to write Sumiyoshi Daimyōjin or the meaning of pillow words such as *chihayaburu* in Tameaki-affiliated texts such as *Gyokuden jinpi no maki* or *Kokin waka shū jo kikigaki*, the content of those secrets is quite different from those in the *Zuinō*. The most likely explanation for these discrepancies is that the author of *Ise monogatari zuinō* borrowed the titles of oral transmissions developed by Tameaki but created his own explanations. Second, *Ise monogatari zuinō*'s identifications of the anonymous "women" in *Ise monogatari* match those in the Reizei school *Ise monogatari shō*, which, although strongly influenced by Tameaki, is generally credited to Reizei Tamesuke and dated to the early fourteenth century, not long after Tameaki's death. Third, in several places *Ise monogatari zuinō* refers to *Suzaku-in zuinō*, a text that does not appear in Tameaki commentaries but shows up in *Ise monogatari shō* and appears in the Reizei school library catalogue of 1317, and so may well have been invented by Reizei Tamesuke himself.

A more important consideration emerges from a comparison of *Zuinō* and a text attributed to Nijō Tameakira.[38] Although *Zuinō* interprets *Ise monogatari* using the kind of religious allegoresis that Tameaki first developed as a critical technique, like Tameakira's *Kokin hikashū Akone den* (The Akone transmission of a collection of secret poems from the *Kokin shū*), *Zuinō* generally refuses to deify Narihira as an avatar of Sumiyoshi Daimyōjin or any other kami or bodhisattva.[39] *Kokin hikashū Akone den*'s "The Matter of *Chihayaburu Kami*" ("*Chihayaburu kami* to iu koto") in particular shows strong similarities to "The Matter of *Chihayaburu*" in *Ise monogatari zuinō*.[40] As in *Zuinō*, *Kokin hikashū Akone den* uses etymological allegoresis to prove that the graphs for the pillow word *chihayaburu* 千葉破る refer to the tearing

37. Katagiri, *(Tesshinsai Bunko) Ise monogatari kochūshaku sōkan*, vol. 2, p. 503.

38. Nijō Tameakira was the son of Nijō Tamefuji; he was commissioned to compile the imperial anthology *Shin Shūi waka shū* (1364) but died before it was completed. His name can also be read "Tameaki," but for obvious reasons I have chosen to use "Tameakira" here.

39. *Kokin hikashū Akone den* has a colophon with Tameakira's name on it and a date of 1331. See Nijō Tameakira, *Kokin hikashū Akone den*, pp. 210–21.

40. Ibid., pp. 211–12.

(*yaburu* 破る) of the thousand-petals (*chi ha* 千葉) of the mother's womb.[41] And it makes the same unusual claim as *Ise monogatari zuinō*: the kami are nothing other than our own souls. In doing so, both *Ise monogatari zuinō* and *Kokin hikashū Akone den* eliminate the *honji suijaku* content that forms such an essential part of Tameaki's interpretive approach. Given the close parallels between the two texts, if we assume that the text was written after 1317, Nijō Tameakira is a strong candidate for authorship of *Ise monogatari zuinō*. He was a friend of Reizei Tamehide (?–1372); he adopted Tamehide's son Tamekuni as his heir, and so he would have had access to both Nijō and Reizei versions of Tameaki texts. In addition, Tameakira was a member of Go-Daigo's circle; he therefore fits Katagiri's profile of a poet with access to the Tachikawa priest Monkan.[42]

It seems probable that *Ise monogatari zuinō* was, as were *Gyokuden jinpi no maki* and *Waka Kokin kanjō no maki*, a high-level waka initiation text. Hints of its use as an initiation text include the title of one section: "Selections from the Initiation Ceremony of the Ultimate Principle" ("Gokuri kanjō sen"). We can also see hints of this in the attention given to a portrait of Narihira: "Those people within our lineage who are to transmit the secrets of *Ise monogatari* must above all preserve the image of Narihira as he appeared on his death bed, wearing the *eboshi* court cap and a blue silk courtier's robe." Clearly the portrait was meant to be hung in the initiation chamber and lend its authority to the initiation ritual of transmission in a way similar to the use of the Hitomaro portrait by the Rokujō. One might therefore consider this text as evidence that Tameakira was attempting to transform Narihira into a poetic ancestor of the Nijō house and thereby unify the family around himself as the leader.

Ise monogatari zuinō follows a legitimizing strategy similar to that used by the Reizei school *Ise monogatari shō* and the Tameaki-affiliated commentaries. It includes a section entitled "Akone no ura kuden" that analyzes episode 117 and makes claims nearly identical to those found in *Gyokuden jinpi no maki* and *Shinsen teisetsu shū*. *Zuinō*'s legitimacy and authority are traced back to

---

41. By way of contrast, Tameaki's *Kokin waka shū jo kikigaki* (pp. 243–44) section on *chihayaburu* uses etymological allegoresis of the graphs of *chihayaburu* to detail five possible readings, all relating to the *Nihon shoki* episode in which Amaterasu hides in a cave. See also "The Profound Meaning of *Chihayaburu*" ("Chihayaburu no shingi"), in Ishigami Hideaki, "Kunaichō Shoryōbu-zō *Kingyoku sōgi*," pt. I, p. 44.

42. Note that Tameaki's grandson, Nijō Michihira, was also a member of Go-Daigo's circle in the 1320s and 1330s.

the Daimyōjin's revelations to Narihira when he accompanied Emperor Montoku to the Sumiyoshi Shrine in Ten'an 1 (857). Narihira is then supposed to have passed this revelation on to his son Shigeharu.

Zuinō is written in the first person and purports to be the words of Shigeharu himself, directly addressing the reader-initiate. Following the title *Ise monogatari zuinō* is the phrase "Respectfully prefaced by the Middle Captain of the Right Division of the Inner Palace Guards, Ariwara no Shigeharu" (*Ukon chūjō Ariwara no ason Shigeharu kinjō*). The general introduction and first seven fascicles of "deep secrets" in *Zuinō* continue this pose. For example, early on in the text we are told: "I, Ariwara no Shigeharu, considering these past matters and pondering them in my own mind, have chosen from among those words of my father, recorded and handed down to me, the seven most essential secret teachings."[43]

Also, like earlier Tameaki-affiliated texts, *Ise monogatari zuinō* uses etymological allegoresis to substantiate its points. First, the author looks for puns and other possible double meanings in poems that then allow him to argue that the poem's hidden meaning (its *kokoro*) is a demonstration of esoteric Buddhism. For example, *Ise monogatari zuinō* analyzes two poems from episode 99 of *Ise monogatari*, "mizu mo arazu" (neither seen nor unseen) and "shiru shiranu" (knowing and not knowing), in order to demonstrate Narihira's profound understanding of radical nondualism, an understanding that is then used to defend ritual sex:

> When Narihira no Ason met the Somedono Lady-in-Waiting[44] at the riding grounds of the Imperial Right Guards, he composed this poem:
>
> *mizu mo arazu / mi mo senu hito no / koishiku wa*
> *aya naku kyō ya / nagame kurasamu*[45]

43. Kariya *Ise monogatari zuinō*, p. 428.

44. Somedono no Naishi: this title probably indicates a lady-in-waiting to the Somedono Empress (Fujiwara no Meishi, Nijō no Kisaki's cousin). She is generally thought to be either the daughter of Fujiwara no Yoshisuke, the minister of the right, or the daughter of Fujiwara no Yoruka, the secretary of the Palace Attendants Office. *Ise monogatari shō* identifies Somedono no Naishi as the anonymous woman of episode 99. See Reizeike-ryū *Ise monogatari shō*, p. 385. The original source for the identification is probably episode 160 of *Yamato monogatari* (pp. 330–31), which states explicitly that Narihira had an affair with her and recounts two exchanges of poetry between them. In English, see Tahara, *Tales of Yamato*, pp. 112–13, 264–65.

45. *Ise monogatari*, episode 99; *Kokin shū* 476, Narihira; *Yamato monogatari*, episode 166, Narihira.

> Longing for someone not unseen, nor yet quite seen,
> will this day be meaningless, spent in melancholy reverie?
>
> The true meaning of this poem is that seeing and not seeing are one. The true meaning of "neither unseen nor seen," is expressed in the phrase "not unseen" (*mizu mo arazu*). . . . Thus, in the poem, to be in a melancholy reverie when beginning Harmonious Union [i.e., ritual sex] is referred to as "meaningless" (*aya naku*).
>
> The reply from the Somedono Lady-in-Waiting:
>
> *shiru shiranu / nanika aya naku / wakite iwamu*
> *omoi nomi koso / shirube narikere*
>
> Why do you meaninglessly distinguish between knowing
> and not knowing?
> Your passionate thoughts alone will be your guide.
>
> The true meaning of this poem is "Why should you distinguish between enlightenment and unenlightenment, calling them by separate names?" The phrase "your passionate thoughts alone will be your guide" signifies that when an unenlightened person experiences Harmonious Union with the enlightened person, their consciousnesses merge into a single enlightened passionate thought (*ichinen* 一念). This enlightened passion becomes the guide, and so the dualism of knowing and not knowing is rendered meaningless (*aya naku*).[46]

Here a flirtatious exchange is transformed into a serious philosophical discussion of the problem of radical nondualism and deployed as an argument for using ritual sex to achieve the enlightenment of Harmonious Union (*wagō* 和合), that is, a state of "having no object of perception or discriminative thought" (*musō munen* 無相無念). This idea is implicitly substantiated via the argument that there is ultimately no distinction between enlightenment and unenlightenment. Since "the passions are themselves enlightenment" (*bonnō soku bodai*), proper use of ritual sex can achieve a state of *musō munen*.

In a second form of etymological allegoresis used in *Ise monogatari zuinō*, important words, usually made up of two graphs, such as "Ise" in *Ise monogatari* or "Kokin" in *Kokin waka shū*, are shown to signify esoteric principles. In the case of *Ise monogatari zuinō*, Shingon nondualism informs the argument that the graphs for *i* and *se* signify a whole series of nondualistic dualities, beginning with female and male:

46. Kariya *Ise monogatari zuinō*, pp. 429–30.

In order that there be no remaining obscurities I will enlighten you to a secret not yet revealed: how the myriad things should be divided between the two aspects of *i* and *se*.

I: female; Meditation; Ultimate Principle Underlying Phenomenal Reality, or What is Known; the Womb-Storehouse Realm; the *A* mantra-syllable; the body; the right hand and leg; earth; fire; moon.

Se: male; Compassion; Correct Understanding, or the Subject Who Knows; the Diamond Realm; the *UN* seed syllable; consciousness; the left hand and leg; heaven; water; sun.[47]

Zuinō also assigns new meanings to graphs and then rearranges them to create meaningful sentences that substantiate an argument. For example, this form of etymological paronomasia is deployed to show the "true" meaning of the graphs for Sumiyoshi Daimyōjin (住吉大明神). "Daimyō" 大明 signifies "greatly enlightened"; "jin" 神 (usually understood as "kami") signifies "soul"; "Sumiyoshi" 住吉 signifies "living easily." Thus, the entire phrase is construed as "A soul that has been completely enlightened (and so no longer has discriminative thoughts or deluded passions) lives easily in this world."[48]

Finally, pillow words and other phrases whose meaning had by the early fourteenth century become obscured with time are assigned homophonic graphs (*ateji*) that are supposed to make clear their true meaning. In *Ise monogatari zuinō*, a whole section is devoted to the phrase *chihayaburu*, which usually prefaces (pillows) the word "kami."[49] In the medieval period, *chihayaburu* was widely written with the graphs 風速振る (wind-swift-brandishing) and taken as signifying the mighty power of the gods. However, for reasons that will become clear, *Ise monogatari zuinō* assigns it the homophonic graphs 千葉破る (thousand-leaves-tearing), a reading more useful for its argument. Clearly the author of *Ise monogatari zuinō* was quite familiar with Tameaki's techniques and put them to good use to substantiate his own ideas.

---

47. Ibid., p. 432; for a slightly different assignment of dualisms, see Hayashizaki *Ise monogatari zuinō*, p. 455.

48. Kariya *Ise monogatari zuinō*, pp. 430–31.

49. Ibid., pp. 431–32.

Conflating the Paths of Poetry and Eroticism

In the first seven sections, *Ise monogatari zuinō* pursues the same polemic as the Tameaki-affiliated commentaries: Narihira wrote *Ise monogatari* as a revelation of the unity of the Paths of Poetry and Eroticism. *Ise monogatari zuinō* declares that Narihira was born in Japan to help guide those wandering in the darkness of the degenerate age of *mappō* to enlightenment through sex. As the first patriarch of a sect of Tachikawa Shingon called I-Se (otherwise unknown), he transmitted *Ise monogatari zuinō* to his son Shigeharu, thereby revealing that the creative Path of Poetry is essentially the same as the procreative Path of Eroticism and that both were originated by Izanami and Izanagi at Akone Bay in Ise Province. Those properly initiated into the secrets of the two aspects of *i* and *se* will be able to achieve sexual enlightenment and write better poetry.[50] According to the preface of *Ise monogatari zuinō*:

> Turning away from the unenlightened darkness [of the present] and looking back [to the distant past], we find that Izanami and Izanagi planted the seed at ancient Akone Bay, from whence the blessings of this practice spread out in waves. The poetry of Susanoo no Mikoto has been handed down through the ages, dipped from the pure stream of the Mimosuso River, unceasing as the upper stream of the Isuzu River. Since the time when the two shrine pillars of the two aspects of I-Se were erected, the needles of the awe-inspiring pine of the Sumiyoshi kami have neither fallen nor faded; deeply green they flourish more and more with the passing years. My father, Ariwara no Narihira, was able to acquire this enlightenment. Since the flow of the secret transmission has never been stopped, although Narihira's poem admonishes us not to speak of it, I have this knowledge.[51]

This passage rhetorically conflates the origin and transmission of the Path of Eroticism with the Path of Poetry by omitting a specific object for the "seed" that Izanami and Izanagi "planted" at Akone Bay. On one level, this passage alludes to the poetic "seed" Ki no Tsurayuki mentioned in his preface to the *Kokin shū*: "The seed of Japanese poetry is found in the human heart and grows into myriad leaves of words." This origin of poetry "came into being when heaven and earth were first separated" in the marriage song of Izanami and Izanagi.[52] It is also the "seed of enlightenment," which lies dormant in

50. I have used the form "I-Se" to differentiate this narrower meaning of "Ise" from the geographical place.

51. Kariya *Ise monogatari zuinō*, p. 427.

52. *Kokin waka shū*, p. 93.

each of us until we come into contact with the Buddhist teaching (here the Path of I-Se), at which point it flowers by means of this karmic link to the Buddha. On a deeper level, this "seed" is the secret of I-Se: all the myriad created things arise out of the Harmonious Union (*wagō*) of the two aspects of I-Se. I-Se is understood simultaneously as the Shinto kami Izanami (I) and Izanagi (Se) and as the Taoist principles of feminine Yin (I) and masculine Yang (Se). The Harmonious Union of Izanami and Izanagi produced the "seed" of cosmogonic creation; the harmonious union of female and male produces the "seed" of human procreation. I-Se is also understood as the Shingon *bīja* seed syllables *A* and *UN* identified with the Womb-Storehouse and Diamond Realm mandalas, which in their non-originary interdependence express the ultimate nonduality of all existence.

This multivalent "seed" forms the basis for the practice of pursuing both the Path of Poetry and the Path of Eroticism as a path to enlightenment, dual paths continued with Susanoo no Mikoto, whose "Manifold clouds rising" (*yakumo tatsu*) marriage poem is quoted in the *Kokin shū* kana preface as the first example of regularized thirty-one syllable poetry. The descriptions of the rivers at Ise Shrine and the pine at Sumiyoshi signify the unchanging, pure, ever-flourishing transmission of the art of poetry and sexual enlightenment. The secret transmission of I-Se was passed down from Izanami and Izanagi in the age of the gods, via Amaterasu and Susanoo no Mikoto at Ise and the Daimyōjin at Sumiyoshi; from Sumiyoshi Daimyōjin, it was transmitted to Ariwara no Narihira and then to Shigeharu, his son.

Ise monogatari is thus understood as the tale of the Harmonious Union of nondual dualities, most especially the feminine and masculine aspects. Narihira wrote the stories of poetic and sexual relations between men and women in *Ise monogatari* as an expedient means to lead ordinary people toward the Path of I-Se (i.e., enlightenment through ritual sex). Those who have been initiated into the secrets of I-Se, by having sexual relations with Narihira or by receiving the secrets of *Ise monogatari zuinō*, will be able to grasp enlightenment immediately.

The idea that Narihira slept with women to enlighten them was first voiced in texts associated with Tameaki. Exactly how this enlightenment occurred, however, was left rather vague. *Ise monogatari zuinō*, on the other hand, provides concrete details. For the most part, the mechanism of sexual enlightenment is based in the same kind of spiritual embryology that formed the theoretical underpinning for *Waka Kokin kanjō no maki*. However, whereas *Waka Kokin kanjō no maki* focused on the first five weeks of fetal development, *Ise monogatari zuinō* is concerned more with what happens to the soul in the period between the physiological death of one body and the biological conception of the next.

Shingon spiritual embryology texts argue that because the soul, floating in the preconception void, exists in a state of "having no object of perception or discriminative thought" (*musō munen*), it is in a state of Originally Enlightened Primordial Buddhahood. Since in this state, the soul is not merely without object of perception but is actually formless, *musō* is often taken to mean "being without material form" (*mushiki* 無色). Furthermore, *musō munen* is correlated with the cosmogonic stage when heaven and earth are still united, and chaos has not yet separated into differentiated forms.

Ise monogatari zuinō employs concepts from spiritual embryology in two ways: it attempts to syncretize them with the Shinto origination myth and, in the process, demythologizes the text as an allegory of human procreation; and they form the basis for the mechanism of sexual enlightenment.

The creation myth analyzed in *Zuinō* is quoted from a text called *Yotsugi*:[53]

The two kami Izanami and Izanagi were at the foot of the Floating Bridge of Heaven and, devising a plan, said, "We wonder, is there is any land below this?" So saying, they thrust the heavenly spear downward, and stirring the blue sea-plain, a drop [of sea brine] from the spear hardened and formed an island. There was something in the midst of the sky-void. It was shaped like the budding sprout of a reed plant. The two kami, descending to this island, became husband and wife. First they created the eight large islands, then the grasses and trees, then the sun and moon, then all the myriad kinds of people; and after that, Amaterasu was born.[54]

The opening paragraph of *Zuinō* makes clear the text's concern with syncretizing this creation myth and the spiritual embryology understanding of conception:

---

53. On *Yotsugi*, see Chapter 8, note 46. Both Otsu (*Ise monogatari kochūshaku no kenkyū*, pp. 30–31) and Katagiri ([*Tesshinsai Bunko*] *Ise monogatari kochūshaku sōkan*, vol. 2, pp. 496–98, 503) argue that the *Yotsugi* mentioned in *Zuinō* is a variant text of the historical chronicle *Mizu kagami* that was affiliated with the Tameaki school and transmitted in the Maeda family. Although for the most part the creation myth analyzed in *Zuinō* follows the standard version in the *Nihon shoki*, the use of *Yotsugi* may explain some minor discrepancies.

54. Kariya *Ise monogatari zuinō*, p. 435.

It is written that the origins of how we come to receive a human body and be born in our Isle of Abundant Autumns, the separation of heaven and earth, and the creation of the sun and moon, all begin with the descent from the High Plain of Heaven. The form is conceived from the dew of the father's spear and the mother's birthing hut by the sea; tearing the thousand-petals, it forcefully emerges at last. When we reflect on this, the fact that we have meaninglessly forgotten our original state when there was neither enlightenment nor unenlightenment and have failed to catch the waning light of the dawn moon at Akashi Bay in the sleeves of our robes seems attributable to nothing other than whether we know or do not know that all arises out of the two aspects of I-Se.[55]

Phrases such as "descent from the High Plain of Heaven" and "dew of the father's spear" clearly allude to the origin myth. However, this opening passage carefully conflates cosmogonic creation and procreation, establishing the basis for the idea that the Shinto creation myth is allegorical. The Japanese language enables this conflation by the use of a tense that could refer either to the past or to the present and the omission of any overarching subject, personal names (such as Izanagi and Izanami), or pronouns. In *Zuinō* two questions combined as one confront the inquiring mind: How did we as human beings / the world come to be formed?

The answer to this question is elaborated fully in the last two sections of *Zuinō*. Izanagi and Izanami are the primordial principles of I-Yin (female) and Se-Yang (male). Not just the cosmos but every living being is born through the Harmonious Union of these two principles:

The phrase "the two kami, descending to this island, became husband and wife" refers to the desire of a mother and father to have sexual relations.[56]

Thus, the "dew on the father's spear" is explained as the phallic "spear of the husband":

Thrusting downward is to have sexual relations. . . . The "drop [of sea brine] from the spear" is the male sexual essence. The word "harden" in the phrase "a drop [of sea brine] from the spear tip hardened and formed an island" means that when the male sexual essence and the female sexual essence combine in Harmonious Union, the male sexual essence "hardens" into the seed of the child.[57]

---

55. Ibid., p. 427.
56. Ibid., p. 435.
57. Ibid.

The "blue sea-plain" is understood as the fluid in the womb:

> Because [the womb] inside is filled with water it is called the "sea-plain." . . . The phrase "an island was formed" refers to the child that is formed when the two sexual essences combine in Harmonious Union within the womb; because the womb is like a sea-plain, the child is referred to as an island.[58]

And the phrase, "There was something in the midst of the sky-void. It was shaped like the budding sprout of a reed plant" is understood to refer to the form the soul takes in the empty void of the postmortem-preconception state.[59] As in spiritual embryology texts, *Zuinō* takes this preconception state to be that of Original Enlightenment. The pressing question becomes "Why have we lapsed from this state?" The answer is that we have failed to understand that "all arises out of the two aspects of I-Se," a lacuna that is to be filled by *Ise monogatari zuinō*.

Internalization of Kami and Buddhas

Although the conflation of the Paths of Poetry and Eroticism and the discussion of the mechanism of sexual enlightenment found in the first seven sections of *Ise monogatari zuinō* build on notions found in Tameaki-affiliated texts, in the last two sections *Zuinō* moves in a new direction. These two oral transmissions not only read the origin myth of Japan as an allegory for the process of sexual procreation but also argue that the "kami" and "buddhas" are fundamentally only projections of our own mind/consciousness. These oral transmissions signal a break with one of the hallmarks of Tameaki-affiliated commentaries: reliance on *honji suijaku* theory. Time and time again in such commentaries allegorical analysis of poems and prose foretexts yields the conclusion that various poets, scholars, and historical figures were the Manifest Traces of the Original Ground of kami, buddhas, and bodhisattvas who had "softened their splendor and mingled with the dust" (*wakō dōjin*) of humanity as an expedient device to enlighten sentient beings. This interpretation of *honji suijaku* creates a three-tiered hierarchy: buddhas and bodhisattvas as Original Ground for kami; both kami and Buddhist deities as Original Ground for human beings.

58. Ibid.
59. Ibid.

As we have seen, Tameaki-affiliated commentaries generally expend enormous energy on identifying Narihira as an enlightened avatar (different in name but one in substance) of various bodhisattvas and kami, including, among others, Izanagi, Sumiyoshi Daimyōjin, Kasuga Daimyōjin, the Bodhisattva of Yin and Yang, the Horse-Headed Kannon, and Dainichi Nyorai. For example, the *Gyokuden jinpi no maki* version of the etiology for the "Akone no ura kuden" analyzes the exchange of poems from episode 117 as explicitly identifying Narihira as an avatar of Sumiyoshi Daimyōjin:

> The meaning of this poem is "You are me: why have you forgotten your Original Ground? In the shadow of this pine I have spent years as a Manifest Trace. During that time how much have I benefited living beings? To benefit and save the multitude of living beings I have been provisionally born in your human body."[60]

Gyokuden jinpi no maki reads the "mutsumashi to" poem in episode 117 allegorically to prove that Narihira is actually an avatar of the Daimyōjin and implies that this is the reason Narihira was selected to receive such important poetic secrets. The identification of Narihira as a manifestation of Sumiyoshi Daimyōjin makes a great deal of sense since it redoubles the poetic authority of the text: the sacred authority of Sumiyoshi combined with the poetic authority of Narihira, who was popularly identified as a Sage of Poetry (*kasen*) in the medieval period.

In contrast, in its description of the same scene *Ise monogatari zuinō* refuses to identify Narihira as Sumiyoshi Daimyōjin's avatar. It indicates only that Sumiyoshi Daimyōjin singled Narihira out for praise ("You are not of the ordinary, ignorant multitudes") and that he is therefore worthy of receiving the "Akone no ura kuden." Although Narihira is said to have written *Ise monogatari zuinō* as an expedient means to "benefit, transform, and guide all living beings," a phrase usually used to denote a bodhisattva's efforts to save sentient beings, he is portrayed only as an enlightened human, the first patriarch of the path of I-Se. At no time is Narihira explicitly identified with any deity.

Underlying this diminution of *honji suijaku* elements is *Ise monogatari zuinō*'s allegorical interpretation of kami and buddhas as in fact nothing other than our own souls (*tamashii* 魂):

> A person's soul is referred to as a "kami." The word "kami" does not refer to something awe-inspiring outside ourselves. It is said that [the kami are] the karmic link of the Buddhist divinities dimming their splendor and mingling with the dust of this

60. *Gyokuden jinpi no maki*, pp. 545–46.

world; when [a kami] is in a state of *musō munen* and has no body or thought, it is a buddha. A kami is a buddha who mingles its light with the dust in order to guide people. Your soul is called a buddha when it is in the midst of the sky-void, because it has neither body nor consciousness to acknowledge anything. It is called a kami when it becomes a human being in order to guide other people. . . . Your own consciousness is, in itself, a kami.[61]

Such being the case, there is no reason to stand in fear and awe of kami: "There is no such thing as a kami that exists in some other place and exacts retribution . . . since the soul is itself the kami, it is your own mind that metes out punishment."[62] *Zuinō* takes the concept of *honji suijaku* and turns it inside out. This rationalization of Shinto and Buddhist deities as nothing more than projections of our own consciousness is substantiated through the analysis, mentioned above, of the pillow word *chihayaburu*. *Chihayaburu* is shown to have a rather different meaning than is usually thought:

The phrase *chihayaburu* 千葉破る means "emerging from the womb"; it refers to the process by which the soul, having been conceived in a human form, is born. The form of the Five Viscera and the Six Entrails of the mother closely resembles petals of the lotus flower. Conceived in the lotus, when born in the tenth month, the child emerges by tearing (*yaburu* 破る) those thousand-petaled (*chi ha* 千葉) membranes. . . . Thus the phrase "chihayaburu kami" refers to the soul.[63]

Since the Originally Enlightened soul in its preconception state is a buddha, birth becomes a process in which the "soul as buddha" dims its splendor and becomes a "soul as kami" by mingling with the dust of this world. This collapses the apparent hierarchy of *honji suijaku* into the continuous cycle of life, death, and rebirth. The conception process, which is usually viewed negatively within Buddhism as a prolongation of suffering, is now seen positively. If two enlightened people have sex and a child is conceived, this is cause for celebration, since the child is an enlightened buddha incarnated to benefit and guide other human beings. It is precisely in this sense that Narihira is described as being born in this world to "benefit, transform, and guide living beings to Nirvana." This explains why, unlike earlier commentaries, *Ise monogatari zuinō* makes no claims for Narihira's divinity.

---

61. Kariya *Ise monogatari zuinō*, p. 431.

62. Ibid.

63. Ibid.

This view of the kami as none other than our own souls did not develop in a vacuum. Kushida Ryōko and Mark Teeuwen have discussed an "Ise *kanjō*" that can be traced back at least to 1289 and perhaps to 1262.[64] Kushida cites a transmission lineage with the name "Keien Shōnin (Miwa)," which he argues means the Ise *kanjō* was probably first performed within the Miwa sect of Shingon, a form of Ryōbu Shinto permeated with Tachikawa elements, including spiritual embryology, that developed in the late thirteenth century.[65] According to Teeuwen, one of the striking elements of the Ise *kanjō* is that as part of the ceremony a waka poem is chanted expressing the idea that "the kami, as an embodiment of one's own inherent enlightenment, dwells within one's heart/mind (*kokoro*)."[66] In the last part of the ceremony, the following waka is chanted three times instead of a mantra:

chihayaburu / waga kokoro yori / suru waza o
izure no kami ka / yoso ni mirubeki

The acts of my own mind, born from the womb—
what kami could one find anywhere else?[67]

Here *chihayaburu*, which usually modifies kami, modifies *waga kokoro* (my own mind), signaling that the kami is none other than the activity of one's own mind. The author of *Ise monogatari zuinō* probably incorporated the concept that the kami dwells within the practitioner's own heart/mind, as well as the unusual reading of *chihayaburu* from Ise-related initiations such as the Ise *kanjō*.

These insights were then used to explicate episodes from *Ise monogatari* as allegories. For example, in episode 71, when Narihira is sent as an imperial envoy to the Ise Shrine, one of the Ise Priestess's ladies-in-waiting makes a poetic overture. His reply:

koishiku wa / kite mo miyo kashi / chihayaburu
kami no isamuru / michi naranaku ni[68]

64. Teeuwen, "The Kami in Esoteric Buddhist Thought and Practice," pp. 102–5; Kushida Ryōko, *Zoku Shingon mikkyō seiritsu katei no kenkyū*, pp. 511–14. For the 1289 date, see Kushida, p. 513; for the 1262 date, Teeuwen cites Itō Satoshi, "Ise kanjō no sekai," p. 64.

65. As noted in Chapter 6, the founder of the Miwa sect, Hōkyō (Rendō), was active at Sambō-in near Ise in the 1270s.

66. Teeuwen, "The Kami in Esoteric Buddhist Thought and Practice," p. 103.

67. Kushida, *Zoku Shingon mikkyō seiritsu katei no kenkyū*, p. 512; translation from Teeuwen, "The Kami in Esoteric Buddhist Thought and Practice," p. 103.

68. *Ise monogatari*, episode 71; *Shoku Senzai shū* 1401, anon.

If you are in love, pray come,
for this is not a path forbidden by the thousand-petals-tearing kami.

According to *Zuinō*, in this poem Narihira is advocating the path of I-Se:

The "thousand-petals-tearing kami" (*chihayaburu kami*) is the human soul. Since this kami/soul is entirely I-Se, as it says in the poem, how could the kami reject I-Se, particularly when Narihira was actually at Ise? The path referred to is the Path of Harmonious Union.[69]

In episode 65, Narihira supposedly implores the kami and buddhas to release him from his passion for his illicit lover, Nijō no Kisaki. He summons diviners and shamanesses to prepare purification offerings to rid him of his obsessive desire, all to no avail. He then composes the following poem:

koiseji to / Mitarashi gawa ni / seshi misogi
kami wa ukezumo / narinikeru kana[70]

Praying "let us stop loving," an ablution ceremony was
performed in the stream of purification,
but alas, the kami has not accepted the prayer.

The usual interpretation of this poem in its *Ise monogatari* context takes Narihira as subject: "Since Narihira was determined to stop loving Nijō no Kisaki, he performed an ablution ceremony in the Mitarashi River. However, the kami refused his prayers." Because this kind of behavior would contradict *Zuinō*'s argument, some clever interpretation was needed. *Zuinō* asserts it is the unenlightened Nijō no Kisaki who asks Narihira to make the prayer and perform the ceremony. Narihira himself, as the patriarch of Harmonious Union, would never have made such a petition. The poem is understood as follows:

Since everything is I-Se, what kami would accept a prayer to not follow the path of doing I-Se? Because Nijō no Kisaki had not acquired the enlightenment that what is called "kami" is actually just your own consciousness, she said, "Perform this rite so we can escape [from this passion]." Although Narihira let Nijō no Kisaki see him perform the rite, he thought to himself: "Because I have acquired the enlightenment [of I-Se], [to stop loving] would be unreasonable to my consciousness, so it will be

69. Kariya *Ise monogatari zuinō*, p. 431.
70. *Ise monogatari* episode 65; *Kokin shū* 501, anon.

unacceptable to the kami as well." Therefore he said, "Alas, the kami has not accepted it."[71]

In other words, since Narihira wants to sleep with Nijō no Kisaki (and knows sleeping with her is actually a path to enlightenment), and since the kami is none other than Narihira's own consciousness, of course her asking him to stop their love affair is unacceptable to the kami. In this way *Zuinō* neatly takes an episode that appears to directly contradict its own premises and transforms it into proof of its argument.

If the kami are actually human souls, other phrases from the origin myth can be explicated as well. For example the "seven generations of Heavenly Kami" and the "five generations of Earthly Kami" mentioned in the *Nihon shoki* and *Koji ki*:[72]

The phrase "seven generations [of Heavenly Kami]" actually refers to the eyes, ears, nose, tongue, body, will, and Dharma. Although the soul/kami is in the midst of the sky-void, when it receives a form, having eyes it sees colors, having ears it hears sounds, having a nose it smells fragrances, having a tongue it tastes flavors, having a body it gets hot and cold, feels itchiness and pain. Having consciousness it is enlightened as to greed for the myriad things. These are the Six Roots of Perception; adding I-Se, they are referred to as the "seven generations." As for the phrase "the five generations of Earthly Kami," when the Five Great Elements of wood, fire, earth, metal and water are used to form the five bodily limbs, they are called the "five generations."[73]

The five generations of Earthly Kami are simply the five material elements out of which our earthly form is constituted. Because in death these five elements disperse back to their original state, there is no real birth or death:

Thus, although while we possess a human form, it may seem that life is brief, in fact our life does not end, for when we are in the midst of the sky-void there is no limit to life. Thus there is no life and no death. It is said that since there is no birth, there is no death. Since there has always already been life, all that is born is the form.

---

71. Kariya *Ise monogatari zuinō*, p. 436.

72. The terms "heavenly" and "earthly" are not found in the *Nihon shoki* and *Koji ki* descriptions of the five and seven generations of kami, but the terms were commonly interpolated in medieval commentaries.

73. Kariya *Ise monogatari zuinō*, p. 434. There are three puns at work here: *godai* (the Five Great Elements), *gotai* (the five bodily limbs, that is, the human body), and *godai* (the five generations).

There is no birth of life. It is said there is only the original life that is neither born nor dies.[74]

Although the human body may perish, the five elements are eternal and disperse back to their original state. Thus death is nothing to be feared; it is merely the gateway back to a state of Original Enlightenment.

Zuinō also uses concepts from spiritual embryology in its description of the mechanism of enlightenment through sex. According to *Zuinō*, when men and women have sexual relations, their bodies and minds merge into a perfect identity at the moment of orgasm. If both partners are unenlightened, this union will cause them to become further mired in the karma of transmigration. When one or both are enlightened, however, the sexual act will lead them further along the path to enlightenment:

When an enlightened person has Harmonious Union with an unenlightened woman, meditating they merge in the perfect identity of Harmonious Union, becoming a single enlightened thought. The unenlightened woman will become one with the enlightened consciousness; at last she will grasp the karmic link to enlightenment and no longer follow the Path of Evil.[75]

This moment of Harmonious Union, in which each participant loses consciousness of his or her body and mental processes, creates a state of enlightened *musō munen*:

When the two consciousnesses and [their bodies which are made up of] the Five Modalities and the Four Great Elements dissolve altogether into perfect identity, the two people's individual thoughts are transformed into virtue and merge into a single enlightened thought . . . which does not discriminate between enlightenment and unenlightenment. Because everything is originally in Harmonious Union, at this moment of Harmonious Union, [the enlightened consciousness] merges with the unenlightened consciousness and they become as they were originally, that is, the Harmonious Union of the innate and eternally existing I-Se. The unenlightened consciousness and the enlightened consciousness become one, the seed of the Buddha buds, and they grasp the karmic link to true enlightenment. This is the true reality of the essence (*zuinō*) of I-Se.[76]

In other words, the orgasmic moment of Harmonious Union creates a state of *musō munen* identical with the primordial void before creation, as well as

74. Ibid., p. 458.
75. Ibid., p. 429.
76. Ibid., pp. 428–29.

with the postmortem-preconception state of the buddha/kami that is the soul. In both of these states, any mental consciousness that is capable of discriminative thought is disabled, and the Five Modalities and Four Great Elements that make up material form are dispersed. The disruption of all consciousness of physical and mental processes by orgasm likewise results in dissolution of the Five Modalities and Four Great Elements into Harmonious Union.

This idea of Harmonious Union is probably related to Kūkai's notion that Dainichi Nyorai is in a state of eternal harmony (*yuga* 揄伽): "The Existence consisting of the Six Great Elements, the essence of the World of Dharma, is free without any obstacle and is in a state of eternal harmony."[77] The goal of esoteric meditation is to become aware of and attuned to this originally existing harmony. In *Zuinō*, sex becomes a form of meditation whose goal is to obliterate the distinction between self and other, thereby bringing the participants to an understanding (however momentary) of the Harmonious Union that exists between all things in the universe and to thereby achieve "buddhahood in this very body."

Ise monogatari zuinō continues to use the etymological allegoresis that developed out of *honji suijaku* thinking but empties it of *honji suijaku* content. In this, it is similar to the Reizei school *Ise monogatari shō*, which deploys etymological allegoresis to find historical rather than religious meaning. In other words, by the early fourteenth century the interpretive method of etymological allegoresis is becoming detached from its origins in esoteric Buddhist attempts to homologize Buddhist and Shinto deities. This method of analysis continued to be used in the Muromachi Nijō school *Kokin denju*, and it even plays a role in the work of Edo period Nativist (*kokugakusha*) and Neo-Confucian scholars. As we shall see in the Conclusion, however, although Muromachi scholars such as Nijō Yoshimoto and Ichijō Kaneyoshi employ a certain amount of etymological analysis in their commentaries, they begin to voice strong suspicions of the esoteric content of the Kamakura commentaries, suspicions that have until recently prejudiced contemporary scholars from paying serious attention to these commentaries.

77. Hakeda Yoshito, *Kūkai: Major Works*, p. 90.

Conclusion

A teleology evident in the construction of the grand narrative of Japanese literary history, both within the premodern Japanese tradition of criticism and in the twentieth century, has ignored the waka initiation pedagogical system and dismissed the esoteric commentaries it produced. It is easy to defend this teleology; after all, the esoteric commentaries appear to have been actively produced during a period of only about a hundred years (1250–1350) and produced little or no literary criticism that we would consider worthwhile today. Already by the mid-Muromachi the poet-scholars considered the finest of their age were not simply criticizing the commentaries as outmoded and useless but condemning them as a positively dangerous mode of criticism.

Ichijō Kaneyoshi, in his *Ise monogatari guken shō*, was the first to attack the commentaries head on:

> Among the *Ise monogatari* commentaries is one called *Chiken shū*, said to be in the hand of Lord Tsunenobu. It is not by him. Also widely read is the *Selections in Ten Fascicles*. Whose handiwork this is we do not know. In the family papers that have been passed down to me, they are treated as "numerous secret teachings" but on examining them myself I have found that not a single one of the Japanese and Chinese sources quoted as an authority is genuine. Not only do these works fail to grasp the original sense (*hon'i* 本意) of the tales, they cannot be relied on as a source of poetic allusion for either style or vocabulary. The untutored should place not an iota of faith in them, for they are bound to lead into mistaken paths.

The *Chiken shū* for instance, claims that Narihira was the manifestation of the Batō [Horse-Headed] Kannon and that Ono no Komachi was the manifestation of Nyoirin Kannon. That is not the least of its idiocies. I can only assume that it is a later forgery by someone obsessed by things sexual (*irogonomi*) who borrowed the name of Tsunenobu to make him seem an ally of the cause. If Tsunenobu really had written it, then Lord Teika must have come across it; but nowhere do we find reference to it, not even when Teika discusses the matter of the title. It is all most suspicious. . . .

According to one tradition Narihira never went east. The references to famous places in the east are said to refer to Higashiyama or somewhere near the capital. This is utter nonsense. The fact that he traveled east is clearly mentioned in the *Kokin shū*, the *Gosen shū*, and the *Yamato monogatari*: one could hardly ask for better proof.[1]

Kaneyoshi attacked *Waka chiken shū* from two angles: first, its attribution to Tsunenobu is spurious; second, all of its authoritative sources are spurious as well. In addition, Kaneyoshi makes it very clear that he has little patience for either religious or historical allegoresis of *Ise monogatari*. As Richard Bowring has pointed out, Kaneyoshi instead "shifts the emphasis back to the poetry: the poems themselves become the focus of attention, rather than the circumstances of their production."[2] Kaneyoshi's interest lies solely in explicating those aspects that will help the reader understand the *hon'i* of the poem at hand and to write better poetry. Everything else is superfluous. Kaneyoshi's new focus is particularly clear in his criticism that the Kamakura commentaries are worthless as a source for poetic allusion.

Despite Kaneyoshi's antagonism, transmission lineages for a number of the Kamakura commentaries indicate they continued to be disseminated quite widely in the Muromachi and early Edo periods. Although each transmission invariably included an admonition against releasing the commentaries to the uninitiated, *Waka chiken shū*, the Reizei school *Ise monogatari shō*, and *Kokin waka shū jo kikigaki* moved rapidly beyond the limited sphere of the Nijō and Reizei poetry factions into popular culture. As mentioned in the Introduction, numerous Noh plays used identifications, secret histories, and esoteric glosses of *Ise monogatari* and the *Kokin shū* taken from the Kamakura commentaries. If the secret interpretations of *Ise monogatari* and the

---

1. Ichijō Kaneyoshi, *Ise monogatari guken shō*, pp. 505–6; translation (modified) from Bowring, "The *Ise monogatari*," pp. 451–52.
2. Bowring, "The *Ise monogatari*," p. 453.

Kokin shū could be used to write plays that were performed publicly, obviously the secrets were no longer very secret. Muromachi scholars such as Kaneyoshi quite openly enumerated the secret matters and oral transmissions of the Kamakura commentaries. There is also some evidence from these commentaries that by the Muromachi period lower-level disciples received the secret commentaries as a kind of primer. One possibility is that by the late fourteenth century they had ceased to be inner esoteric teachings and were widely accessible to any educated person who moved in the first ranks of society.

This hypothesis is borne out by the prose tale *Arokassen monogatari*, which is (ironically) traditionally attributed to Kaneyoshi. At one point in the story a princess learning the art of waka is told, "The Middle Captain [Narihira] was the Bodhisattva of Song and Dance from the heavenly world, actually an avatar of Kannon. Inwardly he maintained his vows in secret, outwardly he seemed to assuage his passion at random. . . . All the women that he slept with eventually attained enlightenment."[3] This statement is followed by a long list of commentaries considered essential for the princess's poetic education, and some of the titles might be sections of *Waka chiken shū* and *Gyokuden jinpi no maki*. If by the mid-Muromachi, a young girl might be taught these commentaries by her nursemaid as part of her literary education, they were no longer seen as top-secret transmissions. Of course, if the story is by Kaneyoshi, it may have been part of his attempt to marginalize and trivialize the secret commentaries, but it does point to a wider dissemination of their supposedly esoteric secrets.

Another example can be found in *Hioke no soshi* (Tale of the brazier), in which two anecdotes from *Kokin waka shū jo kikigaki* are cited in a battle of poetic wits between an elderly husband and wife.[4] This battle employs the commentaries' polemical structure of debate, or *mondō*, but any serious "meaning" is subverted by the structure's radical recontextualization as a conjugal spat over a broken brazier. The use for comic effect of not only secret commentary material but the format of the commentaries themselves is further evidence that the secret commentaries were no longer taken very seriously.

Even before Kaneyoshi's attack, in the hundred or so years after the period of active production of the esoteric commentaries (the Nanbokuchō

3. *Arokassen monogatari*, in Yokoyama Shigeru and Matsumoto Takanobu, *Muromachi jidai monogatari taisei*, vol. 2, pp. 118–19.

4. See Skord, trans., *Tales of Tears and Laughter*, p. 103.

and early Muromachi), gradual changes crept into the commentaries within the Nijō and Reizei lineages, changes that moved the commentaries away from esoteric Shingon and syncretic Shinto. This was a natural effect of the culture of secret transmission, which encouraged the production of difference, even as it asserted what Lewis Cook has called a "sanctimonious rhetoric of fidelity to received authority."[5] Each generation of initiates within the various lineages "reinvented" the transmission according to its own needs, which changed in accordance with shifting political, economic, and religious changes.

In 1471 the gradual shift toward secularization became a major shift when the renga poets Sōgi (1421–1502) and Jōen (or Tō no Tsuneyori, d. 1484?) jointly invented the *Kokin denju,* the system of secret transmission on the *Kokin shū* that dominated poetic pedagogy until the eighteenth century.[6] As recently as twenty years ago, scholars focused (approvingly) on Sōgi's "rationalization" of *Kokin shū* and *Ise monogatari* interpretation and completely ignored his participation in the creation of the *Kokin denju.* For example, scholars argued that a major turning point in the history of *Ise monogatari* reception occurred when Sōgi came down strongly on the side of the fictiveness (*tsukuri*) of *Ise monogatari.* By asserting that "the phrase *mukashi* is a mark of *monogatari,*" he separated *Ise monogatari* from the *Kokin shū* as a historical text and placed it in the same category as *Genji monogatari.* With this one stroke, Sōgi completely invalidated the Kamakura commentaries' historical and religious allegoresis. At the same time, however, a certain amount of ambivalence remains. For example, in his analysis of the first episode, he notes: "The phrase 'shiru yoshi shite' means that Narihira had an estate in Nara. Although this is not substantiated elsewhere, it is enough that it is recorded in this tale. Narihira was the grandson of Emperor Heizei. It would be logical that he would have an estate in the south."[7] What we see here is a careful balancing act: where there is no historical evidence to the contrary, and where there is a certain amount of logic (Emperor Heizei re-

5. Cook, "The Discipline of Poetry," p. 11.

6. What follows benefited greatly from Lewis Cook's meticulous analysis of Sōgi's contributions to literary interpretation and pedagogy. It also benefited from discussions with Steven Carter and Michael Bourdaghs. See also Bourdaghs, "Linked Verse and Literary Scholarship: An Analysis of Sōchō's Commentary on *Ise monogatari*"; and Carter, "'Seeking What the Masters Sought.'" For more general information on Muromachi developments in literary patronage, see Carter, *Literary Patronage in Late Medieval Japan.*

7. Sōgi, *Ise monogatari Shōmon shō,* p. 592.

tired to Nara, and it would make sense that his grandson Narihira had an estate there), the facts as presented in *Ise monogatari* might be taken at face value. The argument seems to be that this fiction must be accepted as inscribed (i.e., as *tsukuri monogatari*); it is not "hiding" some other layer of "reality" of the kind that the Kamakura commentaries substantiated with spurious historical documents and oracular revelations.

In line with this position, Sōgi strongly criticized the commentaries' rampant historicalization of *Ise monogatari*. For example, in his analysis of the first episode we find:

> In the old-style commentaries (*kochū* 古注), the two sisters are said to be Ki no Aritsune's daughters. Our school does not accept this reading. We reveal only those names actually appearing in the text; we do not reveal names that do not appear there. They could be any beautiful women. In the same way we do not reveal the names of the authors of anonymous poems in the imperial anthologies.[8]

Sōgi also, like Kaneyoshi, strongly disapproved of the tantric reading of *Ise monogatari*. In the very first line of *Ise monogatari Shōmon shō*, he rejects the tantric reading of the graphs of Ise as signifying female and male:

> As for the title of *Ise monogatari*, the old-style commentaries claim it signifies tales of [relationships between] men and women. On this basis they read the graphs for *i* and *se* as "female" and "male." From this various other interpretations arise. Our school rejects this.[9]

Finally, Sōgi was the first scholar to recognize different narrative voices in *Ise monogatari*. Rather than decide between Narihira and Lady Ise as putative authors, he simply acknowledged that the authorship is plural. This more subtle understanding of narrative voice (which he probably derived from his close reading of *Genji monogatari*) was also a factor in his position on the basic fictionality of *Ise monogatari*.

Although this approach to *Ise monogatari* would appear to be a sober rationalization of the exuberant historical and religious allegoresis of the Kamakura commentaries, the "irrational" culture of secret transmission lingered on. Sōgi and Jōen played a major role in the continuation of that culture through their editing and authorship of the secret commentaries that came to form the corpus of the *Kokin denju*. How are these two apparently

---

8. From the lecture notes by Sōgi's disciple, Sōchō, *Ise monogatari Sōchō kikigaki*, p. 654.
9. Ibid., p. 653.

contradictory facts (a movement away from oracular revelation as legitimating source of authority on the one hand and a reinforcement of the irrational authority inherent in a genealogy of secret transmission on the other) to be reconciled? One way of thinking of the contradiction productively is in terms of paradigmatic triggers. Tameaki's creation of esoteric commentaries along with a system of secret Shingon-style initiations and their subsequent widespread adoption by the Nijō and Reizei schools were triggered by discursive shifts and challenges specific to the Kamakura period. The most important of these was competition within an aristocratic society focused on patronage from the imperial court. In the twelfth and thirteenth centuries, the various poetry families—the Rokujō and Mikohidari prominent among them—who had been excluded from political power were competing in the cultural sphere for court-sanctioned privileges such as the right to judge poetry contests and compile imperial anthologies. The Rokujō appear to have been the first to attempt to establish a corpus of secret material that could be used to defend their family's right to such privileges, but the Mikohidari were not far behind. Fujiwara no Tameaki, who ironically was for the most part excluded from the Mikohidari patrimony, can be said to have taken his revenge when he transformed the hereditary transmission system into the waka *kanjō* system, supported by spurious transmission lineages and numerous esoteric commentaries that were widely influential for the Nijō and Reizei. By the Muromachi period, however, a combination of changing religious attitudes, as well as new economic and political realities, meant that waka *kanjō* and esoteric commentaries were no longer particularly effective strategies.

First, by the Muromachi period, the intensity of religious commitment to esoteric practices characteristic of the Kamakura period was already fading. The scholar Ichijō Kaneyoshi, who practiced Amidism (in contrast to Tameaki's esoteric Buddhism) and whose moral philosophy tended toward Neo-Confucianism, was undoubtedly typical of his age in finding the Tachikawa content of the commentaries alarming. More pragmatically, the practice of Tendai and Shingon esotericism had always been limited to fairly high-ranking aristocrats; in the Muromachi period the provincial samurai whose economic support was crucial to scholars like Kaneyoshi and Sōgi were no longer particularly interested in esotericism. These pressures led to a certain secularization of literary scholarship, as the older commentaries were replaced by a more "rational" form of textual criticism that concentrated on philological issues and questions of aesthetic appreciation, content more palatable to the Muromachi audience.

In the realm of economics, in the Muromachi period both poetic and political authority were shifting away from privileged blood lines. The reunification in Kyoto of the political and cultural centers of the country by the Ashikaga shogunate opened the way for talented warriors and commoners to take the place of the aristocracy as important cultural arbiters. And the decline of the political and economic power of the imperial court meant that patronage in the form of the conferral of lucrative privileges was also waning. The last imperial anthology (*Shin Shoku Kokin waka shū*, New collection of ancient and modern Japanese poems, continued; 1439) was "commissioned" in 1433 by Emperor Go-Hanazono (r. 1429–64), but it was actually compiled at the request of the shogun Ashikaga Yoshinori. And waka, although still considered a culturally superior art, was losing ground to the new form of linked verse, renga. Professional renga masters, many of whom, like Sōgi, came from commoner backgrounds and so had no connection to the major poetry families, could not hope for patronage from the court, at least initially. They needed to establish the value of their own names in order to attract tuition-paying disciples, commissions to write the opening link for a renga sequence (*hokku* 発句), and invitations to act as judges at renga contests. They therefore had a certain stake in harshly criticizing the esoteric commentaries and advocating a new form of literary criticism. Although the poetic lineages were not completely without value—Sōgi did, after all, feel compelled to get a Nijō certification—one wonders whether this certification had not become merely nominal. At any rate, it is clear that by the mid-Muromachi the authority of the poetry families had already been seriously undermined.

An overall trend toward professionalization of the teaching of literary criticism, as evidenced in the shift from dependence on patronage to dependence on tuition, was reinforced by economic changes: the accumulation of capital in the provinces, the widespread acceptance of hard currency (as opposed to rice for barter), and the impoverishment of the court (probably the most powerful incentive for aristocratic poets such as Ichijō Kaneyoshi to lecture on the Heian classics). On the other hand, Sōgi clearly understood the pedagogical and economic value of the system of secret transmission, as he demonstrated with the development of the *Kokin denju*. In some ways Sōgi's *Kokin denju* could be seen as an appropriation of the esoteric transmission system that simultaneously emptied it of much of its esoteric content and ritual trappings.

Although the period in which the waka initiation system dominated poetry circles was brief, we should nevertheless be suspicious of narrative histories of Japanese literature that simply dismiss texts like *Waka Kokin kanjō no maki* and *Ise monogatari zuinō* in favor of texts that are relatively easy to assimilate into the synchronic discourses (political, religious, rhetorical) of the scholar. The difficulty and apparent irrelevance of these esoteric commentaries to later developments in literary criticism should not lead us to ignore them. For one thing, the use of etymological allegoresis as an interpretive tool continued to be used throughout the Muromachi and Edo periods by both Neo-Confucian and Shinto scholars. For another, when the commentaries began to seep into popular culture in the Muromachi period, they had an inordinate amount of influence.

By way of a polemical conclusion, and to bring this book back to the theoretical concerns with which I began, I emphasize again that if we use a critical method uncritically, what we "find" in the text is all too likely to be fully predictable beforehand; there will be no surprises. It is simply untenable to assume that readers from the Heian period to the present have always drawn the exclusionary line that binds the text as an object of interpretation in exactly the same way. It is equally untenable to assume that the only way to unbind that text is by means of the very latest critical theory or that we have nothing to learn from the very different ways that medieval Japanese readers themselves approached those same texts.

The Kamakura commentaries, seen as an interpretive and aesthetic dead end by both Muromachi and modern scholars, problematize the neat line of literary "influences" that has been so often drawn from Ki no Tsurayuki to the present. They make evident the multiplicity of literary history; it was by no means a smooth, linear climb to the rarified heights of correct interpretation. If, therefore, we want to gain a sense of the true heterogeneity of medieval Japan, we must pay close attention to texts like these: texts that instantiate the turns and twists, the powerful misreadings and occasional dead ends, that are most symptomatic of their historical position.

From a theoretical point of view, I have tried to argue here that we take seriously the alterity of the medieval Japanese. I am suspicious of New Critical treatments of waka poetry as purely aestheticized objects or as straightforward reflections of a Zen aesthetics that accords all too well with twentieth-century secularism. On the other hand, it seems equally problematic to succumb to a currently more pressing temptation and turn Heian and Kamakura literature into a kind of avant-garde *écriture*, without grounding such a characterization in the historical specificity of classical and medieval strategies of reading and writing.

It is only by taking seriously the alterity of medieval Japanese interpretations, especially those that do not fit with our current notions of criticism, that we can begin to historicize our own critical position. I believe, therefore, that the project should be to read Japanese literature against the grain of whatever critical method we employ; only in this way can we make some progress toward the historicization of own critical assumptions, an essential first step toward being able to see the historical specificity of other cultures.

Reference Matter

Bibliography

Works in Japanese

Unless otherwise specified, the place of publication for all Japanese works except periodicals is Tokyo. The following abbreviations are used for titles of collections:

KNKB	*Kanshō Nihon koten bungaku.* 36 vols. Kadokawa Shoten, 1975–78.
NKBT	*Nihon koten bungaku taikei.* 102 vols. Iwanami Shoten, 1957–68.
NKBZ	*Nihon koten bungaku zenshū.* 51 vols. Shōgakkan, 1970–78.
NKT	*Nihon kagaku taikei.* 10 vols. Kazama Shobō, 1958–74.
SGR	*Shinkō Gunsho ruijū.* 24 vols. Meicho Fukyūkai, 1977–78.
SNKBT	*Shin Nihon koten bungaku taikei.* 102 vols. Iwanami Shoten, 1989–2000.
SNKS	*Shinchō Nihon koten shūsei.* 85 vols. Shinchōsha, 1976–89.
T.	*Taishō shinshū daizōkyō.* 85 vols. Taishō Shinshū Daizōkyō Kankōkai, 1960–78.
ZGR	*Zoku Gunsho ruijū.* 71 vols. Zoku Gunsho Ruijū Kanseikai, rev. 3rd ed., 1983.

Texts Affiliated with Fujiwara no Tameaki (in approximate chronological order)

Chikuen shō (ca. 1265–1270). In *ZGR*, vol. 17, pt. I, pp. 1–11.

Chikuen shō (ca. 1265–1270). In Sasaki Nobutsuna, ed., *NKT*, vol. 3, pp. 410–28.

Waka kanjō den (ca. 1265?). In Miwa Masatane, "Ietaka kataku sho no kentō (*Waka chiken shū, Waka kuden shō* o megutte)." *Ōsaka Furitsu Daigaku kiyō (jinbun, shakai kagaku)* 16 (1968), pp. 130–36.

Waka chiken shū (ca. 1260s?). In *ZGR*, vol. 18, pt. I, pp. 442–535.

[Shimabara Kominkan Matsuhira Bunko shozō] *Waka chiken shū* (ca. 1260s?). In Katagiri Yōichi, ed., *Ise monogatari no kenkyū (shiryōhen)*, pp. 198–286. Meiji Shoin, 1969.

[Kyūshū Daigaku Otonashi Bunko zō] *Waka chiken shū* (ca. 1260s?). In Fujishima Aya, "Kyūshū Daigaku Otonashi Bunko zō *Waka chiken shū*." 2 pts. *Bunken tankyū*, no. 28 (1991), pp. 12–31; no. 29 (1992), pp. 55–78.

[Kunaichō Shoryōbu shozō den Tameuji hitsu] *Waka chiken shū* (ca. 1265?). In Katagiri Yōichi, ed., *Ise monogatari no kenkyū (shiryōhen)*, pp. 96–195. Meiji Shoin, 1969.

Gyokuden jinpi no maki (1273–78). In Katagiri Yōichi, ed., *Chūsei Kokin shū chūshakusho kaidai*, vol. 5, pp. 521–87. Kyoto: Akao Shobundō, 1986.

Kingyoku sōgi (1273–78). In Ishigami Hideaki, "Kunaichō Shoryōbu zō *Kingyoku sōgi*: hankoku to kaidai." 3 pts. *Mita kokubun*, no. 15 (Dec. 1991), pp. 37–52; no. 16 (July 1992), pp. 41–55; no. 17 (Dec. 1992), pp. 51–62.

Gyokuden shū waka saichō, *Jinpi kushō*, and *Akone no ura kuden* (ca. 1270s). In Sasaki Nobutsuna, ed., *NKT*, vol. 4, pp. 386–98.

Ise monogatari engi (ca. 1270s). In Katagiri Yōichi, *Ise monogatari no kenkyū (kenkyūhen)*, pp. 579–82. Meiji Shoten, 1968.

Iwami no jo shiki (ca. 1270s). In Sasaki Nobutsuna, ed., *NKT*, vol. 1, pp. 31–34.

Kakinomoto no Hitomaro no koto (ca. 1270s). In Miwa Masatane, *Kagaku hiden no kenkyū*, pp. 486–500. Kazama Shobō, 1994.

Kokin waka shū jo kikigaki: san ryū shō (ca. 1270s). In Katagiri Yōichi, ed., *Chūsei Kokin shū chūshakusho kaidai*, vol. 2, pp. 223–90. Kyoto: Akao Shobundō, 1973.

Waka Kokin kanjō no maki (ca. 1280s). In Miwa Masatane, *Kagaku hiden no kenkyū*, pp. 459–85. Kazama Shobō, 1994.

Unpublished Texts Attributed to Tameaki

Tameie kuden (ca. 1265–66)

Shinsen teisetsu shū (ca. 1265–70)

Waka entei hishō (ca. 1270s)

Other Primary Sources in Japanese

Arokassen monogatari. In Yokoyama Shigeru and Matsumoto Takanobu, eds., *Muromachi jidai monogatari taisei*, vol. 2, pp. 115–84. Kadokawa Shoten, 1975.

Dōgen. *Shōbō genzō zuimon ki*. In *NKBT*, vol. 81, pp. 317–438.

Fujiwara no Atsumitsu. *Kakinomoto eigu ki*. In *SGR*, vol. 13, pp. 53–54.

Fujiwara no Ietaka. *Waka kuden shō*. In Sasaki Nobutsuna, ed., *NKT*, vol. 4, pp. 386–94.

Fujiwara no Kintō. *Wakan rōei shū*. In Kawaguchi Hisao, ed., *Wakan rōeishū zenshakuchū*. Kōdansha Gakujutsu Bunko, 1982.

Fujiwara no Teika. *Eiga no taigai*. In Hashimoto Fumio, Ariyoshi Tamotsu, and Fujihira Haruo, eds., *Karon shū*, *NKBZ*, vol. 50, pp. 493–95.

———. *Kenchū mikkan shō*. In Sasaki Nobutsuna, ed., *NKT* supplement, vol. 5, pp. 137–307.

———. *Kindai shūka*. In *NKBT*, vol. 65, pp. 99–111.

———. *Maigetsu shō*. In Sasaki Nobutsuna, ed., *NKT*, vol. 3, pp. 346–54.

———. *Maigetsu shō*. In NKBZ, vol. 50, pp. 125–39.

Guhi shō (*U no matsu*). In Sasaki Nobutsuna, ed., *NKT*, vol. 4, pp. 291–312.

Guken shō. In Sasaki Nobutsuna, ed., *NKT*, vol. 4, pp. 354–61.

Ichijō Kaneyoshi. *Ise monogatari guken shō*. In Katagiri Yōichi, ed., *Ise monogatari no kenkyū* (*shiryōhen*), pp. 503–87. Meiji Shoin, 1969.

Inui Teijo. *Yōkyoku shūyō shō*. Nihon Toshū Sentā, 1979.

Ise monogatari. In Sakakura Atsuyoshi et al., eds., *Taketori monogatari, Ise monogatari, Yamato monogatari*, *NKBT*, vol. 9, pp. 111–87.

Ise monogatari. Ed. Watanabe Minoru. *SNKS*, vol. 2.

Ise monogatari nangi chū. In Katagiri Yōichi, ed., *Ise monogatari no kenkyū* (*shiryōhen*), pp. 462–87. Meiji Shoin, 1969.

[Kunaichō Shoryōbu shōzō Reizeike-ryū] *Ise monogatari shō*. In Katagiri Yōichi, ed., *Ise monogatari no kenkyū* (*shiryōhen*), pp. 287–400. Meiji Shoin, 1969.

[Jingu Bunko shozō Hayashizaki Bunko kyūzō] *Ise monogatari zuinō*. In Katagiri Yōichi, ed., *Ise monogatari no kenkyū* (*shiryōhen*), pp. 446–59. Meiji Shoin, 1969.

[Jingu Bunko shozō Miyazaki Bunko] *Ise monogatari zuinō* (excerpt). In Katagiri Yōichi, ed., *Ise monogatari no kenkyū* (*shiryōhen*), pp. 882–84. Meiji Shoin, 1969.

[Kariya Chōritsu Toshokan zō] *Ise monogatari zuinō*. In Yoshizawa Yoshinori, ed., *Mikan kokubun kochūshaku taikei*, vol. 8, pp. 426–37. Seibundō, 1968.

[Tesshinsai Bunko (Kōan 5)] *Ise monogatari zuinō*. In Katagiri Yōichi, ed., *[Tesshinsai Bunko] Ise monogatari kochūshaku sōkan*, vol. 2, pp. 399–461. Yagi Shoten, 1989.

Kakinomoto eigu ki. In *SGR*, vol. 13, pp. 53–54.

Kakinomoto kōshiki. In *SGR*, vol. 13, pp. 55–58.

Kamo no Chōmei. *Mumyō shō*. In Ōsone Shōsuke and Kubota Jun, eds., *Kamo no Chōmei zenshū*, pp. 61–107. Kichōbon Kankōkai, 2000.

Kōan jū nen Kokin shū kachū. In Katagiri Yōichi, ed., *Chūsei Kokin shū chūshakusho kaidai*, vol. 2, pp. 341–431. Kyoto: Akao Shōbundō, 1973.

[Bishamondō] *Kokin shū chū*. In Yoshisawa Yoshinori, ed., *Mikan kokubun kochū taisei*, vol. 4, pp. 3–246. Teikoku Kyōikukai Shuppanbu, 1936.

Kokin waka shū. Ed. Saeki Umetomo. NKBT, vol. 8.

Kokin waka shū kanjō kuden. In Katagiri Yōichi, ed., *Chūsei Kokin shū chūshakusho kaidai*, vol. 5, pp. 485–519. Kyoto: Akao Shōbundō, 1986.

Kokin waka shū kanjō no maki. In Kondō Yoshihiro, ed., *Chūsei shinbutsu setsuwa* (*zoku*), pp. 159–81. Koten Bunko, 1955.

Mujū Ichien. *Shaseki shū*. Ed. Watanabe Tsunaya. *NKBT*, vol. 85.

Nijō Tameakira. *Kokin hikashū Akone den*. In Katagiri Yōichi, ed., *Muromachi gokoro*, pp. 210–21. Kadokawa Shoten, 1978.

Nijō Tameie. *Eiga no ittei*. In Sasaki Nobutsuna, ed., *NKT*, vol. 3, pp. 398–401.

Nijō Tameyo. *Etsumoku shō*. In Sasaki Nobutsuna, ed., *NKT*, vol. 4, pp. 146–86.

Nōin. *Nōin uta makura*. In Sasaki Nobutsuna, ed., *NKT*, vol. 1, pp. 69–107.

Ōe no Masafusa. *Gōdan shō*. In Gōdan Shō Kenkyūkai, ed., [Ruijūbon-kei] *Gōdan shō chūkai*. Musashino Shoin, 1983.

Rokujō Kiyosuke. *Fukurozōshi*. Ed. Fujioka Tadaharu. *SNKBT*, vol. 29.

———. *Ōgi shō*. In Sasaki Nobutsuna, ed., *NKT*, vol. 1, pp. 222–370.

Sensai. *Ungō-ji Seinen zan kyōgen kigo waka jo*. In Kuroita Katsumi, ed., *Honchō bunshū*, pt. 55, p. 236. *Shintei zōhō kokushi taikei*, vol. 30. Yoshikawa Kōbunkan, 1966.

Shiban. *Honchō kōsōden (shidenbu)*. Ed. Bussho Kankōkai. *Dai Nihon Bukkyō zensho*, vol. 103. Meichō Fukyūkai, 1979.

Sōchō. *Ise monogatari Sōchō kikigaki*. In Katagiri Yōichi, ed., *Ise monogatari no kenkyū (shiryōhen)*, pp. 651–710. Meiji Shoin, 1969.

Sōgi. *Ise monogatari Shōmon shō*. In Katagiri Yōichi, ed., *Ise monogatari no kenkyū (shiryōhen)*, pp. 589–650. Meiji Shoin, 1969.

Tachibana no Narisue. *Kokon chomon jū*. Ed. Nishio Kōichi and Kobayashi Yasuharu. 2 pts. *SNKS*, vols. 59 and 76.

Toganoo Myōe Shōnin denki. In *Myōe Shōnin shiryō*. *Kozan-ji shiryō sōsho*, vol. 1. Tōkyō Daigaku Shuppankai, 1971.

Utai shō. Ed. Itō Masayoshi. *Nihon shomin bunka shiryō shūsei*, vol. 3. San'ichi Shobō, 1972.

Waka kanjō shidai himitsu shō. In Miwa Masatane, "Ietaka katakusho no kentō: *Waka kanjō shidai himitsu shō* o megutte." *Ōsaka Furitsu Daigaku kiyō (jinbun, shakai kagaku)* 19 (1971), pp. 44–53.

Yamato monogatari. In Sakakura Atsuyoshi et al., eds., *Taketori monogatari, Ise monogatari, Yamato monogatari*, pp. 231–366. *NKBT*, vol. 9.

Yōten ki. In *ZGR*, vol. 2, pt. II, pp. 581–635.

Yūkai. *Hōkyō shō*. In *T.*, vol. 77, no. 2456, pp. 847–51.

———. *Hōkyō shō*. In Moriyama Shōshin, *Tachikawa jakyō to sono shakaiteki haikei no kenkyū*, pp. 572–81. Rokuyaen, 1965.

———. *Hōkyō shō*. In Pol Vanden Broucke, trans., *Hōkyōshō: Compendium of the Precious Mirror of the Monk Yūkai*, pp. 119–50. Ghent: Ghent National University, 1992.

Zeami. *Rikugi*. In Omote Akira and Katō Shūichi, eds., *Zeami, Zenchiku*, pp. 180–82. *Nihon shisō taikei*, vol. 24. Iwanami Shoten, 1974.

Zenchiku. *Myōshuku shū*. In Itō Masayoshi, ed., *Komparu kodensho shūsei*, pp. 279–307. Wan'ya Shoin, 1969.

Secondary Sources in Japanese

Arai Eizo. "*Kokin shū* kanjō hisho to Bukkyō kyōri: *Kokin* denjushi shikō." *Nara Joshi Daigaku Bungakubu nenpō* 26 (1982), pp. 1–13.

Aso Mizue. "Hitomaro shinkō: sono keisei to hatten." *Kokubungaku: kaishaku to kansho*, no. 9 (1974), pp. 18–29.

Fujishima Aya. "Kyūshū Daigaku *Waka chiken shū* ni tsuite." *Gobun kenkyū*, no. 73 (1992), pp. 55–65.

Fukuda Hideuchi. "Guken shō." In Fukuda Hideuchi, Shimazu Tadao, and Itō Masayoshi, eds., *Chūsei hyōron shū*, pp. 55–102. *KNKB*, vol. 24.

Hazama Jikō. *Nihon Bukkyō no kaiten to sono kichō: Chūko Nihon Tendai no kenkyū*, vol. 2. Sanseidō, 1948.

Hirata Toshiharu. *Sōhei to bushi*. Nihon Kyōbunsha, 1965.

Hisamatsu Sen'ichi. "*Chikuen shō* kō." *Nihon Gakushiin kiyō* 15 (1957), pp. 193–211.

Hosaka Miyako. "Tsumori ke no kajin gun (16): Kunisuke no denki." *Gakuen* (1981), pp. 2–17.

Inoue Muneo. *Chūsei kadanshi no kenkyū (Nanbokuchōki)*. Meiji Shoin, 1987.

———. *Kamakura jidai kajin den no kenkyū*. Kazama Shobō, 1997.

Ishigami Hidemi. "*Gyokuden jinpi no maki* kaidai kō." *Shidō bunko ronshū* 26 (1991), pp. 209–64.

Ishigami Hideaki. "Kunaichō Shoryōbu-zō *Kingyoku sōgi*: hankoku to kaidai." 3 pts. *Mita kokubun*, no. 15 (Dec. 1991), pp. 37–52; no. 16 (July 1992), pp. 41–55; no. 17 (Dec. 1992), pp. 51–62.

Ishikawa Tōru. "Muromachi jidai monogatari ni okeru *Ise monogatari* no kyōju." In Tokue Gensei, ed., *Ise monogatari chū*, pp. 169–222. *Muromachi bungaku sanshū*, vol. 1. Miyai Shoten, 1987.

Itō Masayoshi. "*Ise monogatari* to yōkyoku." In Katagiri Yōichi, ed., *Ise monogatari, Yamato monogatari*, pp. 358–68. *KNKB*, vol. 5.

———. "Jidō setsuwa kō." *Kokugo kokubun*, vol. 49, no. 11 (1980), pp. 1–32.

———. "Kokinchū no sekai: sono han'ei toshite no chūsei bungaku to yōkyoku." *Kanze*, no. 6 (June 1970), pp. 3–9.

———. "Yōkyoku Takasago zakkō." *Bunrin* 6 (1971), pp. 111–25.

———. "Yōkyoku to chūsei bungaku." *Chūsei bungaku* 33 (1988), pp. 34–44.

———. "Yōkyoku to *Ise monogatari* no hiden: *Izutsu* no baai o chūshin toshite." *Kongō* 64 (1965), pp. 2–9.

Itō Masayoshi, ed. *Komparu kodensho shūsei*. Wanya Shoin, 1969.

———. *Yōkyoku shū*. *SNKS*, vols. 57–59.

Itō Satoshi. "Ise kanjō no sekai." *Bungaku* 8, no. 4 (1997), pp. 63–74.

Kami Hiroyuki. "Shinku, soku setsu no keisei to hatten." *Waka bungaku kenkyū*, no. 49 (1984), pp. 47–56.

Kamikawa Michio. "Chūsei no sokui girei to Bukkyō." *Nihonshi kenkyū*, no. 300 (Aug. 1987), pp. 44–70. Reprinted in Iwai Tadakuma and Okada Seiji, eds., *Tennō daikawari gishiki no rekishi tenkai*, pp. 105–39. Kashiwa Shobō, 1989.

Katagiri Yōichi. "Chūsei sego chūshakushū kenkyū nōto yori." *Bunrin* 1 (1966), pp. 142–65.

———. *Ise monogatari no shinkenkyū*. Meiji Shoin, 1987.

———. *Uta makura, uta kotoba jiten*. Kadokawa, 1983.

Katagiri Yōichi, ed. *Chūsei Kokin shū chūshakusho kaidai*. 6 vols. Kyoto: Akao shōbundō, 1971–86.

———. *Ise monogatari no kenkyū (kenkyūhen)*. Meiji Shoin, 1968.

———. *Ise monogatari no kenkyū (shiryōhen)*. Meiji Shoin, 1969.

———. *Ise monogatari, Yamato monogatari*. *KNKB*, vol. 5.

———. *Muromachi gokoro*. Kadokawa Shoten, 1978.

———. *[Tesshinsai Bunko] Ise monogatari kochūshaku sōkan*. Yagi Shoten, 1989.

Kawaguchi Hisao, ed. *Wakan rōeishū zenshakuchū*. Kōdansha Gakujutsu Bunko, 1982.

Kidō Saizō and Shigematsu Hiromi, eds. *Renga yoriaishū to kenkyū*. *Mikan kokubun shiryō*, vols. 8–9. Toyohashi: Mikan Kokubun Shiryō Kankōkai, 1978.

Kobayashi Shigeyoshi. "Sumiyoshi no okina no monogatari." *Ōchō bungakushi kō*, no. 12 (1985), pp. 1–24.

Kojima Michimasa and Fukuhara Takayoshi. "Tendai kuden hōmon no kyōdō kenkyū." In *Bukkyō shisō ronshū*. Kyoto: Heiraku-ji Shoten, 1976.

Kubota Jun. "Junkyōbō Jakue ni tsuite." *Kokugo to kokubungaku* 35 (1958), pp. 43–55.

Kumazawa Reiko. "*Kokin shū* to yōkyoku—chūsei *Kokin* chū to no kanren in oite." *Kokugo kokubun* 39, no. 10 (Oct. 1970), pp. 1–20.

Kushida Ryōkō. *Shingon mikkyō seiritsu katei no kenkyū*. Sankibō Busshorin, 1964.

———. *Zoku Shingon mikkyō seiritsu katei no kenkyū*. Sankibō Busshorin, 1979.

Maeda Eun. *Maeda Eun zenshū*, vol. 1. Shujūsha, 1931.

Mitani Kuniaki, ed. *Monogatari bungaku no hōhō*, vol. 1. Yūrindō, 1989.

Miwa Masatane. "*Chikuen shō* karon no seisei to hatten: gisho *Iwami no jo shiki* ni tsuite." *Nagoya Daigaku kokugo kokubungaku* 15 (Nov. 1964), pp. 17–27.

———. "*Chikuen shō* karon no seisei to hatten: *Gyokuden shū*, *Akone no ura kuden* ni tsuite." *Nagoya Daigaku kokugo kokubungaku* 13 (Nov. 1963), pp. 25–40.

———. "*Chikuen shō* karon no seisei to hatten: kashin toshite no Sumiyoshi myōjin o megutte." *Nagoya Daigaku kokugo kokubungaku* 14 (Apr. 1964), pp. 47–60.

———. "*Chikuen shō* no seiritsu ni kansuru futatsu, mitsu no mondai." *Nagoya Daigaku kokugo kokubungaku* 12 (1963), pp. 49–67.

———. "Chūsei kadō ni okeru kanjō denju ni tsuite." *Chūsei bungaku* 12 (1967), pp. 28–32.

———. "*Etsumoku shō* ke karon no seiritsu o megutte." 2 pts. *Kokugo to kokubungaku*, July 1990, pp. 1–13; Aug. 1990, pp. 29 – 42.

———. "Hisho no seiritsu ni kakawaru mondai." In Yokoi Akio and Arai Eizo, eds., *Kokin shū no sekai: denju to kyōju*, pp. 137–59. Sekaishisōsha, 1986.

———. "Ietaka katakusho no kentō: *Waka chiken shū, Waka kuden shō* o megutte." *Ōsaka Furitsu Daigaku kiyō (jinbun, shakai kagaku)* 16 (1968), pp. 121–36.

———. "Ietaka katakusho no kentō: *Waka kanjō shidai himitsu shō* o megutte." *Ōsaka Furitsu Daigaku kiyō (jinbun, shakai kagaku)* 19 (1971), pp. 35–53.

———. *Kagaku hiden no kenkyū*. Kazama Shobō, 1994.

———. "Kamakura jidai gokan seiritsu no *Kokin waka shū* jochū ni tsuite." 2 pts. *Fuguruma* 12 (Dec. 1964), pp. 1–7; 17 (Feb. 1968), pp. 41–50.

———. "Kanjō denju ki no hiji no ruten." *Kokugo to kokubungaku*, Aug. 1989, pp. 30–41.

———. "Teika gisho no sakusha, kyōjusha wa ikanaru hitobito ka." *Kokubungaku* 26, no. 8 (June 1981), pp. 64–69.

Mizuhara Gyōei. *Jakyō Tachikawaryū no kenkyū*. Kyoto: Fuzanbō, 1968.

Moriyama Seishin. *Tachikawa jakyō to sono shakaiteki haikei no kenkyū*. Rokuyaen, 1965.

Nakagawa Shinnichi. "*Ise monogatari* chūshakusho toshite *Gyokuden jinpi* no maki no ichi: *Waka chikenshū* to no hikaku o chūshin toshite." *Shigadai kokubungaku*, no. 30 (1992), pp. 23–31.

Nakagawa Zenkyō. *Bukyōgaku ronshū*. Sankibō Busshorin, 1976.

Nishomoto Yutaka. *Sumiyoshi Taisha*. Gakuseidō, 1977.

Ōgushi Sumio. "Hitomaro zō no seiritsu to Tō-ji Sansui byobu." *Bijutsu kenkyū*, no. 164 (1952), pp. 80–110.

Omote Akira and Katō Shūichi, eds. *Zeami, Zenchiku*. *Nihon shisō taikei*, vol. 24. Iwanami Shoten, 1974.

Otsu Yūichi. *Ise monogatari kochūshaku no kenkyū*. Yagi Shoten, 1986.

Sasama Yoshihiko. *Sei no shūkyō: Shingon Tachikawaryū to wa nani ka*. Daiichi Shobō, 1988.

Suzuki Tōzō and Hirota Eitarō, eds. *Koji kotowaza jiten*. Tōkyō-dō shuppan, 1956.

Yamada Shōzen. "Chūsei kōki ni okeru waka soku darani no jissen." *Indogaku Bukkyōgaku kenkyū*, 16, no. 1 (1967), pp. 290–92.

———. "Hitomaro shinkō: sono keisei to hatten." *Kokubungaku: kaishaku to kansho* (Dec. 1974), pp. 18–29.

———. "Kakinomoto no Hitomaro eigu no seiritsu to tenkai." *Taishō Daigaku kenkyū kiyō*, no. 51 (1966), pp. 83–123.

Yokoyama Shigeru and Matsumoto Takanobu, eds. *Muromachi jidai monogatari taisei*, vol. 2. Kadokawa Shoten, 1975.

Works in English

Abe, Masao. "Dōgen on Buddha Nature." *Eastern Buddhist* 7, no. 2 (May 1971).

Abé, Ryūichi. *The Weaving of Mantra: Kūkai and the Construction of Esoteric Buddhist Discourse.* New York: Columbia University Press, 1999.

Abrams, M. H. *A Glossary of Literary Terms.* 5th ed. New York: Holt, Rinehart and Winston, 1985.

Aston, W. G., trans. *Nihongi.* Rutland: Charles E. Tuttle, 1972.

Barthes, Roland. *S/Z.* Trans. Richard Miller. New York: Hill and Wang, 1974.

Belsey, Catherine. *Critical Practice.* New York: Routledge, 1980.

Benjamin, Walter. *The Origin of German Tragic Drama.* Trans. John Osborne. New York: Verso, 1977.

Bodiford, William. *Sōtō Zen in Medieval Japan.* Honolulu: University of Hawai'i Press for the Kuroda Institute, 1993.

Borgen, Robert. *Sugawara no Michizane and the Early Heian Court.* Cambridge, Mass.: Harvard University Council on East Asian Studies, 1986.

Bourdaghs, Michael. "Linked Verse and Literary Scholarship: An Analysis of Sōchō's Commentary on *Ise monogatari.*" Seminar paper, Cornell University, East Asian Literature Department, photocopy.

Bowring, Richard. "The *Ise monogatari*: A Short Cultural History." *Harvard Journal of Asiatic Studies* 52, no. 2 (1992), pp. 410–80.

Breen, John, and Mark Teeuwen, eds. *Shinto in History: Ways of the Kami.* Surrey, Eng.: Curzon Press, 2000.

Brower, Robert H. "The Foremost Style of Poetic Composition: Fujiwara Tameie's *Eiga no ittei.*" *Monumenta Nipponica* 42, no. 4 (1987), pp. 391–429.

———. "Fujiwara Teika's *Maigetsushō.*" *Monumenta Nipponica* 40, no. 4 (1985), pp. 401–25.

———. "The Reizei Family Documents." *Monumenta Nipponica* 36, no. 4 (1981), pp. 445–61.

Brower, Robert H., trans., with introduction and notes by Steven D. Carter. *Conversations with Shōtetsu.* Ann Arbor: University of Michigan, Center for Japanese Studies, 1992.

Brower, Robert H., and Earl Miner. *Japanese Court Poetry.* Stanford: Stanford University Press, 1961.

Brower, Robert H., and Earl Miner, trans. *Fujiwara Teika's Superior Poems of Our Time: A Thirteenth-Century Poetic Treatise and Sequence.* Stanford: Stanford University Press, 1967.

Carter, Steven D. Introduction to *Conversations with Shōtetsu*, trans. Robert H. Brower. Ann Arbor: University of Michigan, Center for Japanese Studies, 1992.

———. "'Seeking What the Masters Sought': Masters, Disciples, and Poetic Enlightenment in Medieval Japan." In Thomas Hare, Robert Borgen, and Sharalyn Orbaugh, eds., *The Distant Isle: Studies and Translations of Japanese Literature in Honor of Robert H. Brower*, pp. 35–58. Ann Arbor: University of Michigan, Center for Japanese Studies, 1996.

Carter, Steven D., ed. *Literary Patronage in Late Medieval Japan*. Ann Arbor: University of Michigan, Center for Japanese Studies, 1993.

———. *Medieval Japanese Writers. Dictionary of Literary Biography*, vol. 203. Detroit: Bruccoli Clark Layman, 1999.

Ch'en Hsiang-Ch'un. "Examples of Charm Against Epidemics with Short Explanations." *Folklore Studies* 1 (1942), pp. 37–54.

Cleary, Thomas, trans. *Shōbōgenzo: Zen Essays by Dōgen*. Honolulu: University of Hawai'i Press, 1986.

Cogan, Thomas J., trans. *The Tale of the Soga Brothers*. Tokyo: University of Tokyo Press, 1987.

Coleridge, Samuel Taylor. *Coleridge's Miscellaneous Criticism*. Ed. Thomas Middleton Raysor. Cambridge, Mass.: Harvard University Press, 1936.

Collcutt, Martin. "Religion in the Life of Minamoto Yoritomo." In P. F. Kornicki and I. J. McMullen, eds., *Religion in Japan: Arrows to Heaven and Earth*, pp. 95–101. Cambridge, Eng.: Cambridge University Press, 1996.

Cook, Lewis. "The Discipline of Poetry: Authority and Invention in the *Kokindenju*." Ph.D. diss., Cornell University, 2000.

Culler, Jonathon. *On Deconstruction*. Ithaca: Cornell University Press, 1982.

———. *Structuralist Poetics*. Ithaca: Cornell University Press, 1975.

Cranston, Edwin A. *A Waka Anthology*, vol. 1, *The Gem Glistening Cup*. Stanford: Stanford University Press, 1993.

de Man, Paul. "The Epistemology of Metaphor." *Critical Inquiry*, Autumn 1978, pp. 13–30.

———. "The Rhetoric of Temporality." In idem, *Blindness and Insight: Essays in the Rhetoric of Contemporary Criticism*, pp. 187–228. Rev. 2nd ed. Minneapolis: University of Minnesota Press, 1983.

De Poorter, Erika, trans. *Zeami's Talks on Sarugaku*. Amsterdam: J. G. Gieben, 1986.

Derrida, Jacques. *Of Grammatology*. Trans. Gayatri Chakrovorty Spivak. Baltimore: Johns Hopkins University Press, 1974.

Faure, Bernard. *The Red Thread: Buddhist Approaches to Sexuality*. Princeton: Princeton University Press, 1998.

———. *The Rhetoric of Immediacy: A Cultural Critique of Chan/Zen Buddhism*. Princeton: Princeton University Press, 1991.

Field, Norma. *The Splendor of Longing in the Tale of Genji*. Princeton: Princeton University Press, 1987.

Fletcher, Angus. "Allegory in Literary History." In Philip Weiner, ed., *Dictionary of the History of Ideas*, vol. 1, pp. 41–48. New York: Charles Scribner's Sons, 1973.

———. *Allegory: The Theory of a Symbolic Mode*. Ithaca: Cornell University, 1964.

Foucault, Michel. *The Order of Things*. New York: Vintage Books, 1973.

Frow, John. *Marxism and Literary Theory*. Cambridge, Mass.: Harvard University Press, 1986.

Frye, Northrop. *Anatomy of Criticism*. Princeton: Princeton University Press, 1957.

Gaiman, Neil. *The Sandman, nos. 1–75*. New York: DC Comics and Vertigo Press, 1989–96.

Geddes, John Van Ward. "A Partial Translation and Study of the *Jikkinshō*." Ph.D. diss, Washington University, 1976.

Goble, Andrew Edmund. *Kenmu: Go-Daigo's Revolution*. Cambridge, Mass.: Harvard University, Council on East Asian Studies, 1996.

Goepper, Roger. *Aizen-Myōō: The Esoteric King of Lust, An Iconological Study*. Zurich: Artibus Asiae and Museum Rietberg, 1993.

Grapard, Allan G. "Linguistic Cubism: A Singularity of Pluralism in the Sannō Cult." *Japanese Journal of Religious Studies* 14, nos. 2–3 (1987), pp. 211–34.

———. *Protocols of the Gods: A Study of the Kasuga Cult in Japanese History*. Berkeley: University of California Press, 1992.

Groner, Paul. "A Medieval Japanese Reading of the *Mo-ho chih-kuan*: Placing the *Kankō ruijū* in Historical Context." *Japanese Journal of Religious Studies* 22, no. 1 (1995), pp. 49–81.

Hakeda, Yoshito, trans. *The Awakening of Faith*. New York: Columbia University Press, 1967.

———. *Kūkai: Major Works*. New York: Columbia University Press, 1972.

Hare, Thomas Blenman. "Reading Writing Cooking: Kūkai's Interpretive Strategies." *Journal of Asian Studies* 49, no. 2 (May 1990), pp. 253–73.

Harper, Thomas. "Motoori Norinaga's Criticism of the 'Genji Monogatari': A Study of the Background and Critical Content of his 'Genji Monogatari Tama no Ogushi.'" Ph.D. diss., University of Michigan, 1971.

Henderson. John. *Scripture, Canon, and Commentary*. Princeton: Princeton University Press, 1991.

Hirshfield, Jane, and Mariko Aratani, trans. *The Ink Dark Moon*. New York: Vintage Classics, 1986.

Huey, Robert. *Kyōgoku Tamekane*. Stanford: Stanford University Press, 1989.

Jameson, Fredric. *The Ideologies of Theory: Essays, 1971–1986*, vol. 1. Minneapolis: University of Minnesota Press, 1988.

———. "Metacommentary." *PMLA* 86, no. 1 (Jan. 1971), pp. 9–17.

———. *The Political Unconscious: Narrative as a Socially Symbolic Act*. Ithaca: Cornell University Press, 1981.

Kamens, Edward. *The Three Jewels: A Study and Translation of Minamoto Tamenori's Sanbōe.* Ann Arbor: University of Michigan, Center for Japanese Studies, 1988.

Kamikawa, Michio. "Accession Rituals and Buddhism in Medieval Japan." *Japanese Journal of Religious Studies* 17, nos. 2–3 (1990), pp. 243–80.

Katō, Bunnō; Yoshirō Tamura; and Kōjirō Miyasaka, trans. *The Threefold Lotus Sutra.* Kosei Publishing, 1988.

Katō, Hilda. "The *Mumyōshō* of Kamo no Chōmei and Its Significance in Japanese Literature." *Monumenta Nipponica* 23, nos. 3–4 (1968), pp. 321–430.

Keene, Donald. *Seeds in the Heart.* New York: Henry Holt, 1993.

Kermode, Frank. *The Genesis of Secrecy: On the Interpretation of Narrative.* Cambridge, Mass.: Harvard University Press, 1979.

Kitagawa, Joseph. *On Understanding Japanese Religion.* Princeton: Princeton University Press, 1987.

Klein, Susan Blakeley. "Allegories of Desire: Kamakura Commentaries and the Noh." Ph.D. diss., Cornell University, 1994.

———. "Allegories of Desire: Poetry and Eroticism in *Ise monogatari zuinō.*" *Monumenta Nipponica* 52, no. 4 (1997), pp. 441–65.

———. "Fujiwara no Tameaki." In Steve Carter, ed., *Medieval Japanese Writers,* pp. 26–34. *Dictionary of Literary Biography,* vol. 203. Detroit: Bruccoli Clark Layman, 1999.

———. "*Ise monogatari zuinō*: An Annotated Translation." *Monumenta Nipponica* 53, no. 1 (1997), pp. 13–43.

Konishi, Jin'ichi. *A History of Japanese Literature,* vol. 3. Trans. Aileen Gatten and Mark Harbison. Princeton: Princeton University Press, 1991.

———. "Image and Ambiguity: The Impact of Zen Buddhism on Japanese Literature." Unpublished paper, Tokyo University of Education, Program for Comparative Study on Japanese and Chinese Literatures, 1973. Photocopy.

———. "Michi and Medieval Writing." In Earl Miner, ed., *Principles of Japanese Literature,* pp. 181–208. Princeton: Princeton University Press, 1985.

Kuroda Toshio. "Historical Consciousness and *Hon-jaku* Philosophy in the Medieval Period on Mount Hiei." In George J. Tanabe, Jr., and Willa Jane Tanabe, eds., *The Lotus Sutra in Japanese Culture,* pp. 143–58. Honolulu: University of Hawaii Press, 1989.

LaFleur, William. "Buddhism and Japanese Literature." In *Kodansha Encyclopedia of Japan,* vol. 1, pp. 180–82. Kodansha, 1983.

———. *The Karma of Words: Buddhism and the Literary Arts of Medieval Japan.* Berkeley: University of California Press, 1983.

Levy, Ian Hideo. *Hitomaro and the Birth of Japanese Lyricism.* Princeton: Princeton University Press, 1984.

Levy, Ian Hideo, trans. *Man'yōshū: A Translation of Japan's Premier Anthology of Classical Poetry*, vol. 1. Princeton: Princeton University Press, 1981.

Lyons, John. *Introduction to Theoretical Linguistics*. New York: Cambridge University Press, 1968.

Marra, Michele F. *The Aesthetics of Discontent: Politics and Reclusion in Medieval Japanese Literature*. Honolulu: University of Hawai'i Press, 1991.

Matsunaga, Alicia. *The Buddhist Philosophy of Assimilation*. Tokyo: Sophia University, 1969.

McCullough, Helen. *Brocade by Night: "Kokin Wakashū" and the Court Style in Japanese Classical Poetry*. Stanford: Stanford University Press, 1985.

McCullough, Helen, ed. and trans. *Ōkagami: The Great Mirror*. Princeton: Princeton University Press, 1980.

McCullough, Helen, trans. *Kokin Wakashū*. Stanford: Stanford University Press, 1985.

———. *Tales of Ise*. Stanford: Stanford University Press, 1968.

McCullough, William H., and Helen Craig McCullough, trans. *A Tale of Flowering Fortunes*. 2 vols. Stanford: Stanford University Press, 1980.

McMullen, I. J. "The Worship of Confucius in Ancient Japan." In P. F. Kornicki and I. J. McMullen, eds., *Religion in Japan: Arrows to Heaven and Earth*, pp. 39–77. Cambridge, Eng.: Cambridge University Press, 1996.

McMullin, Neil. "The Lotus Sutra and Politics in the Mid-Heian Period." In George J. Tanabe, Jr., and Willa Jane Tanabe, eds., *The Lotus Sutra in Japanese Culture*, pp. 119–41. Honolulu: University of Hawai'i Press, 1989.

———. "On Placating the Gods and Pacifying the Populace: The Case of the Gion *Goryō* Cult." *History of Religions* 27, no. 3 (Feb. 1958), pp. 270–93.

Melville, Stephen. "Notes on the Reemergence of Allegory, the Forgetting of Modernism, the Necessity of Rhetoric, and the Conditions of Publicity in Art and Criticism." *October 19*, Winter 1981, pp. 55–92.

Miyoshi, Masao. "Against the Native Grain." Special issue: Masao Miyoshi and H. D. Harootunian eds., *Postmodernism and Japan. South Atlantic Quarterly* 87, no. 3 (Summer 1988), pp. 525–50.

Morrell, Robert E., trans. *Sand and Pebbles (Shasekishū)*. New York: State University of New York Press, 1985.

Morris, Ivan, trans. *As I Crossed a Bridge of Dreams*. New York: Dial Press, 1971.

———. *The Pillow Book of Sei Shōnagon*. New York: Columbia University Press, 1991.

Morris, Mark. Review of *Hitomaro and the Birth of Japanese Lyricism*, by Ian Hideo Levy. *Harvard Journal of Asiatic Studies* 46, no. 2 (1986), pp. 638–53.

———. "Waka as Form, Waka as History." *Harvard Journal of Asiatic Studies* 46, no. 2 (1986), pp. 552–610.

Morrison, Grant. *The Invisibles*. New York: DC Comics and Vertigo Press, 1994–2000.

Okada, Richard. *Figures of Resistance*. Durham, N.C.: Duke University Press, 1991.

Owens, Craig. "The Allegorical Impulse." In Brian Willis, ed., *Art After Modernism: Rethinking Representation*, pp. 203–35. New York: New Museum of Contemporary Art, 1984.

Perkins, George W., trans. *The Clear Mirror: A Chronicle of the Japanese Court During the Kamakura Period (1185–1333)*. Stanford: Stanford University Press, 1998.

Phillipi, Donald, trans. *Kojiki*. Tokyo: University of Tokyo Press, 1968.

Plutschow, H. E. *Chaos and Cosmos: Ritual in Early and Medieval Japanese Literature*. New York: E. J. Brill, 1990.

———. "Is Poetry a Sin? Honjisuijaku and Buddhism Versus Poetry." *Oriens Extremus* 25 (1978), pp. 206–18.

Pollack, David. *The Fracture of Meaning: Japan's Synthesis of China from the Eighth Through the Eighteenth Centuries*. Princeton: Princeton University Press, 1986.

Ponsonby-Fane, R. *Suminoe no Ohokami*. Kyoto: Nagai Shuppan Insatsu Kabushikikaisha, 1935.

Quilligan, Maureen. *The Language of Allegory: Defining the Genre*. Ithaca: Cornell University Press, 1979.

Rimer, J. Thomas, and Jonathan Chaves, eds. and trans. *Japanese and Chinese Poems to Sing: The Wakan rōei shū*. New York: Columbia University Press, 1997.

Rimer, J. Thomas, and Yamazaki Masakazu, eds. and trans. *On the Art of Nō Drama: The Major Treatises of Zeami*. Princeton: Princeton University Press, 1984.

Rodd, Laurel Rasplica, and Mary Catherine Henkenius, trans. *Kokinshū: A Collection of Poems Ancient and Modern*. Princeton: Princeton University Press, 1984.

Ruthven, K. K. "Etiological Tales." In *The Spencer Encyclopedia*, s.v. Toronto: University of Toronto Press, 1990.

Sanford, James H. "The Abominable Tachikawa Skull Ritual." *Monumenta Nipponica* 46, no. 1 (Spring 1991), pp. 1–20.

———. "Horse Penises and Human Vajras: Some Elements of Tachikawa Ritual." Unpublished paper, University of North Carolina, Chapel Hill, 1988. Photocopy.

———. "Spiritual Embryology in Shingon Buddhism." Conference paper presented at the annual meeting of the Association of Asian Studies, Washington, D.C., Mar. 1989.

———. "Wind, Waters, Stupas, Mandalas: Fetal Buddhahood in Shingon." *Japanese Journal of Religious Studies* 24, no. 1–2 (Spring 1997), pp. 1–38.

Sanford, James H., trans. "Compendium of the Precious Mirror (*Hōkyōshō*)." Unpublished manuscript, University of North Carolina, Chapel Hill, photocopy.

———. "Not One, Not Two, Not Three: Reflections from a Shingon Mirror." Unpublished manuscript, University of North Carolina, Chapel Hill, photocopy.

Sato, Hiroaki, and Burton Watson. *From the Country of Eight Islands: An Anthology of Japanese Poetry*. Seattle: University of Washington Press, 1981.

Saussure, Ferdinand de. *Course in General Linguistics*. Trans. Wade Baskin. New York: McGraw-Hill, 1966.

Seidensticker, Edward, trans. *The Tale of Genji*. New York: Alfred A. Knopf, 1976.

Shirane, Haruo. *The Bridge of Dreams*. Stanford: Stanford University Press, 1987.

Shively, Donald H. "Buddhahood for the Nonsentient: A Theme in Nō Plays." *Harvard Journal of Asiatic Studies* 20 (1957), pp. 135–61.

———. "Tokugawa Plays on Forbidden Subjects." In James R. Brandon, ed., *Chushingura: Studies in Kabuki and the Puppet Theater*, pp. 23–57. Honolulu: University of Hawaii Press, 1982.

Skord, Virginia, trans. *Tales of Tears and Laughter*. Honolulu: University of Hawai'i Press, 1991.

Slawson, David A. *Secret Teachings in the Art of Japanese Gardens: Design Principles and Aesthetic Values*. Tokyo: Kodansha International, 1987.

Smits, Ivo. *The Pursuit of Loneliness: Chinese and Japanese Nature Poetry in Medieval Japan, ca. 1050–1150*. Stuttgart: Franz Steiner, 1995.

Snodgrass, Adrian. *The Matrix and Diamond World Mandalas in Shingon Buddhism*. 2 vols. New Delhi: Aditya Prakashan, 1988.

Soothill, William Edward, and Lewis Hodous, eds. *A Dictionary of Chinese Buddhist Terms*. Richmond, Eng.: Curzon Press, 1995 [1937].

Stone, Jacqueline I. *Original Enlightenment and the Transformation of Medieval Japanese Buddhism*. Kuroda Institute, Studies in East Asian Buddhism, vol. 12. Honolulu: University of Hawai'i Press, 1999.

Swanson, Paul. *Foundations of T'ien T'ai Philosophy*. Berkeley: Asian Humanities Press, 1989.

Tahara, Mildred, trans. *Tales of Yamato*. Honolulu: University of Hawai'i Press, 1980.

Taylor, Mark. *Erring: A Postmodern A/theology*. Chicago: University of Chicago Press, 1984.

Teeuwen, Mark. "Attaining Union with the Gods: The Secret Books of Watarai Shintō." *Monumenta Nipponica* 48, no. 2 (1993), pp. 225–45.

———. "The Kami in Esoteric Buddhist Thought and Practice." In John Breen and Mark Teeuwen, eds., *Shintō in History: Ways of the Kami*, pp. 95–116. Surrey, Eng.: Curzon Press, 2000.

———. *Watarai Shintō: An Intellectual History of the Outer Shrine in Ise*. Leiden: CNWS Publications, 1996.

Teskey, Gordon. "Allegory." In A. C. Hamilton, ed., *The Spencer Encyclopedia*, s.v. Toronto: University of Toronto Press, 1990.

Thomas, Keith. *Religion and the Decline of Magic*. London: Weidenfeld and Nicolson, 1971.

Todorov, Tzvetan. *Symbolism and Interpretation*. Trans. Catherine Porter. Ithaca: Cornell University Press, 1982.

Tsunoda, Ryusaku; Wm. Theodore de Bary; and Donald Keene, eds. *Sources of Japanese Tradition*, vol. 1. New York: Columbia University Press, 1958.

Tyler, Royall. *The Miracles of the Kasuga Deity*. New York: Columbia University Press, 1990.

Tyler, Royall, trans. *Japanese Tales*. New York: Pantheon Books, 1987.

Ury, Marian. *Tales of Times Now Past*. Berkeley: University of California Press, 1979.

Vanden Broucke, Pol, trans. *Hōkyōshō: "Compendium of the Precious Mirror" of the Monk Yūkai*. Ghent: Ghent National University, 1992.

Van Dyke, Carolynn. *The Fiction of Truth: Structures of Meaning in Narrative and Dramatic Allegory*. Ithaca: Cornell University Press, 1985.

Varley, H. Paul, trans. *A Chronicle of Gods and Sovereigns: Jinnō Shōtōki of Kitabatake Chikafusa*. New York: Columbia University Press, 1980.

Vos, Fritz. *A Study of the Ise Monogatari*. 2 vols. The Hague: Mouton, 1957.

Wallace, John R. "Abutsu-ni." In Steven D. Carter, ed., *Medieval Japanese Writers*, pp. 3–9. Detroit: Bruccoli Clark Layman, 1999.

Watson, Burton, trans. *The Lotus Sutra*. New York: Columbia University Press, 1993.

Wellek, Rene. "Symbol and Symbolism in Literature." In Philip Weiner, ed., *Dictionary of the History of Ideas*, vol. 4, pp. 337–45. New York: Charles Scribner's Sons, 1973.

Wixted, John Timothy. "Chinese Influences on the *Kokin shū* Prefaces." In Laurel Rasplica Rodd and Mary Catherine Henkins, trans., *Kokinshū: A Collection of Poems Ancient and Modern*, pp. 387–400. Princeton: Princeton University Press, 1984.

Yamasaki, Taikō. *Shingon: Japanese Esoteric Buddhism*. Boston: Shambhala, 1988.

Yokota-Murakami, Gerry. *The Formation of the Canon of Nō: The Literary Tradition of Divine Authority*. Osaka: Osaka University Press, 1997.

References to 'Ise monogatari' Episodes

Index of First Lines

Index of Subjects

Harvard-Yenching Institute Monograph Series
(titles now in print)

11. *Han Shi Wai Chuan: Han Ying's Illustrations of the Didactic Application of the Classic of Songs*, translated and annotated by James Robert Hightower
21. *The Chinese Short Story: Studies in Dating, Authorship, and Composition*, by Patrick Hanan
22. *Songs of Flying Dragons: A Critical Reading*, by Peter H. Lee
23. *Early Chinese Civilization: Anthropological Perspectives*, by K. C. Chang
24. *Population, Disease, and Land in Early Japan, 645–900*, by William Wayne Farris
25. *Shikitei Sanba and the Comic Tradition in Edo Fiction*, by Robert W. Leutner
26. *Washing Silk: The Life and Selected Poetry of Wei Chuang (834?-910)*, by Robin D. S. Yates
27. *National Polity and Local Power: The Transformation of Late Imperial China*, by Min Tu-ki
28. *Tang Transformation Texts: A Study of the Buddhist Contribution to the Rise of Vernacular Fiction and Drama in China*, by Victor H. Mair
29. *Mongolian Rule in China: Local Administration in the Yuan Dynasty*, by Elizabeth Endicott-West
30. *Readings in Chinese Literary Thought*, by Stephen Owen
31. *Remembering Paradise: Nativism and Nostalgia in Eighteenth-Century Japan*, by Peter Nosco
32. *Taxing Heaven's Storehouse: Horses, Bureaucrats, and the Destruction of the Sichuan Tea Industry, 1074–1224*, by Paul J. Smith
33. *Escape from the Wasteland: Romanticism and Realism in the Fiction of Mishima Yukio and Oe Kenzaburo*, by Susan Jolliffe Napier
34. *Inside a Service Trade: Studies in Contemporary Chinese Prose*, by Rudolf G. Wagner
35. *The Willow in Autumn: Ryutei Tanehiko, 1783–1842*, by Andrew Lawrence Markus
36. *The Confucian Transformation of Korea: A Study of Society and Ideology*, by Martina Deuchler
37. *The Korean Singer of Tales*, by Marshall R. Pihl
38. *Praying for Power: Buddhism and the Formation of Gentry Society in Late-Ming China*, by Timothy Brook
39. *Word, Image, and Deed in the Life of Su Shi*, by Ronald C. Egan
40. *The Chinese Virago: A Literary Theme*, by Yenna Wu

41. *Studies in the Comic Spirit in Modern Japanese Fiction*, by Joel R. Cohn
42. *Wind against the Mountain: The Crisis of Politics and Culture in Thirteenth-Century China*, by Richard L. Davis
43. *Powerful Relations: Kinship, Status, and the State in Sung China (960–1279)*, by Beverly Bossler
44. *Limited Views: Essays on Ideas and Letters*, by Qian Zhongshu; selected and translated by Ronald Egan
45. *Sugar and Society in China: Peasants, Technology, and the World Market*, by Sucheta Mazumdar
46. *Chinese History: A Manual*, by Endymion Wilkinson
47. *Studies in Chinese Poetry*, by James R. Hightower and Florence Chia-Ying Yeh
48. *Crazy Ji: Chinese Religion and Popular Literature*, by Meir Shahar
49. *Precious Volumes: An Introduction to Chinese Sectarian Scriptures from the Sixteenth and Seventeenth Centuries*, by Daniel L. Overmyer
50. *Poetry and Painting in Song China: The Subtle Art of Dissent*, by Alfreda Murck
51. *Evil and/or/as the Good: Omnicentrism, Intersubjectivity, and Value Paradox in Tiantai Buddhist Thought*, by Brook Ziporyn
52. *Chinese History: A Manual, Revised and Enlarged Edition*, by Endymion Wilkinson
53. *Articulated Ladies: Gender and the Male Community in Early Chinese Texts*, by Paul Rouzer
54. *Politics and Prayer: Shrines to Local Former Worthies in Sung China*, by Ellen Neskar
55. *Allegories of Desire: Esoteric Literary Commentaries of Medieval Japan*, by Susan Blakeley Klein
56. *Printing for Profit: The Commercial Publishers of Jianyang, 1050–1700*, by Lucille Chia
57. *To Become a God: Cosmology, Sacrifice, and Self-Divinization in Early China*, by Michael J. Puett